THE REAGAN FILES

The Untold Story of Reagan's Top-Secret Efforts to Win the Cold War

(Based Upon Over 100 Recently Declassified Letters and National Security Council Meeting Minutes)

First published in the United States by Jason Saltoun-Ebin, September 15, 2010.
ISBN-13 9781453633052
Cover design by Karrie Ross (www.KarrieRoss.com).

Cover photo courtesy of the Ronald Reagan Presidential Library.

Class Photo: February 4, 1981

Front row: Alexander Haig, Secretary of State; President Reagan; Vice President Bush; Caspar Weinberger, Secretary of Defense.
Middle row: Terrel Bell, Secretary of Education; Andrew Lewis, Secretary of Transportation, William French Smith, Attorney General; Jeane Kirkpatrick, U.S. Representative to the United Nations; James Edwards, Secretary of Energy; William E. Brock, United States Trade Representative; John Block, Secretary of Agriculture.
Back row: Raymond Donovan, Secretary of Labor; Donald Regan, Secretary of Treasury; David Stockman, Director, Office of Management & Budget; Samuel Pierce, Secretary of Housing & Urban Development; James Watt, Secretary of the Interior; Edwin Meese III, Counselor to the President; Malcolm Baldrige, Secretary of Commerce; Richard Schweiker, Secretary of Health & Human Services; William Casey, Director, Central Intelligence Agency.

For my mother,

Dr. Synthia Saltoun,

For over thirty years she has been inspiring

her college students to pursue their dreams,

and for thirty two years she has been giving me

the opportunities to pursue mine.

CONTENTS

PART II: REAGAN AND ANDROPOV

PART III: REAGAN AND CHERNENKO

PART IV: REAGAN AND GORBACHEV

EDITOR'S NOTE

I titled this series *Discovering Reagan* because that is exactly what I've been doing over the past nine years. Hour after hour, and day after day, my knowledge of Ronald Reagan and the Reagan Administration has come primarily from looking through hundreds of thousands of pages of documents at the Ronald Reagan Presidential Library. After each turn of the page, I still find myself anxiously wondering what the next turn may uncover.

My interest in Reagan started in 2001, fresh out of UCLA with a B.A. in European Studies, when I started working for noted journalist and presidential biographer Richard Reeves as a research assistant, helping with his biography, *President Reagan: The Triumph of Imagination,* (Simon & Schuster, 2005). I was living in Washington D.C. at the time and interning at the United Nations Information Centre, under the direction of Catherine O'Neill. Early in my internship she recommended that I interview with her husband, Mr. Reeves, for the research assistant position.

I spent the next few months interning by day and researching by night. My first assignment: photocopying every front page of *The New York Times* during the Reagan Administration. A few months later, Mr. Reeves offered me what I thought of as a chance of a lifetime. "I need someone in Southern California to conduct research at the Reagan Library," he told me. I don't remember what I said, but I know I was thinking, "I hope he is asking me."

I walked into the Ronald Reagan Presidential Library knowing little about the Reagan Administration, but prepared to find out everything I could. Unfortunately, though it was a few years before Mr. Reeves' book had to be completed, President George W. Bush made the task more difficult. On November 1, 2001, one month before starting our research at the Reagan Library, he signed Executive Order 13,233, "Further Implementation of the Presidential Records Act of 1978." The Executive Order, according to archivists at the Reagan Library, directed the Library to stop releasing documents until directed to do so by the President of the United States. I understood that to mean, "You are wasting your time here; it will be years before anything new comes out." Fortunately, five million pages of documents had already been released by 2001, the staff of the Reagan Library was extremely helpful and professional, and Mr. Reeves had years of Washington insider experience to rely on, in addition to the hundreds of interviews he conducted. President Obama voided the Bush Executive Order on his first day in office, and months later about 100,000 pages of documents were released that President Bush had withheld. This edition of *The Reagan Files* has been able to make use of some of the documents released in 2009.

According to my notes at the time, the first time I looked through the National Security Council (NSC) and the National Security Planning Group (NSPG) meeting minute files at the Reagan Library was in 2002. I noted that the boxes were mainly empty because the material was still classified, and that I subsequently filed both Freedom of Information Act (FOIA) requests and Mandatory Review (MR) requests for much of the material. In fact, I cannot remember finding a single set of meeting minutes in the files, although, a few had already been at least partially declassified because they had been used in the Iran-Contra hearings and investigations. In 2005, immediately prior to the publication of Reeves' biography, *President Reagan*, the boxes were still empty.

I went back to the Reagan Library in the summer of 2008 to follow up on my earlier research. Looking through the research room, I was immediately drawn to a box I had never seen. Inside the box, to my astonishment, were numerous sets of NSC and NSPG meeting minutes. After a few initial inquiries I was told that someone with authority had started selectively declassifying the meeting minutes. I asked a few more questions, because I had never heard of documents being declassified in that manner and because I had filed FOIA requests for many of the documents and was never notified they had been released. I was again told that someone with authority had started selectively declassifying the documents. I then requested all the NSC and NSPG meeting minute files and decided it was best to just drop my inquiry.[1]

Going through all the boxes, I discovered that over 100 sets of meeting minutes (there are about 350 NSC/NSPG meetings) from both NSC and NSPG meetings had been at least partially declassified. I also discovered that about 100 letters between Reagan and the four Soviet leaders had also just become available for research. I was also struck by the fact that most of the meeting minutes had a declassification date of 2005, which made me wonder why they were not available for research until 2008. Although it seems to generally take about 18 months for the Reagan Library to make a document available for research after it has been declassified, I suspected the delay was also due to the White House, which could withhold the release of a document under Executive Order 13,233. Whenever the agency declassification date is known, I have noted it in the heading for each document, although, like I just said, the document was likely not available for research until 2008. I have also, as much as possible,

---

[1] *Reagan's Secret War: The Untold Story of His Fight to Save the World From Nuclear Disaster*, (Crown, 2009) uses some of the same documents presented in this edition. The authors, Martin and Annelise Anderson, thank Karl Rove in their acknowledgments for helping them secure access to the documents while they were still classified. National security laws were apparently not breached, because Mr. Anderson still had security clearance as a one-time member of the Reagan Administration; he had to go to the secure vault at the Reagan Library to read the documents, and he was not allowed to make photocopies. He was, however, permitted to take notes while reading the documents.

included a background and postscript section for each document, in which I have used President Reagan's public statements when I found the statement to contain an important part of the story of Reagan's efforts to win the Cold War.

After reading through the approximately 1,000 pages of minutes, hundreds more pages of background memos, and the hundreds of pages of letters, I realized these documents were likely the most important Reagan Administration documents to ever have been released. I came to this conclusion because, in all my years of research, finding Reagan's thoughts proved to be few and far between, and in the collection of NSC and NSPG meeting minutes, Reagan's thoughts were both uncensored and officially recorded.

I immediately thought to myself, "This is where I might uncover whether Reagan or Gorbachev deserved more credit for ending the Cold War! This is where I'll be able to prove whether Reagan's critics were right: Was he just an old actor reading a script written by his conservative friends?"

The answers to these important questions, and many others like it, are still not entirely resolved, since most of the meeting minutes are still classified. However, reading through the declassified documents presented in *The Reagan Files*, the reader should get a feeling for what it was like to be with President Reagan when he made some of his most important foreign policy decisions: decisions that helped end the Cold War and shaped the twenty-first century. Pending important declassifications, new editions of *The Reagan Files* will clarify some of the missing pieces of the successes and failures of the Reagan Administration.

My goal for this project has always been to let these important letters and meetings speak for themselves. The task was not easy, as the original meeting minutes were not always typed, different note-takers were often used with different note-taking styles, words and names were misspelled, and the conversations were rarely recorded verbatim. My challenge, then, was to recreate these important meetings while making absolutely certain I did not change a speaker's meaning or tone. For readability reasons, transition words, such as "and," or "but," were added when the minutes reflected only the speaker's thoughts. Similarly, when the subject shifted away from U.S.-Soviet relations, I usually noted the shift or used ellipses. I also bolded most of President Reagan's words so that those interested in just what Reagan said can easily find where he participated in NSC and NSPG meetings.

For the above reasons, it is best to approach the material as a summary of these important meetings and letters. I also strongly urge reading the original documents before relying on my account, which is why I have placed the documents online at www.thereaganfiles.com.

With respect to the letters sent from the four General Secretaries of the Soviet Union to President Reagan, the letters reproduced are the translations found at the Reagan Library. Interested scholars can return to the Reagan Library to find the original letters delivered in Russian. Translations are, of course, subject to mistranslation, but my research suggests that the letters reproduced here are the letters President Reagan read and responded to, regardless of their accuracy in translation.

Mistakes are also unfortunately inevitable in a project like this, and I accept full responsibility. At the same time, my re-creation of NSC and NSPG meetings have been based entirely on the official meeting minutes – and the minutes are imperfect. Hopefully, the NSC has devised a better process for recording these important meetings.

Working on this book has been extremely rewarding. It is also the first book I've put together alone; and although most of the work entailed lonely days and nights spent transcribing, the process was made easier knowing the more that is written about the past, the more likely future leaders are to make important decisions based on what is best for the country as a whole.

I joked that I undertook this project because it was the only work I felt qualified to do after graduating from law school, but the truth is that it was the only thing I wanted to do after graduation. For that reason, if you enjoy reading *The Reagan Files* even half as much as I did working on it, I know you will love your journey through the Reagan years. I also welcome all comments and suggestions and can be reached at thereaganfiles@gmail.com.

Jason Saltoun-Ebin
Pacific Palisades, CA
July 1, 2010

INTRODUCTION

To the victor goes the spoils, and following the Nazi surrender in May 1945, President Truman, Prime Minister Churchill, and General Secretary Stalin met in Potsdam and divided Germany into French, British, American, and Soviet zones. Even though the city of Berlin was located within the Soviet zone, it was agreed that Berlin would be similarly divided.

Instead of bringing stability to Europe, the divisions created suspicions, which quickly turned the Soviet Union against the United States, France, and Great Britain. Within a year, Churchill was in the United States declaring that an "iron curtain" had descended across Europe. When Germany was officially divided into East and West Germany in 1949, the resulting split left Soviet forces in the East facing off against American forces in the West, each side expecting the other to start World War III.

To halt the spread of communism and rebuild war-ravaged Europe into a strong economic partner, the United States offered The Marshall Plan to the devastated European countries and the Soviet Union. Not only did the Soviet Union reject American aid, but the Soviets were so mistrustful of American intentions that they urged all the countries within their sphere of influence to reject the American offer. Instead, the Soviet Union imposed its own communist model wherever possible. As a result of the Soviet threat, in 1947 President Truman signed into law legislation creating the Central Intelligence Agency (CIA) and the National Security Council (NSC).

While the CIA was created to implement covert foreign policy, the NSC was formed to help devise foreign policy. The NSC thus consisted of the President's most senior advisers: the Vice President; the Director of the Central Intelligence Agency (DCI); the Chairman of the Joint Chiefs of Staff (JCS); the Secretaries of State, Defense, and Treasury; the Special Assistant to the President for National Security Affairs ("National Security Adviser," "White House National Security Adviser"); and an entire working staff to research issues and draft memorandums for the heads of each department within the NSC. Over the years, with each President of the United States free to add to the composition of the NSC, other positions, such as the Secretary of Commerce and the Chief of Staff, were often invited to attend NSC meetings.

Reagan, like other presidents before him, was not entirely trusting of the leak-prone NSC meetings. He attempted to solve the leak issue by creating an even more senior group, the National Security Planning Group (NSPG), which was limited to only the Vice President; DCI; Chairman of the Joint Chiefs; and Secretaries of State, Defense and Treasury. In contrast to NSC meetings, which spanned all aspects of foreign policy, NSPG meetings usually discussed only covert military activities. Most NSPG meetings are still classified.

Reagan's first Secretary of State, General Alexander Haig Jr., accepted the position with the understanding that he would be the President's "vicar" of foreign policy. Not satisfied with Reagan's word, on inauguration day Haig went to the White House to get the new President to sign a 20-page draft National Security Decision Directive (NSDD) placing foreign policy firmly under the jurisdiction of the Department of State. Reagan refused to sign the draft NSDD, and it was not until NSDD 2, "National Security Council Structure," was signed on January 12, 1982 that Reagan formally defined the foreign policy roles of the Secretary of State and National Security Adviser. According to NSDD 2,

> The National Security Council shall be the principal forum for consideration of national security policy issues requiring Presidential decision... . The Assistant to the President for National Security Affairs, in consultation with the regular members of the NSC, shall be responsible for developing, coordinating and implementing national security policy as approved by me. He shall determine and publish the agenda of NSC meetings. He shall ensure that the necessary papers are prepared and – except in unusual circumstances – distributed in advance to Council members... .
>
> The Secretary of State is my principal foreign policy advisor. As such, he is responsible for the formulation of foreign policy and for the execution of approved policy.
>
> I have assigned to the Secretary of State authority and responsibility, to the extent permitted by law, for the overall direction, coordination, and supervision of the interdepartmental activities incident to foreign policy formulation, and the activities of the Executive Departments and Agencies of the United States overseas.

Neither "foreign policy" nor "national security" was defined in NSDD 2. A recent search on Websters.com defined foreign policy as "a policy pursued by a nation in its dealings with other nations, designed to achieve national objectives." "National security" is defined as "a collective term for the defense and foreign relations of a country; protection of the interests of a country." With no strong delineation of foreign policy control, Haig was left to fight it out with the National Security Adviser. Reagan would not make that fight easy.

First, Reagan took away Haig's exclusive control of critical information by approving the creation of the Crisis Management Center (CMC). Prior to the CMC, the Department of State controlled the flow of information to the President, because critical communications were transmitted only to the White House Situation Room (WHSR), which was run by the Department of State. With the creation of the CMC, which was run by the National Security Adviser, the Department of State lost its control of information because the WHSR and the CMC simultaneously received the same transmissions.

Second, by 1982 Haig had even bigger problems than controlling information, because he fundamentally disagreed with many of the NSC recommendations presented to Reagan regarding actions directed against the Soviet Union, and Reagan had a particular dislike of disagreements. The new National Security Adviser, Bill Clark, (who replaced Richard V. Allen after Allen resigned following allegations he accepted a bribe for securing an interview with Nancy Reagan), was also actively lobbying for Haig's resignation. Compounding Haig's problem, Clark's first job in the Reagan Administration had been to work under Haig at the Department of State.[2]

Inside the White House, Clark manipulated the foreign policy process by virtue of his "friend" status with Reagan, as Clark was one of only a few people able enter the Oval Office unannounced. Clark's impromptu meetings allowed him to discuss whatever pressing issue he had; and Reagan, trusting Clark, usually complied with Clark's recommendations. Haig, on the other hand, had to make an appointment to see the President and even had trouble reaching him on the phone during crisis situations.[3] In July 1982, when Reagan finally accepted one of Haig's many threats to resign, he had already offered the position to George Shultz, who, going back to 1980, had been the transition team's first choice for Secretary of State.[4]

Clark resigned in October 1983 to become Secretary of the Interior, but the position took him both out of the White House and out of NSC meetings. As for Shultz, although he would serve as Secretary of State through the end of the Reagan Administration, events like Iran-Contra demonstrated that the National Security Adviser was at least as influential in creating and implementing foreign policy as the Secretary of State.

---

[2] Clark and Reagan were good friends going back to their days in California. While he was Governor of California, Reagan appointed Clark to the California Supreme Court in 1973. Many think that Clark was sent to the Department of State in 1981 principally to keep an eye on Haig.

[3] A recently declassified June 14, 1982 memo from Clark to President Reagan described how Haig had tried to contact the President while he was at Camp David to get approval of urgent instructions for the Ambassador to the Middle East. But Haig could not get through to Reagan until Monday when he returned to Washington. Not having heard back from the President, Haig issued the instructions anyway.

[4] According to Steven Hayward, Reagan disfavored Shultz in 1980 because he had already chosen Weinberger as Secretary of Defense and Reagan thought that two Cabinet level appointees from one company (Bechtel) would not go over well with the public. (Steven F. Hayward, *The Age of Reagan: The Conservative Counterrevolution: 1980-1989,* [Crown Forum, 2009] p. 46). Reagan likely also favored Haig because he was highly recommended by former President Nixon, whom Reagan considered one of his most important "silent" advisers. During the campaign and after Reagan was elected, Reagan continued to seek out Nixon's advice, and the two exchanged several letters during Reagan's presidency. Many are found in the Presidential Handwriting files at the Reagan Library.

Robert "Bud" McFarlane became the third national security adviser in three years when he replaced Clark in 1983. McFarlane served as National Security Adviser until the end of 1985, probably leaving because he was tired of dealing with the new Chief of Staff, Don Regan, who seemed to be consolidating power since switching positions with former Chief of Staff, James Baker.[5]

John Poindexter, McFarlane's Deputy National Security Adviser, replaced McFarlane as National Security Adviser, yet McFarlane maintained contact with Oliver North (NSC staffer) and Poindexter over a secret White House email system, allowing him to further the Iran-Contra initiative as a private citizen. In fact, just a few months after resigning, Reagan sent McFarlane to Iran to deliver spare parts in exchange for the release of an American hostage. The hostage was not released, but the Iranians still got their spare parts. Against McFarlane's advice, Reagan continued dealing with the Iranians in the hope of securing the release of the American hostages.

When the Iran-Contra Affair broke in November 1986, North, Poindexter, and Regan became the fall guys. Frank Carlucci, who was the number two at the Department of Defense, moved to the White House to replace Poindexter, and long-time Washington insider, Senator Howard Baker, came to the White House to try to salvage the Reagan legacy as the new Chief of Staff. When Secretary of Defense Weinberger resigned in 1987, Carlucci moved back to the Pentagon as Reagan's second and last Secretary of Defense. In his place, Colin Powell became the sixth and last White House National Security Adviser to serve President Reagan.

Despite the high turnover at the position of National Security Adviser, Reagan had continuity in other positions: George H. W. Bush served as the Vice President for all eight years and was a constant presence at NSC and NSPG meetings; Secretary of Defense Weinberger served for nearly seven years; Secretary of State Shultz served for six-and-a-half years; Bill Casey led the CIA from the beginning of the Reagan Administration until his health failed him in late 1986; James Baker III was with Reagan the entire time (Chief of Staff 1981-1984; and Secretary of the Treasury 1985-1988); Donald Regan was with Reagan for six years (Secretary of the Treasury 1981-1984 and Chief of Staff 1985-1987); and Ed Meese for seven and a half years (Senior Counselor to the President and then Attorney General). These individuals are mentioned because they, more than anyone else in the Reagan Administration, could influence Reagan's foreign policy decisions, and NSC and NSPG meetings were the places where foreign policy decisions were debated and often made.

The constant clashes meant that participants frequently left meetings on the losing side of the argument. Not willing to completely let the decision stand, losers often let information leak to the press in a last-ditch effort to sabotage the perceived flawed decision. Reagan saw the leaks as dangerous, and from time to

---

[5] *See* August 1, 1985 memo from McFarlane to Regan in Chapter 6.

time he warned that jobs were on the line. "I want to see an end to the stories of our speaking with different voices," Reagan told the NSC on July 6, 1981. "We only speak with different voices in this kind of briefing. If there is no other way to cure it – other than blowing up *The Post* and *The Star* – then, if I find out about who the leakers are, they are going back to South Succotash Wisconsin in a hurry." But the leaks, both truthful and misleading, continued throughout Reagan's two terms.

Although almost everything Reagan did in foreign policy in the early years of his administration was related to the Soviet Union, the meeting minutes and letters selected for this book were carefully chosen to document the specific meetings and letters focusing on U.S.-Soviet relations.

Chapter 1 discusses Reagan's efforts to implement his foreign policy priorities by pushing through Congress a sweeping military modernization program. David Stockman, Reagan's Director of the Office of Management and Budget, put Reagan's budget into perspective in the March 19, 1981, meeting: "In 1980 the total Department of Defense and security assistance budget was $148 billion. The budget submitted by the Reagan Administration by March 10 called for a total of $233 billion. This represents a 54 percent increase in two years."

Chapter 2 discusses how sensitive intelligence in December 1981 indicated that the Soviet Union was preparing to invade Poland in an effort to suppress democratic reforms gained by the Solidarity labor movement. The NSC met several times, including four meetings in five days, to decide how best to support Solidarity without provoking a Soviet invasion.

"If we don't take action now," Reagan told his advisers on December 21, "three or four years from now we'll have another situation and will wonder why we didn't go for it when we had the whole country with us. I am tired of looking backward." The minutes show that Reagan contemplated the use of force and invoking threats of World War III, but settled on a speech declaring that the United States would take strong economic actions against the Soviet Union if Poland were invaded, martial law was not suspended, and Solidarity members were not released.

Days later, even though the Soviets did not invade, Reagan ordered sanctions against the Soviet Union designed to restrict high-technology the Soviets were believed to need to complete a trans-Siberian oil and gas pipeline. The sanctions policy, the subject of Chapter Three, made for contentious meetings, because allied cooperation was necessary for the sanctions to be effective, and the allies were reluctant to cooperate because European companies stood to lose hundreds of millions of dollars' worth of contracts. Reagan was not pleased: "President Roosevelt called for a quarantine on Germany in 1939," he said in a September 22, 1982, NSC meeting. "He had his brains kicked out. What would history have been like if he had been listened to?"

The declassified meeting minutes and letters show that the Soviet Union saw Reagan's military modernization program as destabilizing but was nevertheless willing to begin arms control negotiations in 1981. Reagan, however, did not believe the offer was genuine: "Do you suppose he really believes all that crud -- or did he even write it?" Reagan wrote after reading General Secretary Brezhnev's October 15, 1981, letter proposing arms control negotiations.

Reagan famously said that he would have started arms control negotiations with the Soviets earlier, but he couldn't because the Soviet leaders kept dying on him – and three died in four years. However, the letters and meeting minutes show that Reagan was unwilling to enter serious negotiations until 1985 because he did not trust the Soviets and did not want to negotiate until he could negotiate from a position of strength.

The October 13, 1981 NSC meeting minutes also show that Reagan wondered whether the United States should be engaging in arms control negotiations at all. On that day he asked his advisors: "Do we really want a zero-option for the battlefield? Don't we need these nuclear systems? Wouldn't it be bad for us to give them up since we need them to handle Soviet conventional superiority?" Reagan's fear, justified or not, was that the balance between the United States and Soviet Union was only possible if the United States maintained a larger nuclear arsenal than the Soviet Union because the Soviets had larger conventional forces. Prime Minister Thatcher agreed, and in a February 1984 Washington visit urged Reagan to move away from his talk of reducing (and eliminating) nuclear weapons.

Starting serious negotiations in 1985 was also significant, because Reagan had won a landslide victory just a few months before; so by 1985 not only was he in an improved negotiating position, but he also had the support of the American people when he went one-on-one with Gorbachev. Although Reagan engaged Gorbachev in nuclear arms control negotiations with the purpose of eliminating nuclear weapons – Reagan also publicly said on many occasions that his goal was the complete elimination of nuclear weapons – the evidence shows that Reagan and most of his advisers misread the global situation as being one in which the Soviet Union would soon disintegrate and the U.S. would lose this once-in-a-lifetime opportunity to put the nuclear genie back in a bottle. Instead, Reagan focused on eliminating offensive ballistic missiles and rejected Gorbachev's call to eliminate all nuclear weapons by the year 2000.

All was not lost, however, and in 1987 Reagan and Gorbachev agreed on the Intermediate Nuclear Forces (INF) Treaty. The INF Treaty was significant because it eliminated intermediate range nuclear weapons which were thought to be the most destabilizing weapons because they had a short flight time and were aimed at all the major European cities. The documents, however, show Gorbachev was genuinely pushing for START, an even more sweeping arms control agreement that he expected would be signed at the Moscow Summit.

The START negotiations began with the premise that both countries would eliminate 50 percent of their nuclear arsenals. The newly declassified documents show that Reagan led Gorbachev to believe that a START agreement was possible at the Moscow Summit, even though he had secretly agreed, on the advice of his National Security Adviser, that "the further elimination of nuclear weapons would be only a long-term goal."

The Reagan Files takes the reader through the initial correspondences between Reagan and Gorbachev, into the NSC meetings discussing a possible summit, and then to Geneva where Reagan and Gorbachev met for the first time. Overall, Reagan and Gorbachev met five times, with the last meeting in New York serving the purpose of more of a farewell gathering than anything else. Although most of the meeting minutes leading up to the summits are still classified, the declassified letters between Reagan and Gorbachev discuss U.S.-Soviet relations, including negotiations leading up to the INF Treaty. The transcripts from the four summits have also been released and are used extensively in this edition.

No discussion of President Reagan's military modernization program would be complete without a review of the Strategic Defense Initiative (SDI). Labeled "Star Wars" by the media or a great "bargaining chip" by others, the documents show that Reagan and some of his advisers saw the development of a fully functioning SDI as a necessary step before the United States could agree to eliminate nuclear weapons. The minutes also show that Reagan was adamant about developing a working SDI system and sharing the benefits of SDI technology with not only the Soviet Union but the rest of the world.

"Why can't we agree now that if we get to a point where we want to deploy we will simply make all the information available about each others' systems so that we can both have defenses?" Reagan said in a September 8, 1987, meeting. "I don't believe we could ever do that," Secretary of Defense Weinberger responded. Ken Adelman, the Director of the Arms Control Disarmament Agency, echoed Weinberger: "Mr. President, that would be the most massive technical transfer the western world has ever known. ... If they understood our system that well it would be easy for them to move to countermeasures."

Throughout these negotiations, Reagan and Gorbachev engaged in what must have been some of the most important correspondences ever recorded between world leaders. In fact, Reagan and Gorbachev exchanged some thirty letters covering all areas of U.S.-Soviet relations. Where relevant, some of the letters have been reproduced to help tell the story of how President Reagan and General Secretary Gorbachev were able to come together to ease world tensions and start down the path that led to the end of the Cold War.

PART I:

REAGAN AND BREZHNEV

CHAPTER ONE

IMPLEMENTING THE REAGAN AGENDA
(FEBRUARY 6 – DECEMBER 3, 1981)

"Do we really want a zero-option for the battlefield?
Don't we need these nuclear systems?
Wouldn't it be bad for us to give them up
since we need them to handle
Soviet conventional superiority?"[6]

---

[6] President Reagan to his NSC advisers in an October 13, 1981 NSC meeting on Theater Nuclear Forces Negotiations.

"Interagency groups are reviewing the items on today's agenda, their work is not complete, but they will have issues for decision shortly," President Reagan opens his first NSC meeting, on February 6, 1981. Although the subject for the meeting was the Caribbean Basin and Poland, Reagan took the opportunity to explain to his foreign policy advisers how he wanted to use the NSC. Reagan continued,

> The NSC should meet frequently and help to formulate our policies. I urge cooperation at all levels. No one should stand on ceremony. During the campaign, I pledged to implement a new foreign policy and restore the margin of safety. I look to this group to help me. The Intelligence Community has a vital role. I intend to restore the vigor and effectiveness of our intelligence services.
>
> I will use the NSC structure to obtain your guidance, but I will make the decisions. Once made, I expect the Departments to implement them. Subcabinet appointments will play a vital role in effective implementation. The NSC is not just another cabinet agency. Although the decisions will be mine, you are the obvious source for good ideas. I want good advice. The NSC staff functions as an integral part of the White House, and Dick Allen places a premium on good management.

The remainder of the meeting discussed Soviet activities in connection with Poland, Afghanistan, Latin America and Cuba and everyone in the room agreed that the United States needed to not only stop, but reverse Soviet gains around the world.

The NSC met again on February 11, and the subject line this time just read "Central America." The discussion focused on how to stop Cuban involvement in the area with Reagan calling Cuba, "the source of the problem." A few weeks later Reagan received the first of many letters from General Secretary Brezhnev.

Date: **March 6, 1981**
Subject: **Letter, Brezhnev to Reagan (U.S.-Soviet relations)**

SUMMARY

Dear Mr. President,

I consider it necessary to turn to you concerning the most vital problems that are raised by the present international situation. I suppose you are aware that the Congress of our Party, which recently took place in Moscow, devoted paramount attention to analysis and evaluation of the international situation; as well as to the practical conclusions stemming from this. The question was, what should be done in order to preserve peace and to ensure for present and future generations the most basic right of each person – the right to life. This is the essence of the decisions that were taken, which will determine the foreign policy course of the Soviet Union in the years ahead.

We are realists, and of course we take due account of the fact that improvement of the international situation, the lessening and liquidation of the threat of war depend not only upon us but also upon the will of other governments, upon the success of establishing more appropriate mutual understanding and effective cooperation, both bilaterally and multilaterally, in resolving the vital problems of present times.

We are convinced that one's attitude toward the strategic military balance that has taken shape between the USSR and the USA, between the Warsaw Pact states and those of NATO, is of fundamental significance here. The Soviet Union has not sought, and does not seek military superiority. But neither will we permit such superiority to be established over us. Such attempts, as well as attempts to talk to us from a position of strength, are absolutely futile.

The existing strategic military equilibrium is objectively serving the cause of preserving world peace. We are for consistently bringing matters to the lowering of level of the equilibrium, without violating its balance. To attempt to win in an arms race, to count on victory in an atomic war – would be dangerous madness. It must be recognized that endless competition and accumulation of ever newer weapons, while keeping the world under tension, is the real source of the military threat that hands over all countries. We are prepared to act, hand in hand with all countries and above all with the United States, in decisive struggle against this threat. It is clear the great extent to which success here depends upon the joint actions precisely of our two countries.

We are in general for normal, good relations with the USA, for the development of these relations in the interests of the peoples of our two countries, in the interests of peace.

The present state of Soviet-American relations, the sharpness of the problems demanding solution, create the imperative need for the conduct and development of dialogue that is active and at all levels. The Soviet Union favors such a dialogue and is prepared to come to agreement regarding mutually acceptable decisions, with account for the lawful interests of the sides.

Soviet-American summit meetings have special significance in all this, and at the Congress we considered it feasible and advisable to speak out directly in favor of such a meeting.

As is known, in recent years the Soviet Union has put forward numerous proposals for reducing the threat of war and for strengthening international security. Many of these have been approved by the UN and other impressive fora. All of our proposals remain in force and we will work toward their realization.

However, the current situation is such that it is necessary to intensify efforts still more in order to improve the international situation radically, to give people confidence in a safe, peaceful future. Guided by this vital necessity, the Soviet Union has come forward with new, large initiatives permeated with deep concern to restrain the arms race, deepen détente, strengthen peace.

I found it necessary to call your personal attention, Mr. President, to these proposals, put forward, as you know, at the Congress of our Party. Apart from the scale and the far-reaching character of these initiatives, I wish in particular to underscore their realism, the account they take of both our own interests as well as the interests of our partners.

Experience shows how complicated and difficult it is to liquidate, to extinguish hotbeds of military conflict. It is therefore important to conduct preventive work to prevent such hotbeds from occurring.

In this context, measures to strengthen trust in the military sphere, carried out at the decision of the all-European conference, play a positive role. The Soviet Union has made proposals for widening significantly the volume of these measures.

We are now proposing to widen substantially the zone of applicability of such measures. We are prepared to extend them to the entire European part of the USSR, on the condition, of course, of a corresponding widening of the zone of measures of trust by the Western states. I would like in this connection once again to emphasize that the Soviet Union favors the successful conclusion of the Madrid meeting. Adoption at it of a decision to call an all-European conference for discussion and solution of problems of military détente and disarmament in Europe would have a particularly importance significance.

We also consider that the working out and adoption of measures of trust could also be useful in the area of the Far East. The Soviet Union would be prepared to conduct concrete negotiations on this account with all interested countries. Without predetermining now all problems relating to such negotiations, attention nonetheless should be called to the fact that in this region not only the USSR, China and Japan are neighbors. As is known, there is also a U.S. military presence. This and other specifics of the region would have to be considered, so that measures of trust would in fact be effective.

In some countries the opinion is expressed that our recent proposals concerning the Persian Gulf cannot be separated from the question of the presence of a Soviet military contingent in Afghanistan. Our position consists of the following: while prepared to reach agreement on the Persian Gulf as an independent problem, and to participate in a separate settlement of the situation around Afghanistan, we also do not object to the questions connected with Afghanistan being discussed in conjunction with the questions of security of the Persian Gulf. Such discussions naturally can concern only the international aspects of the Afghan problem, and not the internal affairs of that country. The sovereignty of Afghanistan must be fully-protected, as must its status as a nonaligned state.

Proceeding from the exceptional importance – not only for the USSR and the U.S.A., but also for other countries – of the problem of limiting and reducing strategic weapons, we for our part are prepared to continue without delay appropriate talks with the United States while preserving everything positive that has been achieved thus far in the field. It is understandable that such negotiations can be conducted only on the basis of equality and equal security of the sides.

As one of the practical measures in this area, we are prepared to reach agreement limiting the deployment of new submarines – in the U.S.A., the Ohio class, and submarines of a similar type in the USSR. We could also enter into accord on banning modernization of existing ballistic missiles and the creation of new ones for deployment on these submarines.

Attempting to avert the dangerous accumulation of nuclear missiles in Europe and to facilitate the speediest possible attainment of a decision regarding such weapons, we propose that agreement be reached on establishing a moratorium now on the deployment in Europe of new medium-range nuclear missile facilities in the USSR and the countries of NATO – that is, to freeze both quantitatively and qualitatively the existing level of such means, including, of course, the forward-based nuclear facilities of the U.S.A. in this region. Such a moratorium could come into force as soon as negotiations on this question commence, and would be effective until a treaty is concluded on limiting, or even better, on reducing such nuclear facilities in Europe. In this we proceed from the position that both sides would cease all preparations for deployment of corresponding additional means, including the American Pershing II missiles and ground-based strategic cruise missiles.

Judging from reports we have received, in certain places attempts are being made to represent the situation as if there were nothing new in this Soviet proposal. Nothing could be further from the truth. Assertions of this sort can only indicate an effort to evade a decision of the matter, a lack of desire to take account of the vital interests of the European peoples.

We consider that informing the general public, indeed all people, of the consequences with which atomic war is fought would have great significance, and would in particular bring additional influence on governments for attainment of agreements directed in a practical way toward averting such a war. With this aim in mind, we propose the creation of an authoritative international committee that would demonstrate the vital necessity of averting a nuclear catastrophe. The committee might include the most prominent scientists from various countries. Very likely the General Secretary of the UN could play a role in the realization of this aim. The conclusions reached by the committee should be made known to the entire world.

Further, for solution of many current international problems a far-sighted approach, political will and courage, authority and influence are required. This is why we believe it would be useful to convene a special session of the Security Council, with the participation of the top leaders of the permanent and non-permanent member states of the Council, in order to seek the key to improving the international atmosphere and preventing war. Leaders of other states obviously could take part in the session, if they wished. Naturally, thorough preparation for such a session would be required to ensure positive results.

Returning to the theme of hotbeds of tension and the task of liquidating them, I would like particularly to single out the question of the situation in the Middle East. No matter how one regards that which has thus far been done in this region, it is clear that political settlement there has been set back. The present situation urgently demands a return to a collective search for an all-embracing settlement on a just and realistic basis, which could be done, say within the framework of a specially convened international conference.

The Soviet Union is prepared to take part in a constructive spirit in such work jointly with other interested Liberation Front, and with Israel. We are prepared for such a joint search with the U.S.A., with which we have had in the past certain experience. We are prepared to cooperate with European states, with all who sincerely desire securing a just and stable peace in the Middle East. The U.N. clearly can continue to play a useful role here.

There are questions that I want to touch upon in this message. We expect, Mr. President, that you will regard our proposals with appropriate attention. As you see, they embrace a wide circle of problems and foresee measures of a political and military character; they concern various types of weapons and military forces; they touch upon the situation in various regions of the world.

We of course understand that time is required for study and consideration. Probably the necessity for some sort of consultations, exchange of views – in short, for various forms of dialogue – will arise. We are prepared for this.

Respectfully,
L. Brezhnev

POSTSCRIPT

Reagan's response to this letter could not be located.

Date: **March 26, 1981**
Subject: **Poland; Nicaragua; Southern Africa**
Status: **Declassified in Part (2005)**

SUMMARY

HAIG: The State Department has reached independent judgment that we are witnessing the most serious crisis in Poland since last August. Sensitive information from a former White House official indicates that there is a strong possibility that there will be an internal takeover by the Polish militia, the entrenchment of the party hardliners and a major crackdown on Polish dissidents, all of which could lead to armed conflict. Our assessments now indicate that Soviet forces are positioning themselves to move into Poland from without. Given the fact that the Polish Central Committee will be meeting on Sunday, with parliament scheduled to meet in an emergency session on Monday, a major move by Polish, and possibly Soviet forces, could occur on Monday.

Some believe that it is essential for the United States to make a strong statement, like the statement last December which helped to deter any move against the Polish workers. In this regard, the Europeans are far out in front of us. A statement by the United States should definitely lay out the repercussions of Soviet action and the consequences of internal suppression, while at the same time holding out the carrot of economic assistance.

The United States should move quickly if it wishes for a U.S. statement to have a preemptive benefit. I have already prepared such a statement, which the State Department can issue, or, in the alternative, can be issued by the President, by the White House press secretary, or some other appropriate individual. In any case, a public statement is much better than a letter.

BAKER:	What did the West Germans say?
HAIG:	They noted the seriousness of the situation.

[The official meeting minutes indicate that Haig starts reading the prepared statement which noted United States concern and hope for a peaceful resolution of the situation on a "basis acceptable to all parties concerned."]

WEINBERGER:	Has the deputy prime minister been invited?
HAIG:	He has been planning to come for some time.
REAGAN:	**Would a quiet indication by us to the Soviets that we might be willing to lift the grain embargo if they exercised restraint with respect to Poland help the situation? The Secretary of Agriculture wants it lifted and I'm now caught between a campaign promise and the need to resolve a domestic issue.**
WEINBERGER:	It would be impossible to lift the grain embargo if the Soviets move into Poland.
REAGAN:	**We need to make a strong statement.**
HAIG:	I'm concerned about mixing domestic and foreign policy issues.
REAGAN:	**It is not a domestic issue to those people affected by the grain embargo.**

HAIG:	There are already a series of agreed-upon measures to be taken unilaterally by the United States and jointly by the NATO allies. A working meeting at the state department this afternoon is going to be held to continue those deliberations.
	While the grain embargo is an important issue, it is a peripheral one and could possibly lessen the impact of the warning statement to be issued by the United States.
CASEY:	It is questionable whether the Soviets are even concerned about the grain embargo at this point in time.
MEESE:	I think that lifting the grain embargo will have an impact.
CASEY:	I think it would have very little impact at this particular time.
ALLEN:	Can we have the proposed text distributed to attendees?
CASEY:	The CIA concurs with the assessment of the situation in Poland presented by Secretary Haig.
REAGAN:	**Can the proposed statement be strengthened with a veiled threat regarding US-Soviet relations in the future, with the implication that while the United States would like to lift the grain embargo, it is impossible to do so under the present circumstances?**
HAIG:	We need to get the message out in a short, sharp fashion. It the Soviets do not move into Poland, the United States could indicate its intentions to lift the grain embargo at some future time.
MEESE:	What are the European allies prepared to do?
HAIG:	They are prepared to do far less than the United States. At the same time, however, it is important to maintain unity with the allies.

[Copies of the proposed statement are distributed to all the attendees].

	With respect to the allies, the United States should tell them it is going to issue a statement. The United States should also send a message to NATO informing them of the importance of maintaining unity.
SMITH:	Sooner or later we knew it had to happen.
HAIG:	The statement might have added impact if it was noted that it had been adopted at a meeting of the National Security Council. Is the meeting underway a meeting of the NSC or a meeting of the NSPG?
ALLEN:	The meeting is listed on the President's schedule as a meeting of the NSC.

[The official meeting meetings say: "With one slight change in wording regarding the visit of the Deputy Prime Minister, the attendees agreed that the draft statement should be issued by the White House Press Office.]

The discussion then shifts to Central America, Nicaragua and South Africa.

POSTSCRIPT

A few days later, on March 30, President Reagan was shot and nearly killed outside the Washington Hilton hotel after giving a speech to the AFL-CIO. The would be assassin, John Hinkley Jr., was a delusional young man trying to get the attention of actress Jodi Foster.

Hinkley's shots missed President Reagan, but one of the bullets ricocheted off his motorcade, and the flattened bullet entered through his left armpit before stopping dangerously close to his heart. Not realizing that Reagan had been shot because the secret service could not find an entry wound due to the flattened bullet, it was not until Reagan started coughing up blood that the car was diverted to George Washington University Hospital where emergency surgery saved his life.

The minutes of the April 11 NSC meeting, the first after the assassination attempt, are still classified. However, before the next declassified meeting on April 30, Reagan and Brezhnev exchanged several letters, including a letter Reagan wrote by hand while recovering in the hospital from his near-death experience.

Date: **April ?, 1981 (exact date could not be determined)**
Subject: **Letter: Brezhnev to Reagan (U.S.-Soviet relations)**

Dear Mr. President:

In connection with your communication of April 4, I am bound to state at the outset, that in our opinion, its content and its form serve no useful purpose either at the level of Soviet-American relations or from the point of view of the normalization of the situation in Poland.

In fact, it repeats again the motif of imaginary "threats" to Poland on the part of the Soviet Union which already for an extended time have been tossed from one American announcement to another.

The more frequently such statements are made the more apparent becomes their true character. It is doubtful that anyone can be deceived by them. Already for a long time – practically from the beginning of the well-known internal events in Poland – it was precisely the United States, and the Administration itself, that has applied crude pressure on the situation in Poland and, in essence, interfered in the internal affairs of that country.

When in Washington, at the very highest official levels, there are issued public "warnings" to the Polish People's Republic against the adoption of measures to stop the actions of those who strive to throw the country into anarchy and at the same time, in no unmistakable terms, there are threats of some kind of punishments, we are faced not just with interference but with open incitement to the continuation of disorders and disobedience of legitimate authority. By virtue of what right is this done?

And is it necessary to recall what is being done for the support of anti-government elements in Poland by way of American secret services and other organizations, particularly through the radio broadcasts to that country by stations which are controlled by the U.S. government? It is no secret that the same purposes are served also by the pseudo-humanitarian assistance to particular groups in Poland on the part of certain American trade unions.

Actions of this kind are impermissible in relations between sovereign states. The USA, after all, has also signed the United Nations Charter which gives no one the right to interfere in the internal affairs of other countries. And in how many authoritative international documents since the UN Charter have the governments of the world decisively expressed themselves in favor of this principle, hallowed by centuries, which no one is allowed to trample?

We wish directly to warn the United States of America: do not interfere in the internal affairs in Poland. If Washington genuinely desires that life in Poland return as soon as possible to normal – as is declared there, from time to time – then one should act accordingly.

As concerns the happenings in Poland, we have proceeded and continue to proceed from the collective position of the states of the Warsaw Pact, which, we assume, is known to you.

It should be clear that socialist Poland which, together with its allies, is a member of the organization of the Warsaw Pact, is going to be protected from all assaults from the outside on its prevailing system, from all claims of external power to intervene in the solution of its internal affairs.

And one more thing. In your communication you make an attempt to link the internal events in Poland with international problems and to issue some kind of warnings on that subject. In this connection one can only express regret that in Washington, apparently, there is inadequate awareness of the truth that any positive achievement can be only the result of the mutual wish of the parties. In the solution of international problems, whether these be questions of European security or arms limitation, all states must be equally interested, including the US, and no one may assume that here one can punish someone else without first punishing himself.

Of course, I am decidedly not in agreement with the manner in which in your communication you interpret the Afghanistan question. Our point of view on this question, we have expressed more than once, is scarcely necessary to do this again.

If one is to touch on the American position in regard to Afghanistan then it is clearly reflected in such facts as the recent public announcement of the intention of the USA to provide weapons to the interventionists and terrorists who are sent into Afghanistan, as well as the pressure exerted by the US on Pakistan for the purpose of preventing the opening of an Afghanistan-Pakistan dialogue with which we sympathize and which would open the way to a political solution of the problem.

Mr. President, I have frankly given you our position on the questions which you have raised. We are indeed ready to discuss any problems which may arise. It seems, however, that it would be counterproductive and not in the interests of our two countries to reduce everything to mutual recriminations and accusations. The situation in the world is such that there is a pressing necessity for a constructive dialogue for the purpose of locating mutually acceptable solutions of the world's unresolved problems. This also applies to Soviet-American relations.

Respectfully,
L. Brezhnev

Date: **April 24, 1981**
Subject: **Letters from Reagan to Brezhnev**

BACKGROUND

While Reagan was in the hospital recovering from the assassination attempt, the Department of State was working on a response to Brezhnev's warning to avoid interfering in Poland and Afghanistan. Reagan really did not like the draft State prepared, and with a belief that he was saved for a reason, decided to take matters into his own hand despite the best efforts of his advisers to stop what they considered a foolish endeavor. Brezhnev, what must have been to his surprise, received both Reagan's handwritten letter and the letter prepared by the Department of State. A typed version of Reagan's handwritten letter can be found in the endnotes. Reagan lifted the grain embargo against the Soviet Union the same day he sent these letters.

[President Reagan's April 24, 1981 handwritten letter to Secretary Brezhnev, pg.1]

SYSTEM II   5
90204

THE WHITE HOUSE
WASHINGTON

My Dear Mr. President

In writing the attached letter I am
reminded of our meeting in San Clemente
a decade or so ago. I was Governor of
California at the time and you were
concluding a series of meetings with President
Nixon. Those meetings had captured the
imagination of all the world. Never had
peace and good will among men seemed
closer at hand.

When we met I asked if you were
aware that the hopes and aspirations of
millions and millions of people throughout
the world were dependent on the decisions
that would be reached in your meetings.

You took my hand in both of yours
and assured me that you were aware of
that and that you were dedicated with
all your heart and mind to fulfilling
those hopes and dreams.

The people of the world still share that
hope. Indeed the peoples of the world,
despite differences in racial and ethnic
origin, have very much in common. They
want the dignity of having some control
over their individual destiny. They want
to work at the craft or trade of their

[President Reagan's April 24, 1981 handwritten letter to Secretary, pg. 2]

2

own choosing and to be fairly rewarded. They want to raise their families in peace without harming anyone or suffering harm themselves. Government exists for their convenience, not the other way around.

If they are incapable, as some would have us believe, of self government, then where among them do we find any who are capable of governing others?

Is it possible that we have permitted ideology, political and economic philosophies, and governmental policies to keep us from considering the very real, everyday problems of our peoples? Will the average Soviet family be better off or even aware that the Soviet Union has imposed a government of it's own choice on the people of Afghanistan? Is life better for the people of Cuba because the Cuban military dictate who shall govern the people of Angola?

It is often implied that such things have been made necessary because of territorial ambitions of the United States; that we have imperialistic designs and thus constitute a threat to your own security and that of the newly emerging nations. There not only is no evidence to support such a charge, there is solid evidence that the United States, when it could have dominated the world with no risk to itself, made no effort

P

[President Reagan's April 24, 1981 handwritten letter to Secretary, pg.3]

7

whatsoever to do so.

When World War II ended, the United States had the only undamaged industrial power in the world. Our military might was at it's peak — and we alone had the ultimate weapon, the nuclear weapon, with the unquestioned ability to deliver it anywhere in the world. If we had sought world domination then, who could have opposed us?

But the United States followed a different course — one unique in all the history of mankind. We used our power and wealth to rebuild the war-ravaged economies of the world, including those nations who had been our enemies. May I say there is absolutely no substance to charges that the United States is guilty of imperialism or attempts to impose it's will on other countries by use of force.

Mr. President, should we not be concerned with eliminating the obstacles which prevent our people — those we represent — from achieving their most cherished goals? And isn't it possible some of those obstacles are born of govt. objectives which have little to do with the real needs and desires of our people?

It is in this spirit, in the spirit of helping the people of both our nations, that I have lifted the grain embargo. Perhaps this decision will contribute to creating the circumstances which will lead to the meaningful and constructive dialogue which will assist us in fulfilling our joint obligation to find lasting peace.

Sincerely
Ronald Reagan

[President Reagan's Typed Letter of April 24, 1981 to Secretary Brezhnev]

Dear President Brezhnev:

Thank you for your letter of March 6.

Your letter raises many complex issues which obviously cannot be dealt with in an exchange of correspondence, except in general terms. Please be assured that our country is vitally interested in the peaceful resolution of international tensions. This Administration is prepared to settle disagreements by negotiations. We are also prepared to observe scrupulously our international commitments.

At the same time I must be frank in stating my view that a great deal of the tension in the world today is due to Soviet actions. As we and our allies have repeatedly stated, two aspects of Soviet behavior are of particular concern to us:

-- First, the USSR's unremitting and comprehensive military buildup over the past 15 years, a buildup which in our view far exceeds purely defensive requirements and carriers disturbing implications of a search for military superiority.

-- Second, the Soviet Union's pursuit of unilateral advantage in various parts of the globe and its repeated resort to the direct and indirect use of force.

These activities raise serious questions about the Soviet Union's commitment to the peaceful resolution of outstanding issues in accord with international law, the "Basic Principles of Relations" concluded between our two countries in Moscow in 1972, and the Helsinki Final Act.

I believe that real progress in relations between our two countries is possible and necessary. But my Administration is determined to judge Soviet intentions on the basis of actions and demonstrated restraint.

This does not diminish our commitment to constructive dialogue. Effective and meaningful communication between our two countries is absolutely essential. I welcome your assurance that the USSR also believes in such a dialogue. We should work together to avoid misunderstanding or miscalculation.

A personal meeting and a direct exchange of views would certainly be a useful way of pursuing this dialogue at the appropriate time. Clearly, however, the success of such a meeting would depend in large measure on careful preparation and a propitious international climate. I do not believe that these conditions exist at present, and so my preference would be for postponing a meeting of such importance to a later date.

All Americans share your concern over the threat to mankind in the age of nuclear weapons. I welcome your statement that the USSR is prepared for discussions with the United States on limiting strategic weapons. I have stated publicly that the United States is ready to undertake discussions with the USSR that would lead to genuine arms reductions. We are presently engaged in a review of arms control and as soon as this review is completed we will be in touch with your Government.

Your acceptance of the principle that confidence-building measures should apply throughout Europe, including all of the European portions of the USSR, strikes me as encouraging. As our delegation at the Madrid Review Conference has made clear, we support France's proposal for a meeting to negotiate a coherent system of measures on European security: obligatory, verifiable and of military significance. Soviet acceptance of these criteria would eliminate important obstacles to the holding of a security meeting within the CSCE framework as part of a balance outcome from the Madrid conference.

I am afraid, however, that I cannot be sanguine about your treatment of other arms control issues, especially your proposal for a moratorium on deployments of theatre nuclear forces in Europe.

At the time it took its December 1979 decision, NATO rejected the concept of a moratorium because it would perpetuate existing Soviet superiority in long-range theatre nuclear forces. The continuing deployment since then of Soviet SS-20 launchers targeted against NATO has worsened the situation. NATO deploys no land-based missiles in Europe that could reach territory of the Soviet Union. The reasoning that prompted the Alliance to reject a moratorium in December 1979 is thus even more persuasive today.

Further to our exchanges on Poland, I must reject charges that the United States is intervening in that country's affairs. This is simply not true. As we have repeatedly made clear, our concern is that the Polish Government and people be allowed to resolve their problems peacefully and free from any outside interference. In our view, recent Soviet military behavior and tendentious propaganda amount to a threat of the use of force which represents interference in Poland's internal affairs.

In this connection I have noted with concern repeated statements by responsible Soviet official suggesting that the form of a country's political, social and economic system bestows upon the Soviet Union special rights and, indeed, duties, to preserve a particular form of government in other countries. I must inform you frankly and emphatically that the United States rejects any such declaration as contrary to the charter of the United Nations and other international instruments, including the Helsinki Final Act. Claims of special "rights," however defined, cannot be used to justify the threat of force to infringe upon the sovereign rights of any country to determine its own political, economic and social institutions.

I was disappointed that in your treatment of Afghanistan, the most important element in the situation was not mentioned – the prompt withdrawal of Soviet forces from that country. There is wide international agreement that the Soviet military presence in Afghanistan is a major source of tension in the area. Proposals for dealing with this by initiating a dialogue between Pakistan and Afghanistan have been firmly rejected by the Pakistanis themselves and by virtually all concerned nations since they fail to deal with the central issue of Soviet withdrawal. Evidence that the Soviet Union is prepared to move toward an acceptable resolution of the Afghanistan problem on the basis of her prompt withdrawal would go far toward restoring international confidence and trust necessary for the improvement of East West relations.

I have spoken frankly in order to convey to you my views and feelings, and give you a clear sense of the basic foreign policies of my Administration. The discussion initiated in this exchange should continue through the full range of diplomatic channels. If you agree, Secretary Haig and Foreign Minister Gromyko might meet for further exchanges on these and related matters. The traditional meeting at the United Nations in September may be an appropriate forum. Perhaps by that time a basis will exist not only for deepening our bilateral dialogue, but for considering how and at what ace we may begin to build a better and happier relationship.

Sincerely,

Ronald Reagan

Date: **April 30, 1981**
Subject: **Theater Nuclear Forces (TNF) Negotiations**
Status: **Declassified (2005)**

SUMMARY

Haig argues: (1) It is vitally important that he and Secretary Weinberger commit the U.S. to a specific date; (2) The United States cannot put conditions on a timetable for negotiations; (3) The negotiations must be conducted using the SALT framework; and (4) The State position on these issues is that we should lay out a timetable to meet with Soviet Foreign Minister Gyomyko by the fall and to negotiate with the Soviets on TNF by the end of the year.

Deputy Secretary of Defense Carlucci tells the President that DOD is not opposed to negotiations or discussions of timetables, but that any negotiations with the Soviet's must be preceded by a common assessment of the threat and of our requirements. Carlucci recommends a public position of hoping to begin negotiations by the end of the year and in the meantime immediately working out the details with the allies.

"We all agree that we need positive movement on modernization before we go into the negotiations," Reagan responds. "If we do not, then the Soviets will drag their feet because of their large advantage in TNF."

Reagan then asks Haig for a clarification of what he meant by the term, "SALT framework." "It implies a linkage between TNF negotiations and the broader SALT process," Haig clarified.

The meeting returns to discussing a proposed date to begin negotiations. Haig repeats his emphasis on the importance of setting a date while Carlucci again argues for first completing the necessary studies. President Reagan then settles the issue:

> We will conduct the studies. We will continue to deploy modern systems. We believe the study can be done by the end of the year, and look forward to negotiations in that time frame. We will discuss with Gromyko in the fall. If the studies are not ready by the end of the year we will take that into consideration. The language "SALT framework" is okay, but needs to be clearly separated from an interpretation that we are resuming the Carter SALT approach.

Date: **May 22, 1981**
Subject: **US-USSR Standing Consultative Commission (SCC)**
Status: **Declassified in Part (2005)**

SUMMARY

The following introductory arguments are presented:

ALLEN: We have a fairly tight agenda today. The issues for discussion are: (1) next week's meeting of the US-Soviet Standing Consultative Commission (SCC); (2) US policy towards Sudan; (3) US policy towards Libya; and (4) a new Central American policy framework.

The SCC is a body created by the signatories to the SALT I agreements to oversee compliance issues. At issue today, is what approach the US will take at the May 27 meeting of the SCC, the first time during this

Administration. Guidelines for such an approach and for instructions to the US Delegation have been worked out in a series of Interagency Group meetings and at the Senior Interdepartmental Group (SIG) level. An outline of the State Department's discussion papers on this approach is attached at Tab A. The Secretary of State, the Secretary of Defense, and others will speak on the proposed approach.

HAIG: The discussion paper reflects sound interagency consensus. Let us review its basic points. The SCC is essentially a technical body reviewing SALT compliance issues. At this forum, we will express some general concerns about non-SALT arms control compliance issues, but we see more detailed expressions of such non-SALT concerns as one to be delivered through our Embassy in Moscow by our Charge, Jack Matlock.

On the ABM Treaty, we will provide the routine notifications, state our adherence, and raise compliance concerns involving concurrent Soviet testing of SAMs and radars. On the Interim Agreement (IA) and SALT II, we will be noncommittal about our observance, using only the general formula that while our policy review is underway, we will take no actions to undercut existing agreements as long as the Soviet Union exercises the same restraints.

At the SCC, we will not raise compliance issues in terms of specific provisions of the Interim and SALT II agreements. But in the general context of compliance concerns will raise three issues: (1) telemetry encryption; (2) reconstitution/reload capability; and (3) ICBM launcher dismantling. Internally we will agree not to seek ratification of SALT II, and will agree that we are prepared to take actions inconsistent with SALT II and the Interim Agreements if required by national security considerations.

Our next steps in developing SALT policy should be to ask the SALT IG, which has done an outstanding job so far, to undertake three further analyses. First, the IG should consider steps by which we would implement our internal policy concerning SALT II and the Interim Agreement, including the modalities of withdrawing the SALT II Treaty from the Senate, how we should officially inform the Soviets, what to say to our Congress and public, and what, if any, planned or proposed US defense programs might be inconsistent with the Interim Agreement or SALT II.

Second, the IG should undertake a formal interagency review of the ABM Treaty and of US ABM options in the arms control context. Third, the IG should initiate a study of long-term US SALT approaches designed to support our strategic force modernization programs and including our policy towards the Soviets and towards our allies.

MEESE: Who is heading our delegation to the SCC?

ALLEN: Brigadier General John Lasater. Secretary Weinberger, do you wish to say something?

WEINBERGER: This will be our first time in the same room as the Soviets discussing SALT. We see the SCC as a technical level discussion, but the Soviets will want to use it for much wider purposes, including probes of our position on the Interim Agreement and SALT II. We should emphasize that this is a lower-level technical forum, and we should stay away from the larger arms control issues.

On the internal policy review issue, I do not think we should say that we will take actions inconsistent with SALT II. After all, SALT II is not in effect. President Carter urged that the Senate not vote on it, and it is in no sense pending. Earlier the Armed Services Committee rejected it by vote of 10-0, and the Senate Foreign Relations Committee favored it by only one vote. SALT II is not alive. Our defense budget does not involve any violation of the SALT II agreement, but that was by chance, and we should retain flexibility.

ROSTOW: In preparing the back-up policy papers for today, over 30 suspected Soviet arms control violations were carefully examined. The proposed instructions to our SCC Commissioner would raise five SALT compliance issues as follows: (1) SAM and ABM concurrent testing; (2) large phased-array radars; (3) telemetry encryption; (4) reconstitution/reload capability; and (5) ICBM launcher dismantling.

In instructions to our embassy in Moscow, we would have them raise four non-SALT compliance issues as matters of U.S. concern, to include: (1) chemical warfare in Afghanistan and elsewhere; (2) biological incidents at Sverdlovsk; (3) the floating radioactive materials; and (4) nuclear testing.

Looking ahead, I would like our arms control policy to accentuate the positive. We should not be talking just about withdrawal but what to do next. In my calls on Senator Percy and other Senators, we agreed that the best way to handle the SALT II Treaty issue would be via a Senate resolution, unanimous if possible, sending it back to the White House, while at about the same time, the Administration would announce its policy of where we want to go in arms control and what we wish to achieve.

JONES: We have found past SCC meetings with the Soviets very useful. It is a rare forum for military-to-military contact.

On the SCC approach proposed before us today, we have no fundamental differences. However, we see a problem in the proposed distinction between our internal and external policy on our observance of SALT II and the Interim Agreement.

Publicly, it is proposed that we would say we will take no action inconsistent with SALT II, while internally we would agree to take actions inconsistent with SALT II and the Interim Agreement, if required by national security considerations. We should recognize that the Soviets can do many things in the near term if they cease to observe current SALT restrictions, such as increasing their SS-18 Reentry Vehicles (RVs) from 10 to 20 or 30. In the short run, we cannot match them. We would, therefore, prefer to see us stay with the language that we will not take actions that would undercut existing agreements as long as the Soviet Union exercises the same restraints. A further consideration is that we probably cannot keep the knowledge of any sensitive internal US Government decision within the confines of this room.

MEESE: We can keep it in this room. Our internal decision would not be communicated to the Commissioner.

JONES: We have not been too successful so far.

HAIG: General Jones has a point – that this formulation may be too negative. I am quite comfortable with the language here in our discussion paper, but I would like to have the old language in any public areas.

WEINBERGER: Several practical issues are involved here. For example, if our 4,600 M-X holes have to be opened up under SALT II verification, this adds three to four billion dollars in cost. As for jeopardizing current SALT II restrictions on the Soviets, there are things the Soviets could chose to do, of course, but I suspect they are doing these things anyway, and I am against restraining our own programs. That's why I opposed SALT II. Also, our Trident program is affected, and a whole host of other programs.

MEESE: Our public posture should be that of taking no actions that would undercut existing agreements as long as the Soviets exercise the same restraints. On the other hand, none of our programs should be inhibited by SALT II.

REAGAN: **What can the Soviets really do that prevents us from telling them now that we cannot go along with SALT II?**

ALLEN: It would indicate to the rest of the world that we are against the SALT process. We've all been imprisoned by the SALT language. We need some new categories, e.g., Strategic Arms Reductions Talks. They would be known as START.

WEINBERGER: We should also be looking at ABM defense as arms control. Let's keep our options open on ABM. On the distinction between real arms reductions, as distinguished from arms limitations, the public does not realize the important differences. For example, in SALT, the Soviets could deploy an unlimited number of missiles and their intercontinental Backfire bomber.

REAGAN: **Why should we preserve the illusion of SALT if we are going to slide around and do what we accuse the Soviets of doing, (violating it)?**

MEESE: The SCC Commissioner will focus on technical matters and will not be addressing these larger issues.

JONES: With SALT restrictions lifted, the Soviets could rapidly deploy more missiles, warheads, and Backfire bombers, and there is little, if anything, we can do to prevent or to match it. There is no SALT impact on our M-X now because we will not begin deployment until 1986. You can forget about the M-X verification port holes until 1984. On Trident, we can make a decision a year from now. Let's stick with the public statement.

HAIG: We have to avoid creating a negative stalemate in the public's mind. We need to express our objectives and clarify our approach on issues like the ABM.

REAGAN:	**But the Soviets are not being restrained by SALT II, are they?**
JONES:	So far, they have not taken no actions inconsistent with the provisions of the Treaty, except, perhaps in the area of verification. On the SS-18, they could go rapidly from 10 to 20 RVs.
WEINBERGER:	However, there are some real concerns about Soviet compliance with the ABM Treaty and the Interim Agreement.
JONES:	Yes, there are.
CASEY:	(Two lines redacted).
ROSTOW:	That dimension is fully taken care of in these papers.
SCHNEIDER:	As a footnote to what Secretary Weinberger said about SALT restrictions on US programs, I recall that the SIG also referred to the Protocol restrictions on our sea-based cruise missile and other programs.
JONES:	The Protocol expires on December 31, 1981. Then it has no programmatic impact.
ALLEN:	The issue before us today is approval of this guidance for the SCC meetings. We will be continuing our review of the larger issues and will be bringing up these issues here at another time. Do you approve?
REAGAN:	**Okay.**

A short discussion follows on the Caribbean Basin, and Libya and Sudan are both left for another meeting. Reagan receives Brezhnev's response to his April 24 handwritten letter just a few days later.

Date: May 25, 1981

Subject: **Letter from Brezhnev to Reagan, (response to Reagan's handwritten April 24, 1981 letter)**

Dear Mr. President,

I gave a careful thought to your personal letter to me and want to respond to it in the same personal and frank manner.

Just as you do, I recall our brief conversation at the reception given by President R. Nixon at "Casa Pacifica" in June 1973. Today, as we did at that time, all Soviet leadership and I commit our hearts and minds to realization of hopes and aspirations of all the peoples of the world for peace, quiet life and confidence in their future.

At the recent congress of our Party it was with all due emphasis stressed once again that not war preparations that doom the peoples to a senseless squandering of their material and spiritual wealth, but preservation and consolidation of peace, and, thereby, implementation of the foremost right of every man – a right to live that is the clue to the future.

I noted that, recalling the year of 1973 you indicated that peace and good will among men never had seemed closer at hand.

And, indeed, precisely in those years our two countries took the path of reaching agreements which marked a radical turn for the better not only in Soviet-American relations, but in the international situation as a whole. Those were the years when the USSR and the USA actively and not without success set about to solve the task of limiting arms, first of all strategic arms, when they started seeking in common solutions to acute international problems, when mutually beneficial bilateral ties and cooperation between our countries in a variety of fields were developing fruitfully.

Why then did hitches begin to appear in that process, why did it pause and even find itself set back? To answer this question correctly one thing is necessary – to take an objective, non-biased look at the course of events.

And then, Mr. President, we shall recall, that even at that time when Soviet-American relations were developing upward voices resounded in the United States of those who did not like such a development and who stubbornly tried to slow down and disrupt this process. And further on, their efforts became ever more active. Those were the efforts that were pulling back, to confrontation, efforts embodied in quite a number of concrete steps directly aimed against the improvement of relations between the USSR and the USA, against the relaxation of international tension. On the contrary, nothing of the sort was taking place in the Soviet Union.

We have differences of opinion between us of philosophical and ideological nature, and it could not be otherwise. But when it comes to the events of international life – whether pertaining to the present day, to the recent or more distant past, -- then an objective approach is not only possible, but necessary. Otherwise it is easy to misstep and to plunge into serious errors.

Here, for example, it is said in your letter that after the Second World War the USA had a capability to dominate the world, but, deliberately, as it were, made no use of that capability. Let me say it straight away, it is hard to find many people among those who are familiar with that time through their own experience or who had seriously studied it, that would share such an affirmation.

Actually, the USA did the maximum it could using a wide array of military, political, and economic means to achieve what American leaders themselves called "Pax Americana", in other words, to restructure the world the way the United States wanted it to be. But this proved to be beyond its possibilities – and this is the way it was. Even the possession during a certain period of time of what you call "the ultimate weapons" didn't make the USA omnipotent.

To follow your logic, we, in our turn, could have said that after the defeat of the Hitler Germany and, incidentally, even before the American atomic bomb emerged, the Soviet Union was in a position to do much of what it didn't do being guided by its principled convictions, true to its word and respecting its allied commitments. However I wouldn't like to go deeper into this subject now and to discuss events that didn't take place.

You are saying that the policy of the USA has never constituted a threat to anyone else's security. Let us go back to the facts again. Hardly three years passed after the end of the war when the USA set about to create the NATO – a closed military block. One would wonder what the need for it was. After all, fascist Germany had been routed and militarist Japan destroyed. The keys to peace were in the hands of the allied powers of the Anti-Hitler coalition. Who was the target of the military block of NATO and the numerous overseas American bases? No secret was made in the USA who all that was directed against.

You made mention of the post-war American economic assistance programs. The USA did really give assistance. But who was the recipient? It was only those countries which chose to submit their policy to foreign interests. On the contrary, the states belonging to a different social system, and, indeed, generally the peoples which did not agree to submit their policy to outside diktat did not receive the American assistance. That is how matters stood. In essence that is precisely how they stand at the present time.

If we are to take the most recent years, when after a period of ascent the relations between our countries began to deteriorate, and deteriorate sharply, it is known that the lion's share was contributed to that by the Carter administration. That was done consciously and purposefully, but in the final analysis, let us be frank, it brought no laurels to Carter. Isn't it so, Mr. President?

However, for some reason or other, the new US administration too had decided to continue on the same path. They, Mr. President, to see what is going on through our eyes. Attempts are being made to revitalize the USA-made military and political alliances, new bases are being added to those which already exist thousands of kilometers away from the USA and aimed against our country, the American military presence abroad in general is being increased and expanded, large areas of the world are being declared spheres of "vital interests" of the USA. Nobody even asks if the peoples inhabiting those areas wish to be under the patronage of other countries. Attempts are made to tell some other peoples what to do with their natural resources, threatening them otherwise with all kinds of punitive actions.

For all their difference, however, the peoples have the same right to be masters of their own destiny. There should be no double standards in this respect. One must not believe that if something is good for the USA then it has also to be good for others. After all, is it good, for instance, for the average American family, not to mention the family of a peaceful Afghan peasant, when the intention is openly announced in Washington to go on with supplying arms to the bands carrying out incursions into the Afghanistan territory from the outside?

It is not for the sake of polemics that I am sharing my thoughts with you, Mr. President. I would like them on the one hand, to give you a better understanding of what actually constitutes the policy of the Soviet Union, and, on the other hand, to help clarify how we and indeed, others as well, perceive certain actions of the USA, especially those of recent time.

The main idea, though, that I would like to convey through my letter is that we do not seek confrontation with the USA or infringe upon American legitimate interests. What we seek is different – we wish peaceful cooperation, a sense of mutual trust, and benevolence between the Soviet Union and the United States of America. Guided by this sincere desire we propose now to the USA and other Western countries honest and constructive negotiations, as well as a search for mutually acceptable solutions of practically all major questions existing between us – be it restraining of the arms race, elimination of most dangerous sources of tension in various areas of the world, or measures for confidence building and developing a mutually beneficial cooperation. These proposals of ours contain no ruse or any ulterior motives. And I would like you to accept them precisely in this way and with no bias.

Thus our policy is a policy of peace. We will never set up the fire of war. You know very well, as we do, what such a fire would lead to. I would want to believe in the wisdom of your people, in your personal wisdom also not to allow anything that would push the world towards a catastrophe.

These are some of the general considerations which I wanted to convey to you, Mr. President, in conjunction with your letter. Maybe it was not possible to express everything in sufficient detail. An exchange of correspondence has its limitations, and in this sense a private conversation is better. In this regard, concerning the possible meeting between us, I would like to say that it is also my view that such a meeting should be well prepared. We could yet return to the question of its timing, I believe, at a moment acceptable to both of us.

Sincerely,

L. Brezhnev

Date:　　　　**May 27, 1981**
Subject:　　　**Letter from Brezhnev to Reagan (response to Reagan's April 24, 1981 typed letter)**

Dear Mr. President,

I carefully studied your letter of April 24. And I will tell you right away of my appreciation of the frank expression of your views and feelings as well as the principle directions of your Administration's foreign policy. It is in the same spirit of frankness that I want to give you my reply believing that clarifying mutually the positions of each other has an important significance in developing a dialogue between us. This, as I understand, corresponds to your intentions too.

Your letter, regrettably, is based upon a general premise of the Soviet Union being responsible for the tensions existing in the world. Such a premise not only is at variance with the factual state of affairs, but leads away from the real causes behind the current situation, and, thus, can only make it more difficult to find ways to eliminate those causes in order to remove the tensions.

All assertions concerning a Soviet military threat or our alleged search for military superiority do not become any more convincing through having them repeated. Aims and intentions which are not ours must not be ascribed to us. After all, we set our goals ourselves. And we, for our part, say in no uncertain terms: the Soviet Union did not have and has no intentions to achieve military superiority. We have no need for it.

Our actions in the field of assuring our country's defense capability – and we are doing nothing beyond that – have always been only a forced reaction in response to the military programs carried out in the West. Indeed, it is a generally recognized fact that every new spiral in the arms race has been initiated by the United States. And what is typical is that each time such thrusts were accompanied by vociferous outcries about the "Soviet military threat", about the US "lagging behind" on a particular kind of weapon. True, it would be admitted later on in a whisper that no "lagging behind" had in fact taken place, that someone, as it were, had made a "wrong calculation." But, by then, what was done was done, new weapon systems had been deployed and the quantity of arms amassed had been significantly increased. This is what the facts testify to, and, indeed, they are accessible to everyone.

We are witnessing today an active propagation of the thesis that the alleged "imbalance of forces" has occurred and that the USSR entertains some "sinister intentions". Your predecessors, however, including the President whom you succeeded, recognized that there was a parity in the military area between the USSR and the USA, between the East and the West. Does it seem that all depends on who does the counting?

It is not in the Soviet Union at all that huge military budgets are being adopted and programs are being started on an unprecedented scale to produce new weapon systems, which does not only exceed the defense requirements but reasonable limits in general. Again, it is not in the USSR that demands are being made to rescind agreements reached earlier on arms limitation, that the intention is loudly proclaimed to surpass militarily all other states, that a definite status is being given to doctrines envisaging the possibility of delivering the first strike and waging "limited" wars with the use of nuclear weapons. And that is precisely the way it is.

Therefore, it is not our side that should be urged to exercise restraint. The Soviet Union is not for the competition in armaments, nor is it for their endless build-up. We stand for the preservation of the existing parity in the military-strategic area, which is the most important guarantee of peace and stability of all peoples, as well as for a gradual reduction of the arms level on the basis of the principle of equality and equal security of either side.

Nor is there any ground, Mr. President, to charge us with having the intention to obtain some unilateral advantage anywhere in the world, to call into doubt our commitment to the principles embodied in the UN Charter, in the Helsinki Final Act or in the Basic Principles of Relations between the USSR and the USA. This simply does not square with the facts.

The Soviet Union is resolutely against interference in the affairs of other peoples, against imposing someone else's will on them. But we are also against anybody arrogating to himself such a right, and when attempts to this effect take place we are invariably on the side of the peoples who stand up for their own independence.

I will address myself briefly to certain specific questions raised in your letter.

You speak positively of our consent to have the zone of application of confidence-building measures in the military area substantially expanded, to include also all of the European part of the USSR. However, the Western participants of the Madrid meeting, including the USA, have up to now been evading the answer to the question what they, for their part, are ready to do in this connection on the basis of reciprocity.

It is to be hoped that the USA will take a more constructive position at the Madrid meeting both on the question of convening a conference on military détente and disarmament in Europe and on the other questions being discussed there, and that it will, thereby, demonstrate its intention to reckon with the hopes of people for the continuation and development of the process of strengthening security and cooperation in Europe in accordance with the Final Act.

It is a matter of regret that the USA reacted negatively to our proposal to place a moratorium on deployment of new medium range nuclear missile systems in Europe by the countries of the NATO and by the USSR. References made in this respect to the necessity of deploying new American medium-range missiles in Western Europe in order to off-set some sort of "superiority" of the Soviet Union simply are not borne out by the actual state of affairs. One might believe that there exist no numerous American forward-based nuclear systems in Europe and near it which are capable of reaching the territory of the USSR or that the nuclear weapons of the US NATO allies have suddenly disappeared. But all that is there, indeed, and we can in no way close our eyes to it.

The objective approach, the principle of equality and equal security require that in making an analysis of the situation one should not limit himself to any single type of weapon, but should see the nuclear potentials in a comprehensive way. A true reflection of the factual state of affairs can be found only in that approach. And this state of affairs is such that the Soviet nuclear weapons in Europe do not exceed the aggregate level of the nuclear systems of the NATO group and, therefore, there exists now in Europe an approximate parity in the respective types of weapons. The replacement by the Soviet Union of the old missiles by the modernized ones has not changed the situation. Accordingly, the moratorium that we propose would merely freeze the existing approximate parity, making it easier to reach agreement on the ways to reduce the level of that parity. We noted that on more than one occasion you expressed yourself in favor of such a reduction.

We cannot view the US desire to station in any case its new missiles in Western Europe as anything but the intention to disrupt the strategic parity and to achieve superiority. It goes without saying that we will have to react to it in a proper way. But wouldn't it be worthwhile giving a thought whether such a turn of events will reinforce anybody's security, including that of the USA? We are convinced it will not.

This is the reason why we call upon the US Administration and you personally to weigh up again, realistically and with all factors in mind, the developing situation and to take steps in order to open the way toward achieving through negotiations an effective limitation and reduction of nuclear arms in Europe. Given the will on both sides, it is possible, I believe, to reach this goal.

A few words on Poland. It appears that some sinister plans on the part of the USSR are perceived by Washington in everything, and sometime there is even talk on the possibility of some "internal aggression" in Poland. A question is in order – what at all is meant by the "internal aggression"? Is it possible, for example, that the USA can commit an aggression against itself?

Earlier I already expressed to you our position as well as our assessment of the US behavior with regard to Poland. It remains the same. The United States must in no way interfere in the Polish domestic affairs.

The United States stated on more than one occasion that it would not like to see the Soviet troops in Afghanistan. It is, in fact, this idea with regard to Afghanistan that is present in your letter too. But the Soviet troops are there not just because we want it to be so. We repeated many times that we would withdraw our limited military contingent, provided the aggression against Afghanistan was ceased and a political settlement of the international aspects of the Afghan problem was found. Should the United States be really willing to facilitate such a development, it could certainly do much in this direction. Mentioning the negative position of the Pakistan leadership doesn't change a thing. It is well known why Islamabad under various artificial pretexts is now avoiding negotiations with Kabul.

Mr. President, in a detailed manner and in the spirit of frankness I have laid down the thoughts which came to me in connection with your letter. I believe this will be useful both for additional clarification of the proposals that had been put forward in my letter of March 6 and for your better understanding of the Soviet position on certain pressing international issues, as well as on questions concerning the relations between our countries.

I hope that our exchange of views as well as the discussions at other levels will help find mutually acceptable solutions which would constitute our common contribution to the strengthening of peace. In this regard I take note of the assurances contained in your letter that the United States is vitally interested in the peaceful resolution of international tensions and that your Administration is prepared to settle disagreements by negotiations.

Sincerely,

L. Brezhnev

Date: **July 6, 1981**
Subject: **East-West Trade Controls**
Status: **Declassified (2004)**

BACKGROUND

Today's meeting is the first of two meetings in four days on East-West Trade Controls. The meeting provides a solid introduction to the subject, and shows that the idea of restricting high-technology to the Soviet Union was important to Reagan at least six months before he ordered sanctions against the Soviet Union in response to events in Poland.

SUMMARY

After Reagan starts the meeting with "a brief account of a letter he had recently received from a Navy man," Allen introduces the subject:

> The items we will discuss today are of great importance. Mr. President, the decisions you make based on today's meeting or perhaps on two NSC meetings this week will set the course of our East-West Trade Policy and will be important in setting the course of our relations with the Soviet Union. Our allies and the Soviets will both see these decisions as setting the course of our economic and strategic trade policy.

> We need decisions before the Ottawa Summit, so that we can inform our allies of our policies. The Summit countries together do more than 70 percent of the West's trade with the Soviet Union.

> The issues to be discussed are complex and interrelated, ranging from our allied (COCOM) national security export controls, through U.S. and allies controls on Oil and Gas Equipment and Technology and U.S. policy on the Siberian Pipeline, to the U.S. decision on a specific export control case – the export of 100 Caterpillar pipelayers to the Soviet Union.

> The complexity and breadth of the issues – heavy in both economic and security context – required enlarging the Council (NSC) for this topic.

> Because of the complexity and enlarged attendance, this meeting will be introductory, with a second meeting Thursday to deal with the detailed issues in more detail.

The objectives of this meeting are to determine the basic positions of each agency and the key factors in reaching those positions and to identify differing views for examination in the second meeting.

The papers to be discussed can be divided into two groups. The first deals with Allied Security Controls. The remaining three papers deal with various aspects of controls on Soviet energy development.

I would like to proceed as follows: In the first round each participant will have two minutes to state his position on the options concerning National Security Controls and to identify the major considerations in his decision. Following that round, the President may wish to ask some questions. Again, we will have to limit the comments to two minutes. Then, we can follow a similar procedure for the second group of papers.

The first paper presents three options for strengthening security controls on exports to the USSR. These options would tighten COCOM security controls by varying degrees. Each would require negotiations with our COCOM allies to implement. The difficulty and length of the negotiations would, of course, probably vary with the degree of tightening of controls.

I suggest we begin with the statements of positions. Secretary Haig, would you like to begin?

The discussion follows.

HAIG: Yes. It is important to know that we are dealing with a group of interrelated – and sometimes contradictory issues, to recognize that the decisions will affect both out relations with our allies and with the Soviets. It is also important in making our decision to balance what we want against what we can do.

Option I maintains controls on equipment and technology and would be much as the policy in recent years. Our allies are comfortable with this policy and it will be difficult to change it.

Option II would add to the controlled items equipment and technology <u>critical</u> to military related industries. For example, shipbuilding and heavy equipment.

Option III would control <u>all</u> military relevant technology.

I believe we should elect Option II, which would significantly broaden restraints. It will be difficult to do this. For two years we have been negotiating in COCOM to make a narrow increase in militarily relevant metallurgical technology with little result. Selling Option II to our allies will be very difficult. We should seek at the Summit meeting a subsequent high-level COCOM meeting. At the same time as we increase these controls, we should loosen up on lower level controls.

WEINBERGER: We must consider our allies' positions, but we must consider whether we wish to aid the Soviet's, or not, and we must not adopt the attitude that if we don't sell to them someone else will. This is sometimes true, but our policy should be very restrictive. Almost everything aids their military and helps their economy. We know that they will only be satisfied with world domination, and we cannot satisfy them by appeasing them.

We should not give in to the argument that "if we don't, others will." To go along with this weakens our ability to lead and to not supply them.

While Option III is not considered feasible, following Option I should be discontinued. Option II is an improvement, but will still continue to help the Soviets. There will be slippages. We should strengthen Option II by an ad hoc examination of things under Option III. They turn against us what we provide them.

BALDRIGE: Mr. President, we have to have a program that works. The present program does not work. We have 5,000 applications in process. Some 2,000 are already legally overdue. Our business people – and our allies – do not understand our current policy.

I think we should go for Option II – tighten controls at the tope (the higher technology) – loosening at the bottom on routine items. With fewer items to process, we can process them faster and give more attention to the more important items at the top.

For example, robots are not on the list now. We would deny some under Option II, but the simple "pick and place" robots would go.

Super alloys – there are some 2,000 of them. We can't control all of them. We would deny the vacuum induction furnaces and technology used to make them, but not the items themselves.

We have the same kind of problem with computes. We would differentiate between the important and the not important – allow shipments of items that can be had from electronic stores.

We believe we could update the COCOM regulations by October.

DAVIS:	I note that restrictions on atomic energy items would be continued under any of these options. We lean to Option II. However, denial may stimulate their own research to develop capabilities in the long term they otherwise would not have if dependent on imports.
BROCK:	I follow Mac (Baldrige) in his recommendations. I feel we should ship almost anything in hardware – deny the technology. That way we can freeze them into a position five to ten years behind us.
CASEY:	It is a mistake to help the Soviets by exporting to them items they need. There is a greater negative impact from the exports than positive economic value to us as an export. We should be concerned not only about technology, but also about products. We should go as close to Option III as our allies will allow.
JONES:	We should impose the tightest possible controls. The policy should be somewhere between Options II and III.
STOCKMAN:	I prefer Option II, but would urge the tightest possible analytical framework as to the effects of the option. We need an estimate of the cost to the Soviets in terms of the impact on military investment and the linkage of our policy to their economic expansion.
KIRKPATRICK:	We need to be concerned about the impact of our policies on our allies. But we also need to be concerned about their impact on the rest of the world. Strengthening Soviet capabilities increases their power around the world and their ability to interfere. I don't believe that denying exports to them will increase their ability to innovate on their own. We should force them to divert productive capacity to developing their own technology. We should follow Option II, plus an item-by-item analysis.
ALLEN:	Mr. President, after your questions, I would propose following the same procedures on the remaining papers.
REAGAN:	**I do have a question. The Caterpillar tractors for the pipeline. Where would they fall in the options discussed?**
ALLEN:	Under Option I, the pipelayers could go. Under Option II, they could go – unless restricted by an ad hoc analysis. Under Option III, they would not go.
REAGAN:	**Is all this predicated on dealing with our allies? It is not much to us economically, but, for example, the whole pipeline thing if the Soviet Union can meet its**

own needs, there is less need to go to the Gulf. But does Western Europe become more dependent?

HAIG: The pipelayers are not related to COCOM controls. I suggest we cover that item, Mr. President, under the next discussion.

WEINBERGER: The question was what would happen under these rules? Under Option II, the would get it. This is the reason that Option II must be strengthened to avoid pre-automatic approval that would strengthen Soviet export capabilities.

BAKER: In other words, energy would not be considered a defense priority item?

WEINBERGER: It could be.

ALLEN: Let's go through the arguments on the remaining papers.

MEESE: This topic controls the others.

WEINBERGER: I continue to have concerns about Option II.

REAGAN: **One more thing. Is this unilateral, or what is the effect on the allies?**

ALLEN: Your decision would be a fit topic for the Summit. We all agree on the need to strengthen controls. The vehicle used (to approach the allies) will be critical. As Al (Haig) said, your decision will have tremendous undercurrents.

HAIG: We might look at the history on this. Carter decided post-Afghanistan on a tightening of the controls. We have been attempting to tighten the controls for the last years, but there are two problems. One was the lack of a coherent U.S. policy. The second is the reluctance of our allies. It will be a strong, uphill battle to strengthen controls (even going for Option II), but it can be accomplished by strong leadership. We would all like Option III, but we can't do it.

BALDRIGE: But they still want to buy from the U.S. Allowing them to have the pipelayers helps them (to solve their problems).

ALLEN: I suggest we go through the same routine on the remaining papers. The remaining three papers examine the U.S. and allied positions on the export of equipment and technology that would assist the Soviets in the exploration and production of oil and gas. However, they do not pose the question of whether it is in the interest of the U.S. and the Western allies to assist development of Soviet energy. The major arguments on this question are:

For

- Developing Soviet energy helps them overcome potential energy and hard currency shortages and reduces their motivation to aggression in the Persian Gulf Oil area.
- Increases the world oil supply and keeps the Soviets from purchasing on Western oil markets, reducing pressure on world oil prices.
- Maintains a cooperative relationship with the Soviet Union in an important economic area to offset the competitive relationship in the military sectors.
- Results in substantial export and employment benefits for U.S. and allied countries.

Against

- It is unlikely that the Soviet Union will ever become dependent on the world market for oil imports; if it decides to intervene in the Persian Gulf, it will do so for reasons other than to obtain oil; e.g., to deprive the West of oil.
- Western equipment and technology reduces the costs of energy development to the Soviet Union and frees resources for application in the military sector.
- Western assistance contributes to an expansion of Soviet energy exports to the West and to Eastern Europe and increases their dependence on the USSR.
- It is inconsistent to seek increases in defense expenditures while making it easier for the Soviets to devote resources to their military.

These are some of the very complex issues. Al (Haig), would you like to begin the discussion?

HAIG: There are five options to consider (referring to Oil/Gas Controls). The first three are so restrictive we cannot get allied cooperation on them. The allies would argue that these options would result in greater Soviet demand on the world oil market and lead to more aggressive Soviet behavior. This is a complex issue. The toughest to be decided today. It involves – is it in our interest to hinder Soviet energy development? What are the implications of decreased Soviet production? What can be negotiated with our allies? The allies will perceive us as rigid. The Soviets will appear to be forthcoming. We give them no incentive to negotiate with us. The question is, do we wish to concentrate on limiting exports of technology, or on end use equipment that is available elsewhere?

We should focus on preventing access to technology – Option IV – but with a case-by-case analysis of end items. But as an overall policy, we should go for controls on export of technology.

ALLEN: That covers the second paper, but are you prepared to state your position on the pipeline?

HAIG: Yes, if you want me to. The first two options are overly harsh and not sustainable. Our allies see Soviet energy as more secure than OPEC. They want to diversity by taking in Soviet energy.

I am concerned about the dependency question. I would recommend a modified Option III, where we could look at end items before licensing. We can put major pressure on our allies at the Summit, but I have talked to Schmidt twice and to Genscher three times on the pipeline and they refuse to give up on it and, Mr. President, you received a call from Schmidt over the weekend. They say they can go for six months in the event of a Soviet cut-off. I favor Option III, vey much toughened on any item.

On the pipelayers, the Japanese are going to sell them anyway. The Soviets have approximately 1,500 of them in inventory. These are replacements for existing equipment. They are not for the Siberian Pipeline. They involve no sophisticated technology. They are not COCOM controlled. They can be used only for pipelaying. They have no other applications. They do not involve a technology transfer. The Japanese would provide them.

WEINBERGER: I feel differently on all three issues. I haven't heard all the Schmidt arguments, but I am weary of defining our policy on what Schmidt wants. Our policy should be leadership – not anticipating what our allies will say and setting our policy on that. The Schmidt government is weak and may not be around long, anyway.

It should be clear to our allies that it is definitely against our (mutual) interests to increase Soviet capabilities by $20 billion per year.

We sent scrap iron to Japan before World War II, and we are doing a great deal to increase Soviet capabilities. We need a harder line position.

We should come closer to Option I on Oil/Gas Export Controls. We need to demonstrate to our allies that it is not in our interest to increase Soviet capabilities. It will take hard work to develop energy substitutes (alternative supplies for them).

The easy way to go is to give up. The Soviet ability to build the pipeline without Western assistance is questionable. Compressors are necessary to the pipeline. We can work with our competitors to develop internal arrangements to make the Japanese less willing to sell.

Komatsu gets a subsidy form the Japanese government. The Japanese can subsidize because they don't have to pay for their own defense. We need to persuade the allies with alternative solutions (to their energy needs) that the pipeline is not in their interest. For example, Komatsu wants into the U.S. market.

I would take a position much closer to our security interests. It seems wrong to authorize equipment they want from us. On the Caterpillar pipelayers, I would elect Option I (deny). On the Siberian Pipeline, somewhere between Option I and II. It is not in our interest to increase allied dependence.

BUSH. Suppose Caterpillar has a French facility, would U.S. restrictions apply?

WEINBERGER: Yes, we can enforce U.S. law on a U.S. company. We can persuade them under U.S. law

BUSH: Suppose the company is 51 percent foreign owned?

WEINBERGER: There are means by which we can control the exports.

BALDRIGE: We want to be as tough as we can, operating in the real world. If we go too far and can't get our allies to go with us, it won't work. I have with me Assistant Secretary Larry Brady, who is known as "the toughest gun in the West" on export controls and he supports this position. The products – pipelayers, compressors, drill bits – are generally available from other sources.

As Al said, there are 1,400 pipelayers in the USSR. Komatsu is 1/3 the size of Caterpillar and had the market targeted. We cannot stop all these countries from shipping to the USSR.

My position is Option IV on Oil/Gas Controls, Option III on the pipeline project.

The pipelayers get to be an emotional argument. The Japanese will sell them to the Soviets. The existing licensing requirements were imposed for human rights reasons.

DAVIS: The theme of the discussion seems to be what our allies will support. We want to restrict export of technology, but this requires allied support. The international oil companies are the transferors of technology. To control them would require strong allied support.

My main concern is the Siberian Pipeline. It will have an important effect on Soviet exports. I would like to delay or restrict it.

On the Oil/Gas Controls, I would prefer Option III, if strongly supported by our Allies; Option IV if we do not get that support. On the pipeline, I prefer Option II, but Option III is more likely practical. The pipelayers should not be supplied, but our decision should depend on the Japanese position.

BROCK: I would recommend Option IV on Oil/Gas; Option III on the pipeline, and Option III on the pipelayers.

There are strong feelings in this room on what should be done. However, I believe there are two threats to our security. There is the Soviet threat and the economic threat.

Increased oil prices have put heavy economic burdens on the Free World. The fact that Schmidt is in trouble and that there are four communists in the French government illustrates the economic weakness. Our allies are all in political jeopardy, including Mrs. Thatcher. We give far more than $20 billion annually to the OPEC countries. A way to break OPEN would be desirable. But we are not working on it. To break a potential dependency on the Soviets, we need to increase exports of coal, nuclear, etc.

REGAN: We want the Soviets to keep producing oil and gas. We could not supply Europe. We are probably going to have a shortage of gas in the mid-80s. Now Western Europe is hostage to Algeria. Their economies are weakened by energy events. It is advisable to keep the gas flowing.

My recommendations are: Oil/Gas – Option IV; Siberian Pipeline – Option III; Pipelayers – Option III.

CASEY: We need to talk turkey to our allies. The OPEC problem is a separate one. We are talking about getting two percent of the energy we need from the Soviets at the expense of increasing their hard currency by 25 percent. The Soviets are a small factor in the allies' trade accounts. We are a larger factor.

The Soviets cannot do without gas. They will have to divert resources to building pipe and compressors if they West doesn't supply them.

I understand there is a Senator Garn letter signed by 40 to 50 Senators opposing the pipeline. We have the right to tell our allies they should not put in the pipeline if they expect us to defend them.

Senator Garn proposes increased exports of coal and nuclear power.

JONES: Oil/Gas has a definite security concern. We recommend on Oil/Gas Controls, Option II; on the pipeline, Option I or II; and on the pipelayers, Option I.

But we cannot restrict everything if the allies let it flow. We should not take unilateral action. We should have some flexibility in getting our allies cooperation.

STOCKMAN: I have grave doubts about frustrating Soviet production of energy for three reasons:

1. There is an asymmetry in oil resources versus world populations, with reserves concentrated in the Middle East and in the USSR. Restrictions on Soviet production would impose a burden on the West, which needs energy.

2. The Soviet Bloc is now a large net exporter. If we impede them, we will reduce their exportable surplus. This would cost them foreign exchange, but would increase Western energy prices.

3. There is a good case for exceptionalism (to other restrictive policies) in Oil/Gas. Exports of Oil/Gas equipment come back to the West in the form of Oil and Gas, improving the energy balance and decreasing world prices.

I favor the same options as Treasury.

KIRKPATRICK: We consistently find that, in our negotiations, the allies are already significantly dependent. France for 15 percent of its gas; the FRG for 30 percent. Our negotiations and discussions with our allies already mention dependency as an inhibiting factor on their actions.

	Increases in energy supplies won't necessarily hold down Soviet prices. They don't necessarily price on a supply-demand basis. We have to think about Option I on each of the three items.
ALLEN:	Mr. President, we will prepare an overview paper for you. We note the urgent requirement for decisions. Because of the size of the pipeline project and its strategic implications, it is the most urgent and important decision.
HAIG:	Much of what has been said about the pipeline is theology. It always is. But we have to go to Ottawa with a strong alternative program. We have to have a strong, skeptical view. We should not support the pipeline. We should stay skeptical and work with our Allies.
REAGAN:	**We are held by our allies to be most rigid in our approach to maintaining a stricter position. Our allies note they have the Soviets next to them. Trade is more essential to them. But, how do we say to our own people that we must continue to sacrifice – and to our allies – if we are not prepared to use all our weapons? Don't we seem guilty of hypocrisy – weak – if we are not prepared to take a strong position?**
	I for one don't think we are being harsh or rigid. The Soviets have spoken as plainly as Hitler did in "Mein Kampf." They have spoken world domination – at what point do we dig in our heels?
ALLEN:	I request that all of you display total reticence in discussion about this meeting and that you do not characterize the positions of other participants. The President makes the decisions – not the NSC.
WEINBERGER:	You do have the Garn letter, do you not?
ALLEN:	Yes.

Date:	**July 9, 1981**
Subject:	**East-West Trade Controls; (CBI); (Leaks)**
Status:	**Declassified (2005)**

BACKGROUND

Today's meeting continues the discussion from July 6 on East-West Trade Controls during which Haig and Weinberger disagreed on how to best impede the construction of a Soviet trans-Siberian oil and gas pipeline. The Caribbean Basin is also briefly discussed, and Reagan ends the meeting with a warning that he will fire anyone caught leaking information to the press. (*The*

New York Times reported on July 2, 1981 that a Senior White House official concluded that strained and sometimes difficult relations with Secretary Haig are "a fact of life" in the Reagan Administration.")

SUMMARY

ALLEN: Mr. President, we have a full agenda today. If you will permit me, I would like to state the objective of today's meeting and then a suggested method of procedure.

We have two topics to cover. We will continue our discussion of East-West controls. We would also like to devote some attention to the Caribbean Basin Policy. Secretary Haig and Ambassador Brock will be going to Nassau this weekend for a Foreign Minister's meeting.

With regard to the East-West portion of our discussion, we have only a short period to make decisions required to be presented to our allies at the Ottawa Summit meeting. We need, at that meeting, to seek their support for important initiatives that will have a profound effect on both near and longer-term military, political and economic facets of our East-West relations.

Our objective today is to complete the NSC discussion of the East-West trade topics, though the President may choose not to make his final decisions for a few more days.

There is a great deal of complex material to be covered and each agency should have an opportunity to advance its key arguments. Therefore, I propose to proceed as follows:

There appear to be substantial areas of agreement on the Allied Security Controls topic. While there is not unanimity on the precise course to be followed, I believe the positions of individual departments are quite well defined. Perhaps some adjustments could be made to narrow if we spent more time. However, I believe it would be better to spend the major portion of time on those key issues where wider divergences exist; that is, on the Oil/Gas and Siberian Pipeline issues. Additionally, we have three new papers to consider on these issues.

Therefore, Mr. President, unless you wish to propose some questions on the Allied Security Controls, I suggest we move on to the Oil/Gas and Siberian Pipeline problems.

REAGAN: **I suggest Mac (Baldrige), Al (Haig) and Cap (Weinberger) get together to work out something. Leaning a little toward Option III would be fine with me.**

ALLEN: Mr. President, I suggest the following procedure for the remaining items. Based on an NSC memo request to Secretaries Haig and Weinberger, they have made two additional submissions, answering certain questions. These two additional submissions have been provided to all the participants here. Additionally, today I sent them two further questions based on their submissions. If you will forgive the somewhat rigid nature of this procedure, I will now pose to them the two questions they were provided earlier and they could then answer these questions.

Following that we could then go around the table for additional comments and questions. Secretary Haig and Secretary Weinberger could collect the questions for a response in one fell swoop.

Is that satisfactory to you, gentlemen?

HAIG: Yes.

WEINBERGER: Yes.

ALLEN: Mr. President?

REAGAN: **Okay.**

ALLEN: Secretary Haig, your July 8 paper proposes a "very tough Option III" under which we would "press our allies to take several specific measures to minimize their dependency on Soviet gas. If we do not ourselves deny licenses on exports related to the project, and if we do not enlist the aid of the Japanese and British in restricting exports critical to the project, what is it that is "tough" about our policy? Also, what kind of pressure would we put on our allies to get them to give anything more than lip service to the program of minimizing dependence you have outlined?

HAIG: We should be clear on the two questions. You have signaled out the pipeline. The other issue is oil and gas controls. On that issue we don't believe we could get allied cooperation on controls of technology <u>and</u> equipment. We want to control the technology, but don't believe we can do the equipment as well.

Related to the original question, "Where are we on the pipeline?" Gentlemen, we have been talking about "jawboning" – that's what it is. And we have been doing it. We have talked with (FRG Foreign Minister) Genscher. We have talked with (FRG Chancellor) Schmidt. They want the pipeline! It is important to them. If we ask them to stop, we are asking them to sacrifice from a goal of diversifying their energy supply and on trade at the same time. We lifted the controls on three-fourths of our own trade with the Soviets when we lifted the grain embargo. It would be inconsistent to put pressure on them when we are loosening our own controls.

We have been trying to get them to stop the pipeline, but cannot get them to do it. Schmidt has committed himself publicly to this transaction. Public arm-twisting by us would be counter-productive. However, I believe intelligent handling can convince them to decrease their vulnerability and to increase their protective measures.

Now, as far as a tough Option III is concerned, tough may be a misnomer. We need to be tough vis-à-vis the Soviets. We need to be tough on our budgeters. We need to be tough on our allies. We need to be tough on getting a program put in place on energy security. We need to press our allies to cut in half the size of the pipeline deliveries. We need to assist them to diversify – to limit their imports of Soviet gas.

In recent weeks the increase in interest rates, the decrease in the projected demand for gas, etc., has been causing consumption problems and a glut in oil.

We should be prepared to give our allies an alternative package that would involve, perhaps, Alaskan oil. We should deregulate natural gas, make provisions to deepen our harbors to expand coal shipments. This may require some federal financing. We should reinforce and increase energy sharing arrangements. We must do this whether or not the pipeline is built. We had to help the Dutch in the last oil crisis.

I think, Mr. President, you should mobilize at the Summit a high level monitoring group.

[Secretary Haig then responded to the following question which was posed to him in writing before the meeting: "Would it be inconsistent with your scenario to press very strongly at Ottawa, especially on the Germans and French, perhaps privately, for their agreement to delay further negotiations on the pipeline for, say six months, pending a thorough inter-allied review of the project and alternatives to it?"]

With regard to the second question, "Would we ask them to delay six months?" We shouldn't do this. If we start the work to demonstrate there are other alternatives, they don't want to spend their money there (on the pipeline). But the pipeline is a public problem for Schmidt. He is publicly committed to it. They will tread water, anyway, without our requiring them to do so.

Mr. President, you will find at Ottawa that our European allies are in a blue funk about their economic situation. They blame us in part for their problems because of our approach to our own economic problems – because of our interest rates. A rigid approach to this problem of the pipeline will bring a repeat of the disastrous Carter Administration confrontation with the Germans over the sale of German nuclear technology to Brazil – with a far more significant effect on our ability to deal on East-West matters!

ALLEN: You asked and answered the second question.

Secretary Weinberger, why couldn't your objectives be best served by imploring – persuading our allies to delay the pipeline, rather than stop it.

[Allen then paraphrased the question he had earlier submitted to Weinberger:

> Your objective, as stated in your paper, is to stop the pipeline or, if that is not possible, to scale it down. Why wouldn't this objective be best served by requesting, at least as a first step, the our allies, especially the Germans, agree to delay further negotiations for at least six months, until a full examination of all aspects of the project can be completed, rather than approaching them now with a statement that the project must be stopped, and with threats to block exports by the U.S. and other allies of critical components?]

WEINBERGER: We are unequivocally in favor of stopping the pipeline. Leadership does not add up the columns on the opinions of our allies then conclude you are defeated. You decide what is needed and you do it. The Europeans should be clear on that.

I suspect that the speculation re a shaky economic base for the pipeline is true. We should drive home that we are unalterably opposed to it.

Nobody here at this table wants it built. We can do all the things listed that have been talked about to provide alternatives to the Europeans. They are all good. We can do all the substitutes. But why do all that and build the pipeline too?

We have the objective of stopping it. That may be impossible, but we must try. If built, it will produce large hard currency earnings for the Soviet Union. It will increase European dependence on the Soviets. We worry, even now, about the course of the Germans.

Realistically, we have persuasive power. We must exercise it. Otherwise, to offer these alternatives is useless. If the pipeline is built, we have lost. We give the impression of a weak, undecided country. We must use all reasonable leadership and tactics and alternatives.

If someone believes we can use delay as means – fine, but our objective should be to stop the pipeline. We need to be firm, resolute, in our objective to stop it. We must use all the proper tactics and strategy.

ALLEN: My second question is: "As you indicated, compressors that must come from either the U.S. or the UK are critical to the pipeline. However, these compressors offer potential sales of as much as $300-$600 million to Rolls Royce, a sick company in a sick British economy with a current unemployment rate of about ten percent. Faced with high levels of unemployment and with a German and French desire to go ahead with the pipeline, what incentive would there be for the British government to block the sales of these compressors? What pressure or incentives could we bring to bear to motivate the British to go along with our desire to block the pipeline? Wouldn't British cooperation be significantly easier to obtain if our stated objective was only to delay the pipeline, pending a review of alternatives and/or steps to minimize European dependency, as compared to a position where we propose to the allies that the pipeline be permanently blocked?"

WEINBERGER: In the last three years we have spent $265.3 million with Rolls Royce. We have under current consideration purchase of the Harrier aircraft. There are many other co-production possibilities. It is very easy to give them other sales. Of course, we must not publicly bludgeon them, but motivating them can be done by giving them other contracts.

ALLEN: Mr. President, we also have a new submission from the CIA providing new information. Bill, would you like to summarize your papers?

CASEY: Yes, Mr. President, I would like to make three points.

First, minimizing their dependence (on OPEC oil) would not be achieved by Soviet gas, which would provide only three percent of Western European energy. More important, this pipeline is the largest East-West deal ever. We have to take this matter very seriously. This is our greatest opportunity ever to force the Soviets to divert resources from military programs.

Second, the $16 billion to be lent to the Soviets for this project should better be lent on this side of the curtain to develop Western resources. There are probably better and less expensive alternatives in the West than the pipeline.

Third, with regard to the tactics at Ottawa, at a minimum we should put it off until we explore other alternatives that will be permanent assets to the West.

ALLEN: Mr. President, the CIA paper was delivered this morning. You may wish to look it over at your leisure. I commend it to you as I do the other papers received since the last meeting.

We can now move around the room for the comments and questions of others.

BALDRIGE: Mr. President, the essence of leadership is to take the strongest possible position, but we are weakened if we fail. We don't believe it is practical to stop compressors and pipelayers and the other equipment needed for the pipeline. There is a cable in today that reports a Japanese sale of 500 pipelayers to the Russians. Caterpillar has been told by the Soviets that if they do not have a license by the 30th of this month, Caterpillar loses the sale. There are 1,400 pipelayers in the USSR now. They can be moved to work on the pipeline. Other smaller equipment alternatives are available now from other than the U.S. and Japan. These other alternatives can be developed over time to build the pipeline.

The same is true of the compressors. There are two sources now, but others can make compressors in the reasonably near future. In the time needed to get the pipeline going – three to four years – many other alternatives can be developed.

CASEY: What about the money?

WEINBERGER:	It they can't get the money, they can't build it. We need to stop the entire European support, including money.
HAIG:	I think Mac (Baldrige) is talking about the technology.
BALDRIGE:	My point is that simple bilateral arrangements with two countries cannot stop the pipeline. I would like to associate my position with that of State. I recommend a strong program to develop alternatives. We have said we want a financing of dredging of harbors by the private sector. We want foreign capital to develop our resources.
ALLEN:	Mr. Davis, please keep your comments to two minutes or less.
DAVIS:	We would like to see it stopped or scaled down. However, we defer to others for evaluations of the prospects of success of doing so.
	In either event, we need to increase other alternative sources. The other alternatives are not necessarily direct substitutes for gas. Nuclear power development takes considerable time. Deregulation of U.S. gas would free supplies for Western Europe. But we need to get going on such programs.
BROCK:	In the last meeting I spoke about the economic aspects of this issue. Now I want to look at it as a politician. There are desperate economic problems in Europe. There is the effect of high U.S. interest rates, which has resulted in a revaluation of the dollar that has brought to Western Europe the equivalent of a "third oil shock." Western Europe has a $13 billion trade deficit with us.
	It is better to go with a request that they delay. I am intrigued with Bill Casey's suggestion of gas from coal. We have lots of coal here, but we can't guarantee it will be economic until we cost it out.
	How we do it to (persuade the allies to stop or delay) is important. I support, essentially, State's position.
HARPER:	I think the points that Mr. Stockman wanted me to make are that by discouraging the pipeline today and subsidizing other sources, we will wind up later with the Soviets having their energy, while we are depleting ours.
	The key question is where are we going on a broad picture basis?
REGAN:	I would support delay of the pipeline.

HAIG: Code words cause problems. We could not (in the State Department) be able to support going to Schmidt with a request for him to delay. We seek delay, but the way we skin that cat is not to go to the Europeans now with a request to stop a project three years along.

We cannot be seen as intervening in their economic fate. It's their money! It's their project! We must be very careful on how we intervene.

ALLEN: There is no intention to use code words. We are talking about <u>our</u> security.

WEINBERGER: Our interest rates won't decrease if the pipeline is built. Their deficit won't be decreased if it is built. We must make our position clear. Is the best way to stop the pipeline to go for a delay?

The alternative supply concept is useful, but not much good if the gas is already coming in.

JONES: We want to stop the pipeline, but others are best qualified to decide how.

CASEY: Our approach should be that we want to show them another way – a way to avoid building the pipeline.

REAGAN: **I don't understand.**

CASEY: I want to spend the $16 billion some other way. We could add to the kitty – do a better job.

ALLEN: Your argument is that we want the $16 billion of investment on our side of the line – not theirs.

HARPER: There are budget implications in "adding to the pot."

KIRKPATRICK: The pipeline would tie Western Europe to the Soviet Union. It's already tied strongly. Three hundred thousand West German jobs are now dependent on East-West trade. If the Federal Republic becomes thirty percent dependent on Soviet gas, the number of jobs dependent on East-West trade will increase.

Will this make the Germans, or us, more secure?

We don't want to increase the tendency toward the Findlandization of Europe. We don't want to help the Soviets. We don't want to sell them the rope to hang us!

HAIG: This is a fundamental foreign policy and security policy issue. We have just lifted the grain embargo. Three-fourths of U.S. trade with the Soviet Union has been decontrolled. We are about to negotiate a new grain agreement with them. We must be careful that we do not follow inconsistent policies.

I have just spent time with Thorn (EC). There are riots in Europe – unemployment, disaffected youth; there are problems in the Federal Republic of Germany.

No one at this table should think we have not taken a hard position on the pipeline – and I have done it personally! I have already told them no. They have gone ahead anyway.

Nobody here wants this pipeline. The question is, how can we best manage this problem. It would be a tragedy even to demand a six-month delay. We must provide alternatives. We must suggest they don't need it. It is interesting that the Department of Defense and State papers use the same statistics, yet we come to different conclusions.

WEINBERGER: There are significant differences. We have not yet done anything unequivocal concerning a position against the pipeline, coupled with a positive alternative program. If they think we are going to plead with them, they will not go along.

The pipeline won't stop the unemployment or the riots. If we are unequivocal, we may stop the pipeline. If we are not unequivocal, we will not have assumed a leadership role.

REAGAN: **Is the idea the Europeans are going to do the financing? If they do not, the Soviets will do it themselves for their own use?**

CASEY: There are two separate projects. This one is for exports. If there is no prospect of exports, they won't build it.

REAGAN: **I'm glad no one has said, "have a happy weekend".**

ALLEN: We would welcome added papers on this topic of three or four pages if you wish to submit them to summarize your arguments. Mr. President, we could devote some portion of Monday's meeting to this subject, if needed.

REGAN: I don't buy the argument that Western Europe is in such tough economic shape. Much of what they are saying is posturing. The French Socialists are finding the money to nationalize their industries.

HAIG: I hope my comments did not indicate that I thought they were in such desperate economic conditions.

WEINBERGER: Building the pipeline won't stop their economic problems.

REAGAN:	**Could the same individuals who worked together on the allies security controls issue get together on this issue, and without bloodshed, work out a solution?**
HAIG:	Mr. President, that would be o.k., but DOD has all the armaments. (Laughing) The arguments are the same. I suggest we handle the problem as State has recommended. If I thought stopping or delaying the pipeline was achievable, I would be leading the charge, but I don't think that it is.
MEESE:	As I see it, there are three basic questions: 1) Should we oppose unequivocally? 2) Should we develop alternatives? 3) Does the President say anything at Ottawa?
BROCK:	Isn't there a fourth? What are we willing to pay in damages?
WEINBERGER:	It is not a function of damages. The pipeline would cause us damage.
MEESE:	It's part of the question.
REAGAN:	**Is this an oversimplification? Sixteen billion dollars to build the pipeline – to buy something that will then come through the pipeline? Is there an alternative in the West?**
CASEY:	Yes.
ALLEN:	It would take some development. But what is the inconsistency of "why don't you look at what we have to offer before you go ahead?"
WEINBERGER:	The ways of saying you oppose vary, but leadership is a firm, consistent position.
ALLEN:	Mr. President, this clearly is a monumental issue. It is very important. Do we need one more attempt at a synthesis position? We can devote time on Monday if needed.
REAGAN:	**It seems we are all saying the same thing.**
HAIG:	Let's be frank. It will take us years to develop alternatives. The Europeans know that. We have been working seven years on alternatives. Nothing has happened! We need to go in with something. Not because we are subservient, but because they are our allies and we need them.
REAGAN:	**How long, if they go ahead, before completion of the pipeline?**
UNKNOWN:	Three-to-four years.

REAGAN:

Why is it impossible, during that same three-to-four year period, to supply them from other alternatives?

WEINBERGER:

If we can say to them, you'd have to wait that long to get gas, why not wait that long for other alternatives? It involves resources for coal and nuclear development.

REAGAN:

It involves harbor development, among other things. I remember those ships lined up at Norfolk.

DAVIS:

In a three-to-four year period, there are small prospects of increase of supply to Western Europe by anything we can do. We are talking eight-to-ten years to accomplish anything.

REAGAN:

What about nuclear? We are the only ones who take eight-to-ten years to build a nuclear plant.

DAVIS:

It takes about six years actual construction time to build a nuclear plant. And electricity is not a direct substitute for all uses of gas.

ALLEN:

We have exhausted all our time with no discussion of the Caribbean Basin.

HAIG:

I don't see this lack of NSC discussion on the Caribbean Basin as a problem. Ambassador Brock and I are going down there this weekend to talk about our Caribbean Basin policy.

REAGAN:

Portillo indicated to me they want to be a conduit for our Latin American policy. He did seem to listen when I said we are talking about the whole area.

As they begin to see some of this in other places, I wonder if Castro won't begin to wonder if he shouldn't get back where he belongs, with the West.

Ask him one thing: We'd have a lot better time if they would take back all those Cubans we have.

ALLEN:

Mr. President, I'm sure you have been pleased not to read this past week about the Monday NSC meeting in *The Washington Post* or *The New York Times*.

REAGAN:

Yes. There are sometimes leaks – perhaps in background briefings. I don't think anyone in this room. Perhaps by persons not here, who know only a little. But if we can get through another week, perhaps it will become a habit.

I want to see an end to the stories of our speaking with different voices. We only speak with different voices in this kind of briefing. If there is no other way to cure it – other than blowing up *The Post* and *The Star* – then, if I find out about who the leakers

are, they are going back to South Succotash Wisconsin in a hurry.

POSTSCRIPT

The next declassified discussion on East-West trade controls takes place on October 16, 1981.

Date:	**September 15, 1981**
Subject:	**Further Economic Aid to Poland**
Status:	**Declassified (2005)**

SUMMARY

Today's meeting is called to decide on both emergency aid to Poland and a policy of long-term support of Polish economic reform and recovery. Clark speaks for the Department of State because Haig is in New York. On Haig's behalf, Clark makes the following points:

- The liberalization process in Poland is the first successful break in the Soviet model of Eastern European communism;
- The potential ripple effect is of major strategic importance;
- The benefits of establishing a more independent and freer Poland can't be quantified ; and
- The failure of Poland's challenge to Moscow for lack of Western assistance would be the modern equivalent of Yalta, a historic act of indifference.

Clark then presents Haig's two recommendations:

1. The West should provide short-term relief of Poland's economic crisis while the political liberalization process proceeds. $50 million in food aid should be provided to Poland.
2. As to longer-term aid for Polish economic reform, it is important that we show our interest and support the historic process at work in Poland, but the President should defer a decision as the long-term outlook is cloudy, as there are reports indicating a heightened possibility that the Polish Government may declare martial law.

Weinberger briefs next:

The critical argument against launching a program of long-term economic aid to Poland now is that the Polish Government lately seems to feel that it is necessary to crack down on Solidarity and follow Soviet orders. We should do what we can to encourage Solidarity to resist such Soviet pressures. Beyond immediate food aid there is not much we can do, except provide for transportation of food. Perhaps the International Red Cross could help to get food directly to the people. If we support the government now, we may find that we have assisted the government to resist making concessions to Solidarity.

Casey generally agrees with Weinberger and tells the President that the intelligence community favors financial aid to Poland if there could be assurances that it would not go down the drain, but at the time being no such assurance could be given. Casey recommends direct food aid, possibly through the Catholic Church, because "western relief-type aid expressing goodwill toward the people of Poland would also serve to show the world the failure of the communist system."

After a few more minutes of discussing the situation in Poland, the discussion continues with President Reagan giving his thoughts on Poland.

REAGAN:	**I question whether there is any benefit to the United States in our bailing out the Government of Poland, a government which may be as hostile to us as the Soviets. I often wonder what would have been the outcome if the U.S. had not bailed out the Soviets.**
ALLEN:	There is the option of waiting until the Soviets invade.
REAGAN:	**Does anyone believe that if the Soviets invade they would be met with resistance?**
CASEY:	The Poles surely would resist.
ALLEN:	The immediate problem is to work out arrangements for Catholic Relief Services and other distribution channels so as to assure that the credit for our food aid would redound to the United States.
CLARK:	That requirement is dealt with constantly in managing AID programs.
ALLEN:	We should make a propaganda contrast between our bountiful food production and food aid and the current Soviet grain crop failure.
MEESE:	(Let me see if can summarize the decision): $50 million from the FY 1982 PL480 budget to provide food aid, preferably through Catholic Relief and other non-governmental channels. The second-best alternative is to provide this food through the Polish government. But in any case, our aid would be accompanied by a propaganda campaign.

DECISIONS

To provide $50 million from the FY 1982 PL 480 budget for food aid to Poland to be distributed through Catholic Relief and other non-governmental channels if possible, otherwise the aid should go through the Polish Government. A propaganda campaign will also accompany the food aid.

President Reagan, however, is concerned that the plan might be criticized as dumping grain on the market.

Date: **September 22, 1981**
Subject: **Cable from Reagan to Brezhnev (U.S.-Soviet relations)**

Dear President Brezhnev,

As we begin the fall session of the United Nations General Assembly and approach the meetings between our foreign ministers, I thought it would be useful for me to describe to you some of my thoughts on the future direction of U.S.-Soviet relations.

Let me say at the outset that the United States is vitally interested in the peaceful resolution of international tensions and in a more constructive and stable relationship with your country. We have repeatedly demonstrated our willingness to settle disagreements by negotiations and to observe scrupulously our international commitments.

I believe, however, that a great deal of the present tension in the world is due to actions by the Soviet government. As we and our allies have repeatedly stated, two aspects of Soviet behavior are of particular concern to us:

-- First, the Soviet Union's pursuit of unilateral advantage in various parts of the globe and its repeated resort to the direct and indirect use of force in regional conflicts. The role of Cuba in Africa and Latin America is particularly disturbing and unacceptable to us.

-- Second, the USSR's unremitting and comprehensive military buildup over the past 15 years, a buildup which in our view far exceeds purely defensive requirements and carries disturbing implications of a search for military superiority.

Despite these trends, we are committed to a dialogue with the Soviet Union. We are deeply concerned over the threat to mankind in the age of nuclear weapons. I have stated publicly that the United States is ready to engage in discussions with the USSR that would lead to genuine arms reductions. The existing stockpiles of these weapons and ongoing programs are such that only a serious effort at arms reductions would contribute to the objective which we both share, namely, lifting the threat of nuclear annihilation which hangs over mankind.

While the United States is committed to a stable and peaceful world, it will never accept a position of strategic disadvantage. Because the Soviet Union has, over the past years, embarked on a major program to improve its strategic forces, the United States must also upgrade its forces. We have no desire to tax our societies with a costly, burdensome, and dangerous build-up of armaments. The United States, however, will invest whatever is needed to maintain a secure strategic posture.

The meetings this month between or foreign ministers will, I assume, set the time and place for negotiations between our two countries on what we term "Theater Nuclear Forces." We are deeply committed to achieving a military balance in this area – a balance which has been upset by the unprecedented buildup of military forces by your country in recent years, especially the deployment of the SS-20 missiles. Furthermore, as we have stated at the Madrid meeting of the Conference on Security and Cooperation in Europe, we are prepared to participate in negotiations to fashion a coherent system of commitments on European Security that are verifiable and militarily significant.

With our allies and other concerned nations, the United States is willing to pursue negotiated solutions to the problems that threaten world peace, including the presence of occupation forces in Afghanistan and Kampuchea. Soviet readiness to resolve the Afghanistan problem on the basis of a prompt withdrawal would go far toward restoring the international confidence and trust necessary for the improvement of East-West relations. The Vietnamese invasion and occupation of Kampuchea has earned widespread condemnation from that international community as a breach of accepted norms of conduct and a threat to peace. I call on your government to exert its influence over the government of Vietnam to withdraw its troops from Kampuchea.

In sum, the United States is more interested in actions which further the cause of world peace than in words. We are fully committed to solving outstanding differences by peaceful means, but we are not willing to accept double standards of international behavior. Words and public statements are, however, important. A major contribution to the reduction of world tensions would be for your country to curb the escalating campaign of anti-Americanism and disinformation both inside the Soviet Union and abroad, a campaign which only serves to poison the political atmosphere.

Mr. President, my country stands ready to begin the search for a better U.S.-Soviet relationship. We are prepared to discuss with the Soviet Union the full range of issues which divide us, to seek significant, verifiable reductions in nuclear weapons, to expand trade, and to increase contacts at all levels of our societies. I am hopeful that the meetings between Secretary of State Haig and Foreign Minister Gromyko will start a process leading toward such a relationship.

For such a process to bear fruit, your country must understand the need for greater restraint in the international arena. At the same time, let me add that the United States is fully prepared to do the same with ours. It we can succeed in establishing a framework of mutual respect for each other's interests and mutual restraint in the resolution of international crises, I think we will have created a much more solid and enduring basis for U.S.-Soviet relations than we have ever had before.

-End Text.

Date: **October 13, 1981**
Subject: **Theater Nuclear Forces**
Status: **Declassified (2005)**

SUMMARY

Today's meeting is called to discuss preparations for the upcoming Theater Nuclear Forces (TNF) negotiations. No decision is required.

Reagan starts the meeting on a different subject, human rights in the Soviet Union, and asks about the status of Professor McClellan's Russian wife who is not being allowed to emigrate to the United States; the Soviet religious groups in the basement of the U.S. Embassy in Moscow; whether or not quiet diplomacy would help to get Anatoly Scharansky[7] released; and if there is anyway to indicate to the Soviets that we would be happier in any negotiations if progress were made with these cases. Haig says he unsuccessfully raised each of these issues with Gromyko.

Moving to TNF, Allen tells the President that negotiations with the Soviets will begin in Geneva on November 30; Haig has been guiding the preparatory work; and the purpose today is not to settle on a negotiating position, but to get an update on where we stand. Haig starts with a summary of the TNF negotiations:

> In their 1979 decision, the allies agreed to a modernization program that is on track everywhere except in the Netherlands. The Germans, Brits, Italians, and Belgians have all shown great courage. Schmidt and Genscher have both threatened to resign on this issue, even though they face substantial pressures, including the 250,000 protesters who marched in Bonn this weekend. We have had increased concern about the Dutch, but in my meeting in Egypt with Dutch Foreign Minister Talboys, I was assured that the Dutch would not withdraw their deployment decision, but only undertake a necessary delay in reaching a decision.

> In 1979, the Allies also agreed to TNF arms control negotiations, and we agreed to consult closely with our allies. The IG, which State and DOD co-chair, with major ACDA participation, has undertaken extensive work on these issues. The alliance consultations are important because the primary purpose of the negotiations is political, i.e., to update the TNF modernization program. An actual arms control agreement is secondary and has little prospect because of the imbalance of forces. NATO's Special Consultative Group, the SCG, is the forum for these consultations. It is chaired by Assistant Secretary Eagleburger and will be meeting next on October 26.

---

[7] Scharansky, a Soviet Jew convicted in 1978 of treason and spying for the United States, was sentenced to 13 years of forced labor. After increasing political pressure, he was released in 1986 and emigrated to Israel when he changed his name to Natan Sharansky. He was awarded a Congressional Gold Medal in 1986, the Presidential Medal of Freedom in 2006, and the Ronald Reagan Freedom Award in 2008. Since his emigration to Israel, Sharansky has worked on behalf of Soviet emigrants to Israel and served as a member of the Israeli Knesset.

Let me summarize where we stand in the IG. There is general agreement that:

1. We will propose a phased, comprehensive approach that seeks reductions to the lowest possible levels on land-based TNF missiles in the first phase;
2. We will insist on equal limits for like systems, and these limits must be global;
3. We will negotiate only U.S. and Soviet systems and will not even compensate for these allied systems – a point we may need to reconsider; and
4. We will insist on stringent verification procedures that will almost certainly go beyond National Technical Means.

More specific elements include IG agreement that:

1. Soviet SS-20's, 4's, and 5's must be limited, and there must also be constraints on shorter system, including SS-21's, 22's, and 23's;
2. .Warheads on launchers will be the unit of account;
3. We want to ban refires; and
4. We will not want to negotiate aircraft in the first phase, but may be required to discuss them in the first phase because of Soviet claims concerning the balance. Gromyko threw the aircraft balance issue at me in our UN talks.

The discussion follows.

HAIG: The issues remaining to be resolved include: 1. The TNF-SALT (START) relationship, which is as of yet undefined. As the talks go on, they will merge.

REAGAN: **What does that mean, merge?**

HAIG: The Soviets will not be allowed to double count us.

WEINBERGER: Then you don't mean merging negotiations?

HAIG: No. I am referring to an interrelationship. You cannot do one thing in one forum without it relating to the other forum.

WEINBERGER: But we may not be ready on an issue in one area and could be dragged into that issue through the other forum.

HAIG: We'll have shrewd negotiators. They can hold the line.

ALLEN: We might remind the President that our chief negotiator for TNF will be Paul Nitze, and that for START, it will be General Ed Rowny.

HAIG: We favor having the two negotiations in the same location to facilitate coordination.

Other issues remaining to be resolved include:
1. Levels of reductions – ceilings and floors;
2. Limits on shorter-range missiles; and
3. Verification issues.

We need to study each of these issues in depth.
Verification could be the most controversial issue for the
allies. We must avoid an allied perception that we are
scuttling the talks at the outset by insisting on verification
criteria the Soviets are unlikely to accept. We must treat
the allies gingerly on this matter. In general, the allies
have been supportive on our approach.

WEINBERGER: We at Defense agree with many of the points
made by Secretary Haig: (1) The emphasis on land-based
missiles, including SS-20's, 4's, 5's, 21's, 22's, and 23's;
(2) Banning the refires; (3) Omitting aircraft in any first
phase; (4) Stringent verification procedures; and (5)
alliance consultations.

There is, however, another point we would also
like to bring out. It is the question of what we would like
to achieve in these negotiations. We are conscious of
several difficult dilemmas. If we are perceived as not
engaging in serious negotiations, our modernization
program will not go through. If we succeed in reaching
only a cosmetic agreement, our modernization program
will also come to a halt, being perceived as no longer
necessary. Or if we are viewed as not making progress in
negotiations, the Soviets will make it seem to be our fault,
and our modernization program will be endangered.

We need to assess the nature of our tasks brought
on by the strength of Soviet programs. They have 750 SS-
20 warheads now. The SS-20's are mobile, accurate,
powerful, hard to find and to hit, and they are targeted
against all of Europe and against China and Japan. The
U.S. has no counter. In addition, a new generation of
Soviet shorter-range systems is on the way. We may find
our 1979 TNF modernization program to be insufficient.

In this light, we might need to consider a bold
plan, sweeping in nature, to capture world opinion. If
refused by the Soviets, they would take the blame for its
rejection. If the Soviets agreed, we would achieve the
balance that we've lost. Such a plan would be to propose
a "zero-option."

Initially, it would, of course, be limited only to
long-range land-based missiles, in which the Soviets are
preponderant. If it were ultimately decided to adopt this
option, it should be proposed by the U.S. in a spectacular
presidential announcement, not at the mid or lower-level
SCG on October 26 or in terms of some "lowest possible

numbers" formula. The zero-option should be considered carefully here, and no parts of it should be given away at the October 26 SCG. We should not be using the "lowest possible numbers" formula at the SCG or in any other forum. If we adopt the zero-option approach and the Soviets reject it after we have given it a good try, this will leave the Europeans in a position where they would really have no alternative to modernization.

REAGAN: **Do we really want a zero-option for the battlefield? Don't we need these nuclear systems? Wouldn't it be bad for us to give them up since we need them to handle Soviet conventional superiority?**

HAIG: The zero-option will not be viewed as the President's initiative. It has already been proposed by the German Social Democrats and by German Foreign Minister Genscher in Moscow, and it is a subject of intense debate in Europe.

There are also some serious problems with any "zero option." We should be looking for the hooker and must study this issue fully. What would happen in one or two years when it comes time to deploy if we have a zero-option on the table? With such an option, the Europeans will surely reject any new deployments.

WEINBERGER: The Soviets will certainly reject an American zero-option proposal. But whether they reject it or they accept it, they would be set back on their heels. We would be left in good shape and would be shown as the White Hats. As to the nuclear battlefield systems we need, we would not be including these shorter battlefields systems, e.g., the Enhanced Radiation Weapons (ERW) systems, only the longer-range ones. Also, we would be insisting on stringent verification criteria and on dismantling.

ALLEN: Genscher told me that verification is a popular issue in Europe. Norm (Terrell), so you want to express ACDA's views in behalf of Eugene Rostow?

TERRELL: Gene Rostow and Paul Nitze regret that they cannot be here today. They are in Europe discussing some of these issues with our allies. ACDA supports the IG consensus positions stated by Secretaries Haig and Weinberger. On the "zero-option," we believe it requires further study, and that it should be considered principally in terms of its impact on our deployment schedule in 1983. We favor keeping the "lowest possible levels" formula for the October 26 SCG meeting. "Lowest possible" includes zero. We also want to stress the importance of accurate data and of effective verification.

REAGAN: **How will we verify an agreement?**

ALLEN: We will have the national technical means, satellites, and so on. But in addition, we will be looking at on-site inspections and other means. The problem is that because of the Soviet obsession against inspections, our insistences may appear to some Europeans to have the effect of scuttling the negotiations.

REAGAN: **Even if you could have inspections, who could really travel and verify in that vast country?**

CASEY: With a zero ban, it would be easier.

REAGAN: **Even then, the Soviet Union is a large country. Couldn't they easily hide something in Siberia or somewhere else?**

MEESE: With a zero ban, we would have an easier indicator of whether or not the Soviets were complying.

WEINBERGER: The Soviets would have to dismantle their systems. Third countries and international organizations might need to be involved, but nothing is guaranteeable.

REAGAN: **Maybe we should be leasing some of the people from the Third World nations at Cancun to help verify the dismantling.**

ALLEN: We are running short of time. General Jones, can you comment on the views of the Chiefs?

JONES: We support TNF negotiations. I think it's important to gain allied confidence so we can proceed with the modernization program. We agree with the outline presented by Secretary Haig and Secretary Weinberger. However, we have two concerns at present. First, on the reference to warheads-on-launchers as the unit of account. We may want to count warheads-on-missiles instead. We will need to study this further. Secondly, and this is a major concern, we do not want the reference to aircraft not being negotiated in a first phase to imply that aircraft could be negotiated in a future phase. That would be a slippery and dangerous slope. Aircraft are required for both nuclear and conventional roles and involve other special considerations as well.

HAIG: General Jones' points clearly get us into the SALT/INF relationship. For example, in the data exchange issue on the balance, we will need to count aircraft somehow. That will be a nightmare.

ALLEN: Cap (Weinberger), you will be gone until the 24th?

WEINBERGER:	Yes, I take it from the discussion that in my NATO meetings, I will be reporting on our preliminary preparations and will reaffirm the November 30 starting time for negotiations, but will say nothing substantively on our negotiating approach. I take it we have agreed on a similar position for the October 26 SCG.

Allen then wraps up the meeting noting that they are out of time and asking Haig and Casey to provide the President with written reports on the situation in Egypt. Allen also notes that preliminary indications show that if embargoed, two U.S. compressor components, which the Soviets want for their Siberian pipelines, would cause a two-year delay in the pipeline's operation. A short discussion followed.

HAIG:	I am not so sure that we are confident of the impact of those compressors. We will need to check it out.
CARLUCCI:	There is a decision pending before the President on national security considerations in technology transfer. This item should be factored in.
WEINBERGER:	Senator Percy talked to me on the plane from Egypt about this issue. He is pushing for 200 more Caterpillar pipelayers to go to the Soviet Union.
	The pipeline brings enormous amounts of hard cash to the Soviet Union, which they use to strengthen themselves militarily.
ALLEN:	Our next meeting, later this week, will focus on the Central America/Cuba issue and on the East-West paper.
CARLUCCI:	The East-West discussion should include the technological transfer issue, right?

(General agreement in the room.)

POSTSCRIPT

See April 21, 1982 for the next declassified meeting on arms control. President Reagan officially announced a zero-option on November 18, 1981 when he offered to not proceed with Pershing deployments in Europe if the Soviet Union removed its missiles targeted on Western Europe.

Date: **October 15, 1981**
Subject: **Letter from Brezhnev to Reagan (Response to 9/21/81 letter)**

Dear Mr. President,

Your letter of September 22 contains thoughts which, as you write, touch upon the future of relations between our two countries. I studied them carefully.

I noted, of course, the statements in your message regarding your readiness to maintain a constructive and stable relationship with the Soviet Union, adherence to the dialogue with it, and interest in peaceful resolution of problems causing the international tensions. Those intentions can only be welcomed. We are fully in favor of proceeding along such a path and, on our part, have been constantly calling upon the United States to act in exactly the same way.

We are convinced that a positive development of relations between the USSR and the USA meets the interests not only of the Soviet and American peoples: leveling off these relations, bringing them back on the road of businesslike cooperation would facilitate lessening the dangerous level of tension in the world and would give a real hope for resolution of many acute international problems.

At the same time, to be frank, it is regrettable that a new attempt is made in your letter to present the matter in such a way, as if the obstacle in the way of improving Soviet-American relations and reducing the general international tensions is the policy of the Soviet Union. In the correspondence between us I already dealt in detail on the absence of any basis for posing the question in such a way. And the fact that this thesis is again present in your message does not make it any more convincing.

Nor any useful purpose is served either by the tendency discernable in your message which suggests in one way or another a linkage between the prospect of development in our relations with some sort of modifications in the Soviet Union's "behavior". To proceed on this premise is to steer clearly the whole matter toward a deadlock.

We, Mr. President, just as many other countries, really have serious and legitimate objections to raise with the United States and its policy. However, we are against replacing the consideration of acute and outstanding issues with mutual recriminations over the behavior of any party on the international scene.

You are speaking in favor of taking mutually into account each other's interests. We are in favor of that, too. But no double standard here should be allowed, whereby one side perceives its interests everywhere and in everything, but any legitimate step on the part of the other side is immediately portrayed as encroachment on those interests, as a desire to get unilateral advantages. Abandonment by the United States of such a double standard will in fact demonstrate readiness to heed the interests of the other side and will be a good contribution to the cause of stabilization of the world situation.

And, of course, each side possesses a sovereign right to have appropriate relations with its allies and friends, and to render them necessary assistance. Let me make a point, if we are to speak of our friends, they threaten nobody. Some people do not wish, however, to leave them alone, but left alone they must be.

Here is an example – the campaign against Cuba – a campaign that is constantly being whipped up. Why, for what purpose, is this being done? One cannot be serious in saying that Cuba can allegedly threaten the vital interests of the United States. We call upon the United States not to aggravate the situation around that country but to embark on the path of establishing normal relations with Cuba.

If the US side is really prepared, as you, Mr. President, write, to seek solutions to international problems through negotiations, there exist all possibilities to start doing that.

Take, for instance, that same question about a political settlement of the situation around Afghanistan. As is known, the DRA Government has been consistently seeking such a settlement, in whose context the question of the withdrawal of the Soviet troops from Afghanistan would also be resolved.

Recently the Afghan leadership came forth with new proposals on a political settlement. We support those proposals and regard them as a good basis for reaching appropriate agreements without any prejudice to the security and prestige of any country. Think about it.

Likewise, why should not the United States take, at last, an unbiased look at what is going on in Campuchea? Is it really that the American interests are infringed there? How is it possible in pursuance of some expedient calculations to try to play with the destiny of a nation, which has, as it is, suffered a terrible tragedy. It cannot be permitted that the leftovers of the Pol Pot regime could again stage a bloodbath for the Campuchean people.

And there is still another question – the one concerning the situation around Egypt. Here too there should be no outside interference. Nobody has any right to tell the Egyptians how they must solve their problems. The pressure, which is being brought to bear on that country and, in so doing, on the adjacent countries, must be stopped.

As we have already stated to the US Government, the developments around Egypt affect the security interests of the Soviet Union. Indeed, there is approximately the same distance from the USSR border to Egypt, as from Boston to Chicago.

In your message you, Mr. President, mentioned as one of the factors poisoning the political atmosphere "the campaign of anti-Americanism", which is allegedly waged by the Soviet Union. However, if anybody has the grounds to bring a charge on account of the raging hostile propaganda, it has to be us, the Soviet side. After all, not a day passes in the USA without ever new fabrications about the Soviet Union and its policy being launched. What is more, the most active part in this unseemly exercise is taken by many representatives of the administration.

For instance, what about the incessant campaign about the so-called "Soviet military threat". All sorts of fantastic fables have been told in this regard on our account.

And why did you, personally, Mr. President, recently need to state publicly that the Soviet Union bases its policy on the calculation to score a victory in the nuclear war? Are you not aware of my repeated and clear statements – may be somebody intentionally conceals them from you – that the nuclear war, should it be unleashed, would turn out to be a catastrophe for the mankind?

I stated on more than one occasion, for all to hear, that the Soviet Union is against any nuclear strike, be it the first or not the first, massive or limited. We are for totally precluding the possibility of using nuclear weapons. This is, indeed, the thrust of our proposals set forth at the current UN General Assembly session. This is our firm and consistent position. It is in this spirit that we are striving to educate also the entire Soviet people.

We are not the ones who entertain thoughts about winning a nuclear duel. We believe such calculations to be an insanity.

Of course, we unmasked and will continue to unmask the calumny against our country and our policy. As far as we are concerned, we are against the use of unpermitted methods in conducting the polemics. We are in favor of a quiet, businesslike and, if you will, respectful dialogue.

Your message quite correctly point out what danger for the mankind is presented by the already existing nuclear weapons stockpiles as well as the need for serious efforts to reduce the armaments. However, it is difficult to match these thoughts with the program of a steep increase in the US strategic forces that you have recently announced. After all, this program in no way leads in the direction of the restraint, which you seem to be advocating. No reasonable grounds for the adoption of such a program exist.

The implementation of this program will mean placing the arms race into a new spiral with all its consequences.

The Soviet Union never sought a military supremacy. But we simply cannot permit the disruption of the military-strategic parity.

Mr. President, a meeting between our ministers has recently taken place in New York. In a certain sense its results are positive. I have in mind the agreement reached to hold negotiations on limiting arms in Europe. It is, of course, only the first step, and serious mutual work is yet to be done in search of solutions that would equally meet the interests of the Soviet Union and the United States and be consistent with the principle of equality and equal security. We are prepared to engage in such a search and would like to hope that the US side too will approach the negotiations in a businesslike manner.

The most important question concerning the continuation of strategic arms limitation negotiations remains open. Regrettably, neither your letter, Mr.

President, nor what was said by the Secretary of State A. Haig, introduce, so far, clarity in the US position in that respect.

These are the thoughts which I wanted to set forth in connection with your letter. Let us hope that the exchange between us will serve the cause of establishing a better understanding on the key issues of Soviet-American relations.

Sincerely,
L. Brezhnev

After reading the letter, Reagan scribbled across the cover memo, "Do you suppose he really believes all the crud – or did he even write it? RR"

Date:	**October 16, 1981**
Subject:	**East-West Trade Controls**
Status:	**Declassified in Part (2004)**

BACKGROUND

In the two meetings on East-West Trade Controls in July 1981, Reagan decided to try and stop the Soviet trans-Siberian pipeline from being built because the finished pipeline would provide the Soviet's with cash critical to their military programs. The two July meetings, however, did not produce a consensus on how to try and stop the pipeline construction. Today's meeting continues the debate on how best to gain necessary allied support for stopping the construction of the pipeline.

SUMMARY

MEESE: Even though everyone is not here, I believe we can accomplish some work before the President arrives.

It seems to me the issues we have to discuss today can be divided into three questions. First, do we want to impede the construction of the Siberian Pipeline? We haven't really examined this.

CARLUCCI: I believe we have decided to impede it.

CLARK: Yes.

MEESE: A second question is, to what extent can we obtain the cooperation of other countries, or impede their participation in the project, and what would the effects be of our actions? Third, what is the balance of the effects of our action on our domestic employment versus our national security?

UNKNOWN: (Line not recorded)

MEESE: Foreign policy and national security are the same only in State. (Laughter)

(Reagan and Allen enter)

Mr. President, we had got started on this matter by posing three questions:

- The first is whether we want to impede the construction of the Siberian Pipeline. The consensus answer to that question seems to be yes.
- The second question is to what extent can we get others – our allies – to agree?
- To what extent do domestic considerations weigh in determining our decision?

CASEY: I wonder if we could go back a bit? We have a new comprehensive analysis of what the Soviets buy from the West in technology and the affccts of these purchases. It is staggering – the things they could not do without western assistance (technology).

ALLEN: Is this a new study?

CASEY: Yes, the Soviets go about the acquisition of western technology in a very organized manner. They lay out what they need and identify where to go to get it. As a result of an increased understanding of the effects of Soviet acquisitions, I see a trend to substantial broadening of COCOM rules and revised methods of control to reduce their technology acquisitions. I believe these new findings will isolate and highlight the technology transfer question as never before.

CARLUCCI: We want to force the Soviets into a diversified investment strategy – to force hard choices on them. However, selling technology to them saves them investment funds and makes their choices easier.

CASEY: This new information shows the value of what they are getting is greater than we had ever conceived.

REAGAN: **It seems to me this gets down to showing that if the free world had not helped them and had let their system deteriorate, we wouldn't have the problems we have today. But we can't do it alone. The question is have we worked in good faith with our allies to get their cooperation? And, if we don't get their cooperation, at what point do we (by unilateral embargo actions) simply cut off our nose to spite our face, and add to our own (economic) problems by not**

selling – by depriving ourselves without depriving them (the Soviets) as was the case with grain. Can we make alone a decision to hold them back?

CASEY: On some things we can – on some we can't. Non-agricultural exports are a small portion of our trade with the Soviets. I believe this new study will promote a new allied attitude. It has not been previously recognized how important this issue is. It has never before been looked at in its totality.

ALLEN: Bill is also talking about the acquisition of technology by means other than purchases, such as theft.

REAGAN: **I know that. Also, what they get by buying one, tearing it apart, and learning how to do it.**

ALLEN: It's called reverse engineering. Bill, what are you going to do with this new information? Are you going to make it available?

CASEY: Yes.

ALLEN: We have some important decisions to make. Would this new information have an impact on the issue of oil and gas technology?

CASEY: This is a broad decision. The Soviet economy is in trouble. The question is, do we want to make it harder for them?

HAIG: (Haig entered after the discussion started.) I'm confused. Are we talking about today's agenda?

ALLEN: Bill has indicated that he has a new study examining the totality of technology transfer to the Soviet Union. (Line redacted.)

HAIG: Mr. President, I believe we need to remember that we had a decision to broaden COCOM from purely military applications, to cover military-industrial items. We hope for a high-level COCOM meeting in November to raise this issue. I hope we understand that we do have an agenda for dealing with this technology transfer matter.

MEESE: (The minutes show: "??????")

HAIG: Why don't we put this new information into the bureaucracy and see what happens?

ALLEN: Yes, that's what we should do. Now, we have to deal with this oil and gas policy issue. It is urgent because we have a backlog of licenses to deal with and because our policy on this matter will affect our position on the Siberian Pipeline. We need a decision on our U.S. exports that would contribute to the construction of the pipeline.

MEESE: We have arrived at four options. Would the Department of Commerce state its position on this matter?

OLMER: Secretary Baldrige, with whom I have discussed this matter today, says we continue to support Option IV. This option would allow us to sell oil and gas equipment items on which there are not national security controls. This policy is desirable because the majority of oil and gas equipment not covered by national security controls is available from other sources and unilateral U.S. controls would achieve little.

ALLEN: What about turbine components? We have new information from the CIA that restricting some items would cause a pipeline delay of 18-24 months. Is this correct?

CASEY: Yes. GE says if a license is not granted for shipment of U.S. components, it would take about two-years for European competitors to get started producing them. How much this would delay the pipeline, itself, is not quite so clear, but it would delay it.

ALLEN: Under Secretary Olmer, how would that coincide with your position on Option III?

OLMER: There is disagreement on how long it would take the Soviets to make up the technology shortages that would result from U.S. controls. In an analysis prepared for recent testimony we found that, with very few exceptions, we do not have a U.S. monopoly.

For example, GE compressors could be gotten elsewhere. Our allies are generally unwilling to go along with restrictions. Thus, we are caught in a position of telling our companies they cannot get licenses because our policy is to impede Soviet production, but not licensing won't impede them (the Soviets) because of availability from other sources. (Line redacted.)

CASEY: I agree we don't have a unique capability. It's a matter of time needed to catch up. But the compressors the Soviets would get from other sources would be less efficient than those built by GE.

HAIG: Aren't we getting wrapped around the axle on one facet of the problem? We have had an options paper since August. We have no decisions as yet. Now we have a basic oil and gas decision to make – not a pipeline decision to make.

Mr. President, your earlier remarks were, I thought, on the mark. The question is <u>whether</u> we have the luxury of denying the Soviet Union essential equipment. Then we can get to the question of the pipeline.

UNKNOWN: (The minutes show: "????")

MEESE: I think we should hear the agency positions.

ALLEN: It seems to me that the agencies have spoken and that their positions have not changed.

HAIG: No, let's discuss the four options and keep the pipeline out of it.

MEESE: No, we need specifics to make it concrete. It's silly to discuss the issue without the pipeline. Under Secretary Olmer indicated Commerce's position. We should discuss what position others take. The key question is, what can we get our allies to do?

HAIG: We should discuss our basic policy on oil and gas controls.

OLMER: I think it should be emphasized that some parts of exports for the pipeline are already covered by national security controls. Much is not, but some items are controlled for national security reasons.

ALLEN: The rest is under foreign policy controls. Mr. President, the options have not changed. They are stated in succinct form in the materials provided. Those recommending Option I include Weinberger, Casey, Kirkpatrick and General Jones.

Essentially the same group also recommends Option II. Energy recommends Option III, while Option IV is recommended by Secretaries Haig, Regan and Baldrige, Under Secretary Davis, Mr. Stockman and Ambassador Brock. Simply stated, Option IV is:

> Rather than attempting to impede oil and gas production and exports, our goal will be to deny exports of technology that allow the Soviets to replicate advanced Western equipment; this technology would give them an independent capability to improve oil and gas output and infrastructure. The U.S. will approve exports of end use equipment.

Some of the end use equipment would be directly affected by your decisions – Caterpillar pipelayers, rotors, shafts. All of this has implications for East-West relations and East-West trade, but requires a decision as to what our basic position should be.

HAIG: Mr. President, Option IV is restricting the transfer of technology while dealing with equipment on a case-by-case basis to see if it does violence to our position.

Option IV is preferable because if we unilaterally deny oil and gas equipment, we will not restrict availability to the Soviets. It will be impossible to convince our allies to join us in such restrictions. Cap has talked with the Brits. They suggested in no way would they go along with us.

ALLEN: This proposal involves giving our allies some running room. It is the same policy followed by Carter.

UNKNOWN: (Minutes show: "????")

HAIG: We are talking about holding technology back while selling them equipment on a case-by-case basis.

ALLEN: It would allow shipments of equipment and continued leakage.

CARLUCCI: Are we discussing the subject in the context of foreign policy or that of national security? No one prefers a unilateral embargo. Options I and II would place security controls on oil and gas equipment and technology. Options III and IV would be foreign policy controls.

The question is, what degree of diplomacy and example we use with our allies. We don't know what they will do until we set an example. We must send our allies a steady signal. They are confused by our actions, such as our ending of the grain embargo. We seem to make decisions on commercial grounds.

HAIG: Yes.

CARLUCCI: But if we don't try, we open up the floodgates.

HAIG: No! We say tighten up on technology transfer! We are proposing important modifications – new controls – to our allies.

ALLEN: No! Option IV is precisely what Carter did.

HAIG: Look! There is a profound difference between what Carter did as a knee-jerk reaction and what we do in encouraging our allies to tighten COCOM controls.

To deal with our allies in a credible way, we have to have a credible position. Options I and II are unilateral control actions while trying to get allied support. We won't get it! The President must be concerned about our credibility.

Option IV says increased controls on technology transfer. Let's sit down and do it. On end items we decide case by case. The President and the bureaucracy are capable of doing it.

CASEY:	There are risks in the process.
HAIG:	Option I is not credible.
CARLUCCI:	Under Options I or II, the U.S. will actively impede and use pressure. The actions would not be unilateral.
HAIG:	Would we permit the sale of oil and gas items during the period we are pressuring our allies?
CARLUCCI:	No, we would not. After a fair period of trial we may need to regroup and change our position (if the allies do not follow us).
MEESE:	The President does not decide export controls on a case-by-case basis. We need clear guidelines for the bureaucracy.
UNKNOWN:	Allows items opens a pretty wide track. Items for the pipeline would not go on I or II. They would go on under III or IV.
CARLUCCI:	Under Option I or II we control on the basis of national security concerns.
MEESE:	Would not it be useful to go around the room for an expression of views and then to ask questions?
ALLEN:	I believe everyone has already spoken.
REGAN:	I am confused between Option III and IV. I thought I understood it, but I am not sure now that I do. We need clear guidance for our customs people.
ALLEN:	Under a strict interpretation of IV, the U.S. will approve exports of equipment. The pipelayers would go. (Looking at Under Secretary Olmer) Without a license?
OLMER:	No, they would be licensed.
MEESE:	If we sent 200 in July, it's hard to say they can't have them in September.
OLMER:	No matter which options, I through IV, at least four areas of oil and gas equipment will be controlled – regardless of what decision today. For example, computer controls, rig design, crew training and (?).
ALLEN:	So these items would be controlled?
OLMER:	Several thousand high technology items would be controlled under any option.
CASEY:	In 1979 the Soviets got 1,000 items that aided in their research and development.
ALLEN:	There are several locksteps involved in this decision. The oil and gas decision relates to East-West

trade. East-West trade in turn relates to East-West relations, which relates to our long-range Soviet policy. Walking up the steps, making these decisions gets more difficult as you get higher up on the steps.

CARLUCCI: Unless we select I or II, we make the pipeline decision already made more difficult to sell to our allies. We would be willing to go from I to II, but let's not capitulate too soon.

KIRKPATRICK: We don't want to help the Soviets develop their oil and gas production. There are long waiting lists for oil and gas equipment. The waits are years long. Putting them off won't cost us sales.

REAGAN: **Do you mean if Caterpillar does not sell to the Soviets, then they can sell elsewhere?**

KIRKPATRICK: Yes, in South America and elsewhere.

HAIG: Why is International Harvester going broke then?

REAGAN: **Do you mean that Caterpillar can sell 200 pipelayers in South America? Then why is Caterpillar pressing so hard on this transaction?**

KIRKPATRICK: The fact that Chrysler is going broke does not mean there is no market for them in the U.S.

REAGAN: **At Ottawa, Suzuki said he would look into it.**

HAIG: The Japanese Foreign Minister later said no, they wouldn't withhold sales. They were very clear on it.

HARPER: On oil rigs there is a long waiting line, but on the high technology we want to protect, we need a definition of the technology issues vis-à-vis policy.

ALLEN: Mr. President, we need a statement of options satisfactory to you. I gather that you feel reluctant to sign off on this issue from this options paper – that it is not yet crisp enough.

Possibly, there is a problem in that we don't have an overall Soviet policy. But that wouldn't address the problem of licenses and the problem of COCOM negotiations, and the fact that licensing pipelayers before the COCOM meeting would complicate negotiations.

OLMER: It is important to have a clear statement of policy before the COCOM meeting even though our oil and gas decision is not a matter to be treated directly there. The Caterpillar pipelayers will be seen as a sign of our intentions.

HAIG: There is an important point to be made. We are seeking a broadening of the controls in COCOM to include not just military use technology, but military-industrial equipment. If we now adopt a brittle attitude on oil and gas, it will not be consistent with our COCOM instructions. Option IV would be consistent with our COCOM negotiating position.

I hope that in the future no summary of the options will be prepared to go to the President.

We are smoking opium if we think we can get allied agreement on Option I. We will begin with Option II. Option II has terrible practical applications. Secretary Regan could not administer it. His customs people will not be able to do it.

We should look at the four options on an interdepartmental basis. The whole matter should go back to the drawing board.

ALLEN: This (options paper) is the same paper that went through the process earlier. It has not been changed.

REAGAN: **I'm the most confused person of anyone. Is it possible to have options paper that says "here's what we'll stop selling – here's where they will get it then – here's what they can't get elsewhere?"**

I'd like to know the effect on our economy and the effect on them. I'd like to know the effect on our businesses – those that wouldn't be able to make it (because of our restrictions) – not down to those who make shoelaces, of course.

But I would like to look and see what it would do to the Soviet Union. Is it worth it to make an economic sacrifice? It is difficult to make a decision without knowing this.

HAIG: We all want to tighten up – to give them the minimum we can. But the doctrinaires here want to cut it off (totally) and to tell our allies to do the same. But they will tell us to go to hell.

The ?? Option is IV. Under that we tighten our technology – go case by case on equipment. Perhaps we can tighten up on the individual cases. But let's not stick our head in the pencil sharpener. Let's have a realist policy!

ALLEN: We are trying to reconstruct COCOM, to construct a realistic policy for the 80's. But what is realism for the 80's. Your concern is to get along with our allies.

HAIG: That's your interpretation of my policy. I want a policy that is credible and effective.

MEESE:	We must finish. We are keeping a number of people waiting to use this room. Mr. President, your suggestion was to flesh out the options with some examples.
REAGAN:	**Let me give two more examples concerning the confusion on this issue.**
	First, my understanding is that the technology that slipped through Commerce on ball-bearings allowed the Soviets to MIRV their missiles earlier than they otherwise would have been able to do so. We should have been able to prevent that.
	Second, on the grain embargo, we saw a breakdown in the embargo. The Soviets were getting it without our help while our agriculture here was in a tailspin.
	We have to look at two considerations: Even though it helps them, does it help us as much or more than it helps them? If it is spelled out that way it will help to make the decision. What is it that we can cut off from them that they can't get elsewhere?
MEESE:	We need to talk about this again as soon as possible – at the next NSC meeting.
REAGAN:	**Can we repossess the KAMA River truck plant from them?**
ALLEN:	Mr. President, Larry Brady here is the person who is responsible for that.

POSTSCRIPT

After the meeting was officially over but before the principals left the room, the minutes indicate that Haig confronted Allen about inserting "staff bias into options papers". No further comments are noted. COCOM controls are discussed again in Chapters 2 and 3.

Date: November 17, 1981
Subject: **Letter from Reagan to Brezhnev (Response to 10/15/81 letter)**

Dear President Brezhnev,
    Your letter of October 15 makes it clear once again how profound are the differences in our respective assessments of the causes of the major sources of tension in the world. I find it difficult to accept your declaration that Soviet actions in other parts of the world must have no bearing on our relations. Soviet actions are having a direct and adverse impact on American interests in many

parts of the world. As I have said in my letter to you of September 22, Soviet resort to direct and indirect use of force in regional conflicts is a matter of deep concern to us as is the continued build up of military strength beyond the need for self defense.

Despite these differences, however, we should strive to find a common ground for agreement on matters of vital interest to our two countries and the rest of the world. The cause of peace, and particularly the threat of nuclear destruction hanging over mankind, require that our two countries make an effort, together with our partners, to resolve our differences peacefully. I assure you the United States is committed to such a process. I therefore welcome an opportunity for businesslike cooperation in addressing world problems. I believe that our exchanges, and the discussions in New York between Secretary Haig and Foreign Minister Gromyko, have laid the essential groundwork for such an effort. The key question now is how we can translate these beginnings into concrete results. We are ready to advance specific solutions and to hear our Soviet proposals aimed at relieving the dangers, as well as the current human suffering, in problem areas around the world.

I am convinced, Mr. President, that we can achieve results in the coming year if there is genuine good will and serious interest on both sides.

Afghanistan remains a major obstacle to progress, beclouding the international atmosphere. It appears from recent communications that we both agree on the need for progress toward an internationally acceptable solution of this issue. We appear to agree on basic goals: a nonaligned, independent Afghanistan, free of any foreign military presence and guaranteed against any outside interference. This calls for a complete withdrawal of Soviet forces from Afghanistan at the earliest possible date. The United States is prepared to continue the exchange of views on questions that bear on a political settlement in Afghanistan. Ambassador Hartman will be in touch with Foreign Minister Gromyko to determine whether there is a basis for a serious dialogue.

Now let me address your assertions regarding US policy towards Cuba. We do not seek to interfere with Cuba's independence nor are we interfering in Cuba's internal affairs. However, we do find entirely unacceptable Cuba's unremitting efforts to export its revolution by fomenting violent insurgencies and terrorism against legitimate governments in Central America.

But to get to the real purpose of my letter, arms control is a vital area where progress can be made toward world peace. The United States is prepared to accept equality in conventional, intermediate-range nuclear and strategic forces at the lowest possible level of such forces. We are also prepared to take other steps to enhance general peace and international security.

Let me begin with strategic forces. The United States will be prepared to open negotiations on strategic arms reductions as soon as possible in the new year. In approaching these talks we should learn from past experiences. In my view, however, the negotiations also will require fresh ideas – to which both sides should devote urgent and serious attention – in order that we can achieve genuine reductions in strategic forces. This will demand political will and a readiness on both sides to accept a higher degree of openness in order to enhance mutual confidence. In this connection, I welcome your important public statement that verification measures going beyond national technical means might be possible.

Concerning intermediate-range nuclear forces, the agreement to begin talks on these systems on November 30 in Geneva marks an important beginning in dealing with the difficult issue of the military imbalance in these forces. We are ready to reach an agreement with the Soviet Union which we believe is straightforward and fair. We are prepared to cancel our plan to deploy Pershing II and ground-launched cruise missiles on the condition that the Soviet Union in turn dismantles all of its SS-20 missiles, retires and dismantles its SS-4, and SS-5 missiles, and desists from further deployments of these or comparable systems.

Opportunities also exist for reductions in conventional forces in Europe. Your offensive forces have become increasingly capable. The Soviet Union could make no more convincing contribution to peace in Europe than by substantially reducing its conventional forces. Now is the time to take actions to achieve equality at a lower level of conventional forces in Europe.

The Conference on Security and Cooperation in Europe offers another practical possibility for increasing confidence and reducing the risks of war. At the Madrid meeting, the Western countries have advanced proposals for a Conference on Disarmament in Europe that could negotiate measures aimed at reducing concerns about surprise attack. At the same time, I would hope we could move the Helsinki process forward in a balanced way in all areas taking favorable action to resolve certain humanitarian matters, such as the reunification of divided families and the individual cases raised during the recent discussions between our foreign ministers in New York. Such action I have no doubt would have a favorable effect on deliberations in Madrid, and on relations between our two countries. I feel I must tell you I am personally concerned with the particular cases under discussion between Secretary Haig and your representative.

There is no shortage, Mr. President, of opportunities for easing world tensions. If the Soviet Union is prepared to move forward in these areas of genuine concern to the United States and its allies, you will find me a ready partner.

Sincerely,
Ronald Reagan

Date: **December 1, 1981**
Subject: **Letter from Brezhnev to Reagan**

Dear Mr. President,

I note with satisfaction that in your letter of November 17, 1981 you have expressed yourself ready to strive in the spirit of businesslike cooperation, despite the existing differences between our countries, to find a common ground for agreement on matters of vital interest to our two countries and the rest of the world.

On our part we believed and continue to believe that it is precisely such an approach that is required of the USSR and the USA if we are to be guided by the task of eliminating the threat of nuclear wear. We cannot and have no right to proceed in a different manner and to avoid responsibility which rests on our States.

The main thing, however, is to substantiate the correct general premise with specific actions by both sides. Mere statements no matter how good they may sound, are not enough to achieve progress in the resolution of no simple problems before us. What is required is realistic positions and practical proposals which would take into account the legitimate interests of the other side rather than be built around the desire to somehow infringe on those interests. Otherwise the declared positive goals will remain at best good intentions if not just an attempt to score a propaganda point. Neither of the two will be helpful.

From this standpoint, I shall tell you frankly, the considerations advanced in your letter on specific issues are, to put it mildly, very far from the objective reality. Suffice it to mention the assertion to the effect that the Soviet Union is allegedly increasing its military power beyond its defense requirements. A conclusion is drawn then from this clearly distorted premise that the Soviet Union has to disarm unilaterally, while the US can continue to build on and on its military might at its own discretion. And this is what in fact is taking place in the United States.

Here we are faced with what is called "the double book-keeping" whereby in counting the Soviet arms in question their numbers are made to look many times higher, and – conversely – when it comes to the US, such numbers are drastically understated. Moreover, hundreds of nuclear systems in the possession of Britain and France are totally excluded from the counting, whereas on the Soviet side even those systems are counted which do not belong to the category of medium-range weapons and, indeed, have nothing to do whatsoever with Europe and still less so with the US.

Why is it necessary, Mr. President, to try to compare things which in their essence cannot be compared? It is difficult to dismiss a thought that the calculation here is based on the fact that most people are poorly versed in such matters and therefore will hardly be able to grasp the subject. The past experience shows, however, that sooner or later people will be able to sort things out for themselves. After all, both you and ourselves know very well that even if either side wished to somehow take advantage of the other in such matters, to do so would be impossible. The guarantee in this respect is provided by the national technical means of verification of the USSR and the USA.

Recognition of the effectiveness of such a principle lies at the basis of the SALT-1 and SALT-2 agreements. Respect for this principle consistently guides the Soviet Union in its practical activities.

As a "straightforward and fair" solution of the problem of medium-range nuclear arms you suggest that all Soviet medium-range missiles – both the new "SS-20's" and the old "SS-4's" and "SS-5's" be eliminated. I wouldn't argue with respect to the "straightforward" nature of this proposal, but to call it "fair" and generally a serious one was, of course, impossible not for us alone but for all those who retained the sense of reality.

As recently as yesterday the US officials acknowledged, and some of them do so today, that there continues to exist an approximate parity in nuclear arms in Europe. But even those among US officials, who are trying despite the facts to question it, keep only saying that the parity has been allegedly upset by the introduction of the "SS-20" missiles. It follows from this that when a considerably larger number of the" SS-4" and "SS-5" missiles was in place compared with their present number, no question of "disbalance" occurred to anybody. Why then, may we ask, are we offered to scrap all our medium-range missiles while the entire NATO's nuclear arsenal remains intact? Is there any logic here, Mr. President?

Let me say it straight away that this is not the kind of basis on which questions related to the national security of states can be resolved. In matters of this nature it is necessary to be strictly guided by reciprocity, the principle of equality and equal security. Our delegation in Geneva has the instructions to proceed exactly on this premise. If the US side also adheres to that principle, then one can expect success in the negotiations. There is no other way to achieve success.

Should the West demonstrate its readiness to reach agreement on a truly complete renunciation by both sides of all types of the existing medium-range nuclear arms deployed in Europe or around it, we on our part will be forthcoming.

We could also agree to free Europe altogether from nuclear arms both medium-range and tactical. That would be a genuine zero-option fair for all sides.

Indeed it really appears to us strange to call on the Soviet Union to make a contribution, as you write, to peace in Europe by reducing its conventional forces there. This call should not be addressed to us. You must be aware of the fact that in recent years we unilaterally withdrew from Central Europe 20,000 troops and 1,000 tanks, while the US, on the contrary, added tens of thousands of men to its troops in Europe. That's the actual state of affairs in real life.

The question is which side is lacking in constructiveness and practical steps?

When you, Mr. President, indicate that the US is prepared to open negotiations on strategic arms reductions as soon as possible in the new year, we would like to understand this to mean that such negotiations will actually resume in the near future. We are for it.

It follows from your letter that the US side stands not just for limitation, but for the reduction of strategic arms. In this connection, I would like to remind you that the SALT II Treaty provides for such reductions, and very substantial reductions at that. We have been and continue to be committed to this approach. It is important, however, that in this respect, too, all the factors determining the strategic situation should be taken into account, and that the principle of equality and equal security should be strictly observed.

With regard to the Madrid meeting of states-participants of the Conference on Security and Cooperation in Europe and, above all, the question of convening a European conference on confidence building measures and disarmament: if the Western countries on their part – and it is now their turn to act – show readiness to travel their length of the distance in response to our far-reaching constructive steps, then one can expect to conclude this meeting with tangible positive results and to ensure a stable development of the process initiated by the Helsinki Final Act.

I am not going to engage now in polemics on the question of Afghanistan, although I cannot in any way agree with what has been said by you on this matter. As to you indication that you are prepared to continue the exchange of views on a political settlement around Afghanistan, on our part we did not have and do not have now any objections to that. Our position on concrete aspects of the political settlement is known to you. However, we have not yet received your views on the substance of the problem which you intended to convey through your Ambassador in Moscow.

A few words about Cuba. It has to be stated that the United States continues to deliberately aggravate the situation around that country and to increase tensions in the entire Caribbean area. This is a dangerous, slippery road. At the same time, we are convinced that any step by the US towards normalization of relations with Cuba would find an appropriate response on the part of that country.

In conclusion, I would like to reemphasize that although differences between our countries will, of course, remain also in the future, our position is not to exacerbate those differences or multiply them and, even more so, not to attempt to overpower each other – which is an unpromising perspective – instead, we favor efforts to expand areas of accord.

I think that at least there gradually emerges a set of really important questions on whose solutions our two countries should primarily concentrate their joint efforts being conscious of our mutual responsibility. We are prepared for such work.

Sincerely,
L. Brezhnev

CHAPTER 2

THE POLISH CRISIS

"The Poland situation is unique: completely surrounded by Warsaw Pact countries, cut off from any direct contact with the West. It is the Pope's belief that change in Eastern Europe would come only gradually and at the same rate in all Eastern European country's. The Pope is convinced that over time such liberalization will occur, but no one could know how long the process would take."[8]

[8] Cardinal Casaroli to President Reagan during a December 15, 1981 White House luncheon. Exec. Sec. NSC Subject Files: Records, 1981-1985. Box 49. Memorandum of Conversation President Reagan (December 1981) (1)(2).

Date: **December 10, 1981**
Subject: **Aid to Poland**
Status: **Declassified (2008), released at the Reagan Library April 13, 2009**

BACKGROUND

Reagan's taking office in 1981 coincided with important democratic reforms in Poland. Led by Lech Walesa of the Solidarity labor movement (which had the support of about 50 percent of Poles), the Polish people were seen by Reagan and Haig as trying to escape the tight fist of communism. However, the Polish Government, which Reagan believed to be a proxy of the Soviet Union, suppressed democratic gains by imposing martial law and arresting Solidarity leaders. Faced with a major foreign policy crisis, Reagan saw the situation as an opportunity to score a victory over the Soviet Union.

SUMMARY

President Reagan opens the meeting thanking Casey for a knife Casey gave him as a gift. Reagan tells the NSC that he took the knife to a budget cutting session, and that "after all these farm bill meetings, I'm an expert on corn." "We've got lots of it," Reagan tells the NSC. "Give it to them!"

NANCE: Mr. President, we have one topic on the agenda today: aid to Poland. We will look at a short-term solution to the problem and a long-term solution.

The short-term solution is to provide $100 million of grain to Poland to prevent slaughter of Polish cattle this winter. Secretary Stoessel, would you like to begin the discussion?

STOESSEL: Mr. President, I'd like to begin with a word about the strategic significant of Poland. Poland lies across Soviet communication lines to the West. As a result of events of the last 16 months, the Soviets cannot count on the Polish army and on those communication lines and the Warsaw Pact has been weakened.

It is in our interest to continue present trends in Poland. However, the economic considerations in the Polish equation are important. The Polish economy is in difficulty. We need to help them keep their economy going. The Poles have requested $200 million in immediate emergency aid in the form of grain to avoid distress slaughtering of poultry and livestock. We think $100 million would be appropriate to keep them going through the winter. Their present supplies of grain, without aid, will begin to run out in January.

We must move quickly now, to pick up the slack, to save them. They need feed grain, mostly corn. In extending this aid we can give credit for our assistance to Solidarity and also respond to the Pope and, in doing so, aid the forces of liberalization.

It can be done without legislation. There need be no immediate budget outlay. There is, however, a cargo preference issue that could cause problems. The program to be used requires cargo preferences go to U.S. ships – which would add significantly to Polish costs. But since this is emergency aid we believe we should not implement the cargo preferences provision of the law. There are ways to accomplish that.

REAGAN: **Will there be any furor from the Maritime interests?**

STOESSEL: If they understand your decision, we believe they will go along with it. We have support in Congress from both sides of the aisle for aid to Poland.

BUSH: What is the difference in cost to the Poles if American bottoms are used? I have heard it is about $30 million. That seems a lot. Is it that much?

STOESSEL: Yes, about that.

LYNG: We are having trouble with the Maritime interests on a recent transaction that did not go in American ships. These earlier transactions were "giveaway" sales. We said cargo preference did not apply, but the Maritime interests are complaining.

This is not, however, a concessionary sale and so cargo preference need not apply.

We do not concur in using CCC corn. There would be grave economic problems in doing so and some political problems. The law requires sale of surplus corn at prices that would be about one-third more than market prices in the current situation. We should go into the market and purchase the corn at current market prices.

But we have done that for three years, using credits and guaranteed loans. The Poles now owe us about $1.5 billion and are not making payments.

We believe it is a misuse of CCC to do this – to use the CCC program for foreign policy purposes. We have discussed this matter in the CCEA. We are sympathetic to Polish needs. We have lots of corn, but use of CCC authority to make this sale is skating on thin ice, particularly for a long-term aid program.

One hundred million dollars – OK, but to suggest that we can do it on a long-term basis is far more erroneous.

REAGAN: **Let me ask – they are buying on credit, but it costs more to buy surplus than from current stocks?**

LYNG: Yes, the sale must be at 105 percent of the acquisition cost. This is a provision in the law to prevent markets from being disrupted by the sale of surplus stocks. Our farmers would resist a sale from surplus stocks, which they would see as depressing current prices. They will want a sale from current supplies, and because of recent price drops since acquisition of the surplus stocks the Poles would have to pay one-third more than current prices if they buy from surplus stocks.

REAGAN: **You mean there is no "stowaway Armenian" provision?**

LYNG: No, not in the agricultural programs. Our programs are designed to develop long-term customers. We do not have aid provisions in our law.

REAGAN: **So the sale would be on credit?**

LYNG: Yes, we would get a bank to put up a loan and we would guarantee that loan, though there may be some problems with finding a bank. The Poles have credit problems, they are now engaged in rescheduling. They are essentially bankrupt.

STOESSEL: (Again, I want to emphasize the strategic importance of Poland and the urgency of Poland's needs.)

REAGAN: **We feel, too. It is a bloodless revolution. We don't want to drive them back to the Soviets.**

REGAN: We were, in the CCEA, unanimous in recommending this $100 million transaction, despite the potential farm backlash and other problems. There is an overwhelming need. There is also a need to lead our allies. We want to ensure they come in, too.

REAGAN: **So we agree this should be done, but from what source?**

REGAN: In the CCEA discussions, we left that to Secretary Block.

REAGAN: **How's he doing? (Laughter)**

LYNG: We recommend another $100 million in sales that will result in potential outlays. But there will be less problems if we use corn out of the market's supplies rather than from surplus stocks.

OLMER: We have little to contribute to the discussion except to note that on a recent authorization of $55 million of corn for the Poles, because they incurred additional cargo preference expenses, they only bought $47 million.

Also, Secretary Baldrige hosted Deputy Prime Minister Madej this week. He restated the Polish need.

BUSH: Why should U.S. bottoms cost $30 million? I strongly favor this deal if we can go this route (referring to the briefing memo) providing we don't get pressure from the Maritime unions. But why should it cost $30 million more to use U.S. bottoms?

OLMER: The law requires that 50 percent of the cargo under this form of sale must go in U.S. bottoms unless the Maritime Administration certifies that U.S. bottoms are not available at reasonable rates.

REAGAN: **Jack (Secretary Block) says something in his paper from December 8 to the effect that this sale would not be subject to cargo preference requirements because of section 4(b) (of the Food for Peace Plan).**

REGAN: It would not be subject because it would not be a concessional sale.

LYNG: A sale at market price would not be subject to cargo preference restrictions. In the case of prior sales, some have been for zlotys, some at concessionary prices. P.L. 480 or concessional sales must follow the cargo preference laws. At market prices, the Poles can use their own bottoms.

BAKER: This is not a concessional transaction (referring to the Block memo).

REAGAN: **I believe we should go forward with the $100 million.**

BAKER: Giving them the best deal that does not represent a concessional sale?

REAGAN: **Yes, Jack (Secretary Block) has it all worked out in the memo.**

NANCE: The best deal possible?

REAGAN: **Yes.**

HARPER: Are we going to discuss authorizing longer-term consultations?

NANCE: Yes, we are. Secretary Haig has requested authority to go ahead with a long-term plan at $2.5

billion, with the U.S. picking up 15 to 25 percent of that total. Secretary Stoessel, would you explain this proposal?

STOESSSEL: The $740 million of the $2.5 billion total that would be provided by the U.S. in 1982 would represent about the same level of aid as the U.S. provided last year. The aid would be primarily for grains.

Given Poland's strategic importance, we should consult with our allies and work out a long-term program that would involve them. Poland's actions are also important. And the Soviet attitude is important. There have been some indications that the Soviets may hold back (on exports and aid to Poland) to throttle the Polish economy. However, we don't want Poland's complete collapse. Poland should be OK in the longer term. It is rich in resources. There are risks (in leading an effort to help Poland), but they are acceptable. Poland can be made economically viable. It is in our long-term interest to do so. We recommend that we go ahead with consultations with our allies on a long-term program.

REGAN: We are opposed to beginning consultations. We don't know the long-term costs of such an effort. In the CCEA we decided to put together a joint paper to discuss the Polish economic situation. In the meantime we should go ahead with the $100 million and see what our allies do.

I suggest we postpone consultations until we see what the CCEA says, then come back there.

REAGAN: **Okay.**

HARPER: I would like to join with Treasury to express my concerns about the costs of a long-term program.

LYNG: I would like to emphasize that we (Agriculture) are not going to do this transaction on an aid basis, but on a business basis.

NANCE: Mr. President, we are giving you back 30 minutes of your schedule.

POSTSCRIPT

Martial law was declared in Poland three-days later, constitutional guarantees were suspended and a curfew was implemented. The Polish Government then imprisoned hundreds of Solidarity members, including Walesa.

A still classified NSPG meeting took place the day after martial law was declared, and on December 15 Reagan held a working lunch with Cardinal Casaroli, the Secretary of State from the Vatican.

After the initial exchange of pleasantries, Casaroli told Reagan that the Polish government acted both because of Soviet pressure and to prevent the Soviets themselves from intervening. Casaroli explained that without Soviet pressure, General Jaruzelski (the leader of Poland) would not have imposed martial law. Based on his personal observations, Casaroli felt that Jaruzelski was "nationalist enough not to want the Soviet Union to intervene directly."

Reagan was surprised and told Casaroli that he found it hard to believe that Polish troops would actually shoot workers for labor violations, as had been reported. Casaroli agreed, and asked if there was any evidence to support the allegations. Haig said the U.S. did not have any evidence of shootings, just reports of the threat.

Casaroli continued:

> When the Pope discussed the imposition of martial law with Polish representatives in the Vatican, the representative characterized the manner of imposition of martial law as moderate, but the measures themselves are extremely strong. The Pope, I think, would have spoken differently if he had believed there to be danger of executions of Polish workers.

Reagan wondered whether there was any confirmation of soldiers in Polish uniforms speaking Russian. No one in the room could confirm if that was the case.

Casaroli again emphasized that violence on the part of the Soviets is unlikely, because, as he was told by Cardinal Wysznski, "the Soviets could kill Poland economically anytime they wished." Reagan suggested a propaganda campaign aimed at reminding the world that the imposition of martial law was the result of Solidarity's demand for a national referendum on the government. "This was a clear comment on the lack of popular support for the government," Reagan added. Casaroli partially agreed,

> It is unrealistic to think that one East European country could be extensively liberalized on its own. The Soviets would simply not tolerate such a development....

> It is important to support movements for liberalization in Eastern Europe, but no country could be far ahead of the others. The Poland situation is unique: completely surrounded by Warsaw Pact countries, cut off from any direct contact with the West. It is the Pope's belief that change in Eastern Europe would come only gradually and at the same rate in all Eastern European country's. The Pope is convinced that over time such liberalization will occur, but no one could know how long the process would take.

Baker asked how the Pope viewed the political situation inside Romania. "Although in foreign policy Romania acts independently of the Soviet Union," Casaroli replied, "the internal regime is more Stalinist than any other Eastern European Country." The discussion follows.

CASAROLI: The events in Poland are unfortunate but predictable. Six-months ago the Polish Minister of Transportation visited the Vatican and decried the economic deterioration in Poland caused by the lack of worker discipline. He spoke openly of Soviet pressure on the Polish government to take action and predicted that the Polish government would be forced to intervene openly.

HAIG: The imposition of marital law had been weeks in the planning. It was not something that had been planned in the half-day after Solidarity called for a referendum. The U.S. policy dilemma is not to appear to welcome a repressive regime of martial law, but not to incite Soviet intervention. Although in reality the effect of indirect Soviet pressure and direct Soviet intervention are the same. The distinction is important in the stance that the United States adopts.

CASAROLI: I would not rule out the possibility that Solidarity has been infiltrated by the Polish government. These infiltrations could have generated the pretext for the imposition of martial law.

BUSH: Is there anything we should be doing now?

CASAROLI: The United States and other Western observers should not act until they know what the real situation is in Poland. It is too bad there is a great lack of good information.

REAGAN: **The Vatican and the Pope have a key role to play in events in Poland and elsewhere in Eastern Europe. The Pope's visit to Poland showed the terrible hunger for God in Eastern Europe. I've heard reports of the fervor of the underground Church in the Soviet Union itself, and stories of bibles being distributed page-by-page among the believers.**

CASAROLI: Yes, there is a hunger for God in specific groups in Eastern Europe, but in general the youth are insensible to God. Also, despite strong religious beliefs among certain minorities, young people in general are apathetic.

For example, when the Pope visited Poland recently, he was in Krakow preparing to address a group of some 30,000 young people, the Pope was told that some of the young people were preparing to demonstrate. So he put aside his prepared speech and improvised his remarks to exert a moderate influence on the crowd. That night the youth held their demonstration in the streets. The police called a priest to tell the demonstrators that there are changes coming in Eastern Europe, little by little, but that the time is not ripe for real change in Eastern Europe. The priest recalled the advice he was given in 1963 by an American diplomat in Budapest, who had said that the policy of the United States was to avoid a nuclear confrontation with the Soviet

Union, and at the same time work for small openings in the Iron Curtain, to plant the seeds of freedom.

Although times have changed since 1963, the same principle still applies. Time is not yet ripe for major change in Eastern Europe.

WILSON (Special Envoy to the Vatican): We will probably only know in retrospect what the time for real change actually was.

CASAROLI: I have, as have others, considered the United States the sanctuary for the future of the world. It is a big responsibility for the President, but Mr. President, you should know that the world relies on your good judgment and wisdom.

REAGAN: **I hope to be able to live up to the challenge. Just the day before, the Papal delegation visited to deliver the study of nuclear war. Currently, the only way to deter nuclear war is to arm as strongly as the potential opponent.**

However, this is not good enough. There could be miscalculations and accidents. It is necessary to reduce the number of forces on both sides. The United States made a start in Geneva, offering to dismantle one type of missile. It is hoped that this start could be turned into wider moves towards arms reductions. I was struck by the Papal report's conclusion that in the event of a war there would be no way to care for the huge number of wounded.

CASAROLI: It is relatively simple to understand the horror of nuclear war. It is less easy to figure out how to keep it from occurring. A credible military deterrent depends on a resolve to incur the horrors of that war if necessary. There should be some better way. Another group of scientists is also meeting with President Brezhnev of the Soviet Union to present him the same report.

REAGAN: **Have you heard the story of an American farmer's opinion of the best place for a nuclear war to take place: far enough away that he could say, "What was that?"**

HAIG: Cardinal Casaroli, I expect the negotiations in Geneva to go slowly because the United States has little leverage in the negotiations with the large imbalance of weapons in the Soviet favor. Some say that it might be better to accept an imbalance so long as the United States and NATO have a small but significant deterrent of their own. We reject such an approach because significant imbalances create conditions for more aggressive diplomacy by the other side, and in addition, they remove the incentive for arms controls and reductions.

CASAROLI: Some way is needed to break out of the arms spiral in which each side wants a little cushion, which spurred the other side to further escalate. Some way is needed to break the cycle, or to find a balance at a lower level.

REAGAN: **There is no miracle weapon available with which to deal with the Soviets. We can threaten the Soviets with our ability to out-build them, which the Soviets know we could do if we chose. Once we establish this, we could invite the Soviets to join us in lowering the level of weapons on both sides.**

CASAROLI: Have you thought of the Chinese aspect of the problem? The Soviets are very worried about the Chinese, especially possible future Chinese weapons systems. This has made them build extra weapons beyond those they thought they needed to deal with the United States

NANCE: The weapons pointed at China would be of considerable less range than those that threatened the United States. We would be able to distinguish those weapons directed against China from those directed against us.

REAGAN: **China is many years away from an ability to threaten the Soviet Union.**

CASAROLI: Yes, but arms reductions either has to be global, including all countries, or they could not be accomplished at all.

REAGAN: **If the superpowers are engaged in a serious process of reducing their armaments, the other nations of the world would feel obliged to join in. President Eisenhower, at a time when the United States had a marked nuclear advantage over the Soviet Union, offered to turn over all nuclear weapons to an international authority. The world would be different today if the Soviets had not refused to join in this offer.**

CASAROLI: It is an extremely difficult question, but one that is vital for the nations of the world to address and solve. The Vatican for its part could not play a major role, but would provide the moral assistance that it could. If an informal channel were needed to deal with the Soviet Union, one that would remain private, the Pope would be available to establish it. It is important that a major power be able to save face, and for that reasons some discreet diplomacy might be valuable. Although the Holy See is politically weak, it is morally strong and might be helpful.

REAGAN: **Quiet diplomacy is often extremely important. President Nixon, for example, without making a public show of it, was able to secure the emigration from the Soviet Union of a large number of Soviet Jews.**

CASAROLI: A Soviet ambassador had been able to accomplish a specific humanitarian action through quiet diplomacy, which would not have been possible through a public campaign. Mr. President, Mr. Wilson is a unique envoy to the Vatican. I can speak for the Pope in expressing his gratitude that an envoy of the quality of Mr. Wilson has been sent by the President.

Date: **December 19, 1981**
Subject: **Poland**
Status: **Classified**

SUMMARY

Today's minutes are still classified, however, the decisions are known because they are reviewed in the December 21 meeting.

DECISIONS

1. Not to invoke the "exceptional circumstances" clause of the 1981 debt agreement at this time.
2. To contact leading banks and advise them that the U.S. does not intend to invoke "exceptional circumstances" at this time.
3. To withhold shipment of $71 million worth of dried milk and butter we agreed to provide Poland which has not yet been delivered.
4. To continue shipment of food packages via CARE.
5. To discuss with the allies the following economic measures against Poland:
    A. Suspending Poland's request for INF membership;
    B. Setting a "no exceptions" policy in COCOM on exports to Poland;
    C. Reconsidering allowing Polish fishing fleets access to U.S. waters.
6. Unilaterally suspend the renewal of export insurance for Poland by the U.S. Ex-Im. Bank.
7. After a discussion of various actions against the USSR, the decision was made to defer the decision until the next meeting.

Date: **December 21, 1981**
Subject: **Poland**
Status: **Declassified in Part (2005)**

SUMMARY

After a review of the December 19 decisions (see above), and a still classified CIA update on the situation in Poland, the discussion follows.

HAIG: I want to go over the political logic of the situation. I share the CIA assessment. There was little change in the situation over the weekend. There is widespread resentment among the people against the Polish government, but no major, overt challenge to it. It has been reported that Walesa has been moved to a military prison headquarters, but this is soft information.

It is most significant that Cardinal/Archbishop Glemp has "walked the cat back." He has shifted from a position of strong condemnation of the military law that has been imposed to a plea for modernization and for no bloodshed. We have reports that the Polish military visited every parish this last week and told the parish priests that there would be no reading on Sunday of a condemnation letter. Most of the parishes appear to have followed that lead, though there are some exceptions. The main message has been one of modernization – no bloodshed. While there have been some strong reactions, they have been isolated.

There are two Papal delegations in Poland as of Saturday night. Ambassador Meehan will be meeting with Cardinal Glemp today. Larry Eagleburger will be meeting in Rome with Monsignor Silvestrini.

We have also received a detailed analysis from our Embassy in Moscow. The theme of this message is that the Soviets are "cooling it." They are not preparing for intervention and, significantly, they are not preparing for intervention and, significantly, they are not preparing the Soviet people for intervention. Our embassy feels that – and on this we may differ with them – the Soviets are now willing to accept a Polish nationalist government as distinct from party rule. Party authority is no longer discussed in Moscow.

American Embassy in Moscow believes the Soviets are afraid to intervene because they know they can't back it. The Soviets are preparing food for shipment to Poland and preparing for a massive bailout of the Polish economy.

In Poland, the crackdown continues. But are the Soviets cracking down on Poland?

The position of our allies is stiffening. There is a popular outcry in Britain, in France, and even Schmidt has been dragged along, kicking and screaming, by a Bundestag resolution.

So far, we have no discord in the Atlantic Community. Of course, we have not asked for any difficulty actions yet.

Yugoslavia has condemned the situation in Poland, while within the Warsaw Pact, Hungary and Romania have been the least enthusiastic in endorsing happenings and Bulgaria has been the most enthusiastic.

Things are calm in Warsaw, perhaps aided by the fact that there was a great deal of snow over the weekend. Together with a communications blackout.

(Three lines redacted.)

It is important that, so far, we have correctly avoided intensifying the crisis (by inflammatory messages to the Poles). RFE (Radio Free Europe) is now being jammed intensively, to a greater extent than in many years. VOA (Voice of America) is getting through somewhat better.

One question to be examined is "Is it time for a strong letter to Jaruzelski and/or Brezhnev?"

With regard to sanctions, we don't want to let the assessment of the situation get out of hand with the actions we take.

I am not one who espouses the "devil theory" that all is lost, that the Soviets are in charge, that Solidarity is dead, that all this is the case with or without Soviet intervention. I don't think we should proceed on these assumptions.

There is a second school of thought: that not all is lost; that we should husband our leverage and use it as the assessment changes.

I am of the second school, that all is not lost. In making our assessments of what to do, we should move before all is lost. However, a first question to be answered is "What constitutes all being lost?"

Some see what is happening in Poland as a fundamental unraveling of the Soviet empire (with that as the goal to be pursued). Others see advantages to us in a partial rollback (from what the Poles had achieved), but retaining many of the gains achieved as a basis for a subsequent evolution toward further gains – that we should preserve the environment in which such gains can be achieved.

The real question is: is some degree of repression tolerable from our standpoint, or, do we stand only for total victory, and, are we prepared to pay the price necessary to achieve total victory?

Another question: Are we going to sit still (while events proceed in Poland), or are we going to apply our own pressure on other fronts? For example, Cuba, Afghanistan?

However, it seems to me the worst thing we could do at this time would be to divert world attention from Poland by U.S. muscle flexing elsewhere. Though, perhaps we could do something in Afghanistan without diverting world attention.

But we don't want to piddle away resources before we have concluded that all is lost. You have authorized some actions. These may seem by some as "beating up on poor little Poland."

You will get criticism from some quarters on this. However, you will have to take a lot of flack no matter what you do, and you will want to make your decision on this matter based on what is right, not on the views of constituencies.

There are now new uncertainties in the situation in the attitude of the Church. I think we will want to delay pressure on the Soviets until we further assess the situation. However, we should go ahead with a letter to Brezhnev, advising the Soviets of the price they will pay if they continue.

That is my viewpoint. However, there may be different analyses from others.

REAGAN: **Let me say something in the form of a positive question. This is the first time in 60 years that we have had this kind of opportunity. There may not be another in our lifetime. Can we afford not to go all out? I'm talking about a total quarantine on the Soviet Union. No détente! We know – and the world knows – that they are behind this. We have backed away so many times! After World War II we offered Poland the Marshall Plan, they accepted but the Soviets said no.**

Let's look at the International Harvester license. Kirkland said in a conversation with him that our unions might refuse to load ships. How will we look if we say, yes (let U.S. exports to the Soviet Union proceed) while our unions – our own "Solidarity" – won't load the ships.

I recognize this is a great problem for International Harvester and for Caterpillar. It may mean thousands of layoffs. But, can we allow a go-ahead (on these transactions)? Perhaps we can find a way to compensate the companies if we say no. Perhaps put the items in inventory and use them by

some other means. But can we do less now than tell our allies, "This is big Casino!" There may never be another chance!

It is like the opening lines in our declaration of independence. "When in the course of human events." This is exactly what the Poles are doing now.

One other thing in addition to the Marshall Plan. The Soviets have violated the Helsinki Accords since the day it was signed. They have made a mockery of it. We are not going to pretend it is not so.

BUSH: I have thought a lot about this problem over the weekend. I agree with the President that we are at a real turning point. I believe the President should really identify in a speech with Walesa and the Polish Ambassador. I really feel that – particularly at this Christmas time – the country is waiting for a more forward position. This is not a political matter but one of the world leadership. If we appear to do nothing, we are not taking that position of leadership. The Church has stepped back, but if we have allies that might act and do nothing, we are sending the wrong signal.

WEINBERGER: I agree. I suggest you, Mr. President, talk to the world. It can have the same strong impact that the zero-option speech had. This is not a time for (undue) prudence or caution. The world needs to be told that it has a leader.

I understand the worry about creating another Hungary situation (referring to the 1956 uprising in Hungary), but while we don't want to give the wrong impression (as to Western support to Poland), we do want to give an impression of support.

Let's not be mistaken. What Poland has now in Jaruzelski is a Russian general in a Polish uniform. The Soviets are getting what they want.

Offering Poland a Marshall Plan may be a good idea. But now we have to stop licenses. We can't have a high moral position while we are licensing (to the Soviet Union).

This is a chance to seize the initiative. It is the time to do it. The President should make a speech Wednesday or Thursday – maybe on Christmas day.

BALDRIGE: I agree with the Vice President and Secretary Weinberger. This is a chance to lead the West. The allies might support us, or we might proceed alone. But my only concern is that our actions may be seen as a slap on the wrist. Cancelling the International Harvester and Caterpillar deals would be a slap on the wrist. We should consider suspension of all validated licenses. This category includes all high-technology material. If we suspend all these licenses, coupled with International Harvester and Caterpillar deals, it would be much stronger. But it will be effective only if the allies go along with at least part of it. Hopefully, there would be a chance of their doing so.

CASEY: We will lose credibility if we fail to follow through now on this situation. We are seeing an unraveling of the communist economic situation. However, the prospects of the allies going along with us are fairly slim. But, leadership is getting our allies to go along. The President should speak to the world. We should go with across-the-board sanctions.

BLOCK: The Soviet communist system is collapsing of its own weight. I believe there should be a presidential message, but we must be careful. If we play our trump card — total economic sanctions — at this time, what else can we then do? We must wait for the time to play that card. Not do it prematurely

We need to learn more about what is happening to Solidarity before we make our move. We need allied support. We should try for that before we move.

REAGAN: **Let me tell you what I have in mind. We are the leaders of the Western world. We haven't been for years, several years, except in name, but we accept that role now.**

I am talking about action that addresses the allies and solicits — not begs — them to join in a complete quarantine of the Soviet Union. Cancel all licenses. Tell the allies that if they don't go along with us, we let them know but not in a threatening fashion, that we may have to review our alliances.

The Helsinki Accords have been violated constantly.

I am thinking back to 1938 when there was a great united effort opportunity. In a speech in Chicago, FDR asked the free world to join in a quarantine of Germany. On that request, his brains were kicked out all over.

But I am also reminded of Warner Brothers action on its movie "Confessions of a Nazi Spy."

Interests that wanted to continue selling movies in Germany – even though the Holocaust had already started – and offered to buy the film, including a profit for the makers, to prevent it from being shown (to protect their position in German markets).

But Warner Brothers refused to do it. The film was run and had as much impact as anything (in alerting world opinion).

If we show this kind of strength – and we have labor and the people with us; if we demand that Solidarity get its rights; if that happens, nothing will be done. But if not, then we invoke sanctions (against the Soviet Union) and those (of our allies) who do not go along with use will be boycotted, too, and will be considered to be against us …

The wheat and Olympics actions after Afghanistan were ridiculous. It is time to speak to the world.

BLOCK: You are saying we expect the Soviets and the Polish government might back off and give Solidarity back its rights?

REAGAN: **Yes, we would expect things to go back to the previous position and negotiations start from there. There could also be appeals to compromise.**

REGAN: I see a problem on three levels. The immediate problem – we want to send some message but we do not want to incite street fighting, but a message of hope – at this season they would particularly appreciate it.

Second, Al (Haig) has to have time to get our allies on board without bullying them. Show them where we stand and where we are heading. This takes time. Third, we go it alone, if necessary.

REAGAN: **I agree, we should not surprise (our allies). But there are some things we can do now, plus we tell them this is what we are prepared to do.**

HAIG: May I comment, please?

This is the first time in my memory that we have a pretty solid consensus that the time has come to do something.

What I have in mind is that we send Eagleburger to Europe to talk tough. Also, your letter to the allies is tough, and mine to the foreign ministers is even tougher.

But if we decide here today to step away from incremental pressure, the pipeline, the pipelayers and the rest – this is all a laugh.

You decide this situation requires you to use all your leverage, but in Moscow they are still uncertain. If you now slap on a full court press the Soviets can say to themselves that they have nothing left to lose. On the other hand, we should know in a matter of hours or days whether there is going to be any pullback by the Polish government.

We had hoped Saturday night, December 19, to get a consensus on your line – isolating the Soviet Union wholly – hopefully with the allies, but alone if necessary. Eagleburger will tell us.

However, we should not do this until we have at least warned the Soviets in an unequivocal way.

We have planned a speech for Christmas eve or Christmas day. It would be nationally televised, but before the speech, … we must decide that we are prepared to act.

REAGAN: **That doesn't bother me at all. If we don't take action now, three or four years from now we'll have another situation and we wonder, why didn't we go for it when we had the whole country with us. I am tired of looking backward.**

BUSH: I agree with Don (Regan) and Al (Haig). We should take the time to consult, but giving a speech now is essential. What is missing is moral leadership.

You should state how strongly you feel about Walesa – about Solidarity – about the Polish Ambassador and the Polish people. You can speak in generalities without spelling out details. We don't want to delay.

We are at an emotional turning point. We can do the speech but leave our options open. Identify with the turn in freedom.

WEINBERGER: My worry is that we will wait too long because a single ally can hold us back. If there is moderation in the Soviet position, the way to find out is not to hold back but to make the speech, then if there are no results, spell out the specifics of what we will do. This would be similar to the zero-option speech.

HAIG: All that is being said is compatible, however, we are not dealing with giving a speech but with setting policy. I would never give a speech unless you are prepared to act. From my viewpoint I don't think we are in such a bad position now.

REAGAN: **No – no litany of items is to be recited. But what we should say is an overall expression of what we will do is an absolute quarantine of all trade as President Roosevelt had proposed in 1938.**

HAIG: To warn them again is an empty threat. When you speak (on this) it should be to inform them that you have decided to do something. It will take three days to find out our allies' position.

REAGAN: **That puts us on Christmas eve.**

DEAVER: There is a Wednesday time set for broadcast.

HAIG: Mr. President, we don't know what the Church is doing, but we might be in trouble if you come down too hard.

REAGAN: **We will make it known that this is what will be done if they do not release Walesa.**

KIRKPATRICK: Mr. President, you must tell the truth. You must stand by the central core of this administration. The speech will be an important act. Your earlier statement was fine, but we, I am sure, have all read George Will's column in which he describes the outrageous fact that we have taken no action. This is important.

Everyday, beginning today, we should have some symbolic affirmation about the loss of freedom in Poland. We don't have to warn anyone about anything. You should receive the Polish Ambassador in front of the TV cameras!

It is also time for a letter to Brezhnev. We must set this event in history. We need to do this vis-à-vis our allies. We need to assure them that we plan to stand against oppression.

We might have to suspend the Helsinki Accords. There are also a number of other meaningful acts that we can take that are not dangerous.

One of our objectives is to prevent our own demoralization by inactivity. It made me ill this morning to read a *Post* article on Afghanistan where the Afghans are still fighting Soviet tanks with ancient rifles. Perhaps one of the things we can do is more effective aid to Afghanistan. We don't have to talk about it – just do it.

We should do something every day on Poland and culminate with a Christmas day speech.

MEESE:	It is important, at this point, to get a list of actions to be taken and a list of actions not to be taken.
	For example, are we going to cut off all trade? Part of trade? All communications, including flights and telephones? Are we going to cut diplomatic and political contacts? Are we going to recall our Ambassador? What is our position in the UN?
	We have to have all these things down in some detail so that we know what we are doing.
	A letter to Brezhnev should be done today. Hartman should be brought home for consultations.
	All departments should hold relevant actions in abeyance. We should slow licensing actions.
	The President is seeing Polish leaders today, the Polish Ambassador tomorrow. We should begin work on the speech. And we should organize for the possibility of sanctions.
REAGAN:	**We have all these things we can do. We don't have to let them out. We can't close our embassy in Moscow. We would have to give back the seven Christians that are there. We should also keep arms limitations negotiations going for the time being but be prepared to walk out.**
HAIG:	We don't want to close our embassy or break diplomatic contact. We don't want to get into a World War III scenario. We don't want to stop the INF talks; we don't want to create riots in Europe. In our talks we should take a position that we are reviewing what to do. The Soviets may – as a result of other actions by us – walk out on the INF talks themselves.
REAGAN:	**Cutting off the talks would not punish the Soviets. The talks should, therefore, go ahead.**
HAIG:	We hope by Thursday to see if they have done enough to justify what we are planning. Of course, if the Soviets invade Poland there can be no continuation of the INF talks.
REAGAN:	**I agree.**
HAIG:	I am still not at the point where I would recommend a speech. You probably will want to give one after events unfold, but if Walesa starts talking with the government we will have a different scenario.
UNKNOWN:	We need to assess the total cost of our actions.
BALDRIGE:	There is approximately $3.8 billion of Soviet trade in 1981.

NANCE: My data shows that exports were $3.854 billion, imports $1.24 billion.

BUSH: I don't see why the speech needs to wait. What has been running is a moral identification with Walesa. No more time is needed to at least match that of Mitterrand, a socialist leader. We have not clearly identified with the historic significance of this event. We need to exert moral leadership.

HAIG: There is a difference between what you are saying and what we are discussing. The President wants to take dramatic action. You want the President to be identified with events in Poland.

BUSH: We need a clear statement of what will happen if repression continues in Poland.

WEINBERGER: Delay avoids leadership. The time we needed this was yesterday.

MEESE: As a practical matter, the President's Wednesday speech cannot avoid addressing the Polish issue.

REAGAN: **Yes, I cannot make a "Santa Clause is Coming to Town" speech in this environment.**

The letter to Brezhnev should contain carrots. It could address the fact that they haven't been able to provide their people the living standard they would like and that they would be in an even worse plight without trade with the West.

We could say that we cannot continue trade if events in Poland continue and that we will press our allies to follow us unless the Polish situation is alleviated, but again holding out our hand.

Can he (Brezhnev) envision what it would be like if trade with the West were open? It would be a different, much better world. He can have that one, giving up nothing, or the one that will result if we are forced to take trade-cutting actions.

NANCE: What about the National Christmas tree?

HAIG: Let us make no mistake. This Polish matter is a matter of life and death for the Soviet Union. They would go to war over this. We must deal with this issue with this in mind and have no illusions. There are no cheap runs. We cannot be concerned with various constituencies.

DEAVER: But haven't we ruled out military action? We did that the first day.

HAIG: But we may not have that option.

WEINBERGER:	Soviets may take military actions against Poland, but this is not world war.
HAIG:	We are talking about the way in which we represent our case.
MEESE:	We are 15 minutes behind schedule for a meeting with a women's group.
REAGAN:	**Remember, everyone, stock up on Vodka!**

Date:	**December 22, 1981**
Subject:	**Poland**
Status:	**Declassified (2004)**

BACKGROUND

Today's meeting is the third in four days on Poland. The discussion continues on whether the President should give a speech on Poland, and if so what should be said about the situation in Poland. The NSC agrees that a speech should include Poland, but disagrees over the strength of a warning to the Soviets if they continue to interfere in Poland.

DISCUSSION

REAGAN:	**They tell me that cars in California are already displaying solidarity stickers.**

[Reagan then leaves for 15 minutes. The minutes continue when he returns.]

NANCE:	(Reviews the discussion between Reagan and Polish Ambassador Spasowski, which took places earlier that day).
CASEY:	I haven't much new to report today. The Soviet plan seems to be working. There are reports of pockets of resistance. The rest of the country is acquiescing. In the coalmines – in some factories. We have a report that many Soviet KGB officers are involved in the operation.
NANCE:	Secretary Haig, will you explain events and the options facing us?
HAIG:	Yesterday I said we would need to discuss why the Church has softened its line. We now have a report from Ambassador Meehan on his conversations with Archbishop Glemp. The Church is under pressure from the government. Government representatives told the Church last week that the message scheduled to be read

last Sunday was too tough. When bloodshed began, the Archbishop felt it necessary to go for moderation.

Walesa is alive and apparently vigorous. But he does not want to negotiate with a Soviet agent (Jaruzelski). Walesa is a card for playing in the future. He is a protégé of Cardinal Wysznski. They don't dare kill him at this time.

We have no indication from the authorities of a willingness to negotiate either with Solidarity or the Church. The Army's role is still fairly subdued. They are using special security forces.

We have a Swedish report that the Soviets and the Czechs intend to intervene on December 26, but no verification of it so far.

The strikes continue in the Silesian coalfields. Thirteen thousand coal miners are holed up in a coalmine. The government apparently intends to starve them out.

The Western bankers in Zurich this morning took a hard line. They refused the Polish request to loan $350 million to the Poles for interest payments and they also refused to begin discussion of rescheduling Poland's 1982 debt payments.

I had a call last night from Irv Brown of the AFL/CIO. He feels that resistance in Poland is strong and will be growing. He says: "Don't be influenced by the banks, don't bail out the Poles." European bankers believe they will be compensated either from the foreign hard currency accounts in Poland or by the USSR.

The Brandt statement of yesterday on behalf of Socialist International was a disaster. A rebuttal press statement is being formulated.

The Brezhnev interview with Marvin Kalb skirted Poland, but it was held on December 4, prior to the recent events, so it is of little significance to this issue.

Larry Eagleburger called me twice this morning. He reports the Italians are vigorous, staunch and supportive of actions to be taken. Colombo is good!

But in Bonn, Genscher is opposed to initiatives now, since the Soviets have not intervened. He agreed to discuss economic sanctions, however, and to consider imposing them before the Soviets intervene. There is vigor lacking, however.

Hormats, in his discussions, sees a spectre of softness and opposition to action at this time. The reactions range from the Brits to the French who are the most vigorous, with the Germans softest.

These papers (meeting handouts) that we have put together present steps that we can consider and provide pros and cons of each step and some assessment.

The first paper outlines actions that can be taken against Poland. The second paper lists measures against the Soviets.

One of the themes throughout the assessment, Mr. President, is a strong emphasis on the Soviet steps on allied unity. As of today, on economic sanctions – and on some political actions – Europe would break with us.

REAGAN: **Well, Al, it seems to me on this we make up our minds on what is right to do. We say to the Soviets tomorrow, right, we will proceed with actions – without spelling them out – actions that will isolate them politically and economically. We reduce political contact, we do all we can to persuade our allies to come along unless and until martial rule is ended in Poland and they return to an antebellum state. We have to deal with our own labor movement. They are shutting off shipments to Poland though church shipments are still going.**

HAIG: Yes, they are still going. Last shipment was one week ago.

REAGAN: **I don't know whether Red Cross aid is going or not.**

BUSH: Cardinal Krol mentioned they were getting receipts for the food deliveries.

HAIG: Another thing I would like to call to your attention, Mr. President, it is vitally important that whatever we do we do officially to Brezhnev and Jaruzelski so that they are on notice. They should be offered an alternative.

We should include a deadline by which we expect a response. Now if we want to get out a list of actions we are taking tomorrow night before we have a response to our threats, we risk losing the Europeans before we even get started.

You can layout the human rights considerations tomorrow night. That keeps us flexible and keeps our options open with no public threats.

You can highlight that you hold the Soviets responsible but it is too soon for threats unless you want to break with our allies.

REAGAN: **The thing that bothers me, the constant question is that we continue to deplore, but isn't there anything we can do in practice? Those chicken little's in Europe, will they still be chicken little's if we lead and ask them to follow our lead?**

HAIG: The answer, Mr. President, is yes and no. The European leaders are not the most courageous people but they have more at stake than we do. They are closer to Poland than we are.

REAGAN: **I know.**

HAIG: We ought to be careful with our demands until we decide we want to break with them over this matter, if that is what it comes to.

REAGAN: **If the Polish government doesn't cancel martial law, can we yet do these things?**

HAIG: We will be in for a long, torturous period with the continuation of martial law and negotiations between Solidarity and the Polish government going on. It is difficult for us to kick over the traces now – to go all out – and then to be accused of triggering what will probably happen anyway – a Soviet intervention into Poland.

WEINBERGER: Concerning our allies and the stakes we have in this matter, we have over half a million people in Europe. It is comfortable for the Europeans to do nothing. If you take the lead and give a strong speech they will be in an uncomfortable moral position and they may be dragged along with our actions.

We should be taking stronger action than just wringing our hands – that's what the Soviets want. The Polish government can begin meaningless negotiations with Solidarity that will please Europe. We should have a list of nine things we can do. Each is, in itself, a pinprick but they cause anguish and pain. They evidence our seriousness. They influence public and industrial labor movements. It is morally right to take a stand – a position of leadership.

It is easy to delay and do nothing. If we delay, we will allow them to crush the movement in Poland. We won't push the Soviets into intervening in Poland. They will do it if it suits their needs. As Ambassador Spasowski has said, they will march in for their own reasons, not because of what we do.

I hope your speech is along the lines of your statement yesterday.

HAIG: We agreed on a tough speech but not on measures. We are not debating whether to do tough things – the timing is the issue.

WEINBERGER: The longer we wait the more the situation solidifies. Tomorrow night you should mention measures, not handwringing. These papers are an eloquent plea for doing nothing. We should be considerably bolder. There is a difference here between our recommendations.

REAGAN: **Ambassador Spasowski, in his talk with me this morning, asked that I make a call for a lighted candle in every window on Christmas night.**

HAIG: That's not the kind of act that Secretary Weinberger is saying we should take.

MEESE: It seems to me the candle is important, but we need something else. The things on the list, as far as Poland, are the very minimum that we can do. We should debate about what we want to put the heat on the Soviets.

KIRKPATRICK: In thinking about dealing with our allies, and if we take significant actions they will break with us, as Al says, I'd like to remind you that they do that frequently. Five of them were against us on a Mexican resolution on El Salvador, counter to our interests. The French Foreign Minister led the effort. All except Britain went along. Britain abstained. On the Abu Ein issue France abstained. They break with us frequently. They don't worry that much about breaking with us.

HAIG: I recommend we stop philosophizing and go down the list one by one. First, Poland, what is the speech to cover? Then the USSR: what actions now? What later?

Roman numeral one is actions already approved. We are suspending consideration of the $740 million Polish request for grain. You could state that in your message.

WEINBERGER: We should emphasize there were no assurances that such assistance would go to the people.

REAGAN: **We could say we'll go ahead in food if allowed to monitor that it goes to the people.**

HAIG: The next item is the pipeline. I (c) is the letter to Jaruzelski, you already read it. I (d) is already done but this should not be raised in the speech.

REAGAN:	**All of that is included in the item about food.**
HAIG:	You have sent a letter to Jaruzelski.
WEINBERGER:	What is the general theme?

[Discussion of the letter to Brezhnev and Jaruzelski. The substance of the discussion is omitted from the minutes.]

HAIG:	You can say in your message that you have sent a letter to Jaruzelski.
REAGAN:	**(Reads to himself a draft letter to Jaruzelski.) This seems to have the right tone.**
HAIG:	(Going back to the list), we have suspended Ex-Im credits.
REGAN:	That is not significant enough to put in your speech.
MEESE:	We should say we are suspending all financial aid.
BAKER:	I suggest we go through the list. Decide what you want to do on each item.
HAIG:	Mr. President, we decided yesterday we should not invoke the exceptional circumstances clause. The unions might disagree with us on this one.
REAGAN:	**Will it affect the people?**
HAIG:	This one will affect the banks. They took a strong position this morning in not backing off (on lending more money to the Poles to pay interest on their debt).
REAGAN:	**(Looking at the list) We can withhold fishing rights, suspend consideration of IMF for Poland, and suspend their aviation rights in the U.S.**
REGAN:	I want to add a footnote on the item in the paper concerning the IMF. The paper is somewhat incorrect. The U.S. does not have an effective veto. We only have 20 percent of the total votes.
WEINBERGER:	But if we don't try, we are giving them hard currency.
REAGAN:	**Then we can oppose consideration by the IMF of Poland's application.**
	The acts on Poland: At the point (in the speech after listing actions against Poland) we say who is responsible – the USSR and Brezhnev. Then we can say what actions we have here (actions against the USSR).
	I like the line "seek to isolate the USSR economically." That may take a lot away from them.
	And I would think – that Marshall Plan thing – then to say if this is done, we will cooperate. This should come near the end.

	I oppose withdrawing from the INF negotiations. That would help them (the Soviets). We are trying in INF negotiations to get them to give up missiles.
	I am looking down the list here. I think to consider Helsinki null and void would hit them hard.
HAIG:	Europe will go bonkers if we do that.
REAGAN:	**Why pretend we have an agreement if they violate it constantly?**
HAIG:	You should warn the Soviets if you are going to do this. You will get their attention if you do so.
CASEY:	We cannot terminate right away.
BLOCK:	I think Al's actions are pretty well thought out. Our allies may not come along with us, but they are closer to Poland. But I believe they may well come along if we consult with them.
DEAVER:	I suggest we go from the top of the page down.
HAIG:	That's what I want to do.
	The UN Resolution. We have talked about it. It would get us a kick in the teeth.
KIRKPATRICK:	We must bear in mind that on January 1, the Soviet Union assumes the presidency of the Security Council. It is a very unfortunate change. It will be more difficult for us to do anything. Also, Poland becomes a member of the Security Council on January 1.
HAIG:	I recommend we hold up on this until we look at the rest of the list.
KIRKPATRICK:	I recommend that if we are going to do it, we do so before December 31.
WEINBERGER:	Isn't there an advantage in doing it – in taking a strong moral position?
KIRKPATRICK:	There is a good chance the resolution would not do very well but there is something to be said for doing it anyway.
HAIG:	I suggest we look at the other items first. The most important thing, Mr. President, is what action you take with China.
REAGAN:	**But we can't do it in a speech.**
HAIG:	No, but we are talking with the Chinese. We might encourage possible Chinese pressure on Vietnam or Laos, for example. It is important for the Soviets to know – if the Chinese are receptive – that we are working with the Chinese. It will drive the Soviets out of their gourds!

WEINBERGER:	The price of doing that is Taiwan. There should be nothing in the speech about this.
HAIG:	Number three is the tough economic issues, including a total economic embargo.
WEINBERGER:	But we don't have to do it all. We can cut the exports of oil and gas equipment, cut their maritime access. There are two licenses – Caterpillar and International Harvester – that can be revoked. We can refuse to engage in long-term grain agreement discussions. We can do much, short of a total embargo.
REAGAN:	**I could go – in the sense of what we are telling the Soviets, not in the speech – with the idea that the total embargo is the price of intervention. They have already intervened. Let them guess what we are going to do next.**
BROCK:	Before we leave this item, if we start down this road – even cautiously – we will not hurt the Soviets much unless our allies join us. My concern is how we posture on this.
REAGAN:	**I know, but if we really believe this is the last chance of a lifetime, that this is a revolution started against this damned force, we should let our allies know they, too, will pay the price if they don't go along; that we have long memories.**
HAIG:	I thought we agreed yesterday we should take strong actions, sweeping ones, not incremental. I thought you approved that yesterday. Did I misread the consensus? My problem is the timing in a speech tomorrow will bring the spectre of the terror of WW III on Christmas Eve.
WEINBERGER:	But when is the right time to warn of WW III?
HAIG:	You've gone incremental. I don't think we want to list, for example, the pipelayers in the speech.
REAGAN:	**I am not talking of the speech, but what we will do. Some of those items I will raise in the speech.**
	For example, we will deliver food provided it reaches the people. We will suspend Ex-Im insurance. We will suspend IMF. We will suspend their fishing rights. Then we can move on to the Soviets as being really responsible, then say what we are willing to do.
	What can we put in a speech to mention Helsinki? O.K., maybe not in a speech, maybe we call our allies to review the Helsinki agreement.

BUSH:	The speech is important, but we should allow diplomacy to work. I don't like sending a letter to Brezhnev and Jaruzelski and reading it in the paper.
	I think we should do three things: First, set the paper's moral tone. Second, tell Jaruzelski what steps we are taking. Third, communicate to Brezhnev we concur. This is not a weak position. It is a responsible position. We should give them a chance to work their way out if they want to. You should get your speech out soon. Set the tone, say what you have done, but stop short of details. It they don't respond you can act.
REAGAN:	**We can tell the people we have outlined specifics and that unless and until...**
BUSH:	Or you can say you have made a series of representations. Not detailing them is the way to do it.
HAIG:	I agree. Another thing to think about is that this letter will likely get public and private rebuttals and we will be accused of intervening in the situation. You may then proceed rapidly.
REAGAN:	**It's like the Air Force plan that was formulated for use in Vietnam. The Air Force had 63 aerial targets, which they wanted to eliminate one by one. But they wouldn't let them do it. It would probably have saved 50,000 lives if we had done it.**
	If he (Brezhnev) answers with that crud about (our) intervening in Poland's internal affairs – bang, bang, we'll take steps. First, their trade reps on the way home; then how many of those are needed before he gets the point?
HAIG:	I believe that will be the outcome. Depending on whether we use an incremental or a full court press – there will be a kickback from Europe. The British and the French will be with us. We may be able to isolate the Germans.
REAGAN:	**What do you mean, full court press?**
HAIG:	In the letter there should be no specifics.
REAGAN:	**Both in the speech and in the other, I like to term it – it could lead to the economic and political isolation of the USSR.**
HAIG:	From the U.S.!
WEINBERGER:	The letters should be mailed before the speech. We would be willing to submit a draft.

NANCE:	We have two drafts of the speech, Mr. President. We can put these options on a list. You can check off which you want to adopt.
WEINBERGER:	The question now is how and what we should put in the letter.
HAIG:	Then we have political options. We can reduce political contacts.
MEESE:	We could detail categorically.
HAIG:	No, I wouldn't even do that. We could use the phrase, "would have a profound effect."
BALDRIGE:	That would be enough. That preserves our flexibility.
WEINBERGER:	We have to say more than "profound effect."
HAIG:	You mean like, "You can't have the pipelayers."
WEINBERGER:	We must be more specific.
BALDRIGE:	We are talking on the whole range of economic and political measures.
WEINBERGER:	At this point we need drafts. We need something more specific.
NANCE:	Mr. President, we will provide you drafts and check lists of the various actions that can be taken.
REAGAN:	**What is the speech time?**
DEAVER:	9:00 p.m.
BLOCK:	Let's remember we are trying to achieve a rollback for the Polish people. We don't want Soviet tanks coming in and blood to flow.
DEAVER:	We need a summary of what we have decided.
MEESE:	We will take all the sanctions on this sheet except the Papal visit. The letter to Brezhnev will indicate that specific steps will be taken unless he responds to our concerns.
	Let me summarize what has been decided: the speech tomorrow night will indicate that letters have been sent to Brezhnev and Jaruzelski; it will list specific steps to be taken against the Polish government; if there is no Soviet response, we will select actions from a list without deciding which actions now.
REAGAN:	**The letter must be definite enough without details. The speech must be definite enough to erase the press accusations that we are doing nothing but talking.**
MEESE:	What about the UN Resolution?
HAIG:	I am not opposed to that option. But I believe it will backfire on us.

MEESE:	Mr. President, this organization bleeds frequently on the human rights issue. Should we not go to them?
HAIG:	If we do, you should put it in your speech.
DEAVER:	Some time tomorrow we should have a redraft of the speech.
HAIG:	We are not making a determination on anti-Soviet measures.
BAKER:	Again, concerning what we have decided, we are going to do paragraph (d)?
REAGAN:	**All of those things that if the Soviets do not reply, which of them do we start goosing them with?**
BUSH:	Concerning the UN, the Soviets will ask for some proof of our allegations of Soviet involvement. We will have to produce some sort of proof. What is our evidence? How much can we declassify to make our point?
CASEY:	(The official minutes show, "?????").
BUSH:	Jeane (Kirkpatrick) will need some of that stuff for her use next week.
KIRKPATRICK:	If we want a meeting on December 26, we will have to request it this afternoon.
HAIG:	I want to be able to tell our allies first.
KIRKPATRICK:	We do it all the time at the UN. We always consult with them on a regular basis. We could cite the situation in Poland in our UN Resolution as a threat to peace without mentioning the USSR.
HAIG:	We can't not mention the USSR. Since we are not going to win anyway, we might as well lose going at the Soviets.
MEESE:	We should produce the information provided to Eagleburger, at a minimum.

Date:	**December 23, 1981**
Subject:	**Poland**
Status:	**Declassified in Part (2005)**

SUMMARY

REAGAN:	**We've been in this room often lately, we need a wardrobe change.**
NANCE:	Mr. President, we have three items to discuss today. First is the letter to General Jaruzelski. It has been approved and State has sent it out.

MEESE:	I thought the letter was on hold.
NANCE:	No, the hold is on the Brezhnev letter.
REAGAN:	**Whatever the problem is, I want it settled and both letters to go out before the speech.**
NANCE:	The second item is the Brezhnev letter on which we have a hold (pending resolution of differences of views). The third item is your speech, Mr. President.
MEESE:	I understand that we worked from a State/NSC draft and that changes had been concurred in.
HAIG:	I have seen only a State draft. If you are talking about the NSC draft letter with profound preamble changes, we have not agreed to those changes.

(Brief discussion of the various drafts.)

HAIG:	The NSC draft is very good but for the rhetoric.
MEESE:	My feeling was that the first draft did not emphasize enough that martial law in Poland is not an internal matter. The rhetoric should be worked on.
NANCE:	The draft being worked on is an NSC/Scanlan (State) draft.
WEINBERGER:	There are three drafts. Which is the current one?
NANCE:	Scanlan, Palmer and I worked until 9:00 p.m. last night on the current draft.
HAIG:	It is not a big deal – the differences between the drafts. The only problem is that some of the rhetoric in the NSC version could detract from the action we are seeking.
MEESE:	We can't draft the letter as a group here. We should have a working group to get an agreed upon draft by this afternoon so that the President can have time to look at it before it goes out.
WEINBERGER:	Which draft do we work from?
HAIG:	Both are the same from the substantive viewpoint.
MEESE:	The Jaruzelski letter has gone. We are now on the speech.
REAGAN:	**(Looking at the speech draft)** **Should we read it so we can then discuss it?**

(The meeting minutes show that the speech draft was read and a discussion followed, but the substance of the discussion was not recorded.)

REAGAN:	**Not enough in this is directed against the Soviet Union. We must say that they are responsible. (Two lines redacted). We can say that martial law was being**

printed in October in Moscow and imposed in Poland in December.

HAIG: I hope we know that this is true.

REAGAN: **If they deny, we will call them liars.**

BUSH: Has the Church expressed moral revulsions or said anything that should be used?

REAGAN: **Ambassador Spasowski said a letter written for delivery at churches last Sunday was not permitted by the martial law forces to be used because it was too tough.**

[General discussion followed about avoiding implied promises that the U.S. might not be able to fulfill and that the U.S. will oppose Polish entry into IMF.]

MEESE: Aren't we in fact suspending all economic relations with Poland? We might wish to say so.

REGAN: No, we have no embargo on imports of Polish hams, for example.

MEESE: This language makes it look as if we are piddling. Can't we say we are suspending major portions of our economic relations?

[General discussion on the exact language.]

REAGAN: **We will suspend the right to fish in our waters.**

MEESE: We should have some sort of general preface statement, such as, "The U.S. is taking immediate steps to halt major portions of our economic relations with Poland."

HAIG: I suggest we make it tougher: "We are reviewing the whole range of our relations."

WEINBERGER: We could end it by saying, "We are prepared to take even more drastic steps."

HAIG: The current airline agreement expires in March. We can be subject to suit for abrogating it earlier. I think I would say we are suspending the right of the Polish government to fish in U.S. waters.

REAGAN: **We are suspending the right of the Polish fishing fleet to fish in our waters.**

HAIG: There will be some Polish-Americans who will resist our suspension of fishing rights.

WEINBERGER: We will restrict high technology exports to Poland and its allies.

MEESE:	Is that a sneaky way to stop pipelayers going to the Soviets?
REAGAN:	**We'd like a little heat on our allies.**
WEINBERGER:	We will urge our allies to join us.

[General discussion of high technology and the position of the allies and how to phrase the proposal in the speech.]

REAGAN:	**I have something to insert when we take note of the letter to Brezhnev. I could note that in the letter to Brezhnev I have indicated that we are prepared to take concrete political and economic steps (if our concerns are not responded to).**
HAIG:	If you do that you are saying you are limiting it to political and economic steps – not that we want to say we are going to take military steps.
DEAVER:	We keep coming back to military steps. I thought we eliminated that last week.
WEINBERGER:	I don't like the phrase "concrete consequences."
REAGAN:	**That was why I used "political and economic" steps.**
REGAN:	Why not quote from the letter to Brezhnev?
HAIG:	Yes, we can't go publicly beyond what is said officially.
DEAVER:	Mr. President, we have people here who will produce a revised version based on this discussion.

[General Discussion on what to say in the speech regarding the CSCE agreement.]

DEAVER:	A suggestion – suppose we say in the letter that we propose that Secretary Haig and Foreign Minister Gromyko meet immediately?
HAIG:	That would not be a good idea because the EC Economic Group has not yet met. Lord Carrington suggested a meeting in January. The Europeans are concerned about a repeat of the Afghanistan episode when the U.S. got out ahead of the allies. So far the only European opposition is the FRG. We are making progress and a meeting with Gromyko should be delayed until after the economic group meeting.
	Concerning the UN Resolution condemning the situation in Poland, I have discussed it with the political directors. They believe it will be meaningless – that it will

show our weakness. They are not ready to vote for it. The Resolution would put a barn into the ribs of people we are trying to bring along with us.

I suggest we say, if asked, that the UN is an inadequate forum for this issue so we are not bothering with it.

WEINBERGER: But we'll be accused of not using it. If we use our leadership and propose a resolution, even if we lose leadership remains with us.

KIRKPATRICK: We can only act in the 15 nations Security Council. We have only four close friends in that group.... We probably can't get the nine votes required to get it on the agenda.

The reasons – there has never been a human rights item before on the Security Council agenda. I'm not saying we shouldn't do it, but we may not get it on the agenda.

REAGAN: **In my view, I am ready to take on the UN at any time. There is hardly a news service in the U.S. that doesn't have a coterie of apologists for the USSR. There is UN refusal to get anything done there – they would just say, "See the situation isn't that bad in Poland...others have refused to go along. The U.S. has no support."**

KIRKPATRICK: If we get it on the agenda a full debate would be useful, but if we can't get it on the agenda the result will be a backlash on us.

REAGAN: **Let us save that for the inevitable moment when they will ask, "Why no UN?" We can reply that we didn't treat it there because the UN is impotent and there is no point in sending it there. We want practical action.**

BUSH: Carter went to the UN on Iran. They did get condemnation by a vote of 114 to 130, then they adjourned. However, I am ambivalent on the issue.

HAIG: I think we can get a Security Council condemnation. The time will come.

KIRKPATRICK: The Brits say, go the General Assembly route sometime in January. There we are at least assured of a day of debate.

HAIG: Yes, I believe we should hold this matter in abeyance until we are sure of support.

REAGAN: **Is there anything further?**

MEESE:	Yes, about Rich Beale's suggestion. If you were to call on all free people of the world to flood food into Poland for distribution via non-governmental channels – the Red Cross to put people in Poland to handle the distribution – you are in a leadership position and the more outside people there are in Poland, the more the tendency to violence is mitigated.
REAGAN:	**In the speech?**
HAIG:	I like handling distribution of food via the Church.
MEESE:	This proposal would not negate use of the Church.
HAIG:	There is some possibility of European resentment if we appear to be trying to take a position of leadership on food aid to Poland. In some respect they are doing more than we.
MEESE:	We would call on the Polish government to allow distribution.
DEAVER:	State says that the Red Cross doesn't want its name used.
BLOCK:	Can we have an update on the situation in Poland?
HAIG:	Yes, I am prepared to do that.
DEAVER:	We need a press plan. Should we have backgrounders before the speech? Should we have someone on Nightline? Someone on the morning shows?
HAIG:	One other thing the President asked about is if we can send food going to Poland to Austria for the refugees there. The problem is that it was sold to Poland for zlotys.
BLOCK:	I am not sure we have legal authority to give it to Austria.
HAIG:	We can say the Attorney General is looking into it.
REAGAN:	**I didn't mean to give the food Poland bought to the Austrians, but it has cost Austria $100 million for refugee aid. Now they are welcoming Polish refugees. At the same time we have all this dried milk and cheese. Why wouldn't we say we are willing to help you?**
HAIG:	We'll get back to you on this, Mr. President.
KIRKPATRICK:	You may want to mention Austria in your speech. Kreisky gave a marvelous speech recently.
HAIG:	Yes, after the terrible one.
KIRKPATRICK:	On the press preparation we must be prepared for a press assessment that this is a "do nothing" approach – that the Carter response to Afghanistan may be seen as more powerful. The candle lighting idea is dangerous. It may be compared to Ford's WIN buttons.

HAIG:	Like tying ribbons on the old oak tree.
KIRKPATRICK:	The press response is likely to be that our response is "too little – too late."
REAGAN:	**Tell them that our response is governed by the fact that we want to succeed.**
DEAVER:	What about Secretary Haig going on Nightline and the morning shows and with backgrounders?
HAIG:	The PR is an important issue. However, your European speech, Mr. President, was one of the best things done and it wasn't accompanied by any lower-level interpretations.
DEAVER:	This is different.
BLOCK:	This is very important.
GERGEN:	I recommend the use of backgrounders tomorrow morning.
MEESE:	Nightline would be useful. Secretary Haig can set the right tone in the backgrounders and appearance – that the President is trying to do things that will not hurt the Polish people.
HAIG:	I don't like the talk shows where the sharks ask questions and I must answer for the President.
DEAVER:	If not our answers to the sharks, then others will answer.
WEINBERGER:	In one of the drafts we use the phrase, "in the next few days," referring to the timing of the response we desire. What do we say concerning the time frame?
HAIG:	In the speech, nothing. In the letter to Brezhnev, yes, we do want to say something. I think we'll have an answer in 48 hours and that we won't like it.
REAGAN:	**(The minutes say: "made comments on editing the 'lighted candle' portion of his speech.")**
BUSH:	If we are concerned about Jeane Kirkpatrick's remarks on the candle lighting, we could link doing this to Ambassador Spasowski's request. This avoids the charge that it is gimmickry. It is the President responding to Ambassador Spasowski. We can repeat the phrase linking it to him. It's in at the beginning. We can repeat it again for emphasis. Let's get away from the "WIN button" problem.
REAGAN:	**Then we'll say, "As Ambassador Spasowski requested."**
HAIG:	(Gives update on Poland indicating that the Polish Politburo met and press and TV coverage of the meeting is expected this afternoon.)

	We may have to adjust the President's speech to what happens.
REAGAN:	**He (Jaruzelski) would cut us off at the knees if he surrenders.**
HAIG:	We should know by 3:00 p.m.

[Haig then tells Reagan that the Danes and Norwegians are hesitant, the French tough, the British are increasingly tough, and the FRG is in left field. However, Haig continues,

> Our allies are coming to doing something tough on Poland. But no one wants to do anything on the Soviets but strong letters. When they see yours, they will know what strong is.
>
> The Polish Ambassador to Japan, Rurarz, is going to defect. We have reports of other defections.
>
> The allies have agreed not to rescind the rescheduling of the 1981 debt payments, and to no commitment on 1982 debt rescheduling. All agree no new credits for the Polish government, but that humanitarian aid should continue.
>
> They do not want to make any decisions on the IMF membership question. The European Community is shifting aid from governmental channels to the church. If the Red Cross is not available, they will use CRS and CARE.
>
> The Economic Community Foreign Ministers will meet next Tuesday and a Brussels meeting is set for the first week in January.
>
> If the situation sours, Mr. President, you may want to think of calling Schmidt up from Florida. He is due in today. He is our soft guy.]

MEESE:	Because we will be dispersed over the next week please keep the signal board advised of your whereabouts. The Situation Room will have daily updates available.
BALDRIGE:	Can we comment on the President's speech?
MEESE:	Yes, tell them it was an outstanding job.
GROUP:	(Laughter)

Date: **December 23, 1981**
Subject: **Letter from Reagan to Brezhnev (Poland)**

Dear Mr. President,
 The recent events in Poland have filled the people of the United States and me with dismay. Since the imposition of martial law on December 13, the most elementary rights of the Polish people have been violated daily: massive arrests without any legal procedures; incarcerations of trade union leaders and intellectuals in overcrowded jails and freezing detention camps; suspension of

all rights of assembly and association; and, last but not least, brutal assaults by security forces on citizens.

The recent events in Poland clearly are not an "internal matter" and in writing to you, as the head of the Soviet Government, I am not misaddressing my communication. Your country has repeatedly intervened in Polish affairs during the months preceding the recent tragic events. No clearer proof of such intervention is needed than the letter of June 5, 1981, from the Central Committee of the CPSU to the Polish leadership which warned the Poles that the Soviet Union could not tolerate developments there. There were numerous other communications of this nature which placed pressure on the Polish Government and depicted the reform movement as a threat to the "vital interests" of all socialists countries. These communications, accompanied by a steady barrage of media assaults as well as military exercises along Poland's borders, were coupled with warnings of intervention unless the Polish Government sharply restricted the liberties and rights which it was granting its citizens.

All these actions represented a clear violation of many international agreements to which the Soviet Union is a signatory. Let me only mention one provision of the Helsinki Final Act which you, Mr. President, personally initialed on behalf of your country in 1975. There you have agreed with other countries to refrain "from any intervention, direct or indirect, individual or collective in the internal or external affairs falling within the domestic jurisdiction of another participating state, regardless of their mutual relations."

Our two countries have had moments of accord and moments of disagreement, but since Afghanistan nothing has so outraged our public opinion as the pressures and threats which your government has exerted on Poland to stifle the stirrings of freedom.

Attempts to suppress the Polish people – either by the Polish army and police acting under Soviet pressure or through even more direct use of Soviet military force – certainly will not bring about long-term stability in Poland and could unleash a process which neither you nor we could fully control.

The only sensible solution is to allow the Polish Government and people to begin a process of reconciliation, and to do so now, before the situation deteriorates further. This cannot be done in the present atmosphere of political terror, mass arrests and bloodshed. Representatives of the spiritual, political and social forces in Poland need to be promptly released from detention and a new national dialogue initiated. This is as essential to solving Poland's major economic problems as it is to healing its political wounds. It is the sole path to long-term stability in Poland and therefore in Europe as a whole.

The Soviet Union can either acknowledge the need for this process or continue to prevent it. The consequences of each of these courses for our relationship should be clear.

Over the course of 1981 we have begun to develop a framework to guide our relations in the years to come. In Secretary Haig's last meeting with

Foreign Minister Gromyko and in my last letter to you, we set forth a concrete agenda for negotiations on critical regional and arms control issues. It has been our hope and intention to proceed in 1982 to try to achieve specific progress on each item on this agenda.

The Soviet Union must decide whether we can move ahead with this agenda, or whether we will travel a different path. The heavy responsibility of the Soviet Union for the present repression in Poland threatens to undermine the basis for an improvement in our relationship. We recognize the interest of the Soviet Union in a stable Poland. But a process of reconciliation and moderate reform in Poland represents no threat to the Soviet Union. The United States cannot accept suppression of the Polish peoples legitimate desire for such a process of renewal, particularly when it is imposed under external pressure. Should the Soviet Union persist in aiding the course of continued suppression in Poland, the United States will have no choice but to take concrete measures affecting the full range of our relationship.

Soviet actions in the days and weeks ahead will determine our decisions. As leaders of two great and powerful nations, we bear a mutual obligation to demonstrate wisdom, moderation and restraint. Let me assure you that I am prepared to join in the process of helping to heal Poland's wounds and to meet its real needs if you are prepared to reciprocate. I call upon you to make clear that you understand the need for national reconciliation in Poland. The alternative is not in the interest of anyone.

I hope to hear from you in the next few days.

Sincerely,

Ronald Reagan

Before General Secretary Brezhnev had a chance to respond, in his prime time speech that night Reagan declared "the martial law proclamations imposed in December by the Polish Government were being printed in the Soviet Union in September." Reagan went on to warn of "serious consequences" "if the forces of tyranny in Poland, and those who incite them from without, do not relent."

Reagan also announced that he immediately suspended "major elements of our economic relationships with the Polish Government," including the renewal of the Export-Import Bank's line of export credit insurance to the Polish Government and Polish civil aviation privileges and fishing rights in the United States.

Not wanting to seem unsympathetic to the Polish people, Reagan also ordered the continuation of food shipments through private humanitarian channels, "but only so long as we know that the Polish people themselves receive the food."

Date: **December 25, 1981**
Subject: **Letter from Brezhnev to Reagan (U.S.-Soviet relations; the elimination of nuclear weapons in Europe)**

Dear Mr. President,

Your address on the direct communications link has made all the more pressing the necessity of calling upon you and the Government of the USA to end at last the interference in the internal affairs of a sovereign state – the Polish People's Republic. This interference in the most diverse forms – overt and covert – has been underway for a long time, already.

Essentially, in your current communication, you have placed your personal signature upon the fact that gross interference in the internal affairs of Poland is the official policy of the United States. We have condemned and continue to condemn such a policy. We consider it unacceptable.

Attempting to conceal this policy of yours, you refer, entirely beside the point, to the letter of the Central Committee of the Polish United Worker's Party. Quite apart from the fact that in so doing you distort the sense of this letter, you again proceed from the position of interference, in this case interference in the mutual relations between two political parties – the CPSU and the Polish Worker's, between which, as between the other parties of socialist countries, there exist their own completely equal and friendly norms and practice of relations. This practice was born not yesterday and not today.

If a frank exchange of opinions between communist parties and the expressions by them of their own opinions to each other is not pleasing to someone in the United States, then, in response, we must firmly say: That is the business of the parties themselves and of no one else, and they have not picked anyone else as a judge to impose his norms upon them.

It is especially important to emphasize this matter of principle.

From the standpoint of our party, antipathy has been and continues to be expressed in relation to those in Poland who are enemies of the existing system there and who violate the laws and order of the country, who are plunging into chaos.

You, yourself, as head of the state and government of the United States, are speaking out against the existing state system in Poland – in other words, calling for the overthrow of this system. This is not an imaginary but a most genuine interference in the internal affairs of another sovereign state.

And this is taking place not only in relation to Poland, similar attempts are being undertaken also in relation to the Soviet Union, American officials, yes, even you personally, are uninterruptedly reviling our social and political system, our internal order. We resolutely reject this.

In the light of these and many other generally known facts what then remains of your arguments concerning our alleged involvement in the internal developments in Poland? Nothing whatever.

Your communication cites the good provision of the Helsinki Final Act under which is affixed both my signature and the signature of the President of the United States. Indeed this provision, which stipulates the refraining from any interference in affairs which come under the internal competence of another state, reminds one better than anything else of the unacceptability of the United States advancing any sort of demands regarding the introduction in their own country of martial law by the highest Polish organs. In accordance with the State constitution, it reminds one of the inadmissibility of the United States attempting to dictate to the Poles what they must and must not do.

No one should interfere with what the Poles and the Polish Authorities are doing and will be doing in their own home.

You claim to have the right to decide for the Poles, instead of the Poles themselves, by what paths and means Polish society should develop in the future. But the social order in Poland was chosen not by Washington, not by Moscow, and not by any other capitol, but by the Poles themselves. No one can direct the leadership of Poland on how to conduct its own affairs, or by which methods to stabilize the situation in the country faster and better.

Attempts to impose ones will on other governments grossly violate the elementary norms of international law. I would go further: They are thoroughly amoral, and no sort of word game regarding the rights of man can conceal this fact.

The Soviet Union rejects the claims of anyone to interfere in the events occurring in Poland.

In your communication mention is made of military maneuvers near Poland. You clearly wish to interpret these maneuvers in your own way, connecting them to the situation in Poland, but this is completely unfounded conjecture.

And if one is to touch on the subject of military maneuvers, then the following question rises: How many maneuvers have the military forces of the countries of NATO, including the USA, conducted and continue to conduct in Western Europe near the borders for example of the German Democratic Republic (East Germany) and Czechoslovakia. Could they not present to the United States their bill in this matter? Couldn't, too, we assess such maneuvers as a threat to the Soviet Union and the other socialists countries?

Such is the value of your references to military maneuvers.

You, Mr. President, hint that if the events in Poland should further develop in a manner which is displeasing to the United States, then a blow may be delivered along the entire range of Soviet-American relations.

But if we are to speak without equivocation, it is your administration that has already done enough to disrupt, or at the very least, undermine everything positive which, at the cost of great effort, has been achieved by previous American administrations in the relations between our countries. Today, unfortunately, not that much remains from the previously attained, mutually beneficial, political capital.

What can one say of such hints? Surely, before having recourse to them, one should calmly take everything into account.

In general it will do no harm to make the following observation: The general tone of your communication is not quite that which the leaders of such powers as the Soviet Union and the United States should assume in conversation with one another. This is especially the case if one takes into account the weight and position they carry in the world, their responsibility for the state of international affairs, such is our view.

It would not be us, not the Soviet Union, that would bear the responsibility in the event Soviet-American relations were to suffer further disintegration.

It seems that it would be much more useful if the leaders of the Soviet Union and the United States responsibly and with composure discussed problems which for the peoples are truly of vital importance – how to slow down and stop the arms race which for a long time already has assumed a senseless intensity and scope, how to preserve peace on Earth. We favor placing precisely these problems in the center of attention of the leadership of our two countries and having them find an intelligent solution. I assume and I'm even convinced that the American people need this no less than the Soviet people and other nations.

Respectfully,
L. Brezhnev

Four days later, on December 29, Reagan officially announced a series of eight sanctions against the Soviet Union. Sanction VI, requiring licenses for the export to the Soviet Union of an expanded list of oil and gas equipment, including pipelayers, served the purpose Reagan articulated in the two July 1981 meetings on East-West Trade Controls (trying to stop the Soviet construction of a trans-Siberian oil and gas pipeline). Getting allied agreement, however, was necessary for the sanction to be effective. Chapter Three discusses the attempt by the Reagan Administration to gain allied support for Reagan's sanctions policy.

CHAPTER THREE

SOVIET SANCTIONS

"I must take the blame for having been careless. At the time that I announced the sanctions, I believed that the United States was the dominant factor in what went into the production of the pipeline. Now, Maggie Thatcher has made me realize that I have been wrong.

"I now realize that the important factors are the subsidiaries and licensees of U.S. corporations. Now it seems to me that if we do it at all, we should figure out whether we want to throw a block at the Soviet Union. If we are not prepared to do that, there will be a split between us and American labor. Labor will refuse to load ships. The question is, can we avoid going all the way? Can we avoid telling Europe that our sanctions apply to subsidiaries and licensees?"[9]

---

[9] President Reagan during the February 26, 1982 NSC meeting.

Date: **January 5, 1982**
Subject: **Poland**
Status: **Declassified (2005)**

BACKGROUND

The following series of meetings discuss the aftermath of President Reagan's decision to order high-technology sanctions against the Soviet Union. The sanctions were a highly controversial policy because American and European companies had existing contracts with the Soviet Union for the sale of high-technology equipment, and both American and European companies stood to lose hundreds of millions of dollars worth of contracts if the sanctions were retroactively enforced.

SUMMARY

Weinberger argues for rescinding the license to International Harvester to sell equipment to the Soviets because the equipment would give the Soviets a unique capability; the U.S. could deny them an increased harvest capability and an increased military capability; and allowing the sale would damage U.S. credibility.

Although he was originally against it, because of the changed circumstances in Poland, Haig is now in favor of rescinding the license to International Harvester. Block argues for the sale because the technology is not unique, and Baldrige favors the sale because International Harvester needs to refinance $1.5 billion in debt and the Soviets are going to pay $300 million. Reagan defers making a decision.

POSTSCRIPT

Reagan wrote Brezhnev ten days after today's meeting concerning the plight of seven Pentecostalists refusing to leave the U.S. Embassy in Moscow unless guaranteed the right to emigrate.

Dear Mr. President,
I wish to direct your attention on an urgent basis to the plight of seven Soviet Pentecostalists who have been living in our Embassy in Moscow since seeking refuge there in June, 1978. These people seek permission from Soviet authorities for themselves and their families to emigrate from the Soviet Union according to principles of the Final Act of the Conference on Security and Cooperation in Europe. We have repeatedly approached the Soviet government on behalf of Petr and Augustina Vashchenko and their daughters, Lidiya, Luba, and Liliya; and Maria Chmykhalov and her son, Timofey; and the other members of these two families, seeking a prompt and humanitarian solution to

their plight. Yet three and a half years later, they still await permission to emigrate.

The families' situation has now taken on a new and potentially tragic aspect. After three and a half years of waiting, in frustration and now in despair, two of the family members, Mrs. Augustina Vashchenko and her daughter, Lidiya, have embarked upon a hunger strike in support of their goals. Despite the efforts and sincere well-wishers in the United States and in Europe to dissuade them from this life-endangering course, the two women have made clear they are determined to continue their fast.

Our embassy in Moscow has discussed this matter with your ministry of foreign affairs, informing the ministry that the two families have agreed to leave the embassy and return to their homes in Chernogorsk for the processing of their applications for emigration, according to Soviet laws and procedures, if their other family members residing in Chernogorsk are first permitted to emigrate, and if the seven family members are guaranteed that they will not be prosecuted by the authorities once they depart the U.S. Embassy and are assured that their applications for exit permission for reunification with their other family members abroad will be granted. Out of deep concern for their lives I ask you to intervene personally in this matter to allow these people to emigrate and thereby bring about a humanitarian solution before it is too late.

Sincerely,

Ronald Reagan

It took Brezhnev less than a week to respond.

January 21, 1982

Dear Mr. President,

With regard to your communication of January 15, 1982, I would like to say the following.

The people whom you are petitioning for have really found themselves in a situation not to be envied. After all, this situation was created and has long been maintained in an artificial manner. A way out of it could have been found a long time ago. At the present time, too, it is possible to resolve this question.

The only thing needed is that the US side rather than detain those people within the walls of its Embassy, take measures for them to leave it. Nothing stands in the way of such a step – nobody intended or intends to prosecute that group of pentecostalists.

As to their departure from the USSR, this question can be considered in accordance with the procedure established under our laws and equally applicable to all Soviet citizens, after those persons return to their place of residence.

However, the group of the sect members that happened to be in the US Embassy is being pushed for some reason or another in a different direction –

toward violation of the Soviet laws, setting forth prior conditions and all sorts of demands that can lead only to an impasse. Thus, the entire responsibility for the existing situation rests with the US side, including the responsibility of humanitarian nature.

We are not the ones to be called upon to exercise humaneness. For that matter, the references to humaneness are not convincing, while, in fact, attempts are being made to manipulate the destinies of individuals and not only those of the sect members who are kept in the US Embassy.

What kind of humaneness can one invoke, when the children are forcefully separated from their parents, as is the case with the Soviet citizens Polovchaks? Indeed, when even an American court rules to return Vladimir Polovchack – a minor – to his parents and the US executive authorities are raising obstacles thereto, it is not simply inhumane but immoral.

I would like to believe that on the part of the US side necessary measures will be taken to discontinue the abnormal situation existing around the group of Soviet citizens who find themselves in the US Embassy in Moscow.

Sincerely,

L. Brezhnev

Date: **February 4, 1982**
Subject: **Scope and Interpretation of Oil and Gas Equipment Controls**
Status: **Declassified (2008), released at the Reagan Library April 13, 2009**

SUMMARY

Today's meeting continues the discussion on stopping the construction of the Soviet oil and gas pipeline. Casey believes that an extraterritoriality decision – attempting to impose U.S. law on American subsidiaries located in foreign countries – could delay construction of the pipeline by three years, resulting in denying the Soviets a significant amount of hard currency until 1986.

Haig argues for considering the position of the allies, who perceive that the sanctions hurt them and not us. Weinberger thinks extraterritoriality is "absolutely the minimum approach … the pipeline is just as militarily significant as a plane … and a total embargo would be effective – not a selective embargo."

Baldrige agrees with trying to stop construction of the pipeline, however, "any 18 month delay is not going to have any effect… we lose $500 million in exports for nothing. If the Russians don't get phosphates from Florida, they'll get them from Morocco. All the General Counsels agree we are on tenuous grounds (with extraterritoriality)."

United States Trade Representative Brock reminds Reagan that allied support is also important to help American companies get national treatment. "This step (extraterritoriality) would destroy that effort," Brock tells Reagan. "We have to have allied support, otherwise we have no possibility of success. They look at it as an assault on their sovereignty."

Regan reminds Reagan that cutting off credit to the Soviets cannot be done unilaterally. "Pipeline financing is all guaranteed credit," the Secretary of the Treasury tells Reagan. "The guarantors are Germany and France. To cut off credit to the USSR, you have to have Germany and France withdraw guarantees."

When the discussion moves to a possible grain embargo, Reagan says that a grain embargo will be of no use and that "farmers always hurt first in recessions." Reagan suggests "charging the USSR with violating the Yalta Agreement" because "they would have to defend themselves on the issue."

"This would never pass at the UN," Kirkpatrick responds.

DECISIONS

Reagan's only decision is to prepare a high level mission to Europe to both persuade the Europeans to restrict credit and stop exporting oil and gas equipment to the Soviet Union. The mission to Europe, "The Buckley Mission," is discussed on February 26 and March 25.

Date: February 26, 1982
Subject: Terms of Reference (TOR) for High-Level USG Mission to Europe on Soviet Sanctions
Status: Declassified (2005)

BACKGROUND

Today's meeting continues the discussion on the implementation of Soviet sanctions and discusses how "The Buckley Mission" should approach the allies in light of the fact that the Europeans stand to lose $874 million if the sanctions are enforced. The NSC participants also continue to disagree on whether the U.S. has the authority to apply extraterritoriality, and if doing so would even stop or delay the construction of the Soviet pipeline.

SUMMARY

Reagan opens the meeting:

I must take the blame for having been careless. At the time that I announced the sanctions, I believed that the United States was the dominant factor in what went into the production of the pipeline. Now, Maggie Thatcher has made me realize that I have been wrong. I now realize that the important factors are the subsidiaries and licensees of U.S. corporations. Now it seems to me that if we do it at all, we should figure out whether we want to throw a block at the Soviet Union. If we are not prepared to do that, there will be a split between us and American labor. Labor will refuse to load ships. The question is, can we avoid going all the way? Can we avoid telling Europe that our sanctions apply to subsidiaries and licensees?

Weinberger suggests going for "the full reach, otherwise we will not appear either as sincere or effective." Haig disagrees, and recommends reassessing the U.S. position after Buckley meets with the Europeans. The Joint Chiefs favor the maximum sanctions that account for a balanced approach with the allies.

Casey reluctantly agrees that extraterritoriality will not work and the pipeline is "an accomplished fact," but suggests invoking the Tank Clause to delay the pipeline and possibly stop the construction of a second pipeline.

Attorney General Smith favors extending the sanctions extraterritorially, however, "If we go retroactive, we may make ourselves liable to having to pay compensation." Baldrige thinks that there is no way to stop construction of the pipeline, "We cannot even delay the pipeline significantly."

POSTSCRIPT

Reagan authorized the Buckley Mission on March 1. The next declassified meeting, on March 25, discusses the results of Buckley's mission.

Date: **March 25, 1982**
Subject: **Debrief of Under Secretary Buckley's Trip to Europe**
Status: **Declassified (2005)**

BACKGROUND

Today's meeting is called to allow Buckley to debrief the NSC following his trip to Europe to persuade the allies to cooperate with high-technology sanctions against the Soviet Union.

SUMMARY

CLARK: Mr. President, Jim Buckley, having returned from his mission to Europe, will report on the results of his consultations with our allies on the subject of restricting government and government-guaranteed loans to the Soviet Union.

BUCKLEY: The purpose of the mission was to show the idiocy of subsidizing the Soviet arms buildup through credits: we wanted to look at credits extended to the USSR in strategic terms, to treat them in the same manner as we do the transfer of sensitive technology. Specifically, we wanted to discuss (1) subsidized credits, offered at below market rates (sometimes as much as 50 percent below), and (2) government-guaranteed loans. Most countries provide both types of loans: the Germans have a peculiar form of loan insurance know as "Hermes" which is private but has government backing, so it amounts to the same thing.

More specifically, the mission wished to accomplish three objectives:

1. To consult with the European allies and Japan on the need for credit restraint and the creation of an appropriate mechanism to achieve this aim.
2. Transparency: the exchange among ourselves of information on loans; and
3. Pause: a moratorium on further credits and credit guarantees until the mechanism to control them has been set in place.

We failed in the third objective. The Germans and French said they could not adopt such a moratorium. The Italians said they have already stopped extending credit anyway, but for purely economic reasons. We obtained cooperation on "transparency". The reaction to our first objective, the request for consultations and a "mechanism", met with a mixed response. It was coolest in Germany where it was said that that country finds it beneficial to extend credit at preferential rates and that "Hermes" is a private organization (although admittedly government-backed). The Germans were also disturbed by the notion of singling out the Soviet Union for discrimination in matters of trade, a practice they described as "hostile." We stressed that indeed one must single out the Soviet Union – such discrimination is implicit in the maintenance of NATO and in our defense buildup.

The French were very French: they were prepared to do away with subsidies but they claimed they could not cooperate in restraining the flow of credits because of a 1981 protocol with the Soviet Union committing them to provide the moneys necessary for Soviet purchases in France. We will try to smoke out this accord: we doubt that it exists in this form. The British expressed a willingness to act as "middlemen". The Italians were a joy: fully willing to cooperate, as long as no country took advantage of the arrangement at the expense of others.

The meeting in Brussels was immensely encouraging. We met with the NATO Council, the EC, and Belgian Foreign Minister Tindemans. The smaller industrial nations are sick and tired of having to compete with larger powers.

In general, one could discern growing allied concern over East Bloc debts and an understanding that easy money helps the USSR solve its critical problems. The idea of doing away with subsidized loans met with sympathy. We stressed President Reagan's sense of urgency: that the President has put the December 30 sanctions on hold until we have reported on our mission. There is also growing congressional impatience. A telling argument was that our ability to cooperate in the matter of the ballooning debt of the Soviet bloc depended entirely on the willingness of the allies to restrict loans to the Soviet Union.

We laid a groundwork to go forward with bilaterals. We will start these bilaterals with the Germans next week. After the bilaterals, there is to be a conference of the leading powers to create a consensus. An agreement should be reached well in advance of the Versailles Summit.

The President has also asked us to raise the matter of energy dependence. We did this everywhere. We spoke of North Sea gas, opening the ears of our allies, especially in Italy and Belgium which are not yet committed to the Soviet pipeline. The Germans may reduce their commitment for Siberian gas by 10 percent.

REAGAN: **Well done.**

CLARK: The question is whether we should continue bilaterals on credits and continue deferring the decision on applying extraterritoriality to sanctions. Al?

HAIG: Jim Buckley spoke for me.

CARLUCCI: Defense favors bilaterals, but also extraterritoriality. We believe we can stop or at least delay the pipeline.

CLARK: There is no doubt of the Defense Department's position on this.

IKLE: If we give up too soon on extraterritoriality, we may lose leverage. We should hold on to it.

BALDRIGE: The position of Defense is wrong. We cannot stop the pipeline. The Russians will delay completion until 1986 (rather than 1984) – any delay based on a 1986 deadline therefore has no value. We have gone on this matter as far as we can. It is unfair to the United States – there is plenty of evidence of cheating, (like the Japanese backdating memoranda). No one is going along with us: this is costing many jobs in the U.S. I have no recommendation to make but we should be aware that (1) the allies are not cooperating with our sanctions, (2) we are losing jobs, and (3) we cannot delay the pipeline.

CLARK: Should the President void the December 30 sanctions?

BALDRIGE: We should think about that. Credits are strong action. I would not propose voiding the sanctions without credit controls.

REGAN: Let us continue negotiating a while longer. No one expected complete agreement from such a quick trip. Some two to three months are needed. Soviet trade and credits go beyond the pipeline issue: there are many other things we want to cut off besides the pipeline. Our lever lies in the fact that all East European countries are coming up for review: Poland, Romania, Hungary. The rescheduling of loans, where the allies want help, can be tied up to their actions vis-à-vis the Russians. If we get no cooperation in two or three months, that will be the time to pull the stops.

CASEY: We have ample leverage on credits. Delaying the pipeline is not adequate: it will be on stream in 1985-1987. We should take advantage of the economic situation. The demand for gas is declining, also in Germany. Our fundamental objective should be to develop energy on our side of the line, not theirs. The allies ought to commit themselves not to support the second pipeline, to keep the gas takes to a minimum, and to develop resources elsewhere. Don't worry about the Siberian pipeline.

BROCK: I completely agree with Bill Casey…. If we push the extraterritoriality game we will lose out on credit constraints.

SMITH: If we enforce sanctions, they should be extraterritorial or they are not credible. Talks (on credits) should go on.

HAIG: We recently had a meeting of some Soviet experts from the universities, including the Wharton School. Their conclusions agreed with the consensus that seems to be forming here.

The Norwegian Government wanted to delay the exploitation of its substantial gas reserves until the 1990s because of the energy glut. However, the new Norwegian Government is different from the old one which opposed large-scale economic development. Let us move away from trying to tamper with contractual agreements (on the Siberian gas line). The Europeans are beginning to feel we are crazy. This takes attention away from the really important issue: the second pipeline and the substitution for it of Norwegian energy, which would give good business to U.S. firms.

On extraterritoriality, I agree with Baldrige: European subsidiaries and licensees must fulfill their contracts. This does not hurt us. But there was an agreement that there would be no undercutting and this is being circumvented (for instance by Komatsu which backdates trade agreements).

I also agree with Bill Casey: trying to stop the pipeline is a secondary objective which irritates Europe. Keep this issue dangling. The same applies to the default.

The academic experts on the Soviet Union said that the U.S. is beginning to acquire a reputation for economic warfare against the Soviet Union. This would be disaster when Eastern Europe is drifting away, when we should want to differentiate (between the Soviet Union and Eastern Europe).

I hit the ceiling when I read a *Reuters* dispatch claiming (French Foreign Minister) Cheysson spoke of "insurmountable" differences with the United States. I telephoned Cheysson and he said there was no truth whatever in this report. The same applies to the Buckley Mission. We began to open Europe's eyes to over-commitments in Eastern Europe: that it is bad business. This awareness causes them to cooperate. They are afraid they will never get back their $80 billion. We must show the same patience here that we have shown in COCOM. In the meantime, things aren't so bad: the private banks are not rushing to lend money (to the East).

REAGAN: **Does anyone believe they will ever get back their money?**

HAIG:	Experts say you can write $40-50 billion off.
REAGAN:	**Should we not cut off credit?**
HAIG:	To the Soviet Union, yes; to Eastern Europe, no.
MEESE:	We should look at credit worthiness.
HAIG:	On occasion you have to make a political judgment to keep a country afloat. The academic experts say: we will not bust the Soviet Union. This is a crazy idea. They are in trouble, but you will not change their system with economic warfare.
BROCK:	We can make them change priorities.
CASEY:	Yes.
HAIG:	Jim Buckley did great work: he established the mechanism for the June meeting.
CLARK:	The President has asked Bill Casey to supply daily data on the Soviet and East European economic situation. Al Haig will report to the President on this next week.
CARLUCCI:	There is a question of interpretation. What is meant by "putting extraterritoriality on hold"? Only one firm is involved, Alsthom-Atlantique. The question is: Will they manufacture the rotors or not? Will they desist if we request them to?
CLARK:	The December 29 sanctions applied only to domestic firms. The President deferred the extension of sanctions to subsidiaries and licensees.
CARLUCCI:	Only one firm is involved, a GE licensee in France.
BUCKLEY:	Also a German firm.
IKLE:	They are waiting for a signal.
BALDRIGE:	That is right. The situation is confusing. There are reports they only have to be asked and they will stop. Other reports say they will expand production.
HAIG:	Keeping the issue hanging gives Buckley great leverage. We threaten Europe that we will apply extraterritoriality if they do not cooperate on credits.
BALDRIGE:	Credit restraints are a far stronger measure.
REAGAN:	**If we control credits, they won't be able to buy.**
REGAN:	The more uncertain the situation, the less credits will flow because the banks will be unsure of government guarantees. They are shortening loan periods as is. We are accomplishing things. Uncertainty restrains banks.
CLARK:	What we have is "organized uncertainty".
REAGAN:	**Let me raise a question from the world of fantasy. So far we are doing things which threaten to deny. But they are still in Afghanistan, they are still**

supplying Cuba, they are still preventing Jews and Christians from emigrating. Is there a right time for the West to cooperate? The Europeans do not understand.

Can we foresee a time when they (the Soviets) are in a desperate plight, when the military deprives the people of food, and we might be able to say to them: "Have you learned your lesson? If you rejoin the civilized world we will help you bring wonderful things to your people. But you must get out of Afghanistan, deal realistically in Geneva. No one wants to attack you."

BROCK: If you tie this to real reductions in arms so that their security does not increase, they must accept the carrot.

CARLUCCI: They are not convinced we mean it.

BROCK: Like the Japanese, they feel that if they can only hold on until the next administration…There has to be a carrot.

IKLE: Economic pressures may force them to deal with us.

REAGAN: Will they be desperate enough to grab Middle Eastern oil and tell Europe you will have to buy it from us?

CARLUCCI: A new generation is coming in: it may be different.

CLARK: You may have a Pearl Harbor in Iran if we press them too hard on credits.

Mr. President, anything further on what appears to be a consensus? We then have two alternatives:
(1)   Prepare a short, low-keyed statement for the press; or
(2)   Await a leak.
I recommend the second option.

REAGAN: Let us write a statement as a courtesy and correct any errors that may appear in the leak.

POSTSCRIPT

The discussion on Soviet Sanctions continues on May 24, 1982.

Date: **April 16, 1982**
Subject: **NSSD 1-82**
Status: **Declassified in Part (2006)**

BACKGROUND

President Reagan ordered a review of U.S. National Security Strategy when he signed National Security Decision Directive (NSSD) 1-82 on February 5, 1982. The NSSD stated that the review should produce a NSDD for decision by the President, which reviews:

- Fundamental U.S. national security objectives;
- Regional security objectives;
- Impact of Soviet military power and international behavior on U.S. National Strategy;
- Role of allies in U.S. National Strategy;
- Strategic Forces: objectives, policies, force application strategy (to include incorporation of NSDD-13), and force development strategy;
- General Purposes Forces:
    o Policies for the use of conventional military power to secure U.S. interests in peacetime and war (to include regional considerations and priorities as appropriate).
- Security Assistance policies and objectives;
- Interim goals: Where existing and programmed capabilities are insufficient to achieve desired objectives, interim objectives should be defined.

Today's meeting, which is still heavily redacted, is the first of two meetings called to discuss NSSD 1-82.

SUMMARY

CLARK: Today we meet to consider the first five parts of NSSD 1-82. The President signed the document on February 5, and this is the first occasion we have had to roundtable parts of it. The President asked Tom Reed (NSC) to chair the effort, and the President has read and commented on papers as they have been produced. There will be one more meeting of the NSC to consider the final four parts of the study. The importance of this study is indeed great; it will guide not only budget decisions but also national security for the balance of the century.

We have general agreement on the first four section; the one issue we have is in the fifth section. I suggest that we focus our attention on that section. I now ask Tom reed to discuss the first four sections and the issue we face in the fifth.

REED: This effort is this administration's successor to the PD-18 and PD-62. As you will see, there are substantial differences between our document and those of our predecessors. I will now run though, very briefly, the first four parts and summarize the principal findings.

Part I outlines our basic national objectives and the global environment in which our objectives must be met. The threats we face and the nature of our objectives are such that we are at a time of greatest danger to our national security since World War II. It is highly likely that, over the course of this decade, fundamental changes in East-West relations will occur. In general, our objectives, as outline in Part I, are more assertive and less passive than the approach of our predecessors. For example, we call for active measures to counter Soviet expansionism, to encourage the liberalizing tendencies in the Soviet bloc, and to force the Soviet Union to bear the brunt of its economic mismanagement. The bottom line is we are helping encourage the dissolution of the Soviet Empire.

Part II is a bridge between the military component and the other components of our national strategy. We cannot rely on military force alone to achieve our objectives. If we are to succeed, we must integrate all components.

Part III-A summarizes the threats that we face to our national security. Soviet imperialism remains the major threat. Some feel that the Soviets have now concluded that they have a window of opportunity and may press their advantage into a confrontation. We do not accept that view; this section concludes that it is unlikely the Soviets will challenge us directly in the near future.

Part III-B outlines the role of the allies. Allies are indispensable; we cannot go it alone. But we need more help from the allies than in the past, and this makes us more vulnerable to allied behavior. This is the reality, however, and we must deal with it.

Part III-C. This section established our regional military objectives. Importantly, it begins by stating that we must plan for global war; the 2 ½ or 1 ½ war strategy of the past is no longer sufficient. The Soviet Union is a global military power and our strategy must deal with that reality. We must, at the same time, set priorities among regions so that we are not forced into a decision on whether to escalate or to sacrifice vital interests. The global priorities laid out in the paper are those that we have had for several decades: North America, NATO, Southwest Asia, the Pacific, Latin America, and Africa, in that order.

The issue in this section deals with Southwest Asia. It asks basically what should we try to do in Southwest Asia by the end of the decade. There are two basic options: either we should plan to retaliate on a worldwide basis if the Soviets attack in Southwest Asia; or we should plan to defend in the Gulf.

Before we address this issue, I invite your comments on the other sections.

MEESE: What about the covert-political components of national security?

REED: The interagency review group concluded that those were really strategies of implementation rather than components of national security.

KIRKPATRICK: Under what general component do covert and political actions fit?

REED: They fit under a number of components; partially under diplomatic, military and economic. But we did not believe it would be correct to treat it separately in this paper. Again, we consider that issues such as arms control and covert action should be treated as implementing measures. The purpose of Part II was to show the other legs of our national strategy and not to discuss implementing tactics. However, this paper does discuss one aspect of this topic; specifically, unconventional warfare in Eastern Europe.

MEESE: I agree that these subjects are tactics of implementation, but I think we can solve the problem by calling the economic component in Part II "economic/political."

CASEY: Covert action is primarily directed against specific insurgent threats. (Line redacted.) Nations which control key choke points are under severe threat, and we need to devote more covert action and security assistance to help them out.

REED: We will discuss security assistance in more detail in ten days at the next NSC meeting on this topic. However, I would argue that it is an enormously cost-effective instrument.

WEINBERGER:	Security assistance is the cheapest and best way of defending the United States. We must convince Congress of this.
REED:	This is a clear example of how Congress is impeding efficient expenditure of defense dollars. We must get rid of the tangle of restrictions.
CLARK:	We will focus on security assistance in ten days.
EAGLEBURGER:	Al Haig shares completely the view that security assistance is crucial. We must take a firm stand in dealing with this on the Hill.
WEINBERGER:	We must take action to increase the number of friends we have around the world. They need to know that we are all in this thing together. We need to increase their cooperation with our efforts even in areas outside their immediate regions.
KIRKPATRICK:	We need a political dimension to our national objectives. The best way to defend our interests is to support friendly governments. It is a conceptual mistake not to think about the political dimension in national objectives.
MEESE:	There are other items which do not fit wholly under the diplomatic component; an item such as South American land reform is an example. It is important, therefore, to add the political component to the economic component in Part II.
CLARK:	It appears to me that we have general agreement on Parts I, II, III-A, and III-B. I suggest that we now move to the issue in Section III-C: what do we do about Southwest Asia?
REED:	I suggest that we go around the table and discuss two questions. First, are the wartime priorities which we have accepted for two decades still our policy; and second, what do we want to try to build for Southwest Asia? Do we want to build the capability to defend in Southwest Asia, or do we recognize the difficulties there and counter-attack in other parts of the world? Would we give up oil for pineapples or bananas?"
EAGLEBURGER:	Al Haig's position is strong support for Option Two as presented in the paper. Southwest Asia is our second most important region for strategic and natural resource reasons. It is necessary to posture our forces to defend in the area. The State Department worries that, if we adopted the first option, we will lose credibility in the region, and our allies will be less inclined to help. We will

be telling them that we are willing to give up this area of vital interest. We need to build a force of seven divisions that could be used in Southwest Asia. Even that force may not be sufficient to stand up against a determined Soviet attack. However, it will provide a much more credible deterrent and reassurance for our regional friends and our European allies.

WEINBERGER: Nobody disagrees with the importance of the oil fields; we need to hold them for our national security. We also do not disagree on the requirements for seven divisions, but we need to understand what we are dealing with. The assumption in Option Two is that we could limit the conflict to the region. In fact, the Soviets themselves might be delighted to do just that. The Soviets could mount 40 divisions in just a few days, and they would enjoy shorter lines of communications. On the other hand, we could project two divisions in 14 days and would then have to worry about resupply and reinforcement.

If we want to have the capability to defend the oil fields in the region, we will need to do three things. First, we will have to increase enormously our defense resources in order to expand greatly our air and sea-lift assets. Second, we will have to expand our force structure. At this point, we have 16 divisions, and resources may force us to deactivate one. Third, we will have to have a far more friendly atmosphere in the region. We cannot defend the Persian Gulf unless we have the full cooperation of regional states, particularly Saudi Arabia. Yet, Saudi Arabia is totally unwilling to associate itself with our military efforts. Jordan is making overtures to the Soviet Union, and Israel remains politically isolated. We do not have the bases we require. (Line redacted.) We have a lot to do before we will be able to defend the oil fields. Considering the way Option B is phrased, we simply cannot do it.

The option DOD would prefer is to work in other theaters to hold the oil fields. It is not a question of giving up the oil fields; the question is how best to defend them. The threat of escalation is the key. We also need to work with NATO to overcome their great reluctance to help us in Southwest Asia. This is somewhat ironic since the loss of Persian Gulf oil would hurt Europe far more than us. The UK is the only country that is thinking about defense outside the NATO area. Option B would require budget and force structure increases, and far more friends in the region than we now have. We would need bases well in advance of a contingency.

JONES: I agree with State; we need to work as hard as we can to get seven divisions to Southwest Asia. In a recent war game, in which we made the most optimistic assumptions, we found that we could hold in Iran for a while, but would eventually lose. We need a credible capability for Southwest Asia but also need the threat of escalation.

[General Jones then distributed suggested language for Section C. The alternative wording reads:

> To enhance deterrence by sufficiently improving our global capability to deploy and sustain military forces so as to ensure that should the Soviet Union attack in Southwest Asia, it would be confronted with the prospect of a major conflict *with the U.S.*[10] in-theater and the threat of escalation.]

WEINBERGER: We cannot give up the oil fields. We need to have the Soviets face the prospects of major conflict with the United States in the region and the threat of escalation. The realities dictate that we cannot defend in-place.

REAGAN: **I have always been of the view that the Soviets, if they think they are ready to engage us, will not need an excuse, but at the same time will not engage us if they feel threatened. What we need is a presence so that they know if they come in, they will have to confront the U.S. Can't we use our presence in Europe to that effect?**

WEINBERGER: That's the underlying theme of the new language that has just been circulated. We need a presence in the region, plus we need a threat of escalation.

REAGAN: **You look at Russian history, protecting the homeland has always been of paramount importance. If they know that we might respond to them by hitting them anywhere in the world, that's a strong deterrent.**

REED: If the Soviets know they will face a war with the U.S. in Southwest Asia and that we will be prepared to escalate if necessary, that will be an effective deterrent. I support the JCS proposal.

EAGLEBURGER: State can live with the language if seven divisions remains our objective. We also need to carefully avoid implying that we will draw forces from the central front in Europe for use in Southwest Asia. That could cause big problems with the allies.

---

[10] "With the U.S." is italicized because it was a handwritten addition to the text.

WEINBERGER:	That's true, but there's a limit to how far you can stretch sixteen divisions.
CLARK:	We should insert in the JCS language "…conflicts with the U.S. …"
WEINBERGER:	Our big problem in NATO is to get our allies to see beyond Europe.
MEESE:	I agree. In fact, NATO has larger interests in Southwest Asia than we do.
EAGLEBURGER:	NATO will be more apt to support our objectives outside of Europe if the allies see the U.S. is serious about keeping up our forces.
WEINBERGER:	That's what we are doing.
EAGLEBURGER:	It will also help with our Saudi relationship.
WEINBERGER:	We desperately need bases in Saudi Arabia.
BURT:	Let me ask a specific question. Does "military forces" mean seven divisions plus support?
WEINBERGER:	Yes, at a minimum. But those divisions are going to need support. The danger is that they might be committed to Southwest Asia and then cut off.
REAGAN:	**What about our oldest ally in the region, Israel?**
WEINBERGER:	We need to do a lot of work to avoid alienating other states (Line redacted there remains the deep suspicion of Israel throughout the region.
JONES:	Let me make clear the implications for broader strategy of another part of the paper. (Three lines redacted.) Resource implications are enormous. This is a far greater objective than those we are now planning for.

[General Jones passes out a graphic illustration of our budgetary shortfall.]

	I want to ensure that everybody understands what it is that we are saying.
REED:	That issue is taken up in Section G, which says that we cannot get there from here, and there is a large gap between resources and plans. There are enormous risks involved.
WEINBERGER:	The FYDP is not the panacea. We have clear constraints and have a long way to go. Our reach is exceeding our grasp, but the gap will become far greater if we do not fund the FYDP.
JONES:	(Two lines redacted) there are enormous problems. Bear in mind that seven divisions we are now allocating for Southwest Asia are seven divisions that will not be available for Europe. (Two lines redacted.)

REAGAN:	**We will do whatever is necessary to meet our objectives. A vigorous defense buildup will also be a great help at arms control talks. The Soviets do not believe that they can keep up with us.**
EAGLEBURGER:	We must continue to push the Europeans to do more.
REAGAN:	**If you compare Western Europe to the Soviet Union, you find that our allies collectively have a greater population and higher GNP – why should the Russians look ten feet tall and our allies like pygmies?**
SCHNEIDER:	We should not have too conspicuous a gap between objectives and programs. We need to ensure a high level of congruence. Otherwise Congress will become unmanageable.
REAGAN:	**We have a far more coherent policy than Congress.**
REED:	To summarize, the NSC has accepted the alternative proposed by General Jones. The President has approved the package.

DECISIONS

1. Parts I, II, III-A and III-B are approved as written, except that Part II will be amended to include an economic/political component of national strategy;

2. Part III-C is accepted and the issue is resolved by accepting JCS language, as amended by the NSC. This language is to be included as peacetime military objectives for Southwest Asia and reads:

   "To enhance deterrence by sufficiently improving our global capability to deploy and sustain military forces so as to ensure that should the Soviet Union attack in Southwest Asia, it would be confronted with the prospect of a major conflict with the U.S. in-theater* and the threat of escalation."

   *"In-theater" means seven divisions plus support.

POSTSCRIPT

The discussion of NSSD 1-82 is continued on April 27, 1982.

Date: **April 21, 1982**
Subject: **Strategic Arms Reductions Talks (START)**
Status: **Declassified in Part (2005)**

SUMMARY

Today's meeting is called to begin discussions on the framework of an opening START position. Richard Burt (Department of State), who has been chairing a START Interdepartmental Group (IG), presents the questions for discussion:

> What element of strategic nuclear forces do we want to reduce? A corollary question is, to what levels do we want to reduce? The basic objectives of a U.S. position, we believe, should be those of: (1) military sufficiency; (2) strategic stability; (3) significant reductions; (4) politically plausible; and (5) verifiable.

Burt divides the "what" element into six categories – (1) ballistic missile warheads; (2) launchers; (3) missile throw-weight; (4) warhead weight; (5) bombers; and (6) bomber armament – and then compares the current strategic balance:

> In deployed missiles warheads, the USSR is slightly ahead 7,500 to 7,100; in SALT-accountable missile warheads the U.S. is slightly ahead, 9,500 to 8,800; in strategic nuclear delivery vehicles the Soviets have a substantial lead, 2,763 to 1,944; in missile throw-weight the Soviets have a substantial lead, 5.1 to 1.9 kilogram; in bombers the Soviets lead 415 to 347; and the U.S. has the lead in the number of bomber weapons.

AGENCY POSITIONS

All the agencies favor cuts in the number of warheads to levels between 4,000 and 5,000. State favors a launcher limit of 1,500 and the other agencies push for no limits on launchers. All agree that the bomber limit should be at 250.

Weinberger favors having: (1) the Soviets reduce down to the U.S. levels, (2) a proposal ready before the European Summit, and (3) a Memorial Day television address to drive the process and demonstrate the seriousness of the administration in terms of arms control.

Weinberger also recommends that the U.S. approach should not build on SALT; launchers should not be the basic unit of account; and because the SALT launcher emphasis permitted an enormous Soviet buildup, warheads are not the proper measure since they do not account for the effectiveness of deterrence or include categories like accuracy, yield or hard-target capability. Weinberger recommends using throw-weight as the overall measure of effectiveness.

Haig recommends reducing launchers to a limit of 1,500, and reminds the President arms control is related to the overall defense policy, "including especially, our strategic modernization program, especially the M-X."

Rostow (ACDA) favors a warhead weight limit and a limit on the number of ICBM warheads and rejects the State recommendation of limiting the number of deployed launchers. Rostow says that the mistake of the 1970's was to think that the Soviets, like we, did not want first strike-capability. "Now we must insist on equal deterrence to the bulk of their threat. At present, the Soviets can knock out our ICBM's with one-fifth of their forces. Our proposal would take away two-thirds of their first-strike capability."

General Jones's reminds Reagan that "we actually need increased and better weapons," because NSDD-13 requires 13,000-15,000 strategic weapons and there are currently only 9,000.

Casey thinks the units of account should be decided on the basis of security requirements, and once we have decided what they are, we will need to see how these affect Soviet capabilities and how these need to be limited. President Reagan then tells his advisers what he thinks:

> We have to reduce the first-strike sudden threat of the missiles. The bombers take 12 hours to arrive and are easier to spot. The submarines are not so accurate, and both the submarines and bombers can be attacked before they shoot their missiles. The ICBM is different. The greatest psychological factor has to be an emphasis on the land-based missiles and their special threat.

POSTSCRIPT

The next declassified meeting on START is on May 3, 1982.

Date: **April 27, 1982**
Subject: **NSSD 1-82; (Security Assistance)**
Status: **Declassified (2005)**

BACKGROUND

Today's meeting is a continuation of the April 16, 1982 meeting in which a general consensus was formed on the first five parts of the draft NSSD for an overall national security strategy. Today's meeting is called to focus on the last four parts of the draft NSDD.

SUMMARY

President Reagan opens the meeting:

> I would like to express my appreciation for the outstanding efforts of everyone who was involved with this study. I want to assure each of you that your efforts have resulted in one of the most significant and meaningful statements of U.S. national strategy. More importantly, this study will undoubtedly serve as the basis for the national security of the United States for the remainder of this

century. As important as this effort is, I recognize that it is but one part of our overall national strategy, and I ask that each agency devote the same energy and resources to other ongoing strategy studies which characterize this study. I also want to take time here to thank Bill Clark and Tom Reed for the effort they have put into this endeavor.

Reed (NSC) then introduces the discussion:

> On April 16 we considered the first five segments which set the foundations of a national security strategy. Part I, which discussed the world environment, looked at the Soviet threat, concluded that both the Soviet Union and the United States have problems, and there is a potential that the decade of the 80's will be the decade of resolution.

> The first part of the study also sets forth our national objectives; an active but prudent program to encourage the dissolution of the Soviet empire. It also set forth the interlocking set of strategies that must execute our national objectives: economic, political, diplomatic, informational and military. We agreed on the nature of the Soviet threat and concluded that it poses significant dangers to the free world. We considered the role of our allies and friends, and we found that our relationship with our allies and friends is indispensable. Finally, we set forth some regional military objectives and theater priorities.

> Today we will look at the specific forces and attempt to answer the question of what are we going to do about the problems we face and the objectives we have. I will also describe what is new in the study as opposed to the Carter program.

> Section D, Strategic Nuclear Forces, states that nuclear deterrence is our most fundamental national security objective. It acknowledges that the U.S. no longer enjoys superiority or parity and therefore there is great danger to the U.S. and our allies. We must fix this condition, we must achieve parity, and for the United States, this is our first priority. … What is different about the treatment of strategic nuclear forces in this section as opposed to the last administration? I would say the answer has three elements: First, we are going about it in an integrated way. Second, we are according top priority to C^3I, and finally, rather than by a patchwork approach, this program is going to persist towards a goal and do it in a balanced and steady way.

> Section E, General Purposes Forces, has three major subsections. The first discusses our employment policies and discusses how we plan to use our general purpose forces. Given force insufficiencies, we can't be everywhere at once, and therefore we have concluded that in a conflict with the Soviet Union, we must undertake sequential operations and establish clear priorities…. The second major subsection deals with force employment strategy – how do we plan on using our resources? In peacetime, we plan to take advantage of forward deployed forces, security assistance, special operations, exercises, and the capability of our rapid deployment forces. In wartime, in a conventional war not involving the Soviet Union, we ought to limit the scope of the conflict,

keep the Soviets out, and end the conflict as quickly as possible. In a conventional war involving the Soviet Union, we ought to be able to halt the Soviet advances and prepare to execute counter-offensives where appropriate, with the words 'where appropriate' being very important.

The paper makes the conclusion that, and I quote, 'the U.S. does not now possess a credible capability to achieve all military objectives simultaneously. In the midterm we will remain unable to meet the requirements for simultaneous global operations.'

The final subsection deals with force development; in other words, what do we want to fix first. The paper opts for the first priority to be given to operational improvements: first, readiness – to be sure what you have works. The second priority is to update C^3 -- make sure what you have works as a team. Then, sustainability – be sure what you have keeps on working. Then mobility – so that what you have can operate where you want it to operate. Finally, force modernization.

There are three new elements in this section. First, the paper treats with global planning; no longer are we talking about 2 ½ war strategy or 1 ½ war strategy. Second, the paper tells our forces to be prepared to respond to non-Soviet contingencies. In Carter documents there was a clear implication that U.S. forces would not be required to respond to non-Soviet contingencies. Finally, the section sets a clear and comprehensive order of priorities.

Section F, security assistance, states that security assistance can be the most cost-effective investment we can make, especially right now. The major problem is that though there are more than 150 nations in the world, 60 percent of our security assistance goes to two countries – Israel and Egypt. It you add Turkey and Greece, 75 percent of our security assistance goes to four countries. Yet there are problems all over the world, and Bill Casey has a map that he will discuss later that points that out so vividly. A second problem is that we are hamstrung by Congress. This section lays out the following proposed solution to our security assistance problems.

Proposed solutions – first, we must establish a full-court press under Congress to pass the FY 82 supplemental and the FY 83 bill. Second, we must plan for steady growth for security assistance as part of the defense pie. Third, we must use more multiyear commitments to our allies and friends. Fourth, we must anticipate foreign military sales by activating and using our Special Defense Acquisition Fund. Fifth, we must undertake a legislative strategy to amend or rewrite as appropriate the Foreign Assistance Act and the Arms Export Control Act. This section is different from the previous administration's approach to security assistance in that it sets a plan of action, recognizes the vital role of security assistance, and unlike the Carter Administration, it is not queasy about security assistance. During the Carter Administration there was an aura of 'security assistance is simply cattle prods for cops.'

The final Section, G, deals with force integration. The purpose of this section is to tie everything together. Included in the analysis is a discussion of the trade-offs between money, strategy and risk. The paper address:

- Unified forces – no one force can win the war;
- Balanced forces – combat as well as support forces and deployed forces and those at home;
- Total forces – active and reserves;
- Mobility;
- Modernization;
- Integration of the entire spectrum of strategic components so that we win at the lowest possible level;
- Worldwide capabilities;
- Integration of nuclear and conventional forces;
- Strategic defense and space.

The paper then looks at the resulting risks and concludes that in the near term in conventional forces we are deficient in nearly every area; therefore there is a need for a steady, orderly plan to reduce risk. In strategic nuclear forces, we are in danger of blackmail if we don't fix our shortfalls promptly. In looking at the mid-term and longer term, our general purpose forces can maintain forward deployments and can deter and fight local conflicts not involving the Soviet Union. However, our general purpose forces for the mid and longer term will remain inadequate for global conflict against the Soviet Union. Indeed, we will be more balanced and more mobile by the end of the 1980s but relative risk in large measure will depend on what the Soviet Union will do. Finally, the report requires annual risk assessments from the Joint Chiefs of Staff. This section is in fact wholly different from the previous administration because it does treat with the concept of integration.

The last thing I would like to do is sum up. We have prepared an interagency study on national strategy. There are three sides to the strategy: money, risk, and strategy. We held that the FYDP is the baseline. We developed the strategy and addressed the risk. We could do three things: we could change our strategy; we could change the money allocations; or we could accept the risk and reallocate it where we want it. This is not a novel approach. It has been done for many years.

I will now summarize the entire study. We have recognized the risk and redistributed that risk to places where we want it. We must assure nuclear deterrence with the modernization program that will allow our strategic nuclear forces to regain parity with the Soviet Union. In peacetime we rely principally on non-military means to achieve our objectives. In conflicts not involving the Soviet Union we seek to limit the scope of any conflict, keep the Soviets out, and end it quickly. If confronted by the Soviet Union, we plan on sequential operations with lesser operations in secondary theaters. We plan to undertake counter-offensives only where they can affect the outcome of the war and are key to our primary objectives.

The discussion follows.

CLARK:	I propose we hold the discussion on security assistance until the end and open the discussion this afternoon on the nuclear, general purposes forces, and force integration sections.
HAIG:	I would like to stress the imperative of a land-based nuclear deterrent. It is critically important in our ability to manage crises, and if we hope to establish arms control incentives for negotiations with the Soviet Union.
WEINBERGER:	I would like to emphasis the points that Secretary Haig has just made. I agree with him completely. A key is survivable land-based systems. The fact that our MINUTEMAN vulnerability is in the order of 80 to 82 percent must be reversed.
	We need to have the MX and must have it get off the production line. We must also put it somewhere – anywhere is better than in warehouses. The Townes Commission gave us three ideas and we are now working on a fourth. It is not enough to put the MX in existing holes where they would remain vulnerable.
CLARK:	I would like to point out that the President is being kept informed on this problem and has a very high interest in it.
STOCKMAN:	I would like to make a generic comment on the entire study. There is no doubt that this study is a step forward and I am not quarreling with it, but I hope it is but a start and not an end. There is an enormous gap between strategy and capability. It is clear that the resources are not satisfactory to execute the strategy. The study does not address the resources implications and I appreciate the fact that the study was not intended to do so. We have identified the issues but now we need to go on to the later steps of figuring out how to resolve the imbalance between strategy and capability.
WEINBERGER:	The process is in place but it is an enormous task. The Soviet Union is in the lead because of its enormous investment, the fact that we gave them too much technology, and the fact that they stole much technology. What we have done and what the report confirms is to begin the long hard process of bringing back the security that our nation demands while recognizing that Defense will never get more than 30 percent of the total budget. That means that the problems will not disappear but the

process is in place. We have developed a budget and the weapons systems. Congress has endorsed our plan – 98 percent of it last year and so far this year, 90 percent. But we must understand the mess we inherited and the huge task that is before us.

BAKER: Are the resources there to do the job?

WEINBERGER: Yes, by the end of the decade we will have a posture which will allow us to achieve reasonable assurance of deterring Soviet aggression. However, today we cannot make such statements.

BAKER: We will have shortfalls at the end of the decade?

WEINBERGER: The answer, of course, depends on the risk. A no-risk strategy would require 80 percent of the budget. Of course, Defense getting that size of the budget would leave us with problems at least as bad in other areas as those we have in the defense sector today.

REAGAN: **What we are saying is that the plan does not require $500 billion more. In other words, the plan is in place.**

WEINBERGER: Tom Reed did an extremely good job. There are of course quicker ways to reduce the risk, but they would be incredibly expensive. The plan of the Joint Chiefs of Staff, which has a price tag of $750 billion, would increase our carrier force from 15 to 23, but that of course would give you additional risk in numerous non-military sectors. By the end of the decade, our plan will allow us to regain the ability to deter. Our problem is the high risk we face today. In sum, the Defense request is modest.

MEESE: What does "sequential operations" mean? Is it similar to the World War II historical example?

REED: It is. It means that you focus your forces at the point where your vital interests are threatened and have strategic defensive lesser operations in other areas.

WEINBERGER: Sequential operations mean that we will have to accept some early losses.

REAGAN: **We should consider attacks at places, which while not confronting the Soviet Union directly could hurt them just the same – such as Cuba.**

HAYWARD: We are doing that kind of planning right now.

STOCKMAN: In reading the document I note that in page after page we require a capability that will not be provided by the FYDP. The statement is made that when the FYDP is fielded, we still will not be able to fully carry out our strategy. There are serious implications for reserve forces and sustainability. What are the cost implications? There is an indication that there is a requirement to add force structure. It seems as though we need to add numbers to needs.

WEINBERGER: We will be less able to carry out our strategy in Year 2 than we will in Year 6. At the end of the plan we will still be risk-free. However, it is all a matter of degree. Our task is large. What we can do we will do, but it will not fix everything. Even the Chiefs' $750 billion plan would take a decade. There is a period of danger and we must rely on our allies and friends.

HAYWARD: The five-year plan does not do it all. We couldn't do it all no matter how much money Defense received. We don't have the industrial infrastructure, we don't have the industrial capacity. However, the study requires that the Joint Chiefs of Staff provide an annual risk assessment that will enable us to better evaluate how we are reducing risk.

CASEY: We just completed a Soviet strategic capability assessment. It is clear that the Soviets have much capability, but they also have much uncertainty. In this regard, it seems to me that we need to emphasize the cruise missile and strategic defensive systems.

WEINBERGER: We should also mention the Soviet Union is having significant problems in Afghanistan.

[The discussion shifts to security assistance. Haig reminds the NSC that there are two dimensions to the security assistance program: (1) our near-term requirement to gain passage of the FY 82 supplemental and the FY 83 packages, and (2) the longer-term aspect to straighten out the confusing set of legislative restrictions and the inability to respond responsively to valid security assistance requirements. Haig thinks there is going to be a battle on the Hill because "we are asking for $1.2 billion over FY 82 figures. …The previous administration let the program falter, and we now have an enormous backlog to fill." The discussion then continues.]

HAIG: The tragedy right now is that most of our security assistance money is consumed by Egypt and Israel. When you add Spain and Turkey, you have the package. It is crucial for the near-term aspect of our problem to gain White House support for the FY 82 supplemental and the FY 83 package. There can be no divergence of views among the leadership of this administration with regard to this requirement for security assistance. Mr. President, we do not have a prayer of securing Congressional approval unless you are involved.

REAGAN: **We are suffering from years of bad aid programs. We are now doing it right. I think it can be done.**

BAKER: The President was able to secure agreement last year because he vetoed the continuing resolution. That scenario can't be easily repeated this year.

DUBERSTEIN: The Congressional obstacles are severe. The $1.2 billion increase is on the minds of many of our Republican friends.

MEESE: We have to be careful in how we approach Congress. Methodology is important. We can no longer use old methods....

BAKER: In approaching the security assistance bill on the Hill we should go at it in stages.

HAIG: We only have three weeks.

CASEY: We also have to restructure the whole concept of security assistance. We must make it more responsive and more timely. We cannot respond to today's problems when we require a two-year lead-time to provide equipment needed to combat today's problems.

HAIG: We must also fix the longer-term. The Defense profile is up and the security assistance profile should go up in tandem. We have to deal with and solve the legislative prohibitions and make the Special Defense Acquisition Fund (SDAF) work.

WEINBERGER: The SDAF is very important and certainly is a step in the right direction. Security assistance can give us added strength at much less cost. There are modest requests from many countries, such as Korea, countries in the Caribbean, Tunisia, Portugal, Kenya and Spain. We need to think about redirections in the security assistance program. Of course it will take a major fight, but security assistance helps to buy our security on a cheaper basis.

CLARK: The President will get the decision directive together by the middle of next week.

POSTSCRIPT

Reagan signed NSDD 32, "U.S. National Security Strategy," on May 20, 1982.

Date: May 3, 1982
Subject: START (Strategic Arms Reductions Talks)
Status: Declassified (2005)

BACKGROUND

The only meeting minutes for today's meeting that could be located are an unknown note-takers handwritten notes. Since the notes are difficult to read, I highly suggest referring to the original minutes before relying on the following summary.

SUMMARY

The two questions presented for discussion in today's NSC meeting on START are:

　　(1) What unit of account should be used in the START negotiations?
　　(2) Should the U.S. seek to limit throw-weight directly or indirectly?

Haig suggests focusing on both military and political aspects and that the major problems with throw-weight are that verification is very difficult, and a reduction by the Soviets of 65 percent is not credible. Haig argues that a ceiling of 850 missiles is the most significant guard against a breakout by the Soviets.

Weinberger disagrees: "If we just limit warheads we'd play into the hands of Senator Kennedy and Senator Hatfield." The Secretary of Defense argues that yield is the real measure of effectiveness and limiting throw-weight could reduce yield.

Admiral Hayward says that throw-weight is important, but we should get at it indirectly through a combination of warhead reductions and an ICBM ceiling of 850.

Rostow recommends that Reagan, in his upcoming speech, talk about the number of warheads and their destructive capacity without going into detail on how "destructive capacity" is measured. Rostow also recommends going in the direction of smaller warheads to decrease the attractiveness of a first-strike.

POSTSCRIPT

General Secretary Brezhnev, just a few days after today's meeting, announced his willingness to begin negotiations on substantial reductions in strategic nuclear arms and freeze strategic arms as soon as the talks begin. Reagan rejected the proposal in a May 18 White House Press Statement explaining, "a freeze now would codify existing Soviet military advantages and [would] remove Soviet incentives to agree to the substantial reductions which President Reagan has identified as our primary objective in START." In private, Reagan sent Brezhnev a three-page letter that proposed the resumption arms reductions negotiations in June.

Date: **May 7, 1982**
Subject: **Letter from Reagan to Brezhnev (Arms Control)**

Dear Mr. President,

I am writing to address a question of critical importance to our two countries and to the world – negotiations to reduce the threat of nuclear war and the burden of nuclear armaments ... the awesome destructive power of nuclear weapons imposes on our two countries both the practical necessity and the moral imperative to do everything in our power to reduce and even eliminate the possibility of their use in war...

We now stand at another historic juncture in the effort to reduce the threat of nuclear war and the burden of nuclear armaments. One of the highest priorities of my Administration has been to undertake a thorough review of these issues in order to ensure that our approach to the problem of strategic arms reductions is fair, equitable, and understandable to the American people. We have proceeded deliberately to avoid the mistakes of the past. We are now prepared to move forward. Therefore, I propose that U.S.-Soviet negotiations on reductions of nuclear arms begin in Geneva by the end of June, and that we immediately begin exchanges in diplomatic channels to fix an exact date.

Our objective in the negotiations will be substantially to reduce the numbers and destructive potential of strategic nuclear weapons, in the framework of equal and verifiable limitations on both sides...We owe it to both our peoples, and to the World at large, to do better....

In closing, I would like to reiterate that my Administration has no higher priority than reducing the threat of war. I will personally spare no effort to achieve this objective, and I hope that I can count on a similar personal commitment from you. Nothing less will meet the obligations imposed upon us by the responsibilities of leadership in the nuclear age.

Sincerely,
Ronald Reagan

Date: **May 21, 1982**
Subject: **START**
Status: **Declassified (2005)**

SUMMARY

Today's meeting continues the discussion from May 3 on formulating a START negotiating position. Reagan asks: "What's good, if anything, in SALT II?" McFarlane says the counting rules are good; Haig notes that SALT II helps to preclude a Soviet breakout.

Weinberger argues against SALT II: "If we say we'll abide by SALT II, I don't think we'll get on with START." Rostow thinks that it is in the U.S.

interest to abide by SALT II because there would not be an advantage to changing policies. No decision is made.

Date: **May 21, 1982**
Subject: **Letter from Brezhnev to Reagan**

BACKGROUND

This letter is unusually important because Reagan both underlined and annotated the letter as he read it. The underlining and annotations, reflected in the transcript, are also significant because they demonstrate the degree of mistrust between Reagan and Brezhnev and the overall differences of opinion over the balance of forces between the United States and Soviet Union.

SUMMARY

Dear Mr. President,

With regard to your message to me of May 7, 1982 I would like above all to emphasize that the Soviet Union...has been steadily and persistently calling on the United States to agree on joint measures aimed at effectively bridling the arms race, first of all, in nuclear weapons. ...

Life itself puts questions of limitations and reductions of strategic arms in the center of Soviet-American relations. We have always favored increasingly radical steps in this direction. And it is not our fault that the strategic arms limitation process was interrupted for a long period of time. (Reagan wrote in the margin: "History does not confirm.")

Brezhnev spends the next page telling Reagan that regional conflicts should not interfere with arms control negotiations. The letter continues:

I deem it necessary to say it with all clarity since the position with which the U.S., judging by your speech on May 9, is approaching the negotiations cannot but cause apprehension and even doubts as to the seriousness of the intentions of the U.S. side.[11] ("He has to be kidding," Reagan wrote in the margin.)

After all, it is obvious that to isolate just any one component out of the totality of the strategic systems and to make it a subject of negotiations with no connection to the others, as you suggest, would inevitably lead to a distorted

---

[11] Reagan gave the commencement address at his alma mater, Eureka College, on May 9. In his address he called the Soviet Union's arms buildup "the main threat to peace" and noted that the U.S. goal in future negotiations is to "enhance deterrence and achieve stability through significant reductions in the most destabilizing nuclear systems...while maintaining a nuclear capability sufficient to deter conflict."

picture of the balance of forces between sides. <u>*Thus, the "substantial" reductions the U.S. side is talking about on the basis of the picture it has itself presented would naturally be substantial only for the Soviet side.*</u> ("Because they have the most," Reagan noted in the margin.)

Only one thing would be the result of such a one-sided approach – an upsetting <u>*of the existing balance of forces*</u> (Reagan wrote: "He means imbalance") *and a breach of that very stability which the U.S. side is allegedly so anxious to ensure.*

There should be no misunderstanding, Mr. President: this is not a realistic position, not the path toward agreement. Besides, as you know, we are not the only ones who hold such a view.

Brezhnev's letter went on to propose that both sides freeze their modernization programs and asked Reagan to "carefully consider this proposal." Reagan again wrote in the margin, this time quoting President Kennedy: "I have, and it's an apple for an orchard." The letter continues:

I am convinced that the American people would understand and support an agreement between the USSR and the USA which would be based on the principle of equality and equal security, and which would meet the objective of mutual limitation and reduction of strategic arms, just as they have supported the previously reached agreements that you citied. <u>*Soviet people   and you can take my work for that – will resolutely support such an agreement.*</u> (Reagan wrote in the margin: "How will they know? They haven't been told the truth for years.")

Skipping a few paragraphs, Brezhnev concludes:

We will, as before, continue to do all we can so that people can look into the future with confidence and calm, without fearing for the threat of war which is not needed equally – I repeat, equally – either by the Soviet or the American people.

Sincerely,
L. Brezhnev

In the margin, next to the signature line, Reagan scribbled, "He's a barrel of laughs."

Reagan announced, just ten days later, that arms control negotiations would resume on June 29. A still classified meeting took place on June 25, but the White House statement that afternoon said:

> We must do all we possibly can to achieve substantial reductions ... that are verifiable, that go to equal levels, and that enhance stability and deterrence and thereby reduce the risk of nuclear war.

Date: **May 24, 1982**
Subject: **Review of Soviet Sanctions**
Status: **Declassified (2006)**

BACKGROUND

Today's meeting continues the discussion on Soviet sanctions. The issue is of particular concern because Reagan will soon be facing the allies in person at the upcoming Versailles Economic Summit (G-7).

SUMMARY

CLARK: Mr. President, this is the time and the place to further consider our sanctions of December 30. The question is whether they should be maintained, expanded or rescinded as we approach the Versailles Conference. Jim Buckley is present here, awaiting further instructions. Secretary Haig, would you please present the State Department's view.

HAIG: Mr. President, as you will recall, you have decided to hold in abeyance the extraterritorial application of sanctions in order to give Jim Buckley the opportunity to see if a mechanism to restrict the flow of government guaranteed credits can be put in place. He and I have worked with the Europeans on this matter. We have not made an explicit offer of a deal, but we have told them that we would be flexible on existing contracts if a mechanism similar to COCOM could be put in place to control the flow of credits for the remainder of this century. Most European countries are very supportive and so are the Japanese. The most negative response comes from the French who claim that they have a private arrangement with the Soviet Union which precludes such measures. There is a problem with the rotors for the Siberian pipeline, but the Europeans are determined to go ahead and find alternate sources if we give them no choice. Cheysson suggested that they would be flexible on this matter, however.

This Thursday, Jim Buckley will have further meetings with the Europeans. I suggest that we make the Europeans a specific, rather than an implicit, offer. The Europeans realize that we are prepared to suspend extraterritoriality if we obtain in return god and hard commitments on the pipeline issue. The first leg of the

Siberian pipeline is a <u>fait accompli</u>: whether or not we help, we cannot prevent its completion. Our leverage applies only to the future. I suggest that we ask Jim to tell the Europeans we are prepared to be flexible on sanctions if they support credit controls and promise to limit future pipeline construction: that is, that they not build a second leg of the Siberian pipeline. They also should be prepared to limit their purchases of Soviet fuel in the future. Then, after the Summit, we should go back and take a look at the whole issue of sanctions because there are serious doubts as to whether they are effective and whether they do not punish us more than the Soviet Union. A good case can be made that they do.

In addition, there is a peripheral question of lesser magnitude. It involves the Japanese participation in the Sakhalin project. The Japanese require critical drilling equipment, worth about $2 million, which they can obtain only in the United States. The Japanese must know before the end of the month whether this equipment will become available to them or they will be in deep trouble with the Soviets. The Soviets threaten that, if they do not get it, they will go elsewhere. We must be consistent. Painful as it may be, we should let the Japanese obtain this drilling equipment, if they give us in return firm support on credits and energy.

CASEY: I have difficulty in understanding what sort of a deal we could obtain from the allies on long-term energy projects. We believe that the probability of the completion of the first leg of the Siberian pipeline is only about 85 percent.

HAIG: We think it is 100 percent. The United States should be constructive. I have talked to the North Sea producers and they think the development of this source is very viable. It will provide business for us and for the Europeans. However, we should move fast.

CARLUCCI: We disagree in general with the State Department's position. We concur that the Sakhalin project is part of an overall problem and that if you give in to the Japanese you will jeopardize the sanctions as a whole and open us up to European pressures. This is no time to lift the sanctions. Martial law continues in Poland and we should continue our pressures. Al Haig is right that our pressure will cause the Europeans to look elsewhere and that GE jobs will in effect be exported to

France, but the alternative is to life the sanctions entirely and this is not the time for that. Credit controls are fine, but we seriously doubt if anything tangible can be obtained on this issue before the Versailles Summit, given the French attitude. Should the Siberian and Sakhalin pipelines be built, this will be as important in the long run as are credits. The pipeline is by no means set, many Europeans have doubts about it. The CIA estimates that the construction of the rotors by Alsthom-Atlantique will push up the price. It is true that we cannot stop the Siberian pipeline, but we can delay it. Some Europeans are beginning to worry whether the construction of the Siberian pipeline will not preempt the development of North Sea oil resources.

BALDRIGE: I am not speaking for any business constituency, but I am convinced that the sanctions won't work in the sense that we want them to work, that is to delay the pipeline construction. The Russians will have many delays in any event. It is unlikely that the pipeline will be completed before 1986. I support the position of the State Department, but I believe we should not make specific promises until we have had a chance to agree with the Europeans on alternate sources and credit restrictions. What we will lose in sanctions will be well worth the gains attained by this strategy. As concerns Sakhalin, we have seen some movement from the Japanese on credit restraints. In general, the Japanese have been cooperative even though there is evidence that they have backdated their Komatsu contracts. I have mixed emotions on the Sakhalin project, but if we can get help from the Japanese on credits and a promise of no further Komatsu sales, then it may be well worth it to let them have what they want.

Murphy: When the Vice President was in the Far East, he was approached on the Sakhalin issue and asked whether we could be helpful. The Vice President would agree with Al Haig and would concur with his position if we can get commitments on credit restraints or, better yet, an agreement on this subject. On the Siberian pipeline, the Vice President would be torn between the two opposite positions, but he would be inclined more toward the position held by Al Haig.

REGAN: We should keep the two problems [the pipeline and credit restraints] separate. If I were you, Mr. President, I would not make any decision today. Let us see what Jim Buckley will accomplish on the 27th on the issue of credits. After that we can give attention to the pipeline. We should send a letter to the heads of state urging an agreement on limiting credits to the Soviets. If we get concurrence on this, then this issue can be removed from the agenda of the Summit. If the Japanese feel that they have to go ahead, let them, as long as they keep the downpayment to 40 percent. But don't let them have the equipment unless they agree – the are desperate for time. I think we can let the GE rotors go but not until we have obtained a real commitment on limiting purchases of gas and the development of the North Sea. As concerns credits, this is not a big deal. There are only $400-$500 million of export subsidies a year. Let us ask the Russians to put up 30 percent instead of 15 percent. The French say they have a protocol with the Russians, but no one has seen it. They claim they are committed in it until 1985 to go on 15 percent. Their credits are mainly government backed. Private sources charge more than the government. By placing the Soviet Union in the top bracket, all one got was a raise in interest rates from 11 ½ to 12 ½ percent. We are really not talking about an awful lot in restraining credits. It will cost the Russians something, but not bring them to their knees. In sum, I urge that a letter be sent to the heads of state, tied to the Buckley mission, to get an agreement. Then we can talk about the pipeline after the Summit.

CLARK: What should one tell Buckley?

REGAN: Push as hard as you can. If we trade, make sure we get something for what we give up.

HAIG: This is precisely what we propose, except we prefer to call in the French Ambassador and write to Mitterand. It is not necessary to write to the other European heads of state because they are already on board. Hence, the President need not write to everyone. But on Thursday, Jim has to be specific rather than general. The French do not want the Summit mucked up.

BUCKLEY: I feel we made a lot of progress yesterday, except for the French. We have secured agreement on a mechanism, but I have not been able to give the Europeans a quid pro quo. We are getting more vibrations on the rotors. We could offer them the rotors. If I have authority, I would have something more concrete to give.

The French do not want Versailles to get bogged down in East-West controversies.

BALDRIGE: The French want specific commitments, but if the French say no to credit controls, do we apply extraterritoriality?

BUCKLEY: Yes, this will have to be our position.

BALDRIGE: In other words, there will be no extraterritoriality if we get concessions [on credit restraints]. We will still keep the sanctions at home. If your mission fails, then we will apply extraterritoriality. This gives you leverage.

BUCKLEY: It has been implicit all along that the President can extend the sanctions extraterritorially. Sanctions will still apply to new contracts.

CASEY: Europe will depend for 20-25 percent of its energy resources on the Soviet Union. If Soviet energy supplies are fully developed, then whoever sits where you are sitting now, Mr. President, ten years from now will confront a situation where Europe obtains 50 percent of its gas supplies from the Soviet Union. The Soviet Union at that time will earn 80 percent of its hard currency earnings from gas sales. Any leverage we have should be used because credit controls are not adequate. It is true that the pipeline cannot be stopped, but we can delay it and make it more costly. We should aim at a swap: develop North Sea resources and give up the pipeline. I certainly agree with Don Regan that no decision should be made before the Summit. Also, we should not relax the sanctions imposed on Poland, where the situation has gotten worse. Norway has great potential to supply energy. It is critical that we do what we can to restrict long-term dependency on Soviet supplies. Credit restraints are nowhere near adequate compensation.

JONES: The Joint Chiefs are concerned over controversies in the alliance: controversies over such issues as nuclear strategy and the presence of troops in Europe. This should be a time of healing at Versailles. We prefer that no pipeline be built, but if we try too much at the Summit we may get nothing. We need a successful Summit at Versailles.

MACDONALD: Brock feels, as does Baldrige, that our first objective should be to convince Europeans to get alternate sources of energy. This objective cannot be achieved by technology restrictions. The latter penalize us.

KIRKPATRICK:	I would like to say that there is a great deal of criticism in France of the gas deal, even in the Socialist Party. The critics agree that anything that can be done to delay the pipeline and develop North Sea resources would be to the good. In other words, we have support inside France. More importantly, I believe that to lift sanctions would be political dynamite. On four specific occasions, Mr. President, you have publicly committed yourself to take stronger measures if there is no easing of the situation in Poland. There has been no easing of the situation there and now we may retract the sanctions. You have been criticized for being too weak. We would be very vulnerable. To permit the rotors to be built abroad would leave us open to the charge that we are exporting U.S. jobs.
SCHMULTS:	This is a bad time politically to lift sanctions. Europe should be passive on the Siberian pipeline and develop closer contacts with Norway.
HAIG:	All this is good stuff. No one is happy with the pipeline: we have been arguing against it for 17 months, but now you have hard choices. British and other European firms can no longer wait to fulfill existing contracts. You may end up where the Europeans will develop alternatives and you will put U.S. manufactures out of business. All this for an enterprise that is already set in place. When you hit a mule with a baseball bat, he will start kicking. The contracts have been signed and there is no use talking about them. [Turning to Casey.] Why do you say that the credit mechanism means nothing? It does. COCOM has for many years meant nothing but Jim Buckley has put some teeth into it after Poland. We are in a cooperative mood. We want something similar on credits. It would be a major advantage to have a credit control mechanism in place. It will not only affect money, but also improve cooperation. We should tell the Europeans to put their money where their mouth is.
BUCKLEY:	What I want meets Bill Casey's objections: a commitment to build no second pipeline and exploration of Norwegian resources. But we must bear in mind that the latter will take ten years.
CASEY:	I believe that unless we can come to an energy and credit agreement with the Europeans on the basis of their

own self-interest, it won't work and won't mean too much anyway. There can be no deals on this matter.

REAGAN: **I will not decide on this matter today but I will tell you how I feel in a manner that perhaps will indicate that I lean one way rather than the other. I felt all along that we imposed sanctions because of Poland and that credit controls were to be a quid pro quo for our not applying extraterritoriality.**

Now it looks as though we are backing off. I am feeling myself like that mule who is ready to kick. How much do we have to give up to get a harmonious meeting at Versailles? What is it worth to go to Versailles? All you get is some jet lag...

We said there would be more punishment coming, and here Walesa is still in jail and we are already talking about relaxing the sanctions. We will lose all credibility.

We talk well, but the Europeans will always back off. The Soviet Union is economically on the ropes – they are selling rat meat on the market. This is the time to punish them. The Europeans should tell the Russians to ease up in Poland, relax martial law, release Walesa. We are not able to afford politically to relax. The Europeans should have a bit of guts. We should tell them: 'we will help you with North Sea energy resources – o.k., have your pipeline, but no second pipeline, and develop Norway.' I had to swallow hard on the sanctions. I care for the U.S. unemployed. How are we going to explain that nothing has improved in Poland, but that business is business? We have arguments on our side. Why don't we provide the leadership and tell the Europeans who is the enemy – it is not us.

We are willing to help the Russians if they straighten up and fly right. We want deeds and they can begin with Poland. We don't even wait for the finale on the credits and are ready to give up.

BUCKLEY: But there is a quid pro quo.

REAGAN: **But this is for extraterritoriality. What happens to our promise that we shall do more nasty things? The Europeans are in a better position because they do business with the Soviet Union: let them tell the Russians we want action on Poland.**

BALDRIGE:	On the <u>quid pro quo</u>, I do not agree with Bill Casey that credit restraints are not significant. They are more significant than restraints on manufactured goods. Today you can always obtain technology in two years or so, but credits cover the entire economy. Control on credits will hurt the Soviets more. This, however, may be difficult to explain politically.
REAGAN:	**I agree. Yes, our sanctions are a leaky sieve and if credit sanctions are imposed, they will have to pay hard cash. Here they are vulnerable. Moscow has to hold out its hand.**
CLARK:	Unless there is something further, we will now adjourn. In sum, there is no decision to be taken, but a strong direction has been indicated. Please hold all this in the family.

POSTSCRIPT

The discussion continues on June 18.

Date:	**June 18, 1982**
Subject:	**East-West Sanctions**
Status:	**Declassified (2005)**

SUMMARY

Today's meeting continues the discussion on Soviet sanctions. Reagan tells the NSC that the decision has not gotten any easier since coming back from the Versailles Economic Summit (G-7), during which he told the Europeans that the USSR is more vulnerable today than we've ever known it to be, and the time has come where someone in the world has to stand on principle. Reagan said he suggested to the Europeans that quiet diplomacy is the way to deal with the Soviets, and that regardless of the fact that we are in a recession, "I don't see how we can retain any credibility if we fall back from this condition (the sanctions)."

Defense recommended extending the sanctions, State argued for lifting the sanctions, and Commerce argued for grandfathering the contracts signed before the sanctions were announced on December 30, 1981.

A memorandum released in 2005, undated and unsigned, titled, "NSC Meeting on December 30, 1981 Sanctions on Oil and Gas Equipment to the Soviet Union," showed that Reagan approved extending the sanctions. The memo reads:

In the NSC meeting of May 24, the President deferred a decision on whether to maintain, rescind, or extend the December 30 sanctions until after the Versailles and Bonn summits. Nevertheless, he used the occasion of the meeting to indicate his general views on this subject. Among the views expressed at the meeting were:

1. The purpose of the December 30 sanctions was to advance reconciliation in Poland through concrete measures;
2. The initiative on East-West credits is solely linked to consideration of extraterritorial controls on oil and gas equipment;
3. Concern that U.S. credibility would be undermined by relaxing the sanctions prior to substantial improvement in the Polish situation and a meaningful allied agreement on credits; and
4. A desire to persuade the allies to move forward with the development of North Sea gas reserves on an accelerated basis and to abandon the second strand of the Siberian gas pipeline.

While the developments at the Summit remain fresh in the minds of the participants, the President wishes to once again review the credit initiative and the December 30, 1981 sanctions and decide on one of the following options:

1. Lift the December 30, 1981 sanctions on oil and gas equipment exports to the USSR governed by existing contract.
2. Maintain the December 30 sanctions as presently constituted.
3. Extend the sanctions to include subsidiaries and licensees of U.S. companies abroad.
4. Approve on an exceptional basis U.S. export licenses for the Sakhalin project.

Next to Option 3, extending the sanctions to subsidiaries, Reagan initiated "RR".

Date: **July 21, 1982**
Subject: **United States Policy Toward Eastern Europe**
Status: **Declassified (2008), released at the Reagan Library April 13, 2009**

BACKGROUND

Today's meeting continues the discussion of Soviet sanctions by discussing whether transferring technology to Eastern European countries would undermine the high-technology sanctions against the USSR because the Eastern European countries could transfer the technology to the USSR.

The meeting is also the first after Reagan accepted Haig's forced resignation and announced that George Shultz would be the new secretary of state.

SUMMARY

SHULTZ: It is important that the United States recognize measures toward liberalization in East European countries, whether these be reflected in domestic or foreign policies. The point should be that while we may not approve of all actions by these countries, it is in our interest to take measures to encourage liberalization wherever possible.

BALDRIGE: With respect to technology transfer, I have a problem. The paper under consideration draws a distinction between technology sold to East European countries versus end products – the former being considered as more easily transferable than the latter. This is not the case. I'm in favor of removing the distinction between technology transfer and the transfer of end products.

I'm also against singling out Romania. I recognize that their record has been good in not transferring technology to Moscow, that could change, and as a consequence, we should not establish as a matter of policy that they should be excluded.

REGAN: It is not clear that Romania has such a good record. With respect to distinguishing between technology and end products, I'm extremely leery about transferring technology to the Soviets and would tend toward a more conservative approach.

BALDRIGE: There is strong evidence that Romania has not been guilty of technology transfer violations. There are instances of Romania holding sensitive technology for more than ten years without compromising it.

KIRKPATRICK: Romania does deserve special consideration. Romania does not pursue as independent a policy line as does Yugoslavia, but it has consistently preserved a measure of independence from the Soviet Union with respect to foreign affairs. For example, Romania abstained on the Afghanistan sanctions.

BROCK: I agree with Secretary Baldrige that Romania has had a good record. Still, I believe it is more proper to focus upon a particular country's internal policies. In that regard, Hungary and Czechoslovakia pursue more liberal internal policies than Romania.

CASEY: I'm in agreement with Secretary Regan to the effect that all East European countries have close relationships with the USSR and do indeed transfer technology to her.

The remainder of the meeting references footnotes and proposed language that could not be located. It is unknown if any decisions are made. The overall agreement is that no more favorable treatment is going to be given to Eastern European countries than to allied countries.

Date: **August 6, 1982**
Subject: **Soviet Sanctions (EC steel dispute)**
Status: **Declassified (2005)**

Regan tells the President that the following questions must be answered:

- Whether to proceed with extraterritoriality or wait for the Europeans to move;
- Whether or not to try and enjoin foreign action;
- What forum to use in a legal action;
- What products the sanctions are in fact supposed to cover;
- What alternative energy sources should be identified; and
- What positive steps might be taken to alleviate the sanctions situation.

President Reagan said he tried to get the Europeans to pressure the Polish Government while he was in Europe, but no one listened. Shultz argues for the importance of finding a solution that causes the least offense to the Europeans while doing maximum damage to the Soviets. Kirkpatrick notes that the French magazine Express wrote that the Europeans did not take Reagan seriously in his call for sanctions, and therefore the Europeans have not made a serious attempt to negotiate. No decisions are made.

Date: **August 9, 1982**
Subject: **START**
Status: **Declassified (2006)**

SUMMARY

Today's meeting is called to continue the discussion on START. The issue for discussion is how to get the Soviets to agree to meaningful verification requirements. Reagan suggests, "Our attitude has to be that of the preacher in church who let the only one-armed man pass the basket."

Weinberger argues that on-site inspections are necessary because anything else "would be hollow and shallow." Adelman says the problem over the years has been calling out violations. Reagan suggests telling the Soviets, "If we find even one (violation), we're back in an arms race and we'll out-build you."

Date: September 22, 1982
Subject: Pipeline Sanctions
Status: Declassified (2005)

BACKGROUND

Today's meeting continues the discussion on Soviet sanctions.

SUMMARY

After Clark introduces the agenda, the discussion follows on the rules being followed in connection with sanctions violations.

BALDRIGE: Temporary denial orders (TDO's) are being issued against alleged violators, whether the violation was a company decision or taken under government duress. They are also applied to subsidiaries and affiliates where appropriate. TDO's do not extend to non-oil and gas related items.

We are getting many requests for exceptions on hardship grounds, such as the Sensor case where a Dutch court has ordered the company to ship. Unintended effects cases are also coming in, such as a case preventing supply for an Australian pipeline. But there should not be any exceptions at this time, otherwise it will be like opening Pandora's box.

After Secretary Shultz returns from meetings with his counterparts in New York, we can reconsider refining the rules. If equipment or technology is for free world projects, if significant hardships are being imposed on innocent third parties and if the project involved reduces energy dependency on the Soviet Union, we should examine a change in rules.

REGAN: There is going to be political fallout because of lost jobs in the U.S. Many of the products involved are interchangeable, so that effects mainly U.S. companies. I agree with Secretary Baldrige, but the domestic implications should not be overlooked.

REAGAN: **We want to hurt the Soviets. Are we stopping the Australian pipeline?**

BALDRIGE: It might be delayed. But we should not make exceptions now. One exception leads to another.

CLARK: Ambassador Hermes (FRG) said last night that they don't agree with the sanctions, but Mr. President, you should not show vacillation now.

BROCK: A number of Europeans have told me that if all of this leads to greater allied unity, it was worth doing. But we are on extremely weak legal grounds if our actions are seen as a punitive rather than deterrent.

How is a pipeline in Australia a deterrent? We must be very precise about the standards on which we make our decisions.

REAGAN: **Can't we buy from Caterpillar and others?**

WEINBERGER: We do. We even have increased purchases from John Brown. But I'm disturbed by the Europeans being unwilling to meet. I support Secretary Baldrige's recommendation.

SHULTZ: Procedurally, you authorized discussions with the Europeans if they want to have a meeting. Foreign Secretary Pym (Great Britain) asked for a meeting. I accepted. Since then they have had trouble getting together – the British, Germans and Italians want to have a meeting, and the French believe if they wait we will fold. We have maintained the posture that we will meet, but they shouldn't believe we're looking for a way out. We're looking for a better approach to East-West economic relations. The British, Germans and Italians understand this. The French don't yet. I have meetings set up in New York.

Secondly, credit restraints on the Soviet Union must be addressed. It is easier to persuade people now not to be too liberal on international lending.

Thirdly, we must try to get agreement on not selling certain key oil and gas technologies and equipment to the USSR. U.S. companies control a major portion of this material, so the Europeans can't say we're being unfair. One possibility might be government guaranteed credit for this material.

Finally, there is concern over the Soviets taking a bigger share of market than implied by the first pipeline. The temptation is there to go ahead and gain a much higher percent of the European market. We must reserve space in the market for additional Norwegian North Sea gas. There have been changes in attitude in Norway due to changed market conditions. We are considering an interesting combination of Dutch/Norwegian gas in the future.

The British don't want to discuss this without discussing food exports to the USSR. We should reply that our policy is no subsidized sales of American grain. There is no all-out trade war planned – we're talking about European vulnerability. The Europeans are out of their minds to put themselves in the position of reliance on Soviet energy they are moving towards.

As I told Geoffrey Howe, they're not offering us something. This is an alliance. We see Soviet behavior, technology transfer and other unacceptable actions. Let's get together and decide what to do about it. The whole atmosphere is cockeyed now.

WEINBERGER:	We are in full and total agreement on this mater. We are not trying to wriggle out of the sanctions.
REAGAN:	**I have no quarrel with this exposition.**
REGAN:	What if something happens in Poland, have we come to grips with this problem?
REAGAN:	**Our pipeline position has to do with European exposure. Poland gave us a reason to act. There is more at stake here than Poland.**
SHULTZ:	The political, strategic and economic factors are related. We will not alter the sanctions until we see moves by the USSR. We will stick to our positions. We can't call off on COCOM and other things. We must move to a strategic posture not necessarily related to Poland.
BROCK:	We must separate what we hope to achieve strategically from the sanctions per se which are related to Poland.
BALDRIGE:	(Looking at Reagan) You have said that if the three conditions are met we would lift sanctions.
REAGAN:	**Yes**.
SHULTZ:	Even if the conditions are fulfilled and we lift sanctions, we still want to do these things.
BAKER:	But by agreement, not unilateral sanctions.
SHULTZ:	Any measure will be much stronger if taken with allied agreement.
KIRKPATRICK:	We hope for improvement in Poland. I was in France and the French press think our legal position is stronger and our companies' licensing contracts more important than we do. But there is confusion on our motivation. Our policy must be made clear.

CLARK:	We were opposed to the pipeline before the declaration of martial law. Favorable developments in Poland would lead to a review of the sanctions, but the issue is broader.
REGAN:	(Looking at Shultz) Be careful. The OECD consensus rates are now at the top of the range and may have to be negotiated downwards.
SHULTZ:	We must move with the market.
BALDRIGE:	The sanctions were imposed because of Poland. We must not be ambiguous. We want other things, of course. But we are giving the allies leadership on high moral grounds on Poland, not to force our allies to do things they don't want to do. Sanctions are a means to an end, not an objective in and of themselves.
REAGAN:	**This is what we indicated at the Summit. The Europeans should go quietly to the USSR and put on the pressure. But they did not agree. We must stick to our position that the sanctions are related to Poland.**
CLARK:	Please review the press guidance.
WEINBERGER:	"No" movement, not "sufficient" movement (text in the press guidance was changed).
BALDRIGE:	Just a final word to emphasize that the measures we have taken are preventive, not punitive. If asked why they are not effective, we should say they represent only the tip of the iceberg so far.
REAGAN:	**President Roosevelt called for a quarantine of Germany in 1939. He had his brains kicked out. What would history have been like if he had been listened to?**
CLARK:	Thank you, Mr. President.

POSTSCRIPT

Arms control negotiations stalled, because, as it turned out, Brezhnev was dying. Before his death on November 10, Reagan sent Brezhnev a letter touching on one of the more sensitive subjects, human rights. Reagan asked Brezhnev to check on the health of Anatoly Shcharansky, a Soviet Jew who had been imprisoned for the last five years on charges of espionage and had been on a hunger strike since September 27. Reagan ended the letter asking Brezhnev to personally intervene "to secure Mr. Shcharansky's release from prison and permission to join his family in Israel."

Brezhnev's response, his last letter to Reagan before his death a few days later, dated October 30, was straight to the point:

Dear Mr. President,

I want to draw your attention to the fact that the question you touched upon…concerns a Soviet citizen, sentenced for espionage and other grave anti-Soviet crimes, and lies within the exclusive competence of the Soviet State. There are neither legal nor any other grounds for resolving it in the manner you would wish.

At the same time, as I understand it, there is no basis for concern in this matter.

Sincerely,
L. Brezhnev

Date: **November 9, 1982**
Subject: **Allied Agreement on East-West Trade and Poland-related Sanctions**
Status: **Declassified in Part (2005)**

SUMMARY

Today's meeting is called because Reagan must make another decision on the Soviet sanctions. Clark tells the President that Shultz needs a decision from the four options presented to him in order to inform the allies.

"The consultations with the allies," Shultz says, "identified common ground in the area of East-West economic relations. This common ground enabled the allies to feel that they had not been negotiating with the United States under duress, and the United States for its part was able to put forward an agreement in a positive, upbeat manner." The bad news, Shultz adds a minute later, "final allied approval depends on U.S. sanctions modifications." Shultz continues to briefs on the details for a few more minutes, after which Clark outlines the public manner in which the President could make the announcement.

Reagan interrupts to say he just wants to know whether the new agreement is better than the current agreement. Shultz says it is basically good, but it is impossible to say whether the agreement would meet all the U.S. objectives.

Weinberger agrees with Shultz: "It is basically an agreement to consider an agreement, with the exception not to sign new gas contracts. … The temporary denial orders can be rescinded and enforcement of the June 18 measures can be suspended pending completion of the studies."

Baldrige thinks the effectiveness of sanctions is now at its height and that "within a couple of years it will diminish as companies and countries figure out ways to work around the sanctions." Baldrige, disagreeing with Shultz, adds: "If the agreement was in fact better than the sanctions, then the clean, unambiguous action of Option 1 should be taken. … Option 2 would solve some but not all of the problems of U.S. companies which had been affected by these sanctions. It would not solve General Electric's problem with its rotors."

For several minutes the principals continue to debate the merits of each option. Finally, Reagan asks for a clarification between Options 1 and 2. Under Secretary Olmer takes the question:

> Under the 1978 Afghanistan sanctions and prior controls, the United States prohibited the export to the Soviet Union of oil and gas exploration and production equipment and technology. It did not, under these controls, prohibit export of equipment for refining or transmission and had not controlled foreign subsidiaries and licensees. The measures taken in June controlled subsidiaries and licensees. The measures of December 1981 controlled refining and transmission equipment. Therefore, under Option 1, two of the four oil and gas equipment areas would remain under controls, whereas under Option 2, all four areas would remain under control. In addition, under Option 2 there would be a small amount of additional leverage concerning extraterritoriality. Concerning G.E.'s rotors, the hope would be that the agreement reached after the studies on high technology items would prevent Alsthom-Atlantique from displacing General Electric in the world market.

POSTSCRIPT

Reagan signed NSDD 66, on November 16, 1982, which officially cancelled the Soviet sanctions. The announcement came a few days earlier, in his November 13 radio address.

CONCLUSIONS

Despite the strict sanctions policy, Walesa was not released until November 1982, and martial law was not suspended until December 1982. Walesa was awarded the Nobel Peace Prize in 1983, and in 1986 he called for the United States to lift all economic sanctions against Poland.

In 1987 Vice President Bush spent four days in Poland telling the Polish government that relations between the two countries would not normalize until the Polish government's respect for law had substantially increased. However, the sanctions were officially lifted on February 19, 1987.

Towards the end of 1989, Walesa was asked to appear before a Joint Session of Congress, the second unelected person ever to be so honored. In his remarks, which were in large part a plea for monetary support, very little was said about the early 1980s. Walesa, however, emphasized nonviolence and the importance of Poland's fixing Polish problems. A year later, in 1990, he was elected the President of Poland with 73 percent of the vote.

PART II:

REAGAN AND ANDROPOV

CHAPTER FOUR

NOVEMBER 18, 1982 – JANUARY 30, 1984

"The message to the Soviets is that if they want an arms race, the U.S. will not let them get ahead. Their choice is to break their backs to keep up, or to agree to reductions."[12]

---

[12] Ronald Reagan to the NSC, November 30, 1983.

Date:	**November 18, 1982**
Subject:	**M-X Basing Decision**
Status:	**Declassified in Part (2005)**

BACKGROUND

Yuri Andropov replaced Brezhnev as General Secretary of the Soviet Union on November 12. Although over one hundred letters were found between Reagan and the various Soviet leaders at the Reagan Library, no letters were found between Brezhnev's last letter, dated October 30, 1982 and a letter on June 17, 1983 from Reagan to Andropov, congratulating him on becoming Chairman. Reagan's June 17 letter and Andropov's response are discussed in the postscript to the meeting on April 29, 1983.

SUMMARY

Today's meeting is called to help Reagan decide if the M-X missile should be deployed, and if so, how and where it should be based. Reed identifies four options and the costs associated with each option:

1. Abandoning the land-based leg of the TRIAD – no cost;
2. Deploy 100 M-X in existing MM (Minuteman) silos -- $17 billion;
3. Deploy M-X in CSB (Closed Space Basing) -- $26.4 billion;
    a. Adding deception to the CSB -- +$5.8 billion;
    b. Adding Ballistic Missile Defense (BMD) with a small area to defend and treaty compliant -- |$8 billion;
    c. Do BMD R&D and Long Lead Procurement -- +$3.5 billion;
4. Proceed back to M-X/Multiple Protective Shelters (MPS) -- $40 to $50 billion.

"The Secretary of Defense has provided a list of suitable basing locations if CSB is selected and an environmental study has been provided to the participants," Reed concludes. "Any location would be legally defendable if challenged on environmental grounds."

Weinberger briefs next:

> M-X basing is a most difficult decision given Soviet technology. The MPS is not suitable because the Soviets would require no new technology to defeat it. At an expected cost of $40 billion for MPS, the President is correct by deciding not to proceed with MPS. The question is, do we give up the TRIAD or do we keep ICBMs? We have to keep the TRIAD because I think the other two legs are not so invulnerable that we can afford not to. The Soviets must not lose the perception that our systems can survive a first strike. The situation is okay now, but our deterrence is weakening. What is left is for the President to conclude in 15 minutes that we are under nuclear attack and then launch – very destabilizing.
>
> We must look at the future. In 1989 the submarines will have survivability and the B-1s can penetrate through the 1990s. Senator John Tower says silo

stuffing will not be supported. ... Congress doesn't like the idea of an airplane, and deep underground basing can't be ready until the late 1990's...I have no hesitancy to recommend CSB.

General Vessey follows:

Security is dependent on both arms control and military strength. Stability comes from deterrence, and deterrence comes from war-fighting ability. Strategic nuclear forces alone will not buy deterrence. The Joint Chiefs supported START with the understanding that M-X would be deployed. All the Joint Chiefs support fielding the M-X, but do not agree on a basing mode.

The Army Chief of Staff and the Chief of Naval Operations worry about M-X survivability and command-and-control problems as well as the fact that fixed basing systems cannot be made invulnerable. The two Chiefs recommend we base some M-X in MINUTEMAN silos but eventually move to the sea-based system, D-5. If the decision is made to go with M-X in CSB, then a BMD system should be included at the outset. The Air Force Chief of Staff recommends M-X in CSB. The Commandant of the Marine Corps worries about the uncertainty of M-X survival with or without BMD.

Shultz keeps his comments short: "The M-X missile is an essential part of what we need if Geneva is to succeed. I will support the M-X/CSB. If we don't maintain our strength – the Soviet stock-in-trade—we will have problems as we urge our allies with respect to the INF."

Casey worries that the Soviets could counter both dense pack and deceptive basing methods, although doing so would take them a considerable amount of money and would not be ready before the early 1990s. Casey also thinks the Soviets are going to have to spend a lot on missile defense or deception and because of that, they might abrogate the ABM Treaty.

Keyworth stresses the need for both the TRIAD and the CSB for the M-X, and Reagan tells his advisers that the United States needs the Triad and the M-X missile, and that he strongly believes deterrence is the correct policy.

POSTSCRIPT

Four days later, on November 22, Reagan announced his decision to deploy 100 M-X missiles in an array of 100 closely spaced, super-hardened silos at or near Francis E. Warren Air Force Base, Wyoming. He directed that the initial operation capability be achieved in 1986 with full operational capability by 1989. He also directed that the deployment be designed with the growth possibility of deceptive measures in mind, and with the recognition that in the future we may have to deploy a Ballistic Missile Defense System.

In his speech announcing the decision, Reagan explained that the deployment was necessary because "a secure force keeps others from threatening us, and that keeps the peace." Reagan continued:

The United States wants deep cuts in the world's arsenal of weapons, but unless we demonstrate the will to rebuild our strength and restore the military balance, the Soviets, since they're so far ahead, have little incentive to negotiate with us. Let me repeat that point because it goes to the heart of our policies. Unless we demonstrate the will to rebuild our strength, the Soviets have little incentive to negotiate. If we hadn't begun to modernize, the Soviet negotiators would know we had nothing to bargain with except talk. They would know we were bluffing without a good hand, because they know what cards we hold just as we know what's in their hand.

The MX missile, later called "The Peacekeeper," is discussed again on April 14, 1983 and December 16, 1986.

Date: **December 16, 1982**
Subject: **U.S. Relations with the USSR**
Status: **Declassified (2003)**

BACKGROUND

Today's meeting is called to review U.S.-Soviet relations and brief the President on a draft NSDD. No decision is required.

SUMMARY

CLARK: (Reviews the study on U.S.-Soviet relations and notes that no decision is required.) There is disagreement on several issues, which will be discussed during the course of today's meeting. (Dam was asked to discuss the study in detail.)

DAM: The differences in opinions on the study are relatively minor given the scope of the study and the importance of the subject.

All agree that U.S. policy should contribute to containing and over time reversing Soviet expansionism, promote internal change in the Soviet system, and should involve negotiation where U.S. interest would be served by such an approach. The major areas of difference are: (1) whether U.S. policy should have as a goal inducing the Soviets to shift resources from capital investment in heavy industry and related activities toward the consumer sector; (2) whether we should adopt as a goal refraining from assisting the Soviet Union in developing their natural resources; and (3) whether there should be boycotts on agriculture as part of total trade.

REAGAN:	**I can save some discussion. I've crossed out contentious lines on pages 2 and 2a of the draft NSDD – they are provocative and should not be allowed to leak.**
	Nothing should be in this paper that we don't want to tell the Russians – we know what our policy is if the situation calls for its implementation.
WEINBERGER:	Yes, we are clear about our policy, it does not matter what is in the paper.
REAGAN:	**This approach is what I've always thought of as a part of quiet diplomacy.**
WEINBERGER:	We have to be careful, if something is taken out of the draft, some may interpret that to be a shift in policy.
CLARK:	Secretary Baldrige, is there anything you would like to add?
BALDRIGE:	I disagree with Secretary Weinberger on the issue of refraining from assisting the Soviets with development of their natural resources. To do that would be to wage economic warfare. I thought that interagency agreement had been reached to take this out of the drafts. I don't understand why it is in the paper.
CLARK:	The general rule is that all significant disagreements should be placed on the table.

[The official meeting minutes read: "At this point, the President received a note which informed him of the crash of an FBI aircraft in Ohio. He expressed his deep sympathy for the families, since there were four FBI agents involved with eleven children among them.

"Discussion continued among Dam, Weinberger, and Baldrige on the question of Soviet natural resource development. Clark asked Regan if he wished to comment."]

REGAN:	I want to shift the discussion to the question of technology transfer. The paper is ambiguous in terms of not specifying whether high or low technology is intended to be covered.
BUSH:	Yes, there are ambiguities in that area which could best be dealt with by leaving the section out.
CASEY:	[inaudible]
KIRKPATRICK:	I am also bothered by the ambiguous way in which technology is discussed in the paper. What, for instance, is meant by "critical" technology? I presume the central goal is to avoid helping the Soviets develop their military establishment.

REGAN:	Perhaps what is intended is "unique" technology – technology that the U.S. has but not its allies.
BALDRIGE:	This discussion shows how complicated the subject is. It would be better to get clarification at the SIG. We cannot give business such ambiguous guidance.
CLARK:	Dr. Pipes, would you please clarify what is meant by "critical"?
PIPES:	The word "critical" was not initially in the draft. It was added at State's insistence.
WEINBERGER:	Going back to Ambassador Kirkpatrick's point – that the central goal is to avoid helping the Soviets develop their military establishment – we should be examining all technology, and if that means the business goes abroad, so be it.
DAM:	Secretary Weinberger, what would be accomplished if the Soviets could get the technology elsewhere?

[The minutes say: "This discussion was continued, with Secretaries Weinberger and Baldrige participating, and with comments from Judge Clark and Ambassador Kirkpatrick.]

REAGAN:	**To summarize the discussion: We should not facilitate a Soviet military buildup.**

[The minutes say: "After brief related comments by Mr. Wick and Secretary Block, Secretary Weinberger turned to the issue of securing allied cohesion.]

WEINBERGER:	That is an attractive goal, but sometimes we pay an awful price to achieve it. Making allied cooperation a course we are committed to may amount on occasion to preemptive capitulation.
VESSEY:	Sensitive technologies have been transferred in the past. Our goal should be to insure that they are not transferred in the future.
REAGAN:	**To summarize, our goal is to not facilitate a Soviet military buildup, but at the same time I don't want to compromise our chance of exercising quiet diplomacy.**

[At this point the meeting shifts to specific wording in the draft NSDD. No decision is reached, and Reagan wraps the meeting up thanking "all the participants for expressing their points of view. Today's discussion, I think, has cleared the air a little."]

Date: January 10, 1983
Subject: U.S. – Soviet Relations
Status: Classified

SUMMARY

Today's meeting minutes are still classified, but Clark's briefing memo (declassified in 2005), told Reagan that the purpose of the meeting is "to obtain views of your advisors on US-Soviet relations and next steps in the Intermediate-Range Nuclear Force (INF) negotiations."

Attached to Clark's memo were separate Defense and State papers on the INF negotiations. The Defense paper, Clark wrote, said it was the wrong time to "abandon our position for zero missiles on both sides. " The State paper, Clark continued, "says we need to deploy the INF missiles in Europe to re-establish the U.S. strategic link to NATO. ... Failure to deploy would be a massive political defeat for the US and the Alliance, with lasting scars here and in Europe."

Date: January 13, 1983
Subject: Arms Control/INF
Status: Declassified (2005)

SUMMARY

Today's meeting continues the discussion on formulating an INF negotiating position. Shultz supports an objective of "zero-zero" with any number between 0 and 572 acceptable. "If we give up on zero-zero as our ultimate objective, the peace movement would take it up so fast that your head would swim," Shultz told Reagan.

Weinberger argues "zero-zero is the best for us, the allies, and the world. We should not lightly abandon it." The Joint Chiefs and Casey also support zero-zero. "The Soviets will not be flexible until deployment of the Pershings are assured," Casey adds. The discussion follows.

REAGAN:	**The last figure I heard for Soviet SS-20s was 315. Is that still the correct figure?**
WEINBERGER:	They now have 333 SS-20s and are finishing nine more sites. They will have 342 by March or April. Moreover, those missiles are mobile and can hit any target in Europe.
BARROW:	The JCS very strongly recommend that we stick with zero-zero at this time. We have some misgivings about defining equality, where the Soviets are bringing up

British and French systems, aircraft, and other such items. Zero-zero is attractive, simple, and understandable. The German defense minister visited recently; he asked that there be no changes in our position, at least until after the election. ... We should reinvigorate our advocacy of zero-zero. ... Deployment is the only way to bring leverage on the Soviets.

CASEY: We should stick with zero-zero. If it is important to show flexibility, the deployments must go ahead but we can say that we are open to negotiations beyond that point.

MEESE: We should continue with zero-zero as our ultimate objective. The Shultz way is the way to do it....

WEINBERGER: The Soviets have a great fear of the Pershing II. It is the only leverage we have on them. It takes only seven or eight minutes and is mobile. The Soviets will do almost anything to get rid of it. Therefore we should push zero-zero.

REAGAN: **Our 572 number – is this a mix? How many of them are Pershings?**

UNKNOWN: 108.

REAGAN: **Then how did we arrive at that figure?**

WEINBERGER: It was a 1979 decision.

REAGAN: **Well, if we have a total of 572 missiles and 108 are Pershings then that means 464 are cruise missiles. We must remain at zero-zero. But based on warheads, we allowed ourselves to be inferior. Is that a deterrent force only?**

GORMAN: The 572 number came right out of the air.

REAGAN: **We must deploy missiles. We will go along with what is needed for the FRG (Federal Republic of Germany) elections for a starting point, but if we sit there with zero-zero in our negotiating position and they then propose some ridiculous scheme, we have to respond. Why not go along with an interim reduction of the forces while continuing the negotiations for zero-zero? We can say we will start with a lower deployment of missiles and make it enough so they will still face Pershing's targets in Russia.**

WEINBERGER: The key phrase is "interim leading to zero-zero. Equality is a critical factor. For an interim approach, we would have to make it clear that we plan to continue deployment of Pershing and continue negotiations for zero-zero. This could only be an interim approach, and not until considerably later. As soon as we move away from zero-zero, it is gone forever.

REAGAN: **This can only be an interim move. Would there be any advantage to giving up cruise missiles and keeping the Pershings, since the Pershings are what they are afraid of?**

WEINBERGER: The Pershing is scheduled for Germany; the cruise missile for other countries. Germany originally stated that it requires one other continental country to deploy simultaneously. Later Schmidt said tow other continental countries. Kohl is being accused of abandoning the "2" criterion. If we abandon cruise missiles, the delicate agreements on deployments with others would be called into question.

REAGAN: **We could take an approach that we need a deterrent force and equality, but that is in interim step only.**

We could beat the drums for more public support. They can't divide the allies from us. We could lose support because we look too inflexible. We could say this is an interim step; reduce our missiles, equality, continued reductions for zero-zero.

CASEY: The Soviets do not want to see Pershings deployed. They will never agree to a deal which permits Pershings. They have been building a 20 minute launch-on-warning capability, but the Pershing only provides 8 minutes.

As soon as we talk about reduced numbers, they will say let's have a further moratorium while we talk. Europe will squabble on where the missiles should go and this will give the Europeans their opportunity to put off the decision. Germany supports zero-zero. We cannot allow Moscow a monopoly. There will be no Soviet flexibility until our deployments are assured. At that point (deployment) we can offer further flexibility.

BARROW: Those are valid points.

REAGAN: **The point I was making is that we would not do that until past that date. The only way there would be no deployment is if we achieve zero-zero. We should deploy on schedule.**

CASEY: That will put pressure on the Soviets.

WEINBERGER: And that will relieve pressure on us from the Soviet proposal.

SHULTZ: We can ask the Soviets how much they will reduce. This proposal puts equality at the heart of the matter. They had mentioned British and French systems and our approach will put them on the spot.

Vogel may wind up as the guy who bought the used car from Andropov.

CASEY: The CDU is using this to put the bee on the SPD and Vogel.

REAGAN: **Well, I think we are all agreed that we want equality, zero-zero, and at some point, talk about reduced numbers as an interim step. The date to start is when we start to deploy.**

SHULTZ: But we don't have complete control over the deployment. It depends to a degree on the imagery in Europe. There needs to be a sense in Europe that we are trying to reach a real result in Geneva. This is why equality is important. We can put it forward as a principle. No numbers are needed on the table. So when their proposal was in, we have put up a standard by which to judge it.

REAGAN: **The Soviets say the British and French systems have got to be considered. But France is not in the NATO military arrangement.**

WEINBERGER: And the negotiations are on intermediate weapons, but the British and French weapons are strategic weapons.

REAGAN: **If they want to talk about other systems, such as aircraft and submarines and the like, we can say that everything is negotiable, but we are talking first about the most destabilizing weapons.**

CLARK: I think it would be useful to raise two points. First, with respect to the partial reorganization of ACDA. It was related to management, not policy or philosophy. Nitze and Rowny were consulted before the decision. George (Shultz) is on top of the management question at ACDA, which reports through State.

Second, we intend to remain on high moral ground. In November Bud McFarlane started on an interim basis a public diplomacy activity. A specific plan has been presented to the President, and there will be a decision in the morning. Bud, would you please discuss this.

MCFARLANE: Mr. President, this dates from your speech in London where you talked about spreading democracy. We had been losing the battle of ideas. We want to foster the proper activities in the labor groups, churches, and so forth. …

An international political committee will be established, chaired by State. It will be an idea factory. It will develop ideas which would better promote our policy overseas. We have already had two activities: the Committee on Free Elections and the American Policy Foundation's "Project Democracy."

Through Ed Meese's help, we have gotten $64 million in the FY 84 budget and $20 million in 83 through reprogramming or a supplemental.

With respect to INF in Europe, we are losing to the Soviet propaganda effort….

REAGAN: **I have gotten so interested in the negotiating position that perhaps I should trade jobs with Nitze. If there are holes in this, let me know. Because of Soviet of Pershing and our advocacy of zero, perhaps they could be persuaded to go for a lower figure on an interim basis, while we continue to go for zero over the longer run. We should not be unilateral on this. We should take the countries into our confidence. Italy seems like a sure bet, and I think Maggie (Prime Minister Thatcher) would go along.**

BARROW: We would need a vigorous analysis on the lesser included points and the timing. Even thinking about other than zero-zero is harmful. If we ever talk about it with others, allies will fall off.

REAGAN: **Once we start deploying, the Soviets will understand.**

WEINBERGER: Currently we are saying we want to eliminate an entire category of weapons. The Soviets are not being responsive. We could ask the Soviets if they have another way to eliminate an entire category of weapons.

KIRKPATRICK: (Looking at Casey) Did you say that the CDU says that no monopoly of Soviet missiles is acceptable?

CASEY: (Read statement which basically answered the question as "Yes".)

The Soviets are simply not going to accept zero-zero. The best thing we can do is reductions.

SHULTZ: Well, that leads to two points. First, their preoccupation with Pershing gives us a good bargaining posture because Pershings would be included in any deployment. Second, we don't need to define equality and put this forward to Europe?

REAGAN: **In the proposal, the Soviet's plan, if there are 1046 warheads on SS20s, could we say that the Soviets can destroy every town in Europe of a particular size We could tell that to the placard carriers.**

MCFARLANE: Mr. Wick has a portrayal of that which he wanted to put in your speech. Every time the numbers of missiles goes up a new light goes on showing, for example, London blowing up. But that was a little too strong for your speech.

CLARK: We have some very good people gathering at State: Larry Eagleburger will be chairing this international committee. We have a short time to explicate the various groups.

REAGAN: **Okay. We will deploy. We will start with zero.**

POSTSCRIPT

NATO started deploying Pershing missiles in 1984.

Date: **January 25, 1983**
Subject: **Preparations for Round III of START**
Status: **Declassified in Part (2006)**

SUMMARY

Today's meeting is called to formulate a negotiating position for the third round of START negotiations scheduled to begin February 2. After question for discussion are introduced based on talking points that could not be located, the discussion follows.

SHULTZ: I was not secretary of state when the idea of two phases of negotiations were developed. However, I have studied the idea and it seems to be a reasonable way to proceed. Nothing has happened in negotiations to alter the basic U.S. decision. I support the desire to draw out the Soviets by talking a bit about all the elements of the U.S. approach as proposed by Ambassador Rowny. However, if the only way to do this is to collapse the phases, I feel that we should not do this. I think that we should be able to approach this issue as suggested by Option 2 and to table the Basic Elements paper without necessarily changing the U.S. position on phases.

MCFARLANE: Mr. President, the logic of the current U.S position is to focus on the most destabilizing systems, ballistic missiles and especially ICBMs. We consciously decided to defer negotiation of both slow flying systems and throw-weight until a later phase. The Soviets now feel that they may have found a weakness in the U.S. position by criticizing us on the grounds that it is not comprehensive. Therefore, the intent in tabling a Basic Elements paper is to show that all things are on the table and will be discussed ultimately, and thus undercut Soviet criticism of the U.S. position.

WEINBERGER: The only way to achieve the basic U.S. goal in these negotiations is to get a direct handle on the throw-weight. Today the Soviets have (redacted) metric tons of throw-weight as compared to (redacted) metric tons for the U.S. the two phases of negotiations should be collapsed. Unless this is done, a direct limit on throw-weight will never be negotiated and we will certainly never get the Soviets to talk seriously about the reductions to below the existing U.S. levels of throw-weight.

Some argue that if we place direct throw-weight limits on the table, they will not be negotiated seriously by the Soviets in any case. This is basically the same position taken by those who refused the zero position in INF. They were wrong, and the Soviets are negotiating the zero position with us today. Our negotiators themselves feel that we should get rid of the artificial distinction between the phases, and I agree with them. Failing to request direct limits on throw-weight, ignores the best way to get to parity.

VESSEY: I have concern that in collapsing the phases we would be expected to be able to fill in all the blanks in the U.S. position, and some of those blanks are simply unknown at this tie. SLCMS are especially a problem. The JCS do not want to lay out a Basic Elements paper with blanks in all the numerical limits. They are not sure that its in the U.S. interest to let the Soviets fill in the blanks. They are prepared to defer to the negotiators on how to tactically use blanks, but they are reluctant to start down the road until we internally have filled in all the blanks.

WEINBERGER: We should be in a position soon to fill in all the blanks. What we are talking about now, however, is whether to table a basic framework. We will certainly need the JCS views on what the specifics numerical limits should be, and this of course should be driven by the targets we need to hit. Some items we need not immediately raise. The Soviets have not yet asked us about SLCMs. We need only be able to talk about SLCMs in general terms at this time.

REAGAN: **Do the Soviets exceed us in the number of SLCMs?**

VESSEY: Yes, they do, but we have more SLBM warheads than they do. Also, the Soviets have more SLCMs deployed today than we do.

ROWNY: All the members of the U.S. delegation agree on the need to capture the high ground in the negotiations by tabling a Basic Elements paper. We can table t this paper with blanks rather than specific numerical limits. All agencies generally felt this was a good idea. The idea of collapsing the phases is a step further than simply tabling a Basic Elements paper. Deciding on whether or not to collapse the phases is a more difficult problem but to do so may help me now in negotiations. You can always instruct me not to give anything away, and I certainly don't intend to anyway. I lean towards the idea of collapsing the phases, but whether you do this or not I really want to table a Basic Elements paper.

In tabling such a paper, a direct limit on throw weight would be included, but the number can be left blank. We would make it clear that we would not agree on cruise missile limits unless we also agreed on direct throw-weight limits. The idea of collapsing the phases as a necessary part of tabling a Basic Elements agreement was not part of my original idea. However, it expanded my horizons and is attractive to me now, and we will eventually have to table everything at some point.

SHULTZ: If you start negotiating Phase II issues you certainly do collapse the phases. The basic idea we have with respect to the Basic Elements paper was to talk about but not negotiate Phase II items. We want to maintain our concentration on Phase I.

The Soviets will likely come back to us on the issue of cruise missile limits. Cruise missiles are our strong suit. We should not deal on this issue unless we absolutely have to. The implications that cruise missiles have for improving our conventional warfighting capability are just too great. We are way out in front in this area. I would resist strongly to moving Phase II items into Phase I.

If we got the Phase I limits we have proposed, we would make a drastic reduction in throw-weight. As a technical matter I have to ask if throw-weight really is that important. I recognize that it is an important measure, but with improvements in accuracy and other items, it isn't the only important measure.

CASEY: If you put Phase II items on the table at this time and negotiate on them, you should recognize that you are putting on the table the toughest items to verify.

REAGAN: **I need this oral session to understand the material that I have read. Is the obstacle that we face here that we need to have a treaty on all items before we can have a treaty on any items? Can't we say that we will accept a treaty on Phase I items only if there is a commitment to negotiate seriously Phase II items?**

ROWNY: That is one of the concerns of the Soviets on our phased approach. The Soviets claim that the U.S. just wants them to cut down in area where the Soviets have strength. They are in effect telling us that they will not agree to talk in these terms until the U.S. is prepared to talk to them about cruise missiles.

SHUTLZ: If, however, the Soviets accepted our Phase I approach would it not be in our interest to agree to them and pocket them immediately? Is it possible that the Soviets fear U.S. technology and that if we go to our Phase I limits leaving cruise missile technology unconstrained we will be superior to the Soviets?

ROWNY: The Soviets fear that we won't really cut anything in Phase II.

WEINBERGER: If in fact we get to limits on SLCMs, the Soviets will not be able to accept the verification measures we will requires. If we ignore direct limits on throw-weight until the end (Phase II) it will be hard to get it back into a treaty at that point. We need to introduce direct limits on throw-weight from the very beginning in any discussions about a treaty. If we do not, we risk getting agreement without equal ceilings on throw-weight. I agree that we should table a Basic Elements paper, but with collapsed phases. The issue of multiple agreements or order of agreements are matters for later discussion.

REAGAN: **You mention SLCMs, don't we also have SLBMs?**

VESSEY: All our SLBMs are already covered in negotiations.

REAGAN: **Couldn't we negotiate a limit on total throw-weight agreement for both sides and then have that limit divided up between SLBMs and SLCMs?**

[The minutes read: "Note: The intent of the President's question apparently was to ask whether we could not have an aggregate ceiling which includes ballistic missile throw-weight and cruise missile throw-weight/payload. Further, his intent apparently was to ask whether we could have a total limit in which we consider ballistic missile throw-weight (an area of Soviet advantage) and bomber and cruise missile payload/throw-weight (an area of U.S. advantage). If this is a correct interpretation of the President's question, it was never directly understood or answered."]

ROWNY: Yes, Mr. President we could, but this would get us directly into a negotiation over throw-weight. To get the Soviets to talk about direct limits on throw-weight, I need to offer some limits on something that bothers them. That something is limits on ALCMs. And I need to offer limits on cruise missiles to cut the threat to MX that the large amount of Soviet ballistic missile throw-weight provides.

SHULTZ: I disagree. I am not sure a full scale discussion of cruise missiles would be in our interest. We need to nurse along the current U.S. cruise missile programs. The phased approach that is in our current position makes good sense today. It would effect throw-weight.

WEINBERGER: The fact that cruise missiles could be discussed does not mean that we should agree to immediate limits on cruise missiles. All things are on the table, and the fact that cruise missiles are on the table is not a serious problem.

MCFARLANE: Mr. President, when we began these negotiations the Soviets were at (redacted) MKG of throw-weight while we were and are at (redacted) MKG. To ask the Soviets to go to an equal ceiling at or below our current level would be a real problem. Your original decision which was reflected in our phased approach, was to get to this low equal ceiling indirectly at first. Our Phase I goals would move the Soviets from about 1400 ballistic missiles to 850 ballistic missiles. This would cut their overall ballistic missile throw-weight significantly. The idea of tabling the Basic Elements paper was to undercut Soviets criticism that our position is not comprehensive.

	Ed Rowny wants to put all items on the table. What should Ed say with respect to cruise missiles and throw-weight?
SHULTZ:	I think he should say all vague things and keep all numerical limits blank.
ROWNY:	That was my original idea.
VESSEY:	We must remember that SLCMs are different from ALCMs. ALCMs are clearly strategic. While they could be launched from a number of different type of aircraft, we are planning to deploy them as strategic systems. The Soviets will be able to recognize them as such. SLCMs are a different problem. They are not obviously strategic weapons. Verification will be a really big problem with respect to SLCMs.
	(Paragraph redacted.)
	The U.S. SLCM is not a strategic weapon; it really is an INF weapon. I don't propose putting SLCM in the INF negotiations, but it is important to see the differences between SLCM and ALCM. We certainly don't want U.S. SLCM lumped into agreement packages, especially in overall weapons or throw-weight agreements.
WEINBERGER:	We do not suggest putting SLCM in the negotiations at all at this time. But like throw-weight, we can't keep it off the table.
	I don't believe we will get to meaningful limits on throw-weight in an indirect way.
REAGAN:	**Is it correct that the Soviets have not brought up SLCM?**
ROWNY:	They have only addressed ALCM, not SLCM. However, they know we plan to buy 4,000 ALCMs. (Three lines redacted.)
REAGAN:	**(If this is true) would they not want to focus on (total numbers of) bombers?**
ROWNY:	Yes. And that is why I think we should be prepared to negotiate to 350 total bombers plus some loading limits on the ALCMs on the bombers.
MCFARLANE:	If I may summarize, it appears that all agree that we should table a Basic Elements paper as suggested with all elements included (cruise missiles and throw-weight). We disagree on whether to collapse the phases of our current position and negotiate on all issues at this time.

The discussion continues on the specific limits involved on slow-flying systems and throw-weight. Weinberger argues limits because, "if we propose

SLCM limits, the Soviets will seize the high-ground by noting the potential high cruise missile numbers that we will need to counter the Soviet advantage in throw-weight."

Reagan asks about Soviet defense capabilities against cruise missiles. Weinberger says the Soviets are developing defenses. General Vessey adds the Soviets are spending a lot in cruise missile defense, which is an easier problem than defending against ballistic missiles.

McFarlane closes the meeting by telling the President that he will have time to reflect on these issues and that a decision document will be provided soon. "I guess all that is left is to wish Ed Rowny well in his negotiations," McFarlane says. Reagan responds: "I guess that's all we have done today because I don't think that up to this point we have helped you much."

Date: **January 28, 1983**
Subject: **Discussion on Defense Program**
Status: **Declassified (2005)**

SUMMARY

Today's meeting is called to discuss how to link the Fiscal Year 1984 Defense Program to policy, strategy, and objectives in order to get a positive Congressional response.

Weinberger does most of the talking, including a half-hour briefing on U.S. national security objectives, threats to those objectives, the U.S. defense strategy, and the nuclear and general-purpose force programs which support the strategy. Weinberger makes the following points:

1. It is essential to regain our military strength if we want to accomplish fundamental security objectives for the United States.
2. With regard to our strategy, the nature of our geo-strategic position requires both forward deployments and a flexible force structure that can move rapidly to a range of global locations.
3. The administration inherited a vulnerable deterrent posture for our strategic nuclear forces. Unless all legs of the Triad are modernized, this vulnerability will reach dangerous proportions.
4. With regard to conventional forces, our first priority is to make ready what we have. We have already made a 40 percent increase in the readiness of our units.
5. The defense program will provide a 70 percent increase in capabilities for our ground forces, should they be required for commitment in Southwest Asia, and a 40 percent increase in air force capability for the same contingency.
6. When looking at the budget figures, it becomes apparent that the charge that the defense budget has been immune to cuts is absolutely wrong. The Five Year Defense Program as of today is already $66 billion less than the program submitted in March of 1981.

Reagan isn't convinced that more defense money is needed, and tells Weinberger that he recently heard critics claiming that the proposed defense budget was "unwise" and that "the Administration did not have a strategy it was attempting to execute." Weinberger dismisses the criticism as coming from a former Under Secretary of Defense who had put together the defense problems this Administration inherited.

Regan wants to know if the Department of Defense has a budget fallback position. "Not at this time," Weinberger responds. "The defense budget is already in its fallback position," Reagan adds.

> We need to stand where we are…dig our heels in and stand fast and together. We have to do a better job in getting our message to the public. It is not simply a fight with the Congress – we need to gather the support of the American people…It is not necessary to have them (Congress) see the light, only to make them feel the heat.

A short discussion follows.

WEINBERGER:	It will be a long struggle, but I will take it on. I feel confident that the entire administration will take it on.
CASEY:	It is important to get a vigorous public affairs effort underway. We need 20 to 30 people – on a full-time basis – presenting our message and rationale to the American people.
REAGAN:	**The Carter budget of January 1981 was clearly underpriced – that means that the programs in the budget could not be purchased for the dollars requested. It would be a good idea to cost-out the Carter budget in order to determine the true nature of the budget.**
KIRKPATRICK:	Public affairs could indeed be the essential factor an determinant in the defense budget battle. I suggest that the President deliver a strong defense speech which provides clear evidence that the defense program being proposed is both prudent and essential. With a clear presentation of the vulnerabilities to American security and wellbeing, we could achieve our objective and secure the defense budget we need. However, it is essential that the President deliver this hard hitting and direct message to the American people.
REAGAN:	**Agreed.**

Date: **February 25, 1983**
Subject: **Briefing on Defense Guidance**
Status: **Declassified (2005)**

SUMMARY

Today's meeting is called to allow Weinberger to update Reagan on the purpose of the Defense Guidance, the Soviet threat policy guidance provided by the President, and top-line budget ceilings. Weinberger's 20 minute briefing highlights comparisons of U.S.-Soviet procurement trends, and points out that if the Defense Guidance is not fully funded, the asymmetries between U.S. and Soviet forces will increase.

Reagan wants to make this force comparison public and suggests that a presentation should include a year-by-year comparison of force strength growth as part of the public affairs effort to demonstrate the need for the defense program. Weinberger notes that "mission capabilities will increase 77% by FY88" and "U.S. force capabilities to operate in Europe and Southwest Asia will improve by FY89 as a result of the Defense Guidance, but everything is contingent on successful funding of the FY84 request."

"All the media criticism of alleged U.S. sabre ratting is ridiculous and harmful," Reagan responds. "I wonder if people appreciate how many men in our armed forces have died unnecessarily in conflict because of previous underfunding of training and equipment modernization."

POSTSCRIPT

On March 23, speaking in a primetime television address from the Oval Office, Reagan announced his intention to go forward with "a comprehensive and intensive effort to define a long-term research and development program to begin to achieve our ultimate goal of eliminating the threat posed by strategic nuclear missiles ... [which could] pave the way for arms control measures to eliminate the weapons." This research program became the Strategic Defense Initiative (SDI).

Date: **April 14, 1983**
Subject: **Strategic Force Modernization (M-X)**
Status: **Declassified (2005)**

BACKGROUND

Today's meeting continues the discussion over basing of the M-X missile. Since Reagan's announcement that he wanted 100 M-X missiles by 1986, Congress asked for studying the different basing modes. Reagan then created the Commission on Strategic Forces to study the issue and present a recommendation. Today's NSC meeting is called to update the President on the work of the Commission on Strategic Forces.

SUMMARY

Clark introduces the meeting by telling Reagan that Weinberger has met with the Commission several times, and will present the DOD position followed by the Joint Chiefs.

Weinberger says the M-X problem has been around for several administrations and that the two previous administrations recommended basing modes different than what this administration recommends. Weinberger supports the Commissions recommendation to continue all of the ongoing strategic programs, place M-X in Minuteman silos, initiate a small missile program, proceed with hardness and fratricide research, conduct Ballistic Missile Defense (BMD) research, and pursue ambitious arms control agreements. Weinberger supports the Commission recommendation because doing so would not be a change in policy.

General Vessey and Shultz support the Commission recommendation. Shultz notes the Commission's report raises – in terms of small missile development – an implicit violation of SALT II even though research and development would be permitted. Casey says they have evidence the Soviets are going ahead with small missile development so "it is essential we get on with a small missile."

Reagan closes the meeting: "The Commission has done a great job; they put aside their diversity to come together, and now the support must be uniform for this. Small differences must be set aside. We must do everything we can to refute the critics."

POSTSCRIPT

Five days later, on April 19, Reagan reported to Congress that he endorsed the recommendations of the Commission on Strategic Forces and urged prompt Congressional action and support.

Date: **April 29, 1983**
Subject: **Briefing on the Soviet Technology Acquisition Effort**
Status: **Declassified in Part (2005)**

SUMMARY

Today's meeting, which is still heavily redacted, is called to brief Reagan on Soviet technology acquisition efforts.

Casey briefs first and describes what the U.S. and West are losing in terms of technology because the Soviets have infiltrated companies all over the world. Casey continues:

> Many KGB officers have recently been expelled in Europe. ...The Soviets made acquisitions in strategic missiles, air defense, aircraft carrier catapults, space reconnaissance, and tactical weapons. The Soviets learned new approaches, raised the technology level, and shortened their development time, as well as saved money for (redacted) of their weapons programs. (Redacted) that about two-thirds of the collection involves US technology, and 90 percent is collected by the KGB and the GRU.

Reagan asks if Congress knows how serious the loss is. The response is redacted. Reagan then talks about how he heard of a Swiss high technology company owned by Libya, which made him wonder how many of these types of operations exist. A "huge amount" Casey responds. "There are hundreds of companies owned by Eastern Bloc countries around the world," Baldrige adds. Reagan ends the meeting thanking the briefers for "a sobering experience".

POSTSCRIPT

The next correspondence between Reagan and Andropov found at the Reagan Library was a June 17, 1983 letter from Reagan to Andropov congratulating him on his election as Chairman of the Presidium of the Supreme Soviet of the Union of Soviet Socialist Republics. "I hope that together we can find ways to promote peace by reducing the levels of armaments and moving toward the elimination of force and threats of force in settling international disputes," Reagan wrote.

Andropov quickly responded on June 22, echoing Reagan's call for peace, with an "unbending commitment of the Soviet leadership and the people of the Soviet Union to the cause of peace, the elimination of the nuclear threat, and the development of relations based on mutual benefit and equality with all nations, including the United States."

Cordial July 4 messages were cabled back and forth, and at the end of August, with another round of Geneva negotiations scheduled to begin, Andropov sent Reagan an offer to reduce intermediate range nuclear forces in Europe to equal levels with the British and French if the United States agreed to not deploy intermediate range nuclear forces in Europe. Reagan, however, never responded because arms control negotiations were put on hold following the downing of Korean Airlines Flight 007.

Date: **September 2, 1983**
Subject: **KAL 007**

Today's meeting is an emergency meeting called to formulate a response to the destruction of Korean Airlines Flight 007, which was shot down by a Soviet fighter jet after crossing into Soviet airspace on its way to Seoul from New York. All 269 aboard KAL 007 were lost, including 53 Americans. Reagan learned of the tragedy while vacationing at his ranch in Santa Barbara, Calif., where he expected to spend the Labor Day weekend. Reagan immediately returned to Washington for the emergency NSC meeting. No official meeting minutes were created according to an archivist at the Reagan Library.

Although the substance of the meeting is still classified, Reagan signed NSDD 102, "U.S. Response To Soviet Destruction of KAL Airliner," just three days later. "This Soviet attack underscores once again the refusal of the USSR to abide by normal standards of civilized behavior and thus confirms the basis of our existing policy of realism and strength," the NSDD starts. Objectives, like seeking justice, and actions, like conducting investigations, were also incorporated into the secret NSDD.

Although the modern consensus for why KAL 007 was shot down is that it was just an accident resulting from a combination of faulty Soviet radar and an undertrained air force pilot (who fired before verifying that the plane was not a commercial airliner), a top-secret message from a senior Yugoslav official thought otherwise. "The Soviet military may have acted independently in downing the KAL 747 in order to poison the East-West atmosphere on the eve of the next INF round," the message delivered at the US Embassy in Belgrade started. "In this view, which the official called 'the most plausible,' the Soviet military is unhappy with several of Andropov's latest moves, including: his August 27 INF proposal which considers destroying expensive and modern military equipment; his anticorruption campaign which includes the military among its targets; and his efforts at economic reform which implicitly question the military's dominant position in the Soviet economy."

Although the above theory is merely speculation, the week before the tragedy Andropov made his most significant arms control proposal: the Soviet Union would reduce their intermediate range nuclear forces in Europe to whatever level the British and French maintain, even if that meant a total elimination of INF in Europe.

Date: **November 30, 1983**
Subject: **Strategic Defense Initiative**
Status: **Declassified in Part (2005)**

McFarlane introduces today's meeting on SDI:

In March, the President expressed hope that emerging technologies could allow a shift from sole reliance on strategic offensive forces to defensive capabilities. Studies directed in the wake of the speech examined relevant technologies and policy dimensions of a defense against ballistic missiles (DABM). These studies involved a broad spectrum of the defense community.

Weinberger starts his briefing after handing out a chart comparing U.S. and Soviet defensive forces, and then continues,

We have no Ballistic Missile Defense system, very little air defense and essentially no civil defense, but instead base deterrence entirely on MAD (Mutually Assured Destruction) with offensive forces. The Soviets, in contrast, have 9,400 deployed SAMs, 2,400 interceptors, one Ballistic Missile Defense deployed and being improved, and a new, probably treaty-prohibited radar installation. This is in addition to very large offensive forces. The Reagan program is comprised of arms control, strategic modernization, and strategic defense. The Reagan modernization program, the DABM system, calls for the development of a multi-layered defense system that would be much more reliable than the defense envisioned in earlier R&D efforts.

There are several considerations relevant to a successful strategic defense program: the program will need strong bipartisan support, it is technically daring, we must avoid adverse impact on the budget, the ultimate DABM program should give increased security over the years. The President should address DABM in the State of the Union speech. The development of DABM would increase stability and would present no treaty problem for the time being. There are uncertainties, and we will also need defense against cruise missiles and other threats, and must continue with strategic modernization and improved conventional forces. An effective defense is feasible for deployment in the late 1990s to 2000. We already have some building blocks, but others, such as large computational capability to deal with big threats, are yet to be developed. Rather than deploy the full DABM system all at once, earlier deployment of a partial defense should be possible. We need to continue with strategic and conventional modernization, and we must make it clear to NATO that a U.S. DABM initiative does not mean we will let these other programs slide.

Of the four options put forward by the SIG-DP, I recommend Option 2, which would proceed with R&D as fast as technology would allow but hold open any commitment to deployment for at least a year. We also can't underestimate the importance of the boost-phase intercept, this change in direction is more significant than the increased costs, which are not enormous. DABM will not shake the 1985 budget bad, resources would be for the most part derived by reprogramming now in progress under Paul Thayer.

This initiative runs against conventional MAD and will need work on Capitol Hill. There will be doubters who will say a DABM program will frighten Europe, or not be technically do-able, or unwise for lots of other reasons. But it must be done because it offers hope, and because it would be disastrous if the Soviets were to develop effective missile defense and we did not.

Shultz follows:

I support the program Secretary Weinberger described, and have no opinion on technologies, or costs. R&D is needed, but at the same time we must carefully take only steps that strengthen our alliances. We should go easy on throwing out a deterrence strategy that has worked well in favor of something new and immature. Military history teaches that the best defense is a good offense. We should not become confident that we can develop a defense that could not be countered.

The proposed program can go over well with the allies and the Soviets if it is handled carefully and appears prudent and gives reassurance that we are willing to spend resources responsibly. But the U.S. should not send the wrong message that we think our current strategy is wrong; to do so would be disastrous.

The discussion follows.

REAGAN: **I agree with George that we are charting a new road. To take an optimistic view, if the U.S. is first to have both offense and defense we could put the nuclear genie back into the bottle by volunteering to eliminate offensive weapons. The pessimistic view is that a meeting similar to this NSC is now underway in the Kremlin. If the Soviets get new defenses first, we can expect nuclear blackmail. Therefore, we do need to handle this initiative as carefully and sensibly as possible, but hope and pray we get there first and can make the offer the Soviets would never make.**

WEINBERGER: We have no intention of handling this carelessly.

SHULTZ: Too much hoopla would be careless.

REAGAN: **I have no desire to see hoopla. I announced my intentions earlier; now we are going into the second phase.**

KIRKPATRICK: I recently had talks with French non-government defense specialists. Half of their discussion centered on an independent European BMD.

ADELMAN: I support the proposed program, but I see three paradoxes. The first has to do with stability: in the long run, successful BMD relies on deep reductions in offenses, but in the short run the Soviets would need to proliferate offense to penetrate a U.S. BMD.

REAGAN: **I assumed the continuation of our missile program had to go along with the DABM program. The message to the Soviets is that if they want an arms race, the U.S. will not let them get ahead. Their choice is to break their backs to keep up, or to agree to reductions.**

ADELMAN:	The second paradox: the most appealing objective of a defense is to defend populations, but the most likely outcome is to defend offensive weapons and command centers. And, the third paradox: the subject of ballistic missile defense inherently leads to exaggerations and to very sensitive subjects: arms control, alliance viability, militarization of space, strategic doctrine. We are faced with a nest of controversial subjects. An M-X-like debate would not be useful in 1984.
VESSEY:	The objective of DABM is not just to defend missiles and command centers. The boost-phase intercept has a large population protection significance.
KEYWORTH:	The DABM initiative keeps up-front the theme of hope the President expressed on March 23. The recent movie, The Day After, had the opposite theme of hopelessness.
	Over the last nine months I've faced many of the arguments against defense made so strongly in 1968-72. We are now in an entirely different era of technology. There is great advantage in boost-phase intercept that was not possible in 1968. The Fletcher Panel started out pessimistic, but most of its members wound up optimistic. The message in the Weinberger/Keyworth letter urging the President to speak soon on this subject is the importance of raising the spirit of hope through a long term DABM progress.
WEINBERGER:	Hope is not hype.
REAGAN:	**The proper time to make another address may be on the anniversary of the March 23 speech.**
MCFARLANE:	Does the degree of current alarm over the prospect for space war argue against putting nuclear weapons in space?
WEINBERGER:	We want the means to do reliable boost-phase intercept. While lasers to do this may need nuclear power, we want to accomplish this mission without using nuclear weapons if we can.
BUSH:	Dr. Keyworth, how confident is the Fletcher Group that defensive technologies in space can be made immune from countermeasures?
KEYWORTH:	The study addressed technologies designed to counter a responsive Soviet threat – one that was designed to defeat the defense – rather than the current Soviet threat. This has provided confidence in their conclusions that a robust defense could be developed.

ADELMAN:	Defense of defensive systems is enormously important.
THAYER:	Several years work would be needed before the technology has developed far enough to allow it to be viewed as a defense system. Things not yet conceived of could arise. It will take some time to get to any decision point. While we will be challenged on the resources needed for this program along with everything else, the current estimate is that DABM will add only about $8 billion to the five-year plan. The $8 billion figure is only an approximation and may not be right. Costs will be clearer after a year or two of work.
WEINBERGER:	Independent of the DABM initiative, we must work to develop ASAT and satellite defense capability because of the Soviet capability.
REAGAN:	**We are not alone – the Soviets really make this decision for us. How are we to face the day when they have both offensive weapons and an effective defense?**

[Paragraph redacted.]

SHULTZ:	I see no difference of opinion on what we ought to do. The differences are over how we sell it. This should not be done by selling short the concept that has worked.
WEINBERGER:	If that argument is taken to its limit, there is no need to do anything different. We must make the case for hope for the DABM initiative, while continuing with established deterrents.
REAGAN:	**We must make Congress understand the risk. Make it clear that we are not alone, that the Soviets have been at it longer and ask if we are to sit and do nothing.**
SHULTZ:	I agree. Ballistic missiles are not the only threat. There are others we already know to defend against. The Soviets have done so, not in violation of any treaties. We are asleep at the switch. But, if handled right, the DABM initiative can be a great plus. If handled wrong, it can blow up in our face.
MCFARLANE:	Agreed. We need great care in preparing and conducting public, Congressional, and allied relations. This will be worked on next. Mr. President, do you want to take the DABM decision under advisement while these actions are carried out?
REAGAN:	**Okay.**

Date: **December 20, 1983**
Subject: **Soviet Noncompliance with Arms Control Agreements**
Status: **Classified**

SUMMARY

Today's minutes are still classified, but McFarlane's briefing memo to Reagan states that the purpose of the meeting is to review the major findings of an interagency study on Soviet noncompliance with arms control agreements and to consider when and in what context these findings should be reported to Congress, the allies and the general public. The memo continues:

> The initial interagency review has focused on seven specific issues to be addressed in a secret-level report to Congress. These include the Chemical and Biological Weapons Conventions, the Krasnoyarsk radar, the SS-X-25 missiles, the SS-16 missile, encryption, the Threshold Test Ban Treaty, and the arms control provisions of the Helsinki Accords. In the days ahead, we also intend to focus our attention on a number of other specific concerns we have identified and tasked for analysis, including additional aspects of the SALT I and SALT II agreements and the Kennedy-Khrushchev agreement on offensive weapons in Cuba. In addition, we are considering the serious implications of these Soviet actions for our national security, and we are reviewing possible diplomatic and military options for subsequent consideration by you and the NSC.

POSTSCRIPT

Reagan sent Andropov a letter three days later.

Dear Mr. Chairman:

On his recent return to Moscow, Ambassador Hartman conveyed to Foreign Minister Gromyko some of my thoughts on the current direction of relations between the Soviet Union and the United States. I continue to believe that despite the profound differences between our two nations, there are opportunities – indeed a necessity – for us to work together to prevent conflicts, to expand our dialogue, and to place our relationship on a more stable and constructive footing....

In considering the issues now confronting our nations, I especially regret the decision of the Soviet Union not to continue serious negotiations toward the reduction and elimination of intermediate-range nuclear forces. Since your August 27 letter to me, both our governments made new proposals. For our part, we have sought to address particular Soviet concerns, but have not yet seen a comparable readiness on the Soviet side. The negotiations have reached a stage which suggests the potential for forward movement in some areas; clearly, however, much more needs to be done. Thus, I see no justification for an interruption of these talks, particularly since for two years we were wiling to negotiate while you deployed new missiles.

As I have pledged, both publicly and privately, the United States seeks and will accept any equitable, verifiable agreement that stabilized forces at lower levels than now exist. We are, of course, prepared to continue to search for such an agreement. It is only through serious negotiations that the reduction and eventual elimination of the weapons over which the Soviet Union has voiced such public concern can be achieved.

This also is true as regards in our respective strategic nuclear arsenals. As you are aware, over recent months we have made significant modifications to our position in the Strategic Arms Reductions Talks. We will continue to insist that any START agreement be meaningful – that it lead to real reductions in the most destabilizing categories of ballistic missile systems, as measured by their warheads, and in the overall destructive power of our two strategic forces. In seeking a lower and more stable strategic balance, however, we do not insist on identical force structures.

Any successful negotiation must eventually embody a balance between the interests and advantages of both sides. If the Soviet Union is prepared to agree to meaningful reductions in ballistic missile warheads and destructive power, where it holds the advantage, the United States is prepared to accept more stringent limits on heavy bombers and air-launched cruise missiles, where it possesses certain advantages. If we could achieve a balance of capabilities in this manner, we would be able to develop a common framework for carrying out strategic arms reductions...

You have pledged to me your commitment to peace and I have made a similar and heartfelt pledge. In your letter of August 27, you wrote of "the need for a broad, considered approach and for taking bold political decisions looking to the future." If you are indeed prepared to take such an approach and to make far-reaching decisions and, by doing so, to address in a tangible way some of the basic causes for divisions between our two nations, then you will not find the United States lacking for a positive response comparable in scope.

I await your thoughts on these matters, and on any others which you feel we should address in a joint search for ways to move relations between our countries in a more positive direction.

Sincerely,

Ronald Reagan

Date: **January 13, 1984**
Subject: **Mutual and Balanced Force Reductions (MBFR)**
Status: **Declassified in Part (2005)**

SUMMARY

Today's NSC meeting is called to help Reagan formulate a negotiating position on MBFR (Mutual Balanced Force Reductions) because the Europeans want the United States to modify its arms control negotiating positions. McFarlane introduces the issues:

> The fundamental prerequisites that we have specified which must serve as the foundation of any agreement on MBFR are: (1) Agreement on data, and (2) Stringent verification measures.

> We have been pressing the Soviets for: (1) clarification of their latest initiatives; and (2) more information on categories for reductions. The President has previously approved greater flexibility in our INF and START negotiations and has directed that a fresh look be given to our MBFR position. We were preparing to demonstrate flexibility in the early fall period, but the shoot down of KAL 007 and Soviet intransigence following the incident made it imperative that we stand firm on our MBFR position.

> We have essentially three options: (1) Stand firm on our present position; (2) Attempt to initial a treaty that addresses the questions of parity and includes a comprehensive verification package; and (3) Initiate initial, asymmetrical reductions, followed by an 18-month freeze, then seek a comprehensive data agreement followed by reductions to parity.

"Now is the time to move forward with Option 3," Shultz tells Reagan. The discussion follows.

SHULTZ: I've discussed the outlines of this option with the allies and found strong support for such an initiative. The issue is verification, and if we can get the Soviets to move on this question, then real progress is achievable. If we can offer preliminary, initial, asymmetrical reductions in order to get them to move on verification, then we should do so.

The problem is to find a way to move from a verification agreement to reductions. The optimal course would be to implement – first – small, token reductions. This would place the onus on the Eastern bloc, provide impetus for forward movement to a full agreement, and it would help us considerably in our dealings with the allies.

I feel strong pressures to demonstrate flexibility, but we don't want to move just for the sake of movement. However, movement does make sense now and will help stem Congressional pressures for troop reductions – which are a constant concern to us. The possibility of reaching an agreement is good if correct preliminary steps are taken. Following these steps, an agreement could be signed – followed by full implementation.

REAGAN: **I feel the most important requirement is to ultimately obtain full agreement on data with respect**

to troop strength and force imbalances. I don't want the West to be in a position of constantly backtracking or adopting a new posture in the absence of Soviet movement. I don't want to be in a position of shifting if they give nothing in return. On the other hand, if they provide new movement, then it would be advisable for us to respond positively.

WEINBERGER: I see no positive movement from the Soviets. In particular, they have not set a date for resumption of the talks. Secretary Shultz should tell Gromyko that if they set a resumption date, we would be prepared to show movement. However, we should not move at this time, now should we shift to Option 3. Prerequisites for movement are preciseness on data and a clear definition of the types of forces we are discussing, which places the focus of our efforts on the reduction of combat forces. Pressure from the British and Germans could be handled simply by explaining that we are studying our alternatives. In sum, Soviet moves to date have been marginal and we must, at least, wait until they set a date for the resumption of negotiations before moving.

VESSEY: We should not move quickly now. Their reinforcement problems are a good deal less difficult than ours. I want to stress that data is absolutely essential to achieve full verification. However, I recognize the political imperative to show movement, and that the FRG, for political and demographic reasons, has an essential requirement to exhibit flexibility. In sum, I recommend that we stay with Option 1.

WEINBERGER: The Department of Defense has prepared an alternative proposal to Option 1, but has not been able to staff it through the IG process prior to this NSC meeting.

GATES: (Speaking for Casey) The intelligence community feels that all options could be verified fairly well, however, with respect to Option 3, the framework for a data agreement is of concern. (Specifically) the intelligence community is concerned with the broad categories of reductions proposed by the Soviets, due to their lack of explicitness. There is also a fear that the Soviets will pocket whatever proposal we place on the table and demand further movement from that point. The new Defense proposal has merit in that it: (1) Doesn't commit us too early; (2) Focuses verification on those forces where our capabilities to monitor are best; (3)

Includes armaments and not just personnel, and (4) Allows the Soviets to get themselves out of the box they have placed themselves in.

In sum, the Defense proposal permits a narrowing of our differences.

ADELMAN: The new Defense proposal has the advantage of focusing on counting combat units. However, with respect to allied concerns, Option 3 is clearly preferred. Recent Soviet proposals had some positive points, including: (1) Exit/Entry points, and (2) progress on verification, including some on-site inspection.

In sum, I feel that Option 3 is the preferred variant – it calls for asymmetrical reductions and it focuses on verification. However, in any case, we do not wish to reward the Soviets prior to their designating a starting date for the resumption of the talks.

ABRAMOWITZ: (Summarizes the Options.) Any shift in our position must take into account broader considerations of our policy toward the USSR, allied concerns, and intelligence community reservations. It is important to keep in mind now that:

(1) The Soviets have displayed considerable movement, especially on verification and they have expressed concern with our failure to respond;

(2) Many of the allies feel that we have been too rigid and must respond to the Soviet initiatives;

(3) The Soviets do not like the MBFR talks because they feel they were cajoled into MBFR talks in exchange for our agreement to begin the CSCE talks, so they would be pleased to see the negotiations collapse; and

(4) The prospects for MBFR are dim and it is uncertain if there exists a replacement forum.

If talks collapse, allied unity would suffer and the Soviets would be ecstatic.

Option 3 has merit – it does not give up anything; it calls for asymmetrical reductions; and nothing would occur until adequate verification is in place. Should we decide, instead, to stick with Option 1 or continue to tell our allies we are "studying" our alternatives, there is a good chance the forum will collapse and allied unity will suffer.

I'm not opposed to changing the unit of account at some point in time, but we had best realize that this would be a very time-consuming process.

WEINBERGER:	I feel that we should first concentrate on getting the Soviets back to the negotiating table, and inform the allies that we are considering movement.
SHULTZ:	I disagree with the previous assertions that a shift to Option 3 would represent a repudiation of our long-held position.
ABRAMOWITZ:	The attributes of Option 3 are clear: It calls for asymmetrical reductions; it demands adequate verification at the outset; it calls for no treaty signature or reductions to parity until this is accomplished.
MEESE:	The reductions called for by Option 3 are token. Tabling this proposal enables us to reoccupy the psychological high ground. It is not necessary to cling to a position just because we have held it for over ten years.

The discussion continues with Weinberger and Adelman arguing over the merits of Options 1 and 3, after which McFarlane gives a brief summary of the conversation. Reagan then warps up the meeting with his own observations:

o We have received sufficient movement from the Soviets in their proposals to warrant a response from the West;
> o We will not make a proposal simply to bring the Soviets back to the negotiating table;
> o We will respond to the Soviet proposals, but not before they have agreed to set a date for the resumption of the talks; and
> o We have something concrete in hand that demonstrates Western responsiveness and flexibility to discuss with our allies. Following allied agreement, we will be prepared to table a new proposal at the resumption of the MBFR negotiations.

POSTSCRIPT

Andropov responded to Reagan's December 23 letter with a letter hand-delivered on January 30. Though there does not seem to be any indication of this at the time the letter was delivered, Andropov's response was really a dying mans last wish: An offer to eliminate intermediate range nuclear weapons in Europe if Britain, France and the U.S. would do so as well. Andropov also suggested smaller steps, like a moratorium on nuclear testing and discussions on reducing the threat from space-based nuclear warfare.

Dear Mr. President,
*   I have given careful thought to your letter of December 23. ... If one must state today that the affairs between our two countries are taking on, to put it frankly, an extremely unfavorable shape, then the reason for it is not our*

policy. We did not and do not want it to be so. On the contrary, we have been trying persistently not only to straighten up our relations but also to act in such a way that they develop constructively and in a stable manner. ...

The Soviet Union conducted serious and meaningful negotiations on the nuclear arms, doing the maximum to reach a mutually acceptable agreement. Unfortunately our efforts continued to run against a stonewall. In no way were we able to feel a desire on the part of the U.S. side to reach agreements. I will even add that while assessing the U.S. negotiating posture and practical actions, one cannot fail to draw a conclusion that the U.S. pursued a goal of a different nature – to challenge the security of our country and its allies. There has been nothing so far that convinces us otherwise. ...

We were prepared to accept very deep reductions both of the strategic and European nuclear weapons. With regard to the latter – even to the point of ridding Europe entirely of medium range and tactical nuclear weapons. The Soviet Union continues to be in favor of this. Having started the deployment of its new missiles which are strategic systems, as far as the USSR is concerned, the U.S. side destroyed the very basis on which it was possible to seek an agreement, we have only one view of this step – it is an attempt to upset both the regional and the global balance. So we are reacting accordingly. ...

Let us be frank, Mr. President, there is no way of making things look as if nothing has happened. There has been a disruption of the dialogue on the most important questions, a heavy blow has been dealt to the very process of nuclear arms limitation. The tension has grown dangerously. We know this, and you know this, too. In order to correct the situation, practical steps are required on the part of the U.S. side. ...

We see, so far, no signs that the U.S. is prepare to do so. ...

One cannot, we are convinced, speak of a desire to work for restraining the arms race and at the same time refuse to seek an agreement on the complete and general prohibition of nuclear weapon tests. Such a measure, large as it is, would effectively help slow down the qualitative and quantitative build-up of nuclear arms. This has long been a ripe issue. Many states speak in favor of having it solved.

A definitive step in this regard could also be the ratification of the Soviet-American treaties on the limitation of underground nuclear weapon tests and on nuclear explosions for peaceful purposes signed a decade ago. We have not seen and cannot see now convincing reasons why the United States does not do just that.

And why not try to look for a mutually acceptable solution to the problem of preventing militarization of outer space, while it is not too late to close this extremely dangerous channel of the arms race? We raise this issue as an urgent one which brooks no delay. In this context it is necessary also to solve the issue of banning and abolishing anti-satellite weapons. We have put forward our proposals. We would like you to read them once again with more attention.

They are based on the premise that the United States must have no less interest in solving this problem than the Soviet Union has. ...

Briefly, one more matter. It would be only natural if the desire to improve relations and establish a productive dialogue were accompanied by the creation of an appropriate atmosphere. At any rate, the inflation of animosity is not helpful.

Mr. President, I will be ready to listen to what you think with regard to the thoughts and specific points expressed in the present letter, which have occurred to me in connection with your letter.

Sincerely,

Y. Andropov

Andropov and Reagan, however, were nowhere near coming to an agreement. "The Soviet Union's unwillingness thus far to consider true arms reductions, and its massive increases in strategic offensive forces have necessitated continued U.S. actions to preserve our deterrent capabilities," Reagan ordered in a secret NSDD (NSDD 119) on the Strategic Defense Initiative, which he signed on January 6, 1984. Reagan, in NSDD 119, also ordered "Research on new strategic defense concepts utilizing nuclear devices … as a hedge against a Soviet ABM breakout." NSDD 119 can be viewed in full on The Reagan Files website.

PART III:

REAGAN AND CHERNENKO

CHAPTER FIVE

FEBRUARY 11 - DECEMBER 17, 1984

"It is my belief that the United States and the Soviet Union may be coming together more than many people realize."[13]

---

[13] Ronald Reagan to his NSC advisers during a December 5, 1984 meeting on U.S. Arms Control Objectives.

Konstantin Chernenko officially became the General Secretary of the Soviet Union on February 13. Two days earlier, Reagan signed off on a letter to Chernenko (in his capacity as Secretary of the Central Committee of the Communist Party) to be hand-delivered by Vice President Bush, who was traveling to Moscow for Andropov's funeral.

"I believe that this dialogue (between the U.S. and the Soviet Union) is so important that we should proceed with it as soon as your government is ready to do so." Reagan's letter, the first of what would turn out to be a series of letters with Chernenko, continues,

One area where practical steps are possible is the reduction of strategic arms. When you are ready, we have ideas on concrete ways to narrow the differences between our respective positions. The common framework we are prepared to discuss would incorporate elements of the current proposal of both sides and permit forces that are not identical, while providing for a more stable strategic balance at lower levels.

We are prepared to talk about such a framework in diplomatic channels. But we also believe that we need to return to the negotiating table. This applies to intermediate range as well as strategic nuclear forces. Here too, the world expects us to resume our discussions and find solutions.

Another area where practical steps are possible is the Vienna negotiations on conventional force reductions...

A practical and business-like approach could also be helpful in reducing the dangers of wider confrontation in the many regional problems in which our two nations' interests are involved...

Let me conclude by seeking to lay to rest some misunderstandings which may have arisen. The United States fully intends to defend our interests and those of our allies, but we do not seek to challenge the security of the Soviet Union and its people. We are prepared to deal with you in a manner that could establish the basis for mutually acceptable and mutually advantageous solutions to some of our problems.

Sincerely,
Ronald Reagan

Reagan did not even have to wait two weeks for a response.

February 23, 1984
Dear Mr. President:
We appreciate the kind feelings transmitted on your behalf by Mr. Bush....
I told Mr. Bush and would like to reaffirm it to you personally that our approach of principle to dealing with the United States remains unchanged.

This approach reflects a joint view of the Soviet leadership and enjoys a full support of the entire people of our country.

In conducting our foreign policy we will continue persistent efforts with the aim of strengthening the peace and lessening the danger of war. .....

In practical terms, this means also that our positions laid down, in particular in our message to you of January 28, remain in force. Therein, we clearly expressed our view as to the present state of affairs concerning the issues of nuclear weapons in Europe and in the area of strategic weapons, as well as with regard to the arms limitation and reduction process as a whole. We are expecting your reaction.

I would like, Mr. President, that you and I should have a clear understanding from the very beginning on the central matters of the relations between the USSR and the USA. These are the matters of security. The Soviet Union does not seek a military superiority, nor does it seek to dictate its will to others, but we will, of course, be safeguarding the interests of our security and those of our allies and friends from any attempts to damage those interests.

I believe, you will agree that in a nuclear age we must not allow the irreparable to take place, be it through design or mistake. We are not seeking a confrontation with the U.S. Such a confrontation would hardly be in the interests of your country, either. If you and I have a common understanding on this point, then it should be put into effect also in practical deeds.

From this standpoint it is important that restraint be exercised in everything, in matters big and small, and that both sides display the high degree of responsibility which is required by the interests of international security and stability. As a minimum, it is necessary to do nothing in the practical policy, that could exacerbate the situation and cause irreversible changes in Soviet-American relations as well as in the international situation as a whole.

We are convinced that it is impossible to begin to correct the present abnormal and, let's face it, dangerous situation, and to speak seriously of constructive moves, if there is a continuation of attempts to upset the balance of forces and to gain military advantage to the detriment of the security of the other side, if actions are taken prejudicing the legitimate interests of the other side.

There is another important point which the U.S. leadership must clearly understand: not only the U.S. has allies and friends. The Soviet Union has them too; and we will be caring for them.

We look at things realistically and have no illusion that it is possible to carry on business in total abstraction from the objective differences which exist between a socialist country and a capitalist country.

For instance, our morality does not accept much of what is endemic to the capitalist society and what we consider as unfair to people. Nevertheless, we do not introduce these problems into the sphere of interstate relationship. Just as we believe it is wrong and even dangerous to subordinate our relations to ideological differences.

These are the considerations of a general nature which I thought necessary to convey to you. As to the specific areas where the Soviet Union and the U.S. could, right now and with no time lost, move in a constructive way, those have been outlined by us, including in the message that I mentioned. I would like to expect that a positive reaction on your part will follow.

We have always been resolute advocates of a serious and meaningful dialogue – a dialogue that would be aimed at searching for common ground, at finding concrete and mutually acceptable solutions in those areas where it proves realistically possible.

In conclusion I will emphasize once again: a turn toward even and good relations between our two countries continues to be our desire. And such a turn is quite feasible, given the same desire on the U.S. side.

Sincerely,
K. Chernenko

Reagan responded two weeks later.

March 6, 1984
Dear Mr. General Secretary...
The strategic arms talks have always had as an important stumbling block the fact that our forces are not constructed – for understandable reasons of history and geography – along the same lines. We are concerned about the current imbalance in large, MIRVed (Multiple Independently-targetable Reentry Vehicles), land-based systems in favor of the USSR, which we consider to be the most destabilizing category of nuclear systems. You have criticized our proposals as one-sided and an attempt to restructure your forces without attendant change in our forces. This is not our intent.

Our purpose is to achieve significant reductions in the strategic systems of both sides. Such reductions need not result in identical force structures. The balance we seek must obviously take account of the interests of both sides. That is why in my earlier communications I suggested that we explore what types of reciprocal concessions might bring our interests into better balance.

In my letter presented by the Vice President I went further and suggested that we have ideas on concrete ways to narrow differences between our respective positions. The trade-offs we are prepared to discuss would, I believe, bridge the proposals of both sides and provide, as I said, a more stable balance at lower levels.

Reagan went on to suggest areas where improvements could be made: the hotline; more embassies; getting back to INF talks in Geneva and MBFR talks in Vienna. The letter then continues,

Mr. General Secretary, following his visit to Moscow, Vice President Bush conveyed to me your message that we should take steps to ensure that

history recalls us as leaders known to be good, wise and kind. Nothing is more important to me, and we should take steps to bring this about. For example, last year the agonizing situation of the Vashchenko and Chmykalov families was resolved. I was touched by this gesture. In my view, this shows how quiet and sincere efforts can solve even the most sensitive problems in our relationship. Similar humanitarian gestures this year also would touch the hearts of all Americans.

Therefore I conclude, as you did, that a "turn toward steady and good relations between our two countries" is desirable and feasible. I am determined to do my part in working for that end.

Sincerely,
Ronald Reagan

Chernenko's response, dated March 19, put the blame squarely on Reagan. "This step (the deployment of Pershing missiles in Europe) has become the main obstacle on the path of negotiations, it has undermined in general the process of limiting and reducing nuclear arms."

Chernenko also challenged Reagan to take concrete steps towards real reductions and listed four steps "the USSR and the U.S. should undertake on a priority basis."

1. *Initiate without delay – making a public announcement to this effect – a concrete discussion aimed at reaching an agreement on the prevention of the militarization of space and the prohibition of the use of force in outer space and from outer space against the Earth. We are prepared to conduct such negotiations at the level of specially appointed delegations and at the beginning stage through diplomatic channels if the U.S. side finds it more convenient. ...*

2. *Make, jointly or in parallel, a statement on the intention of the USSR and U.S. to implement the idea of nuclear weapons freeze and on their readiness to begin in this regard a meaningful exchange of views on the matter. The subject of such a discussion could be possible forms of freeze accord (a bilateral agreement, unilaterally taken obligations), the scope, thereof, etc.*

3. *Resume, in agreement with the British government, the trilateral negotiations on the complete and general ban of nuclear weapon tests. We believe that, given the goodwill, it would be possible to count here on rapid progress, considering a substantial amount of positive work done at the previous stage of the negotiations.*

4. *You know, Mr. President, that in my speech of March 2 I spoke in favor of having the nuclear powers adhere in their mutual relations to certain norms. This would meet the urgent requirements of the present day and help create such a climate that would raise the level*

of trust in international affairs, thereby facilitating the prevention of nuclear war and curbing the arms race.

The next page focuses on "regional issues" – the Middle East, South Africa and Central America – after which Chernenko continues,

In conclusion I would like to touch briefly on the area of bilateral relations between our countries. We have always been and remain to be advocates of active and really meaningful ties in a variety of fields, mutually beneficial and equal ties. The experience of a relatively recent past shows that this is possible.

If the U.S. side is truly ready at the present time to correct the abnormal situation that has developed in our bilateral relations as a result of its actions, it could be a welcome thing. We will judge if such a readiness is there by the practical steps the U.S. side will be taking in furtherance of the general concepts contained in your letter. We are instructing our Ambassador in Washington to discuss in greater detail these questions with the Secretary of State.

Sincerely,

K. CHERNENKO

Reagan, perhaps for the first time, thought the Soviet leader must have actually been serious. "I think this calls for a very well thought out reply and not just a routine acknowledgement that leaves the status quo as is," Reagan wrote on the top of the letter. Reagan's response, dated April 16, is discussed in the postscript to the March 27 meeting on nuclear arms control discussions.

Date: **March 27, 1984**
Subject: **Nuclear Arms Control Discussions**
Status: **Declassified (2006)**

SUMMARY

McFarlane introduces today's meeting by presenting the two questions for discussion:

1. What is the Soviet strategy toward arms control?
2. What does the Soviet strategy imply about our behavior for arms control and for dealing with our allies and for handling Congress?

McFarlane continues,

The CIA paper indicates that the Soviet Union is following a two pronged strategy aimed at diverting attention away from their walkout of START and INF and yet permitting them to keep the high ground by treating other issues such as ASAT, CDE, "no first use," etc. The Soviet Union has been implementing that strategy through private groups and Congress to get the United States to engage on the Soviet agenda. We also have a positive agenda: CBMs, Hotline, MBFR, CW, and others.

The United States can compile a positive agenda as well. We have the community of advisors looking at CIA study and asking how we should deal with the Soviet Union in arms control. Mr. President, you have received from your advisors and have read a number of papers expressing views as to how best to proceed. Overall, there is much agreement. For example, everyone agrees that we should reject the Soviet agenda and establish our own agenda. However, there is also some disagreement on what should be our positive agenda and how we should deal with negative Soviet behavior such as non-compliance and the walkouts. In short, we do not have complete agreement on how we validate the record of three-years of effort. Today, we will hear from the President's key advisors.

The discussion follows.

WEINBERGER: My paper begins by asking the question, "What is the interest of the Soviet Union in reaching an agreement this year? And it concludes with the answer that there is very little evidence that they are interested in an agreement. We need to focus on the content of an agreement, not on agreement for agreement's sake. The Soviet Union has little interest in giving the President a victory. They would only give him an agreement for which he could not take credit. What are they interested in? A SALT II agreement that did not provide for reductions?

To get an agreement they will require us to make major concessions. Those who talk of a new framework are really talking about going back to SALT II ½. The Soviet Union has walked out on three talks. We should make our case based on the merits. The zero-option was very popular and the only reason it was rejected was because the Soviet Union wanted a monopoly. They walked out because we would not agree to their having a monopoly. We want more than a piece of paper; we want real reductions. They are now violating SALT II; SALT II means we won't worry about throw-weight. We should be vigorously defending our proposals and pressing the Soviet Union to return to the table. That doesn't mean that there are not things we can negotiate now. We should press to renegotiate the TTBT (Threshold Test Ban Treaty). We can negotiate a full ban on chemical weapons with full verification. We can negotiate notification of ballistic missile tests and Hotline improvements. If we become too eager the Soviet Union will sense weakness.

And even if we get them back to the negotiations, they can set you up for a later walkout when it will hurt most. The reality is that no one across the table is in charge – they have a collegial organization. General Secretary Chernenko is not only not responding, he wouldn't even receive the letter that Scowcroft carried. We should emphasize our proposals, we should make clear that we are ready, and we should speak out on the compliance issue.

SHULTZ: I have a list of ten do's and don'ts, really, six don'ts and four do's.

1. Don't base policy on speculations about the Soviet Union.
2. Don't negotiate with ourselves or Congress.
3. Don't make concessions for the purpose of getting the Soviets back to the table, but we can reorganize our positions to make them more presentable.
4. Don't get into the position where you need an agreement.
5. It is a mistake to change our positive posture on arms control into a negative one because this risks loss of public support, the Congress, and our allies.
6. Don't rest on past work; let's keep working to be prepared. The process is veto prone and therefore we can't let fear of leaks delay the effort.
7. We must continue to set positive messages that we are prepared to deal across the board – look at START and INF for better ways to present our position.
8. We should be prepared to take parts of the Soviet position and shouldn't be against everything in SALT. The Secretary of Defense uses the word "framework" as if it were a swear word. We need to move on MBFR and we need to go further, depending on the Soviet response. We should move quickly on the CW (Chemical Weapons) Treaty and the Hotline. We should move on CDE (Confidence and Security-Building Measures and Disarmament in Europe) and we could move on TTBT if we could manage a decision to take it on forthrightly.
9. We should look at the fundamental differences between us and the Soviets in START. You can debate over whether START or INF is more

important, but I don't see how you can move on START without considering INF.

10. We should look to see what is important for us, and with all due respect to the CIA analysis, they could be wrong.[14]

ADELMAN: I agree with much of what has been said, but I want to remind you, Mr. President, that I worked with the campaign during the hostage crisis and negotiations with Iran and saw the dangers of setting oneself up for an agreement – the risks are great. To answer the mail, we must show that we have sound policies and are serious about arms control. We need to identify areas where movement is possible.

In INF, we've identified a proposal that would have the Soviets reduce to a level which we would stop at. We could negotiate such a step or it could be a declaratory policy. We could attempt to reach a US-Soviet understanding on non-proliferation. We could develop rules of the road or proper behavior through space-CMS in the CDE. We could work with our allies to set the stage for a policy of no early use of nuclear weapons – we could look at different ways to package this and move slowly and cautiously.

VESSEY: We must maintain the momentum of our defense build-up at the highest levels possible. We must protect the President's strategic modernization program. We must keep the alliance together, and we must cap or reverse the Soviet military buildup – Soviets can't or won't negotiate until after elections. The Scowcroft coalition and support on the Hill need tending. The allies are not carrying the load.

CASEY: We must make judgments about the Soviets, but we have a fair amount of history. We can assume that Moscow is not anxious to help the President, but they don't want to appear intransigent. They believe that treaties in START and INF are out of reach. Clearly, the prospects for getting an agreement are remote. We should

---

[14] Shultz is likely referring to a December 30, 1985 CIA paper entitled, "Soviet Thinking on the Possibility of Armed Confrontation with the United States." The CIA concludes that the Soviet's "do not appear to anticipate a near-term military confrontation with the United States…Soviet policymakers, however, almost certainly are very concerned that trends they foresee in long-term US military programs could erode the USSR's military gains of the past fifteen years, heighten US political leverage, and perhaps increase the chances of confrontation." (RRPL: WHSOF of Jack Matlock. Folder: Matlock Chron Jan. 1984 (2/3) Box 90887.)

continue to assess our own interest. We can accomplish something on second order issues. At CDE, we can trade Western confidence building measures for a non-aggression pact.

ROWNY: It is clear there is not a consensus on how to get the Soviet Union back to the table, but I believe they might even return on their own. The Soviet's didn't really explore what was in the trade-offs for them. They may come back when they see that there is really something in it for them. If we show a little ankle, maybe a little thigh, then you can get movement.

There is no chance for a full START agreement this year, and speculation on an Interim Agreement is dangerous. Vladivostok[15] is better precedent, an aide memoir is safest. The Soviet Union never closed the door on START.

NITZE: We should seek U.S. objectives, but we are already clear on that. The issue is tactical. It is not impossible to get an agreement, but 90% chance you won't. It is wholly unlikely that Moscow will negotiate seriously in an election year. What does one do? One does the CW Treaty – that is a perfectly solid thing to do. There is no chance the Soviets will agree to that. But it is dangerous to be solidly engaged in START or INF in an election year.

WEINBERGER: I don't disagree with Secretary Shultz's 10 points, only with the interpretation of them. At this time, we will have to pay a very high price to get an agreement. We have all agreed that we shouldn't make any concessions to get them back to the table. All agreed that we don't want to get into a position where we must have an agreement. We can keep up our work, but we don't want to further weaken our proposals. We can keep sending messages that we are ready to negotiate, but that is hard to do in an empty room. I agree that we should do what we can do in lesser areas, but I'm very worried about space arms control. Also, talk of a START "framework" is a codeword I'm opposed to.

REAGAN: **We are all not as far apart as it might seem. There is no question that the Soviet Union is trying to make us look non-cooperative. I believe the Soviets**

---

[15] Site of the 1974 Strategic Arms Limitation Talks at which President Ford and General Secretary Brezhnev agreed to freeze construction of land-based ICBM launchers.

want to avoid the onus for having walked out of Geneva.

In my answer to the letter from Chernenko, we should recognize that we have opposite views on who is threatened. We should cite their quotations that are threatening to us; we should cite their buildup. Then we could cite the fact that in the 1940's we proposed to do away with all these systems and they said no. Nineteen times since then we have tried to reach agreements, for example, Eisenhower's open sky proposal. We can't go on negotiating with ourselves. We can't be supplicants crawling, we can't look like failures.

I've read the papers and made some notes. Let me share them with you. They want to avoid the onus of walking out, therefore, it is unlikely that they will give us anything in START and INF right now. We want an agreement but we want a good agreement. I do not intend to make unilateral concessions to get them back to the table, but I believe we must have a full credible agenda on arms control. Maybe we could build a record.

Mitterrand believed that they would give us the cold shoulder for several months; therefore, we will need to do lesser things – MBFR, chemical weapons, confidence building, notification of all ballistic missile tests, agreement not to encrypt, and CDE. But we shouldn't let them off the hook on START and INF; we must keep the pressure on. To do this we need solid, flexible positions, on both START and INF.

I don't want to fall into the trap of SALT II, but if there are some things that are good, then we shouldn't ignore them simply because they are part of SALT II. For example, having a launcher limit isn't wrong, so long as it is matched by warhead and throw-weight limits. In short, we need a position which takes part of their approach and melds it with ours so that they have a fig leaf for coming off their position.

I think that my letter to Chernenko should be substantive and positive along these lines and stressing that they have an obligation to resume START and INF talks. Perhaps we should offer to have Ed Rowny and Paul Nitze engage in private talks with the Russians.

I would like to table the chemical treaty before we set off for China. I think the Senior Arms Control Policy Group should accelerate their work and present me with options for new START/INF positions within a few weeks. This is for us, not for the INF public (position). Maybe we should consider a speech in a few months to bring out our record. George (Shultz), I want you to be our public spokesman on arms control. Leaks and gratuitous backgrounders have got to stop. I understand we have procedures for dealing with clearing testimony. I think we should work in private channels but we will not crawl, we will build a record.

MCFARLANE: We have our instructions, now we have to get down to work.

REAGAN: **Are there any disagreements?**

WEINBERGER: I'm concerned that your guidance not be misunderstood. In a few days *The New York Times* may be reporting that the President has ordered new proposals on START and INF -- aren't we talking about what we didn't say, but could say about our proposals?

ROWNY: The Soviet Union has not listened to all that we had to say in Geneva.

NITZE: What we are really talking about is fleshing out our positions.

REAGAN: **Ken Adelman has a good idea on INF about their reducing to a level which we would reach at the end of 1985. Something like that might be an option worth looking at.**

WEINBERGER: Some of our allies might use this as an excuse not to do what must be done on deployments.

ADELMAN: I agree.

WEINBERGER: We should agree that we will fill out our position.

REAGAN: **My letter to Chernenko is an opportunity to get their attention. Have we given enough attention to the fact that they have a climate of insecurity?**

MCFARLANE: Mr. President, we will press on with the guidance. We will make no pre-emptive concessions, flesh out our positions and be ready if they return, and prepare to table a chemical weapons treaty before the China trip.

POSTSCRIPT

The letter discussed in today's meeting, sent on April 16, is reproduced below.

Dear Mr. General Secretary...

As you know, your country's deployment of the SS-20 has been of especially grave concern both to the United States and our allies. Since NATO's December 1970 decision, when your country asserted that a "balance" existed in intermediate-range nuclear forces, the Soviet Union has deployed 238 additional SS-20's with over 700 additional warheads. These missiles constitute a far greater threat to the security of the western alliance – both in quantitative and qualitative terms – than previous Soviet missiles, which had fewer warheads and lower accuracy. ...

If the Soviet Union is prepared to negotiate seriously on such concrete confidence-building measures, the United States will be prepared to discuss the question of reciprocal assurances against the use of force and the context in which such an agreement can be reached. You have asked for a "concrete signal" in the area of arms control, and your representatives have specified that U.S. willingness to agree on non-use of force would be considered such a signal. In this connection let me add that I am pleased that our Ambassadors to the Stockholm conference have agreed to get together soon. This will provide an opportunity to discuss an agreement that would meet both countries' concerns.

Skipping a page, Reagan finally answered Chernenko's offer to reduce intermediate range missiles in Europe to equal numbers.

I am well aware of your views regarding the impasse in these negotiations. You are, I am, sure, equally aware of the fact that we and our allies do not agree with your analysis of the balance in intermediate-range missiles or your assessment of the "obstacles" that supposedly stand in the way of further negotiations. For our part, we are prepared to consider any equitable outcome, and to halt, reverse or eliminate entirely our deployment of Pershing and cruise missiles in the context of an agreement between the two sides.

After a few pages on regional issues and another paragraph on human rights, Reagan closes the letter,

To conclude, let me state once again that the United States is ready for a turning point in our relations with the Soviet Union. We have made a concerted effort to put content into our dialogue. We have a number of specific ideas to explore with you on questions of vital importance to both our peoples. We intend to continue our efforts in this direction. Real progress, however, will require similar efforts on the part of the Soviet Union.

I look forward to receiving your comments on the thoughts I have expressed.

Sincerely,
Ronald Reagan

Underneath his signature, paying tribute to his concern at the March 27 meeting that the U.S. has not "given enough attention to the fact that they have a climate of insecurity," Reagan handwrote the postscript. A typed version can be found in the endnotes.

His Excellency
Konstantin Ustinovich Chernenko
Chairman, Presidium of the Supreme
Soviet of the Union of Soviet
Socialist Republics
Moscow

Shultz received Chernenko's response on June 6.

Dear Mr. President,

I, of course, took note of the pledge of commitment to the lessening of tensions between our countries made by you in the handwritten addition to your letter. In turn, I can affirm once again what I wrote in my letter to you – namely, that it has been and continues to be our wish that there be a turn toward steady, good relations between the USSR and the USA. As a matter of fact, the numerous specific proposals submitted by our side, including those proposals put forward in my letters to you, have been aimed at reaching that objective.

As regards interpreting a certain period in the history of our relations, about which you had already written once before, here our views differ. We have presented our point of view in this regard, so I will not repeat myself. I will note, however, that one side's having military superiority or seeking such superiority cannot be perceived by the other side as an indication of good intentions. There can be only one indication – a willingness to conduct affairs as equals, a willingness reflected in practical terms. The position of the Soviet Union in this regard is clear and precise: we are not seeking superiority, but we will not allow superiority over us. I do not see anything here that should be unacceptable to the United States, if one wants stability and a lessening of tensions. It is from a position of equality that it is possible to agree on really mutually-acceptable solutions, when neither side can have reasons to believe that it is making unilateral concessions.

Let us take the current situation. There is, it seems, an American idiom "to turn the table." Try to look at the realities of the international equation from our end. And at once one will see distinctly that the Soviet Union is encircled by a chain of American military bases. These bases are full of nuclear weapons. Their mission is well known – they are targeted on us. Nothing like it can be found around your country.

And what about the fact that entire regions of the globe have been proclaimed spheres of American vital interests? And not only proclaimed, but made the object of a U.S. military presence. And this is done, among other places, at our very doorstep. And again we, for our part, are not doing anything like it. What conclusions should we draw from this as to the intentions of the U.S.? I believe the conclusions readily present themselves. Such an approach is nothing other than a hypertrophied idea of one's interests in which the legitimate interests of others are completely ignored, an effort to gain, to put it mildly, positions of privilege at the expense of the other side. This approach is not compatible with the objective of ensuring stability. On the contrary, such an approach as a matter of policy objectively helps to create and sustain tensions.

Or let us take strategic arms. Here, too, no claims can be directed toward the Soviet Union. The fact that there is rough parity between the USSR and the USA and, in a wider sense, between the Warsaw Pact and NATO, can be disputed by no expert familiar with the situation. The SALT-2 Treaty was a reflection of this fact. It was not the end of the road, and we did not consider it as such. But the merit of the treaty was, among other things, that it established, I would say, with mathematical precision the strategic balance that has evolved.

Your military experts can tell you that the Soviet Union has done nothing to upset this balance. At the same time we see what kind of attitude is displayed toward the Treaty by the other side. Is it not the criterion by which to judge its intentions?

The same applies as well to medium-range nuclear forces in Europe. I will recall only that it was we who offered to reduce their number to the minimum on the side of the USSR and NATO. In response, "Pershings" and cruise missiles are appearing near our borders. How would you regard it, Mr. President, had something similar happened with respect to the U.S. I believe but that your assessment of the intentions of the other side under the circumstances could only be one – as regards both the other side's approach to negotiations and the essence of its intentions.

But even under these circumstances we have displayed and continue to display utmost restraint. The response we were forced to take, in terms of its scope and character, has not gone beyond the limits necessary to neutralize the threat posed to us and our allies. Moreover, we propose to return to the initial situation and, instead of further unleashing an arms race, to address ourselves in a decisive fashion to curbing the arms race, and to radically limiting and reducing nuclear arms. This is far from imposing conditions. As a matter of fact, what is unfair about the two sides cancelling those measures whose effect was to heighten the level of nuclear confrontation and, conversely, to lessen global security? There can be nothing unfair or damaging for either side in this. A return to the previous situation in the present circumstances would constitute forward movement by both sides toward stabilizing the situation, toward the practical renewal of the entire process of limiting nuclear weapons that is of decisive importance for the future of international relations and for peace as such.

So far, however, we see no indication that the American side proceeds from such an assumption. Regrettably, nothing new on this major issue of the day can be found in your letter either. I say this not for the sake of polemics, but rather in the hope that you will still find it possible to appreciate the way out of the extremely grave situation that we are suggesting.

Chernenko goes on to remind Reagan that he previously proposed "renouncing the construction of large-scale anti-ballistic missile defense systems, entering into negotiations on preventing the militarization of outer space and on banning anti-satellite weapons, a freeze on nuclear weapons, resuming talks on a complete and comprehensive ban on nuclear" but "we have not received a response to these proposals".

Two-more pages followed on possible areas of progress in Stockholm at the CDE, including a chemical weapons treaty, before Chernenko concluded with a strong rebuke of Reagan's latest attempt to interject human rights issues into U.S.-Soviet relations.

I do not want to conclude this letter on a negative note, but in view of some of the remarks in your letter, I must point out that introduction into relations between states of questions concerning solely domestic affairs of our country or yours does not serve the task of improving these relations – if this is our goal. I wish questions of such a nature did not burden our correspondence, which both of us, as I understand it, value.

Reagan, however, continued to quietly raise human rights issues, and his persistence was rewarded as over time several soviet citizens were allowed to emigrate. Reagan also responded with a letter dated July 2 to let Chernenko know that he was still thinking about a response to the June 6 proposals, but wanted to quickly respond to his June 29 proposal for a conference in Vienna to talk about the "militarization of outer space."

First, let me say that I believe your proposal for a conference is an excellent idea. I am prepared to have a delegation in Vienna September 18...

Let me describe my concept of the way a useful conference might be organized. I believe that each of our delegations should be free to raise questions of concern to its side which are relevant to the overall topic. However, these should not be raised merely for the sake of exposition and debate, but with a clear mandate to seek out and find mutually acceptable negotiating approaches which hold promise for concrete results.

I have studied the position you have taken regarding the resumption of negotiations on nuclear arms. Even though I cannot agree with your reasons, I am not asking you to change that position in order to start discussions. But inasmuch as strategic and intermediate-range nuclear weapons systems are the most lethal systems and are intimately associated with those other space weapons on which you propose to negotiate, it is clear that it will be difficult to move very far in solving some of the problems without addressing the others. It would, therefore, be difficult to understand a refusal even to discuss ways that negotiations on nuclear systems might be resumed. As I have pointed out to you several times, I have a number of ideas as to how these problems might be resolved to the advantage of both our countries. I believe that it is in our mutual interest to resolve our current impasse on offensive nuclear weapons.

Regarding the other space weapons referred to in your proposal, I am optimistic that we can find significant aspects of anti-satellite weaponry which would be a fruitful object for negotiations. In sum, I am agreeable to a conference without preconditions of any sort, but one based on a commitment by both of us to find mutually acceptable negotiating approaches to the important question before us.

You spoke in your last letter about the necessity of dealing with each other as equals. Naturally, I agree, and I believe the approach I have outlined for a conference embodies this principle in both form and spirit. As we have both often observed, it is time for deeds. Finding ways to make progress on the central issues I have outlined would be a deed for which the whole world would thank us.

Of course, we need not wait until a conference is organized to discuss the issues before us. I will be pleased to continue our discussion of these and related topics, on a confidential basis, both in our correspondence and through our respective representatives.

Mr. Chairman, I look forward to receiving your thoughts on these matters. It is my earnest hope that you will join me in seizing the opportunity we have to make a major step toward improving relations between our countries and creating a safer world for all.

Sincerely,

Ronald Reagan

It took just five days for a response.

Dear Mr. President:

I have carefully read your letter of July 2, 1984. Let me say frankly that I was looking in it for a positive response to our proposal to hold Soviet-American negotiations this September on preventing the militarization of outer space. Regrettably, there is no such response in the letter.

One has to reach such a conclusion despite the fact that you express readiness to start negotiations in Vienna. For from your letter it clearly follows that the U.S. is not agreeing to participate in the kind of negotiations which the Soviet side proposes and in which it is prepared to participate.

Let me recall that the Soviet Union favors the adoption of urgent measures which would enable us effectively to block all channels for extending the arms race into space. This can be done by banning all space attack systems, which is precisely what we propose to have negotiations about, and by establishing a moratorium, simultaneously with the start of negotiations, on testing and deployment of such systems.

The American side essentially is talking about conducting not negotiations on space, but some sort of "conference" without a definite agenda, i.e. there would be a conversation about everything and about nothing specifically.

We are far from underestimating the importance of questions of nuclear armaments, which in your letter are linked with the problem of space. You know our position with regard to how to solve these questions. But as before, nothing points to the readiness of the American side to take into account this position and open the way out of the present impasse. Banning space weapons is a problem of great importance in its own right. To tie it to questions of limiting and reducing nuclear arms, which are in fact currently blocked, would be to put negotiations on space attack weapons into a stalemated position as well. At the same time, the deployment of space attack weapons would inevitably lead to a sharp escalation of the arms race on earth too, and would complicate all the more the possibility of undertaking effective measures for limiting and reducing armaments in general. We are convinced that such a development of events would serve nobody's interests.

As for space weapons themselves, the emphasis here should, of course, not be on studying something. It is necessary to reach agreement on practical measures in order to prevent the appearance of space attack weapons of any kind. This is also what determines the concrete questions put forward by the USSR for negotiations, in order to resolve the problem in all its aspects and in a radical way.

We approach these negotiations seriously and responsibly, and we expect the same attitude from the American side. If, however, for some reason it is difficult for you to give consent to such negotiations at the time we suggested, we would have to take that into account. It is important that we be in agreement that such negotiations are necessary, and that we will conduct them without unjustifiable delays.

In conclusion I wish to emphasize the main point once again. There cannot be any doubt that it is more sensible to exclude space from military competition in advance, rather than trying later on to eliminate the otherwise inevitable, serious and perhaps even irreparable damage to stability and security. I appeal to you, Mr. President, to look at this whole problem once again from this perspective. I would like to hope that you could give a positive reply to our proposal, which remains in force.

Sincerely,

K. Chernenko

Reagan's response, on July 18, clarified that he accepted "your Government's proposal to begin talks in Vienna on September 18" without any preconditions. Reagan also suggested that their diplomatic representatives immediately get together to define the agenda, but that it was not reasonable to talk about the "militarization of space" without also resuming "negotiations on offensive nuclear arms." Reagan added: "These are in fact the most destructive weapons in our hands, and if we cannot find ways to reduce the dangers they present, whatever efforts we make in other areas will be severely hampered."

Chernenko tried to get Reagan to be more specific, and on July 21 proposed a joint-statement that the U.S. and Soviet Union had agreed "to begin negotiations with the aim of working out and concluding an agreement on preventing the militarization of outer space, including complete mutual renunciation of anti-satellite systems, and to establish from the day of the beginning of the negotiations a mutual moratorium on testing and deployment of space weapons."

Five-days later, on July 26, after receiving the American response Chernenko sent off another angry letter attacking Reagan for not really accepting without preconditions the June 29 proposal to discuss the "militarization of outer-space". Chernenko got straight to the point:

The draft statement proposed by the American side has nothing at all to do with the negotiations which we proposed. Instead of negotiations on outer space, it speaks of some "meeting to discuss and to define approaches for negotiating" and it is absolutely unclear what the negotiations will be about.

To put it briefly, Mr. President, no doubt whatsoever now remains that the American side is not prepared to conduct negotiations with the aim of preventing the militarization of outer space.

If his earlier statements were unclear on how he really felt, Chernenko left no doubt in his concluding paragraph:

I repeat, we regret that the current American position makes it impossible to conduct the negotiations. Should this position subsequently change – and we would like to hope this will happen – and should the wish be expressed on the part of the U.S. to start negotiations with the aim of reaching agreement on the complete and unconditional prohibition of space weapons, we would be ready to return to consideration of this issue. In other words, our position, as it was presented in the statement by the Soviet Government of June 29, remains in force.

Reagan was not about to let Chernenko off the hook, and just two-days later signed off on a letter agreeing to a conference on the "militarization of outer space". "The concept of the 'militarization of outer space' is a broad one, and as I have indicated previously, in my view accommodates offensive as well as defensive systems," Reagan told Chernenko. "Your side may have a different concept, but the important thing at this stage is for our negotiators to meet in Vienna and work out whatever differences may exist." Reagan also sent a proposed joint-statement that differed from the Soviet version in that it did not mention an immediate moratorium on testing.

Chernenko, again, was not going to let Reagan push him into agreeing to something that he did not propose. His response, three-days later, made clear how far apart the differences of opinion were on what should be negotiated in Vienna.

Dear Mr. President,

I agree completely that the subject of our correspondence requires complete candor.

In the spirit of such frankness, I cannot but object categorically to the fact that the American side continues with its persistent attempts to distort the very essence of our proposal of June 20. This is evident from your letter, too.

You write, for example, that we supposedly proposed that negotiations begin on questions of the "militarization of outer-space." We have, however, proposed and continued to propose that negotiations be conducted on the prevention of the militarization of outer-space. These things are different in principle.

Further, an integral part of our proposal of June 29 is the establishment of a mutual basis, beginning from the date of the opening of the negotiations, of a moratorium on the testing and deployment of space weapons. It was also stated quite clearly in my letter to you of July 7.

Since in your reply of July 18 you wrote that you accepted our proposal without preconditions, we naturally were entitled to believe that you agreed to introduce a moratorium as well. Now, however, the American side refuses to include in the joint statement a provision regarding a moratorium. The question of a moratorium is also passed over in complete silence in your last letter. The conclusion from this is inescapable.

The case is exactly the same as regards the attitude of the American side toward another integral part of the proposal – to the effect that, within the framework of the negotiations, the issue of complete, mutual renunciation of anti-satellite systems also be resolved.

Such is the actual state of affairs, Mr. President. The facts show that, stating its acceptance of our proposal without preconditions, the American side actually speaks about negotiations with the aim not of prohibiting but, in fact, of legalizing space weapons. And in addition, it also drags into them weapons which have nothing to do with the subject of the negotiations we have proposed.

You are certainly free, Mr. President, to put forward any proposal of yours. But why should the public be misled by purporting that the U.S. accepts our proposal? Why should the impression be created that the Soviet Union were backing away from its own proposal?

As far as we are concerned, our proposal continues to remain in force, but it is precisely the proposal which was made public in the Statement of the Soviet government of June 29 and which was outlined in my letters to you. We did not put forward any other proposal which could be construed simply as an invitation "to go to Vienna." Anyone who familiarizes himself with our correspondence can easily see that.

K. Chernenko

This was the last letter found between Reagan and Chernenko until November. The next declassified meeting, on September 18, also discusses these correspondences and why the Vienna negotiations never materialized.

Date: **September 18, 1984**
Subject: **Next Steps in the Vienna Process (MBFR)**
Status: **Declassified in Part (2005)**

SUMMARY

MCFARLANE: Over the last four months we have worked in developing a position on anti-satellite systems that would be in the U.S. interest and aid stability. On June 29, the Soviets offered to talk to us about the militarization of space. We agreed, but reformulated their offer so as not to let the Soviets off the hook on discussing offensive systems. Since that time the interagency has concluded its work in planning against two contingencies:

1.   What should be the U.S. position if the Soviets agree to the talks?
2.   How should we handle the situation if they do not agree to the talks?

Three alternative approaches were developed. Each addresses both anti-satellite capabilities and offensive systems.

The first option suggests that we use a Vienna meeting to simply discuss with the Soviets issues of concern to both sides. Option II suggests that we use such a meeting to negotiate an incidents-in-space agreement. Such an agreement would provide rules of the road for space operations and would largely depend upon goodwill. It would be more of a statement of intent to abide by these rules of the road than anything else. Option II also suggests that we could possibly offer not to test our anti-satellite systems against high-altitude objects if others show similar restraint, and to suspend testing of the F-15 system after completing some certain number of tests.

With respect to offensive systems, this option would have us encourage the Soviets to return to the negotiating table by signaling our willingness to discuss possible trade-offs, e.g., limits on bombers and cruise missiles. This approach would have us implicitly link negotiations on ASAT limitation or changes to other arms control positions to specific progress in negotiations.

This approach would also make it clear that we are willing to talk about the offensive – defensive force relationship and to discuss how we could both move toward a greater reliance on defensive forces while maintaining stability.

Option III suggests a comprehensive proposal envisioning two phases. In Phase One, we would suggest to the Soviets that we agree to a temporary moratorium on the testing of specific ASAT interceptors and an interim agreement to cap or limit offensive systems. This cap could perhaps include INF forces. This agreement would also involve a commitment to certain objections for later phases of negotiations.

Phase Two would involve a long-term ban on the testing and deployment of ASAT interceptors. This would require the Soviets to dismantle their existing ASAT systems. It would also involve the negotiating of an incidents-in-space agreement. On the other hand, with respect to offensive forces, we would expect progress toward deep reductions, a discussion of the offensive-defensive force relationship, and in the context of these items, we would consider whether we would accept limits on defensive systems.

Beyond the content of these specific options, we must consider how the Soviets are currently looking at arms control and what the Soviet calculus may be. For example, when will it be in their interest to engage the U.S. across-the-board in this area? It may be that our assessment will argue against any proposals being made right now. To make such proposals may cause us to appear too anxious and may signal to the Soviets that they could coerce us into concessions. The other view that one could hold is that pursing any initiatives now would demonstrate U.S. leadership and put the Soviets on the defensive. Could we have agency views on the issue?

SHULTZ: We should try to move the ball along now. To do so, we need to make reasonably concrete proposals.

First of all, unconstrained military growth by the Soviet Union is not to our advantage. We have more difficulty with the politics of modernization than they do. Reductions are to our advantage.

Secondly, the Soviets' Vienna proposal has some interesting aspects. For example, it provides us the opportunity to change the venue from Geneva, and it provides a way to rearrange the situation to permit them to go back to the table at a different place (i.e., saving face).

Third, the idea of holding simultaneous discussion of offensive and defensive systems is good. They are worried about our SDI program.

We should take timely action on this. We should show to the Soviets where they could go with the U.S. at this time. We need to put out enough concreteness to demonstrate to Gromyko that we are interested in serious negotiations.

I think a quick interim agreement would be to our advantage. We could go on from there to a better agreement. Short-term constraints may be a real benefit to us.

With respect to your upcoming UNGA speech, any arms control initiatives offered in such a speech would not be viewed by the Soviets as serious. I feel we should make our points privately and make them directly to Gromyko.

MCFARLANE: We are all agreed on that point.

WEINBERGER: Now is a very inappropriate time for any proposals (for the following reasons):

- There is no interagency position on ASAT or defensive systems;
- The Soviets most fear SDI and that will be what they urge us to give up;
- What we limit on an interim basis now could harm us in the future. This applies to a temporary ASAT moratorium as well as an interim agreement on offensive forces;
- We will find it impossible to back away from an interim agreement;
- We are not ready to set the trend which a set of interim agreements establishes;
- We would be binding ourselves at a time when the Soviet leadership is in a state of turmoil.

With Gromyko, Mr. President, I would recommend that you affirm your commitment to genuine reductions. Make it clear you are prepared for general discussion but discussions aimed at framing specific negotiations. Note the advantages and disadvantages of our different force structures…

Now is the worst time in the world for a temporary ASAT moratorium interim agreement proposal. It can lead us to preclude SDI development, and interagency agreement is lacking.

We should use the Gromyko meeting to reaffirm U.S. commitments and the need for resumption of START/INF. Beyond this, we should stay flexible. We could set the stage for more substantive talks later.

Given the total lack of verifiability associated with ASAT options and no real Soviet government, any accord would prematurely bind us to patterns of behavior not in our interest.

KELLEY: I echo the Secretary Weinberger. We should avoid a premature accord which binds our SDI activity. Our understanding of the relationship between offensive and defensive systems and SDI is vague at best.

ADELMAN: I would recommend Option Two once we are in the negotiations. But the real problem is, how do we get back into negotiations? If the Soviets are serious, we need to find a way. We could have a delegation go to talk about offensive and defensive systems, SDI, START, INF, and ASAT, along the lines of SALT I.

I would avoid concrete proposals now. We should only pursue general discussion because the Soviets will pocket specific proposals. On interim accords – it's a good idea to seek reductions, but the reductions should not be interim. It's too optimistic to hope for militarily significant reductions any quicker by approaching the project as an interim accord.

With respect to your meeting with Gromyko, we should revisit the idea of on-site inspection of our sites and theirs, and move on a Threshold Test Ban Treaty (TTBT).

KIRKPATRICK: (I don't have any comments.)

CASEY: I agree with Cap (Secretary Weinberger) and General Kelley. The Soviets want to cut SDI. Bellikov is here in the U.S. trying to build Backfire as a counter to SDI. There are two in Geneva who tell that there has been a fivefold increase in science to counter SDI; trying for counter measures by cutting IR plume of ICBMs by 60 percent or by a small nuclear explosion in space; they are worried about optics.

This degree of open discussion is unusual in the amount of detail concerning Soviet plans. It is authorized to create a public backwash.

The Soviets see ASAT as an opening wedge to SDI. We could entangle ourselves on SDI via ASAT. There could be an opportunity if we are able to handle ASAT as a part of discussions of the range of offensive and defensive systems; then ASAT weapons would be only a small portion of all weapons.

Option One is an approach which could provide a framework for the future. We should work toward the future.

SHULTZ: I agree with most but not all of this. We should use ASAT both as a stalking horse to protect SDI and as a way to get limits on offensive systems.

The idea of waiting for the interagency group to agree is a non-starter. The IG never agrees. It we wait for it to agree, nothing will go to the President. The IG is not a fourth branch of government. We can't give it a veto power.

The idea of a general palaver now and specifics later is unreal. We have been around four years, what have we been doing?

REAGAN: **Gromyko's visit may have an effect. I had not anticipated specifics.**

I have to believe that the USSR (mainly its leaders) has a world aggression program, but in meetings we have to show an understanding of its concerns: a fear of invasion, a fear of being surrounded. It's the only country in the world with an internal passport. During World War II, no allied planes were routinely permitted to land in the USSR. Since World War II they approach us with suspicion; they're not getting soft. Maybe we have tried too hard for specifics; we fear world aggression.

Maybe we need a general discussion to clear the air, telling them here are the reasons why we fear your actions. We are not going to seek advantage, but we will keep our defenses up.

The Soviet must be made to have a healthy respect. They must know we will stay even. This being the case, our mutual choices are: We can keep going up and up, or reduce down to a point neither side is a threat.

We should avoid an arms race which impoverishes both sides. We should explore in a general way how to get agreement, and if there is any agreement, then discussions on specifics can follow later.

WEINBERGER: It's important that you let them see your desire for reducing but also that we are not going to permit them to maintain an advantage. If we get into specifics we are likely to preemptively preclude areas where our greatest hopes lie. We could be playing into their hands, limiting what they fear – like Pershing II.

About the IG: My point is not that they decide; my point is they haven't sent you options on this subject so that you can see options and agency positions.

Viewing this meeting as a theater for progress is wrong. Let him (Gromyko) leave knowing that we have strength and will, then lets discuss reductions.

REAGAN: **We need to understand the other actors pushing us to make reductions. We have weaknesses we must correct soon – they don't. Without us honestly moving on track, Congress will prevent us from doing what's needed.**

We can't ignore developing specific proposals.

You are tempting me with the idea of having no IG papers to review.

We need to take care. We are moving toward defense programs that could make certain destabilizing offensive weapons useless. We don't want to be trapped from that path. However, with respect to ASAT – maybe we could make some progress, maybe through some high-level informal discussion.

The idea of an interim agreement is aimed at carrying us until we can find a way back to a more comprehensive agreement.

WEINBERGER: The Soviets did cave in the face of U.S. resolve during the Cuban missile crisis. But, of most importance is the simple fact that an interim agreement is not interim; as a first stage, it has total lack of verifiability. They have no public or Congress to deal with. They can engage in interim policies that we can't. They need to see and know your resolve.

REAGAN: **During the Cuban missile crisis we had an eight to one advantage. They said they'd never be in that position again.**

WEINBERGER: We must recognize that our ASAT program is linked to SDI in many ways. The Soviets are working on defense just as hard as we are.

KIRKPATRICK: The Russians think we do everything for a purpose. If we don't say something, it means something. They worry about CW and BW. In your meeting with Gromyko you must include some reference to CW and BW and to the problem of verifiability.

REAGAN: **That is a good point.**

CASEY: (Three lines redacted).

ADELMAN: The Soviets have shown us they are able to shift their positions. For example, in 1979 they argued they would never negotiate on the basis of NATO's dual-track decision and reversed themselves. The U.S. should not make their return to START and INF more difficult.

REAGAN: **I agree. But when they reversed themselves we had not yet deployed weapons.**

ADELMAN: If there are general discussions in a grand setting, the discussion of the relationship between offensive and defensive systems would be a good springboard back to negotiations on offensive systems.

[The minutes read: "Richard Pipes notes that the USSR did not move from a small duchy to eleven times zones by being invaded. In 1898 the Czar's General Staff did a study that concluded that 80 percent of the wars fought by Russia were okay since Russian started them."[16]]

REAGAN: **Gentscher told us that they still have left the World War II barbed wire up near Moscow, to show how far Hitler got in World War II. The U.S. is allied with the FRG. The Soviets have great fear of U.S.-FRG capacity. How do you argue with this fear?**

WEINBERGER: That's what we need to tell the Soviets: make them understand that we understand their fear, yet we still can't let them possess enough force to dominate the world.

SHULTZ: But suppose Gromyko says "okay; let's talk. Why not set a date before the end of the year?" Could we take "yes"?

ADELMAN: Yes, the preparatory work is laid out.

WEINBERGER: No, we have not figured out a full approach.

SHULTZ: We don't need the full approach. We need agreement on end points.

MCFARLANE: Mr. President, you have already reviewed the options for START and INF.

REAGAN: **Yes.**

NITZE: I'm a skeptic on interim agreements. They are all poison. If you want a useful agreement, don't go down the interim agreement path.

REAGAN: **Concerning the ASAT thing, all theirs are ground-based. Ours are on a plane. I don't know how limits on either ground-based or airborne ASAT systems interfere with SDI.**

---

[16] I am unclear whether Adelman makes this statement referring to what Dr. Pipes told him, or whether Dr. Pipes is at the meeting making this statement. Dr. Pipes is not recorded on the list of participants, but often times people where at these meetings who were not on the official list.

WEINBERGER:	Because you offer a moratorium, they won't move. It puts us on a slippery slope. If we could limit the final agreement to matching our opening position, fine, but we can't. By beginning we must open the entire area for discussion.
	We need to have final limits in mind before entering into negotiations, therefore we must avoid a three-year moratorium or incidents-in-space.
MCFARLANE:	It is their ability to argue that an ASAT is a system that hits a satellite; but that SDI systems can do so too. They are difficult subjects to keep separate.
SHULTZ:	We're not ready to take "yes".
WEINBERGER:	No.
CASEY:	I want us to be able to say "yes," but we need to be ready to take on negotiations on all areas. We must not negotiate just ASAT and mortgage SDI. We risk being out-traded. If we start in ASAT, they will push into SDI.
WEINBERGER:	They should go home sincerely convinced of the President's desire for arms reduction.
MCFARLANE:	Mr. President, I think you have heard it all.
REAGAN:	**Ed (Ambassador Rowny)?**
ROWNY:	The Soviets are interested in trade. You should make clear we are ready to discuss trade-offs in START.
REAGAN:	**No matter what happens, no one should consider giving away the horse cavalry.**

POSTSCRIPT

A few days later, on September 24, Reagan addressed the United Nations General Assembly on "the cause of peace and the cause of human dignity."

After talking about the importance of respecting human rights, Reagan moved on to U.S.-Soviet relations:

Last January 16, I set out three objectives for U.S.-Soviet relations that can provide an agenda for our work over the months ahead.

First, I said, we need to find ways to reduce -- and eventually to eliminate -- the threat and use of force in solving international disputes...

Our second task must be to find ways to reduce the vast stockpiles of armaments in the world. I am committed to redoubling our negotiating efforts to achieve real results: in Geneva, a complete ban on chemical weapons; in Vienna, real reductions to lower and equal levels in Soviet and American, Warsaw Pact and NATO conventional forces; in Stockholm, concrete practical measures to enhance mutual confidence, to reduce the risk of war, and to reaffirm commitments concerning nonuse of force; in the field of nuclear testing, improvements in verification essential to ensure compliance with the threshold test ban and peaceful nuclear explosions agreements; and in the field of nonproliferation, close cooperation to strengthen the international institutions and practices aimed at halting the spread of nuclear weapons, together with redoubled efforts to meet the legitimate expectations of all nations that the Soviet Union and the United States will substantially reduce their own nuclear arsenals. ...

The third task I set in January was to establish a better working relationship between the Soviet Union and the United States, one marked by greater cooperation and understanding. We've made some modest progress. We have reached agreements to improve our hotline, extend our 10-year economic agreement, enhance consular cooperation, and explore coordination of search and rescue efforts at sea...

Now, all of these steps that I've mentioned – and especially the arms control negotiations – are extremely important to a step-by-step process toward peace. But let me also say that we need to extend the arms control process to build a bigger umbrella under which it can operate – a road map, if you will, showing where, during the next 20 years or so, these individual efforts can lead. This can greatly assist step-by-step negotiations and enable us to avoid having all our hopes or expectations ride on any single set or series of negotiations. If progress is temporarily halted at one set of talks, this newly established framework for arms control could help us take up the slack at other negotiations....

How much progress we will make and at what pace, I cannot say. But we have a moral obligation to try and try again.

Some may dismiss such proposals and my own optimism as simplistic American idealism, and they will point to the burdens of the modern world and to history. Well, yes, if we sit down and catalog year by year, generation by generation, the famines, the plagues, the wars, the invasions mankind has endured, the list will grow so long and the assault on humanity so terrific that it seems too much for the human spirit to bear.

But isn't this narrow and shortsighted and not at all how we think of history? Yes, the deeds of infamy or injustice are all recorded, but what shines out from the pages of history is the daring of the dreamers and the deeds of the builders and the doers. These things make up the stories we tell and pass on to our children. They comprise the most enduring and striking fact about human history -- that through the heartbreak and tragedy man has always dared to perceive the outline of human progress, the steady growth in not just the material well-being, but the spiritual insight of mankind...

One of the Founding Fathers of our nation, Thomas Paine, spoke words that apply to all of us gathered here today. They apply directly to all sitting here in this room. He said, ``We have it in our power to begin the world over again."

Date: **November 30, 1984**
Subject: **Soviet Defense and Arms Control Objectives**
Status: **Declassified in Part (2006)**

BACKGROUND

Reagan's landslide reelection, just weeks before today's meeting, interjected new life into arms control negotiations.

"I see no more important task before me than ensuring peace and greater security, not only for the United States, but for all the countries of the world," Reagan cabled to Chernenko on November 15. Reagan also proposed beginning high-level negotiations immediately, and told Chernenko that the United States is prepared to discuss "all arms control proposals both sides offer." In another effort to persuade Chernenko to accept talks on more than just space-based issues, Reagan repackaged his approach with the term "umbrella talks," which he explained would have the objective of creating "a firmer foundation for negotiations on the whole range of specific issues involved in the process of reducing arms and increasing stability."

On November 22, McFarlane announced that the United States and the Soviet Union had agreed to resume talks in Geneva starting in January.

SUMMARY

McFarlane introduces today's meeting:

Today we will discuss the Soviet strategy on arms control and look at the status of Soviet forces and what we expect them to look like in the future. On Wednesday, we will focus more specifically on U.S. objectives in January in contrast to Soviet objectives. Following that we will review substantive options, including questions of how to approach START, INF, space systems, and related issues. We will also look at how to present the United States' view of the relationship of offense and defense. We will stress how strategic defenses can be stabilizing and why they ought to learn to love defense. Our basic analytical work is complete on START and INF and our thinking on space has come a long way.

(Meeting participants) will receive a decision paper only after we have conducted these foundation meetings.

McFarlane then turns the meeting over to Casey who introduces Doug George (CIA) to present the George/Gershwin paper. "The Soviet Union has over 2,500 SNDVs (strategic nuclear delivery vehicles) and a vigorous development and deployment program," George starts his briefing.

The centerpiece of Soviet offensive systems is the large MIRVed (multiple independently targetable re-entry vehicles) ICBM force, especially the heavy missiles such as the SS-18. The Soviets also have a follow-on missile under development for each of their existing types including the SS-18.

The Soviet Union is removing SS-11s to make room for the addition of new ICBMs, probably the SS-X-25. The Soviets will replace most of its strategic offensive systems in the early-to-mid 1990s, addressing survivability through mobilized ICBMs such as the train-mobile SS-X-24 and the land-mobile SS-X-25. The Soviets will place greater emphasis on diversity, especially in developing a modern bomber force which will include the B-1 equivalent BLACKJACK bomber and the modern AS-15 air-launched cruise missile. The Soviets also continue to build-up SS-20 missiles and deployments of the SS-21, SS-12 mod 2, and SS-23 in Europe.

1985 is the year of decision for the Soviet Union based on the schedule of their five-year plans. The Soviet Union can live without SALT II limits for at least another year, but because of their hot production lines are well positioned to move beyond those limits in the future....

The Soviet Union desires to preserve its near-monopoly in strategic defense capabilities – including recently upgrading the Moscow ABM system – and has the potential for widespread ABM defense in the 1990s. The Soviets have also improved their air defenses and indeed, the Soviet SA-X-12 surface-to-air missile blurs the differences between air defense and ABM.

The Soviet Union is doing vigorous research on direct energy and anti-submarine warfare technology. In ASW they are using their manned space mission. At the present time the Soviet Union has some difficulty countering cruise missiles and advanced bombers, especially stealth weapons....

Mr. President, the Soviet space program is large and involves many programs including the Soviet space shuttle. The Soviet Union has an operational ASAT interceptor which can be launched in as little as sixty minutes after preparations begin. The Soviet Union has an advanced SDI program of its own, but would likely also respond to the American SDI program with greater resources and offensive counter-measures, including decoys and missile hardening.

Moving to the strategic challenge which U.S. programs present to the Soviet Union – the Soviets are afraid that U.S. gains will erode the advantages which they have achieved. The Soviet Union has a launch on warning capability which the P-II puts in jeopardy. The Soviet Union recognizes that no amount of capital that the Soviet Union can invest would permit them to compete successfully with the United States in terms of SDI because of their inability to develop modern computers at the rate at which they are being developed in the United States. Stealth, B-1, the cruise missiles, the Pershing II, all present problems for the Soviet Union....

In terms of arms control, the Soviet Union wants to continue to negotiate but wants progress on Soviet terms. SALT I and SALT II accepted the status of the Soviet Union as a superpower equal, but the Soviet Union retains as its goal compensation for all of the forces of all its opponents. Their goal is to protect their strategic gains while delaying the U.S. strategic response and especially to undercut ICBM modernization and SDI. ASAT is the stalking horse for SDI. Moscow remains committed to the principle of 'equality and equal security,' which means that they will continue to focus heavily on the INF issue, particularly this year when the Belgian and Dutch deployment decisions are pending.

Soviet leaders plan numerous visits, including a visit by Chernenko to Paris this year. These visits will be used for the propaganda purpose of stopping the U.S. INF deployments. It is quite possible that the Soviet Union will manipulate its SS-20 bases in order to get the Dutch to pause in their decision on deployment of ground-launched cruise missiles.

The Soviet leadership has agreed on a new course for U.S.-Soviet relations but General Secretary Chernenko or his successor will have little leeway to alter the thrust of Soviet strategic programs and arms control policies. The Soviets do not expect major agreements soon, but will use the arms control process to pursue political goals. One can expect the Soviet Union to be very active in trying to influence U.S. policy through allies, our publics, and the Congress. They may well prove quite sophisticated in exploiting differences within the West and in encouraging restraints on U.S. defense spending. Moscow also hopes to inhibit U.S. actions elsewhere, such as in Nicaragua. In Geneva, Gromyko (Soviet Foreign Minister) will have a political agenda of setting the stage for the Soviet European visits in early 1985 and his announced goal will be to halt the arms race, especially in space. Gromyko's substantive agenda will focus on stopping SDI through an ASAT moratorium and trying to get an INF moratorium as well. He will be looking for unilateral restraint by the West but will attempt to use SALT II as the point of departure in the strategic modalities, the Soviets probably will have a plan for Geneva but they are likely to expect the U.S. to take the lead in proposing modalities.

There are also economic factors influencing Soviet behavior. Despite difficult economic times, the economic situation is not likely to cause the Soviet Union to forego strategic programs or make concessions. On the other hand, they have an interest in slowing down the pace of strategic arms competition, in particular because they cannot compete with the United States in an open-ended high-technology competition such as would be associated with SDI.

In conclusion, the Soviets appear to have achieved successful re-entry into strategic arms control talks. They believe the process is beneficial to their interests, although they have stated that they do wish to achieve agreements. Clearly, they view the talks as a means to influence U.S. and allied behavior. These talks in the next year take place as the Soviet Union is deciding on the size, composition and capabilities of forces planned for the 1990s. The Soviet Union looks to arms control to slow down U.S. technological development, while it protects advantages they have achieved. The Soviet Union can live with SALT II for at least another year, and they are well positioned to go beyond its limitations in the near future. The Soviet Union is gearing up for a major public affairs battle, their emphasis on ICBMs has not changed, they are well positioned to go beyond existing agreements in both offensive and defensive systems, and they have a vigorous space program.

The discussion follows.

WEINBERGER:	Strategic defense is what gives the United States its leverage on the Soviet Union and may prove to be our best response.
VESSEY:	The Soviet Union gets a tremendous amount of military leverage from its ICBM force; it is important that we develop a counter to that. At the same time, the Soviet Union is developing diverse strategic forces such as the United States has done.
MCFARLANE:	We should set aside the detailed discussion and focus on the big picture. The President should recall his policy of commitment to a military force structure which the Soviet Union would respect. In 1980 the President talked about "the window of vulnerability," and today the United States is still faced with problems in resolving the threats. For example, our problem in getting Congressional support for the M-X.

Today, the Soviets Union has 6,000 ICBM warheads to our 2,000, and all of ours are vulnerable. The Soviet Union has done all that it could to derail the President's efforts, but we have tried to get everyone to recognize the trends. The President's program in arms control has been to restore a stable balance, but we still have a long way to go even though we are better off than we would have been had we continued the policies of four years ago.

As bad as it is today, it is going to get worse. What does that mean for arms control? In my view, either you must persevere in getting offensive reductions, or you must defend the United States. It is imperative that the Soviet Union understand that.

What the Soviet Union wants is high levels of re-entry vehicles and no defenses for the United States. The notion that you must choose between arms control and the strategic defense is nonsense. Strategic defense gives us the capability to restore stability in this century. The other point about SDI is that it permits us to move away from emphasis on nuclear weapons, and this is most appealing to publics. SDI is defensive and it is non-nuclear.

REAGAN:	**Does the Soviet Union fear our economic capability?**
MCFARLANE:	This is different than during World War II – in World War II Congress was on our side.

VESSEY:	The Soviet Union has a greater military and industrial base but the United States has the lead in high technology.
WEINBERGER:	SDI is the key. We don't have the time to mobilize an industrial base the way we did in World War II.
REAGAN:	**I have another question. I wonder whether or not deterrence would be enhanced if we made clear to the Soviet Union that we might "launch-under-attack." (At the same time I wonder) whether we have the warning capacity to be certain that we would have warning, (so) that we would not be caught by surprise.**
WEINBERGER:	There are certain gaps in our radar coverage.
VESSEY:	The gaps refer to attack by SLBMs.
MCFARLANE:	Mr. President, we have no ability to rely on "launch-under-attack" because we do not have the kind of attack assessment capability that we would need to rely on such a policy.
CASEY:	"Launch-under-attack" would make SDI look very good indeed.
WEINBERGER:	Submarines are very close to American shores and would make it very difficult to execute.
VESSEY:	The JCS feel it would be difficult to rely on "launch-under attack."
NITZE:	"Launch-under-attack" is a policy of weakness.
MCFARLANE:	We don't have the right kind of capabilities for such a policy. We don't have the ability to distinguish between attacks on military facilities and attacks on our cities.
WEINBERGER:	SDI is the best response to the Soviet threat.
ROWNY:	Any Soviet attack would be against our missile bases.

POSTSCRIPT

The discussion continues on December 5.

Date:	**December 5, 1984**
Subject:	**U.S.-Soviet Arms Control Objectives**
Status:	**Declassified (2005)**

SUMMARY

McFarlane introduced today's meeting saying that the purpose of today's meeting is to discuss U.S. and Soviet objectives for the arms control process that will start next month in Geneva. McFarlane then summarizes the key recommendations of the Senior Arms Control Group (SACG):

- We should first come to understand our long-term objective – we are meeting with the Soviet Union in order to begin the process of discussing how we can in the years ahead use strategic defense to make the world safer;
- SDI is most likely to be successful in achieving greater stability if the United States and the Soviet Union conduct a dialogue which would continue through the transition to the use of strategic defenses, but during that process we must protect our SDI options and in particular avoid unilateral restraint and moratoria;
- SDI is not only important to our future, but it provides a hedge against a Soviet breakout of the ABM Treaty;
- A major public affairs program on SDI is essential to explain to people that this is a prudent, sensible moral program;
- One of the options before us is to look at smaller steps in the reductions of offensive arms, but before we decide what specific approaches we should take, we should have a clear understanding of Soviet objectives;
- The Soviets will seek to put the onus on us in order to make the U.S. grant concessions;
- The Soviets will test us to determine whether or not we will agree to concrete limitations on space weapons and will try to draw out new proposals;
- The Soviets will attempt to protect existing Soviet advantages and superiority while preventing the U.S. from gaining advantages for its technologies, in particular they will try to stop SDI R& D;
- Clearly the Soviets top priority will be to seek limitations on SDI through a moratorium on ASAT;
- The Soviets will probably argue that we must agree to limitations on space systems first;
- The Soviets will attempt to avoid compliance issues in this forum and are unlikely to show great flexibility on offensive systems.

Moving to the U.S. goals, McFarlane continues,

Our goal is to get a useful process going and to achieve formal negotiations on offensive systems while we discuss the relationship of defense to offense. We must protect and support our options to shift to greater reliance on defense, and we must seek equal and reduced levels of offensive arms, while protecting options for our modernization program. In summary, our objective is to enhance stability by altering the existing imbalance through our own programs and through arms control.

"We should also review certain difficulties associated with verification," Casey interrupts. "The discussion of offense and defense is also very important. Either we must teach the Russians to like defense, or else we must prepare our publics very carefully. Defense is the only alternative to getting stabilizing reductions."

Shultz came to this meeting more prepared to listen than to speak, but raised some questions:

Is our agreement to discuss defense an agreement to negotiate on defense, and isn't it the case that the Soviet Union already likes defense because they have a large air defense network, and it is clear that defense of the homeland is dear to the Soviet

Union. They are likely to say that they already know that defense is important. I am the person who is going to do the talking, but I don't know what it is that I am supposed to say. We need to find some things that both sides are prepared to talk about.

Reagan had heard enough:

It is my belief that the United States and the Soviet Union may be coming together more than many people realize. We have never believed that we would find ourselves at war with Russia except to defend ourselves against attack. We have to look at defensive measures just the way the Soviet Union does; we have to look at civil defense and air defense and ABM. In this regard, the Moscow subway is significant to civil defense.

Everything they have says that they are looking at a first-strike because it is they, not we, who have built up both offensive and defensive systems. We could build on the Soviet preoccupation with protecting the homeland by making clear that we have no intention of starting a nuclear war; that it is our view that they may want to make war on us. We have no objections to their having defenses, but we have to look at defenses for ourselves and we need to look at reducing and ultimately eliminating nuclear weapons.

Relative to the goal of eliminating nuclear weapons, an initial reduction of 1,000 is meaningless. Both sides have indicated that they would like to get rid of nuclear weapons entirely, but they are afraid of SDI. We must show them how defenses are not threatening. The Soviet Union is ahead of us in ASAT capability and we should first talk about getting rid of these offensive arms like this F-15 ASAT. We must make it clear that we are not seeking advantage, only defense.

The discussion continues.

MCFARLANE: Stability is the theme that we must develop, and we must make clear that we are looking to defense to counter offensive systems. We must also talk with the Soviet Union because it would be helpful to have an agreement on how we can proceed towards this goal on both sides.

SHULTZ: I applaud the President's notion of setting our goal of zero nuclear weapons. I believe that it is important that the President said that. We must move towards the basis for the elimination of nuclear weapons. My instincts tell me that unconstrained offensive systems can overwhelm a defensive system and therefore without constraint on offense, there can be no successful SDI.

MCFARLANE: Stability is a Western concept. It is imperative that we not forget that we need to deal with the Soviet effort to gain superiority.

REAGAN: **It would be silly if we go into these talks without being realistic.**

The quotation attributed to Brezhnev in Prague, namely, that the Soviet Union has gained a great deal from détente and that therefore, in 1985, the Soviet Union should have its way around the world. I doubt they have in mind Pearl Harbor, but I expect they believed that they would be so powerful that they could coerce us into achieving their objectives peacefully.

WATKINS: We must work hard to prepare for strategic defenses. They are an important hedge against verification and compliance difficulties and they provide the basis for greater stability and reductions in arms controls.

Now is the time to articulate our approach to SDI and to make a statement that makes clear the role SDI plays in achieving stability. We must make certain that SDI is not made analogous to ASAT. We need to have SDI well underway. There is a solid case for SDI, but we will always have problems in dealing with public opinion on space and ASAT. We must link research on SDI to making nuclear weapons obsolete.

REAGAN: **It is important to link research on SDI to making nuclear weapons obsolete. We are behind in ASAT, which is the ability to knock down satellites, but we are willing to negotiate the end of ASATs because they are offensive weapons. SDI is a non-nuclear defensive system. I still wonder whether or not we could give them the technology.**

WATKINS: ASAT, stealth technology and SDI are all inter-related – we must move carefully. The F-15 system is not the answer to the military's prayer, and the MV could be given up, from a military point of view, but it must be remembered that this is closely related to SDI.

REAGAN: **Couldn't we distinguish between offensive and defensive systems? Can we limit ASAT as an offensive systems?**

MEESE: The technology is the same – a treaty on ASAT testing could kill both ASAT and SDI.

CASEY: We must focus on the difficulties of definition and verification in space arms control.

SHULTZ: We could try to limit testing to just those existing systems and to try to protect our research and development.

WATKINS: An ASAT moratorium would inevitably create difficulties for SDI.

TAFT: I want to stress the importance of our making the case for SDI and its role in maintaining the peace. We should do nothing in the negotiations which would prejudice the development of SDI.

ADELMAN: The elimination of nuclear weapons should not be considered a near-term goal, rather, we should focus on the goal of reducing the number of nuclear weapons. However, an important question is, how ambitious should our arms control objectives be? How deep should the reductions we seek be, and how much verification should we require? On SDI, Congress has cut our program by one-third, down to a level of spending below what had been planned even before the President's speech. I want to stress again the need to mention the goal of reinforcing deterrence as we know it.

REAGAN: **SDI gives us a great deal of leverage on the Soviet Union.**

MCFARLANE: The Russians may bet that the United States cannot sell its SDI program. We need to get support for strategic defenses.

REAGAN: **We could start by canceling our subscriptions to *The Washington Post.***

POSTSCRIPT

Two days later, on December 7, Reagan sent a letter to Chernenko expressing his hope that the Geneva meetings will result in "mutually acceptable agreements to begin reductions." The discussion continues on December 10.

Date: **December 10, 1984**
Subject: **Discussion of Geneva Format and SDI**
Status: **Declassified in Part (2005)**

SUMMARY

McFarlane starts the meeting by posing the questions for discussion:

Do we want to separate START and INF negotiations or should they be merged? What shall we do about space – negotiations or discussions only? Should space issues be dealt with separately or merged with START and INF? Should we combine everything together in one large negotiation, perhaps having separate working groups? How do we deal with the objectives of Umbrella discussion? Should we view these as "Umbrella talks" or perhaps "Stability talks" ...

In discussing format, we must remember that the U.S.-Soviet announcement gives us some guidance. The meeting in Geneva is to set the subject and objective and we should remember that we are and the Soviets have agreed to the "new negotiations" in general terms. In the short term, our objective is reduction of offensive nuclear weapons. Our long term objective is the elimination of nuclear weapons.

"Yes, that's right," Reagan interrupts. McFarlane continues,

The advantages of separate START and INF and Space discussions would be to not reward the Soviets for their walkout, could build upon established delegations, would be easier, would be better for allied consultations, and would give us an opportunity to exchange views without committing to negotiations on space. As a disadvantage, it would be unacceptable to the Soviet Union and would draw charges of bad faith, perhaps even a walkout because the Soviet Union is under the impression that we had agreed to new negotiations which include space negotiations.

Reagan doesn't think the Soviets will go for Option 1 – separate START and INF negotiations – and asks Shultz what he thinks. "The Soviet's would be upset if there were no space negotiations at all," Shultz responds. "They believe that is what they agreed to." The discussion follows.

WEINBERGER:	We can deal with space but we must look out for preconditions, especially moratoria.
SHULTZ:	We need to consider the possibility that the Soviet Union might walk out of these talks and we must consider our response. I would hate to have to go to the meeting having to reach an agreement – we should avoid a walkout but be prepared to try again if we don't reach an agreement.
REAGAN:	**Chernenko and Gromyko quoted my words supporting the goal of the ultimate elimination of nuclear weapons.**
MCFARLANE:	They have agreed to negotiations on nuclear and space arms. First of all, they have agreed to negotiations and we must hold them to that. Second, this includes negotiations on space arms.
REAGAN:	**On space arms, can we discuss only offensive and not defensive arms?**
WEINBERGER:	It is important to talk about the relationship of offensive and defensive arms, but ASAT can be defined so broadly that SDI would be impossible.

REAGAN:	**Can we oppose the offensive systems that attack satellites while protecting defensive systems?**
WEINBERGER:	We should discuss all of these issues, but we must recognize that the Soviet Union will call for a moratorium on ASAT in order to undercut SDI and our efforts to get reductions in offensive systems. The Soviets already have an ASAT system, we do not.
ADELMAN:	There are three problems with an ASAT moratorium.
	First, any SDI deployment would be an ASAT, therefore, SDI research could be hurt.
	Second, the Soviet Union has an ASAT already tested. Third, ASAT arms control involves extremely difficult verification and defense issues, all of which means that the Soviet Union will retain an ASAT capability.
	There are not many areas in space arms control in which we want to negotiate. The real incentive for space talks come from publics, allies, and in providing trade-off incentives to the Soviets.
REAGAN:	**We don't need SDI if the Soviet Union agrees to zero, except for security because of verification uncertainties. I suggest we move on to the other options.**
MCFARLANE:	I recommend moving the discussion directly to Option 4 which deals with the question of START and INF merger and provides a negotiating forum for space.
	A START and INF merger has been finessed in our discussion of Umbrella Talks. The disadvantages of a merger are that it makes negotiations more complex, could result in undue influence by the allies in negotiations less central to their interests, and might permit the Soviets to divide us from our allies through proposals to trade off START and INF issues.
REAGAN:	**The Soviet Union cannot justify not counting the SS-20.**
WEINBERGER:	With a merger the Soviet Union would focus more on the British and French systems. (Two lines redacted).Moving to Option 5, combined negotiations, it is complex and might bring great pressure on defensive systems.
REAGAN:	**Going back to INF, the Soviets have warheads in Eastern Europe and the allies requested our deployments.**

MCFARLANE:	Under the Soviet definition of "strategic" systems, they consider our systems in Europe strategic, but do not consider their systems, which cannot hit the U.S., "strategic."
REAGAN:	**The P-II is really for our allies.**
ADELMAN:	The SS-20s are not, in fact, in Eastern Europe but could reach all of Europe. The SS-12s, 22s and 23s (sic) have been moved into Eastern Europe.
SHULTZ:	The SS-20 is a terrific weapon. We need to deal with these issues and we need to manage our allies.
REAGAN:	**(Looking at Shultz) You should be on guard for what the Soviets want and what we want.**
SHULTZ:	Substance and procedure are interrelated. The Soviet Union has many advantages in offensive systems. Those advantages are unlikely to diminish. Soviet forces are destabilizing and threatening and we need to get some limitations on that threat.
REAGAN:	**We cannot exclude SS-20s. Is there a consensus on Option 4? (Should we) go in with Option 2?**
SHULTZ:	Options 2, 4 and 5 are similar – they involve Space negotiations and would inevitably involve separate working groups. Options 2 and 5 would be quite similar as long as there is someone over all to deal with all the questions and make tradeoffs.
ROWNY.	There is much to be said for opening with Option 2 and then having Option 4 as our fallback position.
WEINBERGER:	Options 5 and 6 would be difficult to manage; we need to find out what the Soviet Union wants. Formal negotiations are acceptable, but we need tight rules.
ROWNY:	Gromyko will bring his START representative, Ambassador Karpov and Deputy Obukov, but not anyone from INF.
WEINBERGER:	The question is, do we want to deal with procedure only or do we have to deal with substance?
WATKINS:	The Chiefs are united in the view that we should keep space negotiations separate because Option 5 would give the Soviets too much of a handle on SDI. The Chiefs could support a merger such as Option 4, but would prefer to keep START and INF separate. We should consider a procedure merger before a merger on substance.
CASEY:	We much protect our intelligence assets – the Soviet ASAT talks present a specific danger for sensitive sources and methods. During the talks in Helsinki in 1979

and 1980 (sic), special rules were established including no use of non-secure phones and no post-plenary sessions. Ambassador Buchheim had carefully protected U.S. intelligence interests. SDI should be dealt with in the offensive negotiations.

ADELMAN: I agree with that point and with the suggestion that we go in with Option 2 because of the concern over complexities and allied consultations, but Option4 is acceptable. I believe Umbrella Talks should continue at the Foreign Minister level. The Soviets mentioned "medium range" systems in their proposal, this means that we can hold them to this.

SHULTZ: (I agree) that we need Umbrella Talks to discuss what Heads of State had agreed, namely, that there is an organic relationship between offensive and defense and other issues.

WEINBERGER: Discussions of these organic relationships is mainly something we need to do internally.

REAGAN: **We need talks which can eliminate suspicions. I'm willing to admit that the USSR is suspicious of us.**

MCFARLANE: Our presentation for the January 7 meeting must include a discussion of offense and defense and how to achieve a more stable world in the future. Both sides must reconsider the postwar history of strategic defense. We must explain the role of defense, both to the publics and to the Soviets. We must discuss why we agreed in the past to mutual vulnerability, namely because we had no other option and because we lacked confidence in defense. That is why the ABM Treaty constrained defense.

Our view then was that vulnerability was not only desirable but that basic assumption would reduce pressures to insure offensive arms. In SALT I, we expected a limitation on offensive arms that would leave both sides vulnerable to counter city attacks, but not vulnerable to first strike counter-military attacks. Instead the Soviet Union has invested heavily in achieving a first strike capability and has worked on improving defenses as well. Not only were our assumptions wrong, but circumstances have changed, and now technologies are available to increase the possibilities of defense. We must review the foundations of our thinking, indeed, we may be where the Russians were 15 years ago, looking at defense.

ADELMAN:	The Soviet Union is not abiding by the ABM Treaty. I suggest that we go in with Option 2 and fall back to Option 4 with Secretary Shultz continuing general discussion at the Foreign Ministers' level.
WEINBERGER:	Agreed.
REAGAN:	**Life in the United States is too good for anyone to consider starting a war. I hope that life doesn't get so boring in Russia that they would consider starting a war.**
WEINBERGER:	We must focus on reducing offensive systems. I want to remind everyone that the ABM Treaty is supposed to make it unnecessary for the massive Soviet buildup in offensive systems.
REAGAN:	**I agree that there should have been reductions in weapons in conjunction with the ABM Treaty.**
WEINBERGER:	There has now been a breakthrough in defense technology. We have moved away above the old systems of defense that were 50% effective and ground based.
REAGAN:	**We are now talking about non nuclear systems.**
WEINBERGER:	We are talking about non-nuclear systems that are very popular because people can understand about destroying weapons and not people.
MCFARLANE:	Even if we had never heard of SDI, we would have had a problem – the American people don't like land-based missiles and this presents a military problem. We need another solution other than simply building up land-based missiles.
REAGAN:	**(Looking at Shultz) I want to make sure that you have the Brezhnev quotation from Prague in which he said that because of détente, by 1985, the Soviet Union would have their way in the world. They were wrong.**
SHULTZ:	Agreed.
REAGAN:	**The situation today is like a duel between two gunfighters. Our policy of MAD (Mutual Assured Destruction) could get us both killed. It is just too dangerous, however, that is the situation today. Would deterrence be strengthened if we told the Soviet Union that we would not wait out an attack?**
CASEY:	That is what the Soviet's would say.
ADELMAN:	All the warning systems would have to be fool-proof.

MEESE: Yes, if you are talking about Launch-on-Warning, but what we are talking about is Launch-Under-Verified-Attack, which is quite a different thing.

WEINBERGER: The Soviets know that this might be an appropriate response.

ADELMAN: Paul Nitze said that this is a policy of weakness, a policy that we would adopt only if we were driven to it.

MCFARLANE: The question of whether attack assessment capabilities for Launch Under-Verified-Attack are sufficient is important. Monday we will be talking about the specifics of the negotiations.

POSTSCRIPT

The discussion continues on December 17.

Date: **December 17, 1984**
Subject: **Discussion of Substantive Issues for Geneva**
Status: **Declassified (2005)**

SUMMARY

Today's meeting continues the discussion from December 10 on formulating a negotiating position for the upcoming arms control negotiations and is the last declassified meeting before negotiations start in January.

McFarlane opens with a reminder that today's meeting deals with discussions of the substantive content of the Geneva talks – START, INF, Space, and the relationship between offense and defense. McFarlane continues,

> Our immediate objective is to set into motion formal negotiations and discuss the relationship between offense and space generally. The Soviet Union will try to prevent U.S. SDI research and will urge various moratoria. They will seek to get commitments from us in advance not to develop SDI. The question before us, therefore, is how to sustain SDI, especially with publics, in the face of sustained pressure from both the Soviet Union and the Congress.

> The Soviet Union is returning to the talks because they have seen the success we have had in getting through the President's modernization program, including M-X, TRIDENT, and SDI. They also have come back to the table to block the Belgian and Dutch INF deployments. They expect to block those deployments by being at the negotiating table. They believe that there is an impulse on the Left, perhaps in the Congress, to stop programs and have a moratorium, as long as the superpowers are talking. They fear that the deployments will upset the talks.

Turning to specific recommendations, in START we have sought deep reductions to the level of 5,000 ballistic missile warheads and to stress movement away from destabilizing systems, particularly emphasizing the importance of slow-flying systems such as bombers, as opposed to fast-flying ballistic missiles. In the past year we have done an enormous amount of work and in Geneva we may wish to be in a position to discuss the trade-offs between areas of U.S. and areas of Soviet advantage (between fast-flying and slow-flying systems). Ambassador Rowny has done much work in this regard. For Geneva, Secretary Shultz will need instructions which permit him to discuss our ideas on trade-offs.

In INF, Abassador Nitze has played an important rule on the question of Belgian and Dutch deployments. We have a solid position and we are prepared to agree to any number between zero and 572. Our current proposal has demonstrated our flexibility in our readiness not to deploy our complete entitlement under an equal global ceiling in Europe. In agreeing to reduce both P-II and GLCM, and in our willingness to discuss aircraft limitations, these all addressed Soviet concerns.

The most difficult issue will be space. There is a close relationship between ASAT and SDI research. Unfortunately, we have had the statements by Mrs. Thatcher and Mr. Mitterrand in France accusing us of over-arming and of needing to avoid the space arms race. Both France and Great Britain have independent nuclear deterrence based on SLBMS and they are afraid that SDI will be viewed as negating their independent forces. There is a genuine ignorance of what SDI is all about. I want to remind everyone of the importance of stressing our interest in a non-nuclear system. We need to make the case for SDI not only to our allies but to the American people and to the Russians themselves. We have been living under a concept of deterrence based on the threat of massive offensive retaliation. For twelve years, really longer than that, this concept of deterrence has continued, but has been influenced by certain assumptions, which are no longer true.

First is the assumption that we can't build effective defenses. The second is the notion that if we agreed to limit defensive systems, we would be able to get limitations on offensive systems. The third is an assumption that the Soviet Union would limit their defensive systems as well. Fourth, there is a commitment that neither side would seek unilateral advantage over the other. However, that commitment has been violated by the Soviet Union in a quest for both offensive and defensive superiority.

In defense they have continued to modernize their ABM system and air defense system, indeed, two of their air defenses, the SA-10 and the SA-12, may be dual-capable. They have also built an ASAT system. Therefore, it is imperative that we make the case that Soviets have violated these basic premises and therefore they must reduce offensive systems or else we will have no choice but to deploy defenses.

In addition, however, we must persuade the Soviet Union that it is good to deploy defense, to move away from our total reliance on offensive systems. We must recognize that the Soviet Union will not take easily to this view, so we must show them that we are headed in the right direction. We all agree on the necessity of putting down a marker on SDI. In the next week or two we will be making decisions on the substantive issues.

"I want to put something forward without pride of authorship concerning what has been said by Mitterrand on outer space," Reagan interrupted.

I've been reading what Gorbachev and Thatcher have been saying. I believe that the United States and the Soviet Union should join in discussions of ASAT and weapons in space that can be directed at earth, such as nuclear weapons. My goal is the total elimination of nuclear weapons, and I believe that we are not saying anything that they have not also said recently. SDI is going to be the main target of the Soviet's in Geneva. They are coming to the table to get at SDI. We need to stay with our SDI research program no matter what.

International control of SDI for world protection might be possible at some point, but for now SDI will help alleviate the dangers associated with the impossible job of verification. For example, someone like Qadhafi could develop nuclear weapons and perhaps smuggle them into the United States. Therefore, we need a wide range of measures to handle the threat of covert nuclear weapons, and to ensure that outlaws or other nations cannot gain an advantage.

People now understand how to build nuclear weapons – you cannot make mankind unlearn what it already knows. There was recently a test flight of an SS-X-24 with ten warheads.

There is no price on SDI. We must be frank with the Soviet Union on the need to go down the path towards defense, to eliminate nuclear weapons, but clearly we are not going to give up SDI.

"Defense is important, even if you don't have the elimination of nuclear weapons," Shultz adds.

(There are) examples where nuclear weapons are eliminated, but conventional systems exist. We must also deal with cruise missiles and bomber defenses and expand our program beyond the current SDI effort. I've just spent two and a half hours with the British Foreign Minister, Geoffrey Howe, and Howe expressed the same views as Mrs. Thatcher. Nevertheless, my meetings with NATO Foreign Ministers had gone extremely well using the formula that Paul Nitze developed. I'm confident that we will have no problem persuading people of the value of SDI if we put the right twist on it, like we had done at NATO, where nobody had a counter-argument.

I welcome Bud (McFarlane's) emphasis on public diplomacy, and note that we have agreed on a forum which includes ASAT and weapons in space. There is an overlap between ASAT and SDI, and this means we must be careful.

Geneva is going to be a public diplomacy event, whether we like it or not. Some one thousand reporters are expected to be there along with the anchor people from the three networks. The State Department reporters are very unhappy because they will not now be the primary reporters for their news services. But there will actually not be much of a story for them in Geneva because we will hope to keep some element of confidentiality.

We must be prepared that the meeting may break up, and we must be ready, right there immediately, to deal with this situation. We need to sound an appealing note to protect ourselves from a possible Soviet walkout. Therefore we need to lay out our position quite clearly. It must have content, and we must go beyond a bull session. There is a lot of content in the area of offensive systems negotiations, but there is also content in the space area. It is important to bring up the issue of how we will be evolving towards defenses. We must go out and make clear our position.

The discussion follows.

REAGAN:	**We must stress that in a context of the Soviets' having already said that they want to give up nuclear weapons. If they walkout of Geneva because of SDI, we can emphasize that they are not serious.**
	We must be prepared to make clear to the American people that this is a system which does not kill people, that, it would free the world from the threat of nuclear weapons.
	The Soviet Union will have difficulty walking out when we have made a sound case.
SHULTZ:	We should not assume failure; that will only lead to failure. Instead, we need to look at our position so that we are not afraid of failure.
CASEY:	We must be ready for the prospect that they will put us on the defensive and even walkout.
SHULTZ:	We have the basis for avoiding that possibility if we make the right decisions.
MCFARLANE:	There is in existence a public diplomacy plan being prepared by the NSC staff. The central element is the so-called SDI bible. The book will be available within a couple of weeks and will be made public before the negotiations in Geneva. Public speaking engagements will help us in our effort to promote SDI. The President should give a speech on SDI sometime after the Geneva talks, and address SDI in the State of the Union as well. It is important that everyone get out on the stump to speak for SDI.
MEESE:	We must distance the space issue from the SDI issue. They are not the same. The President's idea is not simply a space question.
REAGAN:	**We are looking to see what these technologies can do.**

BAKER:	There is confusion about SDI…
WEINBERGER:	There is confusion about SDI because many people have not examined the issue carefully and because of the Soviet disinformation campaign. Our SDI program is going to be a non-nuclear system. We don't have SDI technology available yet, but we need to work on it. Some people say that it is expensive, but SDI will not be as expensive as all of the offensive systems that we would need absent SDI. It might cost one-tenth as much.

Many people are not aware of the consequences of not having defenses. SDI is in the same position with respect to negotiations as was the Pershing–II. The Soviet Union fears it and will do everything they can to encourage delay and to try to stop the program. Instead, we have to make the case that SDI will even encourage reductions.

REAGAN: **I have been reading about the phenomenon of nuclear winter, and of the volcano Timbora which erupted in 1816 creating a cloud which created winter conditions – snow and ice – around much of the world there was no summer. Nuclear winter ought to encourage reductions.**

ADELMAN: Nuclear winter should also increase support for SDI. SDI is also important to prevent horrible consequences from an accidental war, such as described in the novel <u>Fail-Safe.</u>

It is important to distinguish SDI from space, we could do that by negotiating rules of behavior for anti-satellite systems and satellites themselves. That gives us something to negotiate about.

Our theme would be that we need to make the world safer through the controlled use of space, that negotiations along these lines would be better than doing nothing. The Defense Department has generated some interesting statistics since the ABM Treaty: the Soviet Union has spent more money on defense than on offense while the United States spent six times as much on offense as on defense.

MCFARLANE: We still don't have an ICBM in the ground.

REAGAN: **Many of those who are for the small ICBM now will turn against it after they have killed the M-X, when they hear complaints about missile trains and missile trucks moving around the United States. I can**

imagine what the environmental complaints will be. That is another reason why we must have SDI.

WEINBERGER: The Soviet Union has the mobile SS-X-24 and SS-X-25. The Soviets have come close to stopping the mobile Pershing II's and GLCMs, and they have still not given up trying to stop them.

The Soviets are continuing to try to stop our M-X system, despite the fact that they have three or four similar new missiles. The Soviets will try to blame us for a breakup in the talks if we don't agree to give up SDI.

We must be careful about ASAT. The Soviet Union has an ASAT system, and they are trying to prevent us from developing one. If we have a moratorium, our scientists will drift away from the project and we will become further and further behind. A moratorium is bad, and in any case, it is not verifiable.

With respect to space, we should take the affirmative position, that we are going ahead with SDI and we are not going to be stopped. We should be prepared to talk about permissible changes to the ABM Treaty. There are worse things than signing a bad agreement, it is no victory to sign a bad agreement.

REAGAN: **I've been talking with a number of experts who are critical of SDI. They all seem to think that it is a nuclear weapon. We need to explain to them that it is not a nuclear system we seek.**

SHULTZ: I'm not sure SDI is truly a non-nuclear program.

WEINBERGER: Certain types of terminal defense systems based on older technologies are still nuclear. We are hoping to move beyond these.

ADELMAN: A terminal defense system could be non-nuclear, but the older systems are nuclear.

NITZE: What about EXCALIBUR?

SHULTZ: I think some of these systems are nuclear.

WEINBERGER: The defenses against ballistic missile systems that are space-based are intended to be non-nuclear.

ADELMAN: Some of these space-based systems might be powered by nuclear reactors.

WEINBERGER: We must stress that these are systems to defend the United States. I'm often asked whether we are defending cities or weapons and I say that we are defending the United States by destroying the weapons.

ROWNY: We are not talking about putting nuclear weapons in space, only nuclear reactors.

MCFARLANE:	That's not the case. Approximately $200 million is in the DOE budget for EXCALIBUR, which involves a nuclear explosion in space.
WEINBERGER:	That's not the kill mechanism.
MEESE:	Secretary Shultz is right. We didn't want to prematurely limit the technologies involved.
SHULTZ:	I thought that there are nuclear weapons involved.
WEINBERGER:	We are seeking a non-nuclear system, a non-nuclear kill option.
MCFARLANE:	We can describe the program as heavily focused on non-nuclear systems.
WEINBERGER:	Our theme must be to reduce offensive systems as we evolve towards defensive systems.
REAGAN:	**(Looking at Shultz) We should get the Soviet Union to agree to work towards the elimination of nuclear weapons and then throw this commitment back at them if they stand in the way of strategic defenses.**
	(I want to) get this process of reductions going.
NITZE:	We might make progress in INF towards reductions if we would begin with a proposal of equal reductions on each side.
REAGAN:	**The Soviet's are continuing to build up their forces.**
WEINBERGER:	What we are in favor of is not equal reductions, but reductions to equal levels. Paul (Nitze), you meant reductions to equal levels?
NITZE:	I indeed meant equal reductions.
REAGAN:	**I thought proportional reductions were acceptable?**
BUSH:	Mr. President, did you not, in fact, propose to Gromyko proportionate reductions?
REAGAN:	**It seems that if we are willing to live with 572 for us and over 1,000 for the Soviets, then we ought to be able to live without equal numbers on both sides.**
MCFARLANE:	We are looking for a definition or approach that makes a compromise look better. The Pershing II has one warhead on its launcher, the GLCM has four warheads on its launcher, the SS-20 has three warheads on its launcher.
	We are looking for a formula which might describe an equal reduction in launchers that would also result in an equal warhead outcome.
NITZE:	That's correct.

REAGAN:	**We need to emphasize the idea of elimination of nuclear weapons in the end; the zero-option for INF would be a great step in that direction.**
NITZE:	We may need to make specific proposal to the Soviet Union. It would be useful if we could make general statements, even if we don't present specific proposals. For example, we could say that we would accept in principle equal reductions even if we don't give them the details.
ADELMAN:	We will need a response to charges that we are not serious about negotiating on space issues either.
SHULTZ:	It is important that we not get into the lingo of simply protecting SDI. We need to word it in the right way, as, for example, Paul Nitze suggested. We need to find a way of defending SDI without appearing inflexible.
REAGAN:	**Whatever we do, we must be resolved among ourselves that SDI is not the price for reductions.**
SHULTZ:	The problem of MIDGETMAN and railroad cars made one thing clear: arms control is important to the United States. We must reach arms control agreements because it is not clear that we can contemplate an unrestrained race with the Soviet Union. We need reductions and we need to trade for them. They won't come for free.
MCFARLANE:	We'll prepare instructions for a decision by the President over the next couple of weeks. Mr. Casey will prepare a presentation of the problem of verification.
CASEY:	Verification has been built up as an absolute. We need to prepare public opinion for what it is that we are likely to achieve.

President Reagan then concludes the meeting with a joke about an American in the Moscow subway. Paraphrasing the official notes, which paraphrased President Reagan, the American is shown the beautiful marble work in the Moscow subway and, asks, "Where are the trains?" The American wasn't given an answer, just more demonstrations of the beautiful marble. Finally, after asking, "Where are the trains" several times, his Soviet counterpart responds, "What about the Negro problem in the South?"

POSTSCRIPT

Chernenko sent another letter to Reagan, hand-delivered to Shultz on December 21. Shultz, as he usually did, summarized the letter before sending it to the White House. The basic thrust of the letter, Shultz wrote, is that "its tone is positive and it looks toward the Geneva meeting."

PART IV:

REAGAN AND GORBACHEV

CHAPTER SIX

THE ROAD TO GENEVA

"We seek the total elimination one day of nuclear weapons from the face of the Earth."[17]

---

[17] President Reagan during his second inaugural address. January 21, 1985, Public Papers of the President of the United States.

Date: **March 11, 24, and April 30, 1985**
Subject: **Letters between Reagan and Gorbachev**

BACKGROUND

The start of Reagan's second term also brought changes to the composition of the National Security Council. Meese moved from his position as Senior Counselor to the President to the Department of Justice as Attorney General after William French Smith resigned; Secretary of the Treasury Regan, feeling like he could do more inside the White House, convinced Chief of Staff James Baker to switch positions. Reagan approved the switch without expressing any reservations, and both Baker and Regan were content with their new jobs as Baker was elevated to a Cabinet position and Regan, though taking over a traditionally non-cabinet level position, was allowed to retain his Cabinet spot.

In terms of negotiations with the Soviet's, "As you are aware," Reagan said in his January 9 press conference on arms control,

> [Secretary Shultz's] meeting with Mr. Gromyko has resulted in agreement between our two nations to begin new negotiations on nuclear and space arms. Our objective in these talks will be the reduction of nuclear arms and the strengthening of strategic stability. Our ultimate goal, of course, is the complete elimination of nuclear weapons.

Reagan's call for the elimination of nuclear weapons did not go over well with Prime Minister Thatcher. In their joint-statement following her February 20 White House visit, the word "eliminate" was never used, and Reagan called the discussion "cordial" with an agreement for "significant reductions in the number of nuclear weapons." Thatcher publically called the discussion a "thorough one, especially about the prospects for arms control negotiations." On the issue of nuclear weapons, she said they shared a "sincere wish to get down the number of nuclear weapons in the world in a way which is still balanced and which still keeps our security."

Privately, on February 22 Thatcher sent Reagan a short letter urging him to stop his calls for the elimination of nuclear weapons because doing so was harming her attempt to modernize the British defensive forces "by giving the impression that a future without nuclear weapons is near at hand." Thatcher added, "We must continue to make the case for deterrence based on nuclear weapons for several years to come."

The day after Chernenko's death in March 1985, Reagan started the most important official correspondences of his presidency.

March 11, 1985
Dear Mr. General Secretary:

As you assume your new responsibilities, I would like to take this opportunity to underscore my hope that we can in the months and years ahead develop a more stable and constructive relationship between our two countries. Our differences are many, and we will need to proceed in a way that takes both differences and common interests into account in seeking to resolve problems and build a new measure of trust and confidence. But history places on us a very heavy responsibility for maintaining and strengthening peace, and I am convinced we have before us new opportunities to do so. Therefore I have requested the Vice President to deliver this letter to you.

I believe our differences can and must be resolved through discussion and negotiation. The international situation demands that we redouble our efforts to find political solutions to the problems we face. I valued my correspondence with Chairman Chernenko, and believe my meetings with First Deputy Prime Minister Gromyko and Mr. Shcherbitsky here in Washington were useful in clarifying views and issues and making it possible to move forward to deal with them in a practical and realistic fashion.

In recent months we have demonstrated that it is possible to resolve problems to mutual benefit. We have had useful exchanges on certain regional issues, and I am sure you are aware that American interests in progress on humanitarian issues remains as strong as ever. In our bilateral relations, we have signed a number of new agreements, and we have promising negotiations underway in several important fields. Most significantly, the negotiations we have agreed to begin in Geneva provide us with a genuine chance to make progress toward our common ultimate goal of eliminating nuclear weapons.

It is important for us to build on these achievements. You can be assured of my personal commitment to work with you and the rest of the Soviet leadership in serious negotiations. In that spirit, I would like to invite you to visit me in Washington at your earliest convenient opportunity. I recognize that an early answer may not be possible, but I want you to know that I look forward to a meeting that could yield results of benefit to both our countries and to the international community as a whole.

Sincerely,
Ronald Reagan

Gorbachev was quick to respond, and on March 25, Shultz was handed a letter in which Gorbachev agreed to a summit "to search for mutual understanding on the basis of equality and account of the legitimate interests of each other." Shultz, in his cover letter to Reagan, thought Gorbachev had in mind an August meeting in Helsinki "on the occasion of the tenth anniversary of the CSCE Final Act."

The same day the Gorbachev letter arrived, Reagan, in a White House press conference before the House vote on the M-X missile, called the M-X "absolutely essential to our national security and our hopes for peace." "And if we fail," Reagan said, "we'll be signaling to the world that on this key issue we are irresolute and divided. And the Soviet Union will see that, in dealing with the United States, propaganda and stonewalling are much more profitable than good-faith negotiations."

In a letter dated April 4 (hand-delivered by House Speaker O'Neill during his congressional visit to Moscow), Reagan told Gorbachev that he very much appreciated the importance of continued correspondences and would soon be responding to his March 24 letter.

Reagan's eleven page response, dated April 30, started by criticizing Gorbachev for not taking responsibility for the death of Major Arthur D. Nicholson, 37, who was shot to death on the afternoon of March 24 by a Soviet soldier while on a monitoring mission in East Germany.[18] Reagan then moved to the Soviet invasion of Afghanistan[19] before addressing arms control negotiations and SDI.

A particular obstacle to progress has been the demand by Soviet negotiators that, in effect, the United States agree to ban research on advanced defensive systems before other topics are dealt with seriously. I hope that I have misunderstood the Soviet position on this point, because, if that is the Soviet position, no progress will be possible. For reasons we have explained repeatedly and in detail, we see no way that a ban on research efforts can be verified. Indeed in Geneva, Foreign Minister Gromyko acknowledged the difficulty of verifying such a ban on research. Nor do we think such a ban would be in the interest of either of our countries. To hold the negotiations hostage to an impossible demand creates an insurmountable obstacle from the outset. I sincerely hope that this is not your intent, since it cannot be in the interest of either of our countries. In fact, it is inconsistent with your own actions – with the strategic defense you already deploy around Moscow and with your own major research program in strategic defense.

In this regard, I was struck by the characterization of our Strategic Defense Initiative which you made during your meeting with Speaker O'Neill's

---

[18] Major Nicholson was one of 14 officers assigned to East Germany under a 1947 US-Soviet agreement that provided for the exchange of intelligence-gathering missions in East and West Germany. The Soviets maintain that Nicholson was trying to take photographs in a clearly marked restricted area, a charge the State Department denied. Major Nicholson's death is now considered the last casualty of the Cold War.

[19] Reagan wrote on Afghanistan: "One situation which has had a profoundly negative impact on our relations is the conflict in Afghanistan. Isn't it long overdue to reach a political resolution of this tragic affair? I cannot believe that it is impossible to find a solution which protects the legitimate interests of all parties, that of the Afghan people to live in peace under a government of their own choosing, and that of the Soviet Union to ensure that its southern border is secure. … I fear that your present course will only lead to more bloodshed, but I want you to know that I am prepared to work with you to move the region toward peace, if you desire."

delegation – that this research program has an offensive purpose for an attack on the Soviet Union. I can assure you that you are profoundly mistaken on this point. The truth is precisely the opposite. We believe that it is important to explore the technical feasibility of defensive systems which might ultimately give all of us the means to protect our people more safely than do those we have at present, and to provide the means of moving to the total abolition of nuclear weapons, an objective on which we are agreed. I must ask you, how are we ever practically to achieve that noble aim if nations have no defense against the uncertainty that all nuclear weapons might not have been removed from world arsenals? Life provides no guarantee against some future madman getting his hands on nuclear weapons, the technology of which is already, unfortunately, far too widely known and knowledge of which cannot be erased from human minds.

Reagan then spent a page on human rights before concluding by thanking Gorbachev for agreeing to a summit, leaving it up to him to pick a time and place. The eleven page letter received a ten page response on June 10.

Date: **June 10, 1985**
Subject: **Letter from Gorbachev to Reagan**

Dear Mr. President,
    I noted the intention expressed in your letter of April 30 to share thoughts in our correspondence with complete fairness. This is also my attitude.

Gorbachev then quickly called Major Nicholson's death "deplorable" and changed the subject to the "major problems" – the fact that the Soviet Union has nuclear weapons pointed at it from every direction while the United States does not, and the fact that SDI research is leading to the militarization of space.

The attempts to develop a large-scale ABM system inevitably set in train a radical destabilization of the situation. Even the factor of uncertainty as such will not only prevent any limitation of nuclear weapons, but will, instead, lead to their build-up and improvement. Therefore, when we resolutely raise the question and state that the militarization of space is impermissible, it is not propaganda and not a consequence of some misunderstanding or fear of "falling behind technology." It is a result of thorough analysis, of our deep concern about the future of relations between our countries, the future of peace.

Gorbachev then denounced SDI research – "All facts unambiguously indicate that the U.S. embarks upon the path of developing attack space weapons capable of performing purely offensive missions" – and criticized the American negotiating positions in Geneva – "On the subject of preventing an arms race in space the U.S. delegation did not present a single consideration at all. I emphasize, not a single one."

Gorbachev also denied any Soviet violations of the ABM Treaty and reminded Reagan that both countries share a common interest, "to avoid war." Moving to "stimulating" the Geneva negotiations, Gorbachev suggested a moratorium on all nuclear weapon tests; trilateral negotiations with Britain "on the complete and general prohibition of nuclear weapon tests"; discussing the problems of chemical weapons at the Stockholm Conference (CDE); and suggested that Reagan reevaluate his negotiating positions on MBFR because doing so "would be in your and in our interests, in the interests of a military relaxation in Europe."

In terms of human rights, "[T]here should be no misunderstanding concerning the fact that we do not intend and will not conduct any negotiations relating to human rights in the Soviet Union," Gorbachev informed Reagan. "We, as any other sovereign state, regarded and will regard these questions in accordance with our existing laws and regulations."

Concluding on a positive note, Gorbachev reiterated that he still wants a summit even though "holding it in the United States is unrealistic."

The same day of Gorbachev's June 10 letter, Reagan issued a public statement saying he had sent Gorbachev a letter detailing Soviet noncompliance with arms control agreements, and threatening that the United States would breakout of the SALT II constraints if Soviet violations were not soon corrected.

The Soviet response was quick and to the point: "President Reagan's statement pledging continued adherence to the 1979 arms treaty confirmed his intention to destroy the entire system of arms-control accords."[20] A more thorough, but no less direct, response came from Gorbachev on June 22.

Dear Mr. President...

I shall start by stating that your version of the past and present state of affairs in the key areas of Soviet-American relations, that of the limitation and reduction of strategic arms, cannot withstand comparison with the actual facts....

It is not for the sake of polemics, but in order to restore the full picture of what has occurred, that I would like to return briefly to what has been done by the United States with regard to the current regime for strategic stability.

One cannot dispute the fact that the American side created an ambiguous situation whereby the SALT II Treaty, one of the pillars of our relationship in the security sphere, was turned into a semi-functioning document that the U.S., moreover, is now threatening to nullify step by step...

The chain ensuring the viability of the process of curbing the arms race, put together through great effort, was consciously broken...

---

[20] *NYT:* June 12, 1985: "Soviet's Say Reagan is Gradually Ending Pact." A8.

It is no secret as to what guided the American side in taking this step: it wanted to gain an advantage by deploying long-range cruise missiles. As a result, already today one has to deal with thousands of such missiles. The U.S. sought to sharply tilt in its favor the fine-tuned balance of interests underlying the agreement. Now you see, I believe, that it did not work out this way. We too are deploying cruise missiles, which we had proposed to ban. But even now we are prepared to come to an agreement on such a ban, should the U.S., taking a realistic position, agree to take such an important step.

The deployment in Western Europe of new nuclear systems designed to perform strategic missions was a clear circumvention, that is non-compliance, by the American side with regard to the SALT II Treaty. In this, Mr. President, we see an attempt by the United States, taking advantage of geographic factors, to gain a virtual monopoly on the use of weapons in a situation for which our country has no analogue. I know that on your side the need for some regional balance is sometimes cited. But even in that case it is incomprehensible why the U.S. refuses to resolve the issue in a manner which would establish in the zone of Europe a balance of medium-range missiles, whereby the USSR would not have more missiles and warheads on them than are currently in the possession of England and France. Such a formula would not infringe upon anyone's interests, whereas the distortion caused by the American missiles in Europe is not a balance at all.

In broader terms, all these violations by the United States of the regime for strategic stability have one common denominator: departure from the principle of equality and equal security. This and nothing else is the reason for the lack of process in limiting and reducing nuclear arms over the past 4-5 years.

However, I would like you to have a clear understanding of the fact that, in practice, strategic parity between our countries will be maintained. We cannot envisage nor can we permit a different situation. The question, however, is at what level parity will be maintained – at a decreasing or an increasing one. We are for the former, for the reduction in the level of strategic confrontation. Your government, by all indications, favors the latter, evidently hoping that at some stage the U.S. will ultimately succeed in getting ahead. This is the essence of the current situation.

Should one be surprised, then, that we are conducting negotiations, yet the process of practical arms limitation remains suspended? It would probably not be too great a misfortune if this process simply remained frozen. But even that is not the case. The "star wars" program – I must tell you this, Mr. President – already at this stage is seriously undermining stability. We strongly advise you to halt this sharply destabilizing and dangerous program while things have not gone too far. If the situation in this area is not corrected, we shall have no choice but to take steps required by our security and that of our allies.

We are in favor, as you say, of making the best use of the chance offered by the Geneva negotiations on nuclear and space arms. Our main objective at those negotiations should be to reestablish the suspended process of limiting the arms race and to prevent its spread into new spheres.

The SALT II Treaty is an important element of the strategic equilibrium, and one should clearly understand its role as well as the fact that, according to the well-known expression, one cannot have one's pie and eat it too.

Your approach is determined by the fact that the strategic programs being carried out by the United States are about to collide with the limitations established by the SALT II Treaty, and the choice is being made not in favor of the Treaty, but in favor of these programs. And this cannot be disavowed or concealed, to put it bluntly, by unseemly attempts to accuse the Soviet Union of all mortal sins. It is, moreover, completely inappropriate in relations between our two countries for one to set forth conditions for the another as is done in your letter with regard to the Soviet Union.

I am saying all this frankly and unequivocally, as we have agreed.

One certainly cannot agree that the provisions of the SALT II Treaty remain in force allegedly as the result of restraint on the part of the United States. Entirely by contrary. The general attitude toward the Treaty shown by the American side and its practical actions to undermine it have given us every reason to draw appropriate conclusions and to take practical steps. We did have and continue to have moral, legal and political grounds for that

We did not, however, give away to emotions; we showed patience, realizing the seriousness of the consequences of the path onto which we were being pushed. We hoped also that sober reasoning, as well as the self interest of the U.S., would make the American side take a more restrained position. That was what in fact happened to a certain, though not to a full, extent. And we have treated this in businesslike fashion. Without ignoring what has been done by the American side contrary to the SALT II Treaty, we nevertheless at no time have been the initiators of politico-propagandistic campaigns of charges and accusations. We have striven to discuss seriously within the framework of the SCC the well-founded concerns we have had. We also have given exhaustive answers there to questions raised by the American side.

Unfortunately, the behavior of the other side was and continues to be utterly different. All those endless reports on imaginary Soviet violations and their publication did not and cannot serve any useful purpose, if one is guided by the tasks of preserving and continuing the process of arms limitation. Why mince words, the objective is quite different: to cast aspersions on the policy of the Soviet Union in general, to sow distrust toward it and to create an artificial pretext for an accelerated and uncontrolled arms race. All this became evident to us already long ago.

One has to note that your present decision, if it were to be implemented, would be a logical continuation of that course. We would like you, Mr. President, to think all this over once again.

In any event, we shall regard the decision that you announced in the entirety of its mutually-exclusive elements which, along with the usual measures required by the Treaty, includes also a claim to some "right" to violate provisions of the Treaty as the American side chooses. Neither side has such a right. I do not consider it necessary to go into specifics here, a lot has been said about it, and your military experts are well aware of the actual, rather than distorted, state of affairs.

One should not count on the fact that we will be able to come to terms with you with respect to destroying the SALT II Treaty through joint efforts. How things will develop further depends on the American side, and we shall draw the appropriate conclusions.

The question of the approach to arms limitation has been, is, and will be the central issue both in our relations and as far as the further development of the overall international situation is concerned. It is precisely here, above all, that the special responsibility borne by our two countries is manifested, as well as how each of them approaches that responsibility.

In more specific terms it is a question of intentions with regard to one other. No matter what is being done in other spheres of our relationship, in the final analysis, whether or not it is going to be constructive and stable depends above all on whether we are going to find a solution to the central issues of security on the basis of equality and equal security.

I would like to reaffirm that, for our part, we are full of resolve to strive to find such a solution. This determines both our attitude toward those initial limitations which were arrived at earlier through painstaking joint labor, and our approach to the negotiations currently underway in Geneva and elsewhere.

I wish to say this in conclusion: one would certainly like to feel tangibly the same attitude on the part of the United States. At any rate, as I have already had a chance to note, we took seriously the thought reiterated by you in our correspondence with regard to a joint search for ways to improve Soviet-American relations and to strengthen the foundations of peace.

Sincerely,
M. Gorbachev

POSTSCRIPT

The next declassified letter is not until September 12, but just a few weeks after Gorbachev's letter the announcement came on July 3 that Reagan and Gorbachev agreed to a November arms control summit in Geneva.

The summer continued with press statements and radio addresses on the upcoming negotiations and the importance Reagan placed on SDI research. Reagan was also dealing with the hostage situation in Lebanon and, as later revealed, arm sales to Iranian intermediaries to secure the release of the hostages.

Following through with a May 1985 suggestion from Pat Buchanan – Reagan's Director of Communications – on July 15 Reagan ordered the creation of a Blue Ribbon Commission on Defense Management to drum up support for his defense program. A short statement came the next day on the ongoing negotiations in Geneva: "In sum, we are about where we had expected to be. …We hope the Soviet Union will be more forthcoming in the next round of negotiations." Two weeks later, in another White House statement, Reagan did not pull any punches:

> We regret that the Soviet Union to date has been unwilling to negotiate in concrete and detailed terms to achieve such reductions in Geneva. In this respect not only have they failed to address our desire for deep reductions and enhanced stability, but they have not been willing to present specific numerical levels supporting their own approach.

Gorbachev, on a public relations tour of his own, sat down with *Time* magazine on September 3 for his first interview with western journalists. Asked about the prospects for a successful arms agreement at the Geneva Summit, Gorbachev responded that without an agreement restraining the SDI program, no other agreements would be reached.

Gorbachev was not bluffing. In his next letter to Reagan, on September 12, he proposed a 50 percent reduction in nuclear arms if Reagan agreed to "a complete ban on space attack weapons." For Europe, Gorbachev also announced, he would reduce, counting by numbers of warheads, to whatever level of intermediate range nuclear forces Britain and France possessed.

Date: **September 20, 1985**
Subject: **Visit of Soviet Foreign Minister Shevardnadze**
Status: **Declassified in Part (2008)**

BACKGROUND

Today's meeting, the first in a series of meetings before the Geneva Summit, is called to formulate a response to Gorbachev's proposal to reduce all nuclear weapons by 50 percent if the U.S. agreed to ban "space attack weapons".

SUMMARY

MCFARLANE: This NSC session is going to be a forum to provide the President with a strategic overview of the broad direction we hope to pursue in dealing with the Soviet leadership between now and the meeting in November. We will also be reviewing the major issues on our bilateral, human rights and regional agendas. Arms control has been dealt with earlier, and we are going to take it up again next week.

The process was set in motion two months ago by the President's invitation to the soviet general secretary. Our preparations for these meetings have enabled us to prepare solid positions in the four areas that will be on the agenda. These include bilateral issues, such as air safety, the opening up of new consulates, and the renewed exchanges agreement; human rights concerns; regional issues like Afghanistan, Central America and other parts of the globe will be on the table; and security issues, particularly arms control.

Before moving to the substantive issues, it would be helpful to review the major public diplomacy events leading to the Geneva meetings. Our program is designed to ensure that the President has solid support from three key audiences – our allies, the Congress, and the U.S. public. We have selected activities and events that will demonstrate that we are prepared for substantive results in Geneva and that we go there with a comprehensive and reasonable agenda. We feel the Soviets moved quickly and early to seize the high ground in this area with a blistering propaganda campaign. However, we feel that the Soviet effort has been perceived for what it is – old propaganda in new packaging – and has made no lasting impact on allied or American public opinion.

The secretary of state speech in New York next week, followed by his meetings with Shevardnadze, will initiate a series of critical events in our game-plan for Geneva; this will be followed by the President's vey important meeting with Foreign Minister Shevardnadze on Friday. We believe that the foreign minister will bring a fairly elaborate and concrete arms control proposal, to be revealed either during his UN speech or presented here on Friday. General Secretary Gorbachev will be in France from October 2-5. We can expect a flurry of media attention, but we doubt that any concrete results will come from his meetings with Mitterrand.

We believe the tide of public opinion will be shifting to our favor given the substantive thrust of our proposals. While most of the media attention to date has been on arms control issues, these events will enable us to demonstrate that our agenda includes efforts to engage the Soviets on the other sources of tension between us –

human rights, Afghanistan and their expansionist policies. We will make it clear that our themes for the November meeting – <u>Realism</u>, <u>Restraint</u>, and <u>Reciprocity</u> – offer real hope for substantive progress.

I am now going to turn to the secretary of state who will provide us an overview of the three issue areas that are the focus of today's meeting – human rights, regional concerns, and bilateral issues.

SHULTZ: I am not ready to fully discuss the issue areas that are at the heart of today's meeting. (Instead), I'm better prepared to carry the discussion to the issues and objectives we have for the Shevardnadze and Gorbachev meetings.

We have not achieved substantial progress on any of our bilateral issues – most remain on dead center. The most fruitful discussions have been on the North Pacific Air Safety Agreement, but we still have not reached any operational understandings with the Soviets on improved procedures. A cultural agreement, providing for a resumption of our formal exchange program with the USSR, shows some promise of being ready for signature prior to November. The proposal to open up new consulates in New York and Kiev is proceeding but we remain concerned with the increase of Soviet personnel this would place in New York. A boundary dispute in the Bearing Sea is also under intense discussion.

Under the regional concerns there are four principal areas we will want to address. We have had extensive discussions with the Soviets on Afghan, Asian and African problems, and expect to discuss Central America prior to the President's meeting with Gorbachev. While no substantial progress has been achieved, we are interested in institutionalizing the concept of these meetings on regional concerns. This will help promote the idea that we and the Soviets are seriously talking about problems around the world.

There is a general feeling that the area that might best lend itself to substantial progress is Afghanistan. The Indians, in particular, have made this point to us. In the President's meeting with the General Secretary, he should, on the one hand, stress our readiness to seek a resolution of the Afghan situation. At the same time, the President will want to demonstrate the depth of our concern with the continuing Soviet ·occupation. It is important for the President to demonstrate to Gorbachev that he has steel in his backbone.

Human rights are certain to be the thorniest issue on the agenda. The Soviets resent the perceived intrusion into what they regard as internal matters and have roiled at our linkage with their behavior in this area to bilateral trade. We have traditionally made it clear that there is a direct relationship between Soviet compliance with agreements that have been signed with regard to human rights and the extent to which we are willing to increase non-strategic trade.

REAGAN: **Bob Michel has sent over a pertinent excerpt from Forest Pogue's biography of General George Marshall. In a discussion with Marshall near the end of World War II, General Deane made an interesting comment on the traditional Soviet way of dealing with foreigners. (Quoting Pogue)**

> **In a careful analysis of the situation Deane explained that part of the trouble arose from Russian suspicions of foreigners. They simply cannot understand giving without taking, and as a result even our giving is viewed with suspicion. Gratitude cannot be banked in the Soviet Union. Each transaction is complete in itself without regard to past favors. The party of the second part is either a shrewd trader to be admired or a sucker to be despised. He made it clear that the picture was not all bad – the individual Russians were likeable, and he thought that they would be friendly if they dared.**

SHULTZ: We must be careful in the language we use in our public presentations; we need to avoid using the phrase that we are "flexible." To the Soviets, this would connote a weak stance on our part. It would be much better to use the phrase, "We are prepared for a serious give-and-take."

REAGAN: **I agree. Just think about the Soviet historical fear of invasions and suspicions of foreigners that reaches extreme paranoia in some cases. During World War II the Eighth Air Force suffered extensive casualties flying bombing runs over German troop positions, and particularly when they had a return over the same routes. This was because the Soviets denied them permission to land in Soviet-controlled areas.**

SHULTZ: The most useful instruments we have to break down those suspicions are the exchanges and exhibits we send to the Soviet Union.

Jack (Matlock), how did you evaluate the utility of these exhibits?

MATLOCK: These exchanges have considerable value. One exhibit drew 250,000 visitors from a single city. The exhibits were staffed with Russian-speaking American guides providing Soviet citizens with perhaps their most informative look at the American way of life.

REAGAN: **A defector recounted the story of when his father, a high-ranking general, was driving along a narrow mountain road and encountered another car. While there was room for the general to move over further, he directed his driver to stand fast. In the general's mind, any concession to move from his position would have been degrading.**

MCFARLANE: Director Casey will now present an intelligence perspective on Soviet objectives for the Shevardnadze and Gorbachev meetings.

CASEY: It is difficult to say with confidence precisely what the Soviets seek to achieve. We are fairly certain that their principal concern at the present time is our SDI program. A second major concern to the Soviets will be alleviating drains on their sluggish economy.

Overall, there are three primary Soviet objectives: 1) limiting our strategic defense program, particularly preventing any testing or deployment of weapons with real potential; 2) creating the public impression that progress in the arms control area is directly dependent upon American willingness to cooperate; and 3) reducing tensions between the superpowers. The rationale for doing so is not because of a desire to improve relations per se, but to increase trade between the USA and the USSR, which they realize depends on better ties.

The Soviets will try to prevent SDI through technical means, but if they are unsuccessful, they will seek to halt our program politically by influencing American and European public opinion. Thus, we understand that Shevardnadze will be bringing a major arms control proposal with him. We believe that he will introduce the proposal during his address at the United Nations, but he could make it public as early as this Sunday, or to increase the attention to his Washington visit, present it to the President during their meeting next Friday.

The intelligence community sees little chance for progress in the arms control area and speculates that the Soviet proposal will provide little in the way of substance. It is important to the Kremlin to convey a picture of reasonableness at this time. On trade, the Soviets will not be coming hat-in-hand, but will seek to promote trade by stressing the mutual advantages such an increase might bring.

The Soviets strongly wish to avoid any discussions of human rights. However, we have some indications, principally from Edgar Bronfman's discussions in Moscow, that they may create a publicity windfall by permitting the emigration of a few well-known Jewish activists. Finally, the Soviets will not stress bilateral issues during these meetings.

MCFARLANE: Secretary Weinberger, would you like to provide a defense perspective on the upcoming meetings and the three areas under discussion?

WEINBERGER: We can't underestimate the importance of our SDI program in Soviet thinking. They will be looking for ways in which they can secure an advantage. The consular agreement currently under discussion presents serious concerns to us because the Soviets send over only fully-equipped spies, reporting directly to either the KGB or the GRU.

Both Shevardnadze and Gorbachev will be seeking to blame us for contributing to the creation of a charged atmosphere prior to these meetings. They will allege that this was the rationale behind our raising the Spy Dust issue, when this was in fact a blatant Soviet violation of standard diplomatic custom.[21]

We believe that attention should also be addressed to the Soviet failure to resolve satisfactorily all of the problems revolving around our military liaison missions (MLMs) in the Berlin area. The latest incident was not serious, but could have been.

I agree with CIA that they will be seeking oil and gas equipment from us, and it is imperative that we not allow them to use our technology to their own advantage.

---

[21] Weinberger is likely referring to the fact that 1985 became the "Year of the Spy" after the United States arrested and accused several U.S. Government personnel of spying for the Soviet Union. Several convictions followed and many sensitive U.S. operations, including the wiretapping of undersea cables to monitor Soviet military communications and the locations of submarines, were compromised.

Finally, we should be prepared to counter strongly any allegations they will accuse us of in the human rights area by stressing the nature of our free society and Soviet non-compliance with the Helsinki Agreement.

The President should be firm on Afghanistan. The Soviets should understand that this is a matter all Americans feel strongly about. The Soviets need to withdraw from Afghanistan and we should be prepared to assist them in doing so. In Kampuchea, Moscow should be using its influence on Hanoi to get the Vietnamese to withdraw. And in Central America, we should tell the Soviets to stop interfering in the region.

REAGAN: **(Returning to the best way to handle human rights), in studying our successes and failures in the past, quiet diplomacy has produced substantive results. However, when the glare of publicity was brought on these negotiations the Soviets quickly hardened their position. We might speak privately to the Soviets and indicate that we are prepared to cooperate on this issue. In particular, we would not publicize their concessions if they complied fully with the Helsinki Agreement.**

MCFARLANE: I'm in basic agreement with the President, but for the sake of discussion will play the devil's advocate. If Gorbachev wished he might play this private dialogue back to American public opinion to create the impression that we are not sincerely interested in pressing this issue. Still, the thought has considerable merit. Perhaps the best tactic would be to approach the Soviets at the ministerial level.

REAGAN: **I agree. (The quiet arrangement worked in the past), whereby we had rescinded the grain embargo with the result that there are some happy people now living in the West. That one we worked quietly through Ambassador Dobrynin.**

BUSH: I agree that human rights will be one of the most divisive issues on the agenda. In my meetings with Georgy Arbatov, it was clear that the Soviets will either seek to avoid discussion or launch a concerted counterattack on us. Many of these problems could be resolved along the lines the President suggested; through quiet agreements by high-level diplomats working privately.

SHULTZ:	The CIA produced a very useful paper suggesting that the Soviets may have a serious interest in reaching an arms control agreement. Economic conditions, their situation in Afghanistan, and Gorbachev's focus on his domestic agenda, could impel them to seek resolution of some of their international difficulties. We need to treat this possibility seriously and decide how best we can take advantage of potential opportunities.
	It is important for us to strive to achieve our objectives. If we earnestly do so, it is very possible we can bring them to realization. We simply can't just continue claiming that all the Soviets have in mind is creating a propaganda screen.
CASEY:	I agree, but the Soviets will still focus on stopping our SDI program.
WEINBERGER:	They will also seek to preserve their lead in areas where they are ahead.
REAGAN:	**The Soviets traditionally only make agreements where they see clear advantages. I agree with George (Shultz) that the most acute problem facing the Soviets at this time is the state of their economy. The question is how far Gorbachev will be prepared to go because of this (their economy).**
	We must be prepared to seize any opening presented to us. In this regard, President Nixon's recent statement is entirely apropos. He said, "We want peace. They need peace." Thus, the Soviets will have some motivation to reach agreements.
WEINBERGER:	The Soviets will perceive a need for reducing their arms burdens, but only at a later date will they be persuaded to move in this direction.
REAGAN:	**Yes, SDI may very will be our most important leverage. I am prepared, once any of our SDI programs prove out, to then announce to the world that integrating these weapons in our respective arsenals would put international relations on a more stable footing. In fact, this could even lead to a complete elimination of nuclear weapons.**
	We must be prepared to tell the world we are ready to consult and negotiate on integrating these weapons into a new defense philosophy, and to state openly that we are ready to internationalize these systems.

MCFARLANE: That concludes this NSC meeting. More sessions will be held the following week as we finalize our preparations for Foreign Minister Shevardnadze's visit.

POSTSCRIPT

Several more still classified meetings on arms control were held before the Geneva Summit, and Reagan and Gorbachev exchanged at least four more letters prior to meeting in Geneva. In one of Reagan's letters, dated October 13, he suggested they could reach "radical and stabilizing reductions in strategic offensive arms and a separate agreement on intermediate-range nuclear missile systems." In terms of SDI research, Reagan proposed "that both sides provide assurances that their strategic defense programs are and will remain in full accord with the ABM Treaty."

The problem with Reagan's SDI proposal, Gorbachev noted at Geneva, was that Reagan's staff was in the process of undermining the ABM Treaty by urging the least restrictive interpretation (as opposed to the restrictive interpretation) under which SDI research and testing could be conducted in space (as opposed to just in laboratories).

Date: **November 21-22, 1985**
Subject: **The Geneva Summit**
Status: **Declassified**

SUMMARY

The Geneva Summit, the first meeting in seven years between a President of the United States and a general secretary of the Soviet Union, started with a private meeting (interpreters and note-takers only). Reagan characterized U.S.-Soviet relations as "peaceful competition" and Gorbachev emphasized cooperation rather than confrontation" and the importance of halting the arms race. Reagan, perhaps already sensing that a deal was not in reach, suggested starting with confidence-building measures. "In the meeting with the larger group, where we should soon move," Reagan told Gorbachev, "the sides can explain why there is mistrust, but can also begin to try to eliminate this mistrust."

Moving into the big conference room for the first plenary session, Gorbachev welcomed Reagan's proposal for further exchanges in the areas of science and technology to help remove the distrust that currently exists. Moving to SDI, Reagan called it a "shield" and criticized Gorbachev for trying to curtail SDI when the Soviet's already have "the same kind of research program." "If one or both of us come up with such a system," Reagan added, "then they should sit down and make it available to everyone so no one would have a fear of a nuclear strike." Gorbachev held his response until the afternoon session.

"We think SDI can lead to an arms race in space, and not just a defensive arms race, but an offensive arms race with space weapons," Gorbachev told Reagan after lunch. The General Secretary continued,

> Space weapons are harder to verify and will feed suspicions and mistrust. Scientists say any shield can be pierced, so SDI cannot save us. So why create it? It only makes sense if to defend against a retaliatory strike....
>
> I know that you, Mr. President, are attached to SDI, and for that reason we have analyzed it seriously. Our conclusion is that if the U.S. implements its plan, we will not cooperate in an effort to gain superiority over us. We will have to frustrate this plan, and we will build up in order to smash your shield.
>
> You say the Soviet Union is doing the same, but this is not the case. Both of us do research in space of course, but our research is for peaceful purposes. The U.S., in contrast has military aims, and that is an important difference. The U.S. goal violates the ABM Treaty, which is of fundamental importance. Testing is also inconsistent with the Treaty, and can only exacerbate mistrust.
>
> If the U.S. embarks on SDI the following will happen: (1) No reduction of offensive weapons; and (2) We will respond. This response will not be a mirror image of your program, but a simpler, more effective system.

Three more private meetings and two plenary sessions followed over the next two days, but both Reagan and Gorbachev were committed to their positions. All was not lost, however, because Gorbachev agreed to visit Washington in 1986 and Reagan agreed to go to Moscow in 1987.

Stopping at NATO headquarters on the way home, Reagan called SDI "one of the most important developments of this century... it was clear that we could not reconcile our differences over SDI." With respect to a possible INF agreement, Reagan reported an interim agreement capping NATO missiles at the level deployed at the end of this year with the Soviets reducing down to the same level within range of NATO Europe as well as proportionate reductions in Asia. Foreshadowing an INF agreement, Reagan also said they agreed to separate out INF talks so that INF "would not be held hostage to progress in space talks."

CHAPTER SEVEN

PREPARING FOR REYKJAVIK

"Modernization must be seen as modernization, not as a buildup. I'm willing to bring the number of missiles down if the Soviets will reduce. We can come down to any equal levels if they join us."[22]

---

[22] President Reagan during an April 16, 1986 NSC meeting.

Date: November 28, 1985
Subject: **Letter from Reagan to Gorbachev**
(See endnotes for transcription)

THE WHITE HOUSE
WASHINGTON

Nov. 28 '85

Dear Secretary General Gorbachev

Now that we are both home & facing the task of leading our countries into a more constructive relationship with each other, I wanted to waste no time in giving you some of my initial thoughts on our meetings. Though I will be sending shortly, in a more formal & official manner, a more detailed commentary on our discussions, there are some things I would like to convey very personally & privately.

First, I want you to know that I found our meetings of great value. We had agreed to speak frankly, and we did. As a result, I came away from the meeting with a better understanding of your attitudes. I hope you also understand mine a little better. Obviously there are many things on which we disagree, and disagree very fundamentally. But if I understand you correctly, you too are determined to take steps to see that our nations manage their relations in a peaceful fashion. If this is the case, then this is one point on which we are in total agreement —— and it is after all the most fundamental one of all.

THE WHITE HOUSE
WASHINGTON

As for our substantive differences, let me offer some thoughts on two of the key ones.

Regarding strategic defense and it's relation to the reduction of offensive nuclear weapons, I was struck by your conviction that the American program is somehow designed to secure a strategic advantage -- even to permit a first strike capability. I also noted your concern that research & testing in this area could be a cover for developing & placing offensive weapons in space.

As I told you, neither of these concerns is warranted. But I can understand, as you explained so eloquently, that there are matters which cannot be taken on faith. Both of us must cope with what the other side is doing, & judge the implications for the security of his own country. I do not ask you to take my assurances on faith.

However the truth is that the United States has no intention of using it's strategic defense program to gain any advantage, & there is no development underway to create space-based offensive weapons. Our goal is to eliminate any possibility of a first strike from either side. This being the case, we should be able to find a way, in practical terms, to relieve the concerns you have expressed.

For example, could our negotiators, when they resume work in January, discuss frankly & specifically what sort of future developments each of us would find threatening? Neither of us, it seems, wants to see offensive weapons, particularly weapons of mass destruction, deployed in space. Should we not attempt to define what sort of systems have that potential and then try to find verifiable ways to prevent their development?

And can't our negotiators deal more frankly & openly with the question of how to eliminate a first-strike potential on both sides? Your military now has an advantage in this area — a three to one advantage in warheads that can destroy hardened targets with little warning. That is obviously alarming to us, & explains many of the efforts we are making in our modernization program. You may feel perhaps that the U.S. has some advantages in other categories. If so, let's insist that our negotiators face up to these issues & find a way to improve the security of both countries by agreeing on appropriately balanced reductions. If you are as sincere as I am in not seeking to secure or preserve one-sided advantages, we will find a solution to these problems.

THE WHITE HOUSE
WASHINGTON

Regarding another key issue we discussed, that of regional conflicts, I can assure you that the United States does not believe that the Soviet Union is the cause of all the world's ills. We do believe, however, that your country has exploited and worsened local tensions & conflict by militarizing them and, indeed, intervening directly & indirectly in struggles arising out of local causes. While we both will doubtless continue to support our friends, we must find a way to do so without use of armed force. This is the crux of the point I tried to make.

One of the most significant steps in lowering tension in the world — & tension in U.S.–Soviet relations — would be a decision on your part to withdraw your forces from Afghanistan. I gave careful attention to your comments on this issue at Geneva, and am encouraged by your statement that you feel political reconciliation is possible. I want you to know that I am prepared to cooperate in any reasonable way to facilitate such a withdrawal, & that I understand that it must be done in a manner which does not damage Soviet security interests. During our meetings I mentioned one idea which I thought might be helpful & I will welcome any further suggestions you may have.

THE WHITE HOUSE

WASHINGTON

These are only two of the key issues on our current agenda. I will soon send some thoughts on others. I believe that we should act promptly to build the momentum our meeting initiated.

In Geneva I found our private sessions particularly useful. Both of us have advisors & assistants, but, you know, in the final analysis, the responsibility to preserve peace & increase cooperation is ours. Our people look to us for leadership, and nobody can provide it if we don't. But we won't be very effective leaders unless we can rise above the specific but secondary concerns that preoccupy our respective bureaucracies & give our governments a strong push in the right direction.

So, what I want to say finally is that we should make the most of the time before we meet again to find some specific & significant steps that would give meaning to our commitment to peace & arms reduction. Why not set a goal — privately, first between the two of us — to find a practical way to solve critical issues — the two I have mentioned — by the time we meet in Washington?

Please convey regards from Nancy & me to Mrs. Gorbacheva. We genuinely enjoyed meeting you in Geneva & are already looking forward to showing you something of our country next year.

Sincerely yours,   Ronald Reagan

Date: **December 24, 1985**
Subject: **Letter from Gorbachev to Reagan**

DEPARTMENT OF STATE
DIVISION OF LANGUAGE SERVICES

(TRANSLATION)

LS NO.   118545
DZ/GT/WH/LB
Russian

His Excellency
Ronald W. Reagan
President of the United States
Washington, D.C.
The White House

Dear Mr. President:

I consider your letter important and also value the form you used in writing to me.

I say this to you because I see the desire to continue and to strengthen what we achieved in Geneva. I am glad that we began there -- both in substance and in spirit -- a direct and frank discussion. I attach special significance to the fact that we have been able to overcome the serious psychological barrier which for a long time has hindered a dialogue worthy of the leaders of the USSR and USA.

I have the feeling that now you and I can set formalities aside and can get down to the heart of the matter -- establishing a specific topical agenda for discussion over the next few years on the basis of our understanding, and straightening out Soviet -American relations. I visualize this task very concretely: we have to broaden areas of agreement, strengthen the elements of responsibleness in our policy, and make the appropriate practical decisions. In my opinion the ideal situation would be one in which you and I would give impetus to a constant forward movement. I agree with what you said: in the final analysis no one besides us can do this.

The first thing we should do is to take upon ourselves the task of undoing the knot which has been tied around the issues of nuclear and space weapons. I was encouraged by the fact that you, Mr. President, also consider that this is of key significance.

I think you understood from what I told you in Geneva that our decisive opposition to the development of space-strike weapons is dictated by the fact that weapons of this class which, due to their specific nature, possess the capability of being used both for defensive and offensive aims, represent in the final analysis an extremely dangerous build-up of offensive potential, with all the consequences inevitably ensuing therefrom from the point of view of further escalating the arms race.

/Released/
597-001 #118
BY _____ 10/99/90

You say, Mr. President, that the U.S. has no intention of using the SDI program to obtain military superiority.

I do not doubt that you personally may really have no such intentions. But you must agree that the leadership of one side has to evaluate the actions of the other in the area of developing new types of weapons, not in accordance with intentions, but in accordance with the potential cababilities which may be attained as a result of the development of these weapons.

Examining the SDI program from this perspective, the Soviet leadership comes to the same conclusion every time: given the realities of the current situation, only a country which is preparing for a first (disarming) strike needs a "space shield"; a country which does not base its actions on such a concept should have no need for such a weapons system.

After all, space-strike weapons are all-purpose weapons. The space-strike weapons that are being created in the U.S. are kinetic energy weapons and also long-range, directed energy systems (with a range of several thousand miles and great destructive power). As our experts and scientists and yours confirm, those weapons are capable of destroying in space, as well as from space, within a very short time, in great quantities and selectively, objects which are thousands of miles away. I stress -- thousands of miles away.

For example, how should we regard the space weapons of a country which have the capability of destroying another country's centers for controlling space objects and of destroying its space devices for monitoring, navigation, communication etc. within very short time intervals measured in minutes? Essentially, these weapons can only be intended for "blinding" the other side, catching it unprepared and depriving it of the possibility of countering a nuclear strike. Moreover, if these weapons are developed, the process of perfecting them and giving them even better combat characteristics will begin immediately. Such is the course of development of all weaponry.

How then, Mr. President, should the Soviet Union act in such a situation? I would like to repeat what I already told you in Geneva. The USSR cannot simply reduce and will not reduce nuclear weapons to the detriment of its security, when the SDI program is being implemented in the U.S. Whether we like it or not, we will be forced to develop and improve our strategic nuclear forces and increase their capability of neutralizing the U.S. "space shield." At the same time, we would also have to develop our own space weapons inter alia for the purpose of

- 3 -

a territorial ABM defense. Probably, the U.S. would in turn
then take some other additional steps. As a result, we will
not get out of the vicious cycle of measures and
countermeasures, out of the whirlpool of an ever-increasing
arms race. The consequence of such competition for our peoples
and for all of mankind is unpredictable.

I am convinced that the only sensible way out is not to engage
in this at all. From every point of view the correct path for
our countries is negotiation on the prevention of an arms race
in space and its cessation on earth. And we need to come to
agreement on the basis of equal and mutually acceptable
conditions.

You and I agreed to accelerate the negotiations. I took
satisfaction in hearing you say that the U.S. would not
"develop space-based offensive weapons."

As I see it, some kind of common basis is emerging between you
and me for a very significant part of the problem of preventing
an arms race in space. Let us have our representatives at the
negotiations proceed on this basis to begin working out
specific measures to prevent the development of offensive space
weapons, i.e., all space-based weapons which can destroy
targets in space and from space.

In the spirit of the frankness in which we are talking, I would
like to say that this issue has now become very acute: either
events will determine policy or we will determine policy. In
order not to be governed by events, it is especially important
once again to conduct a profound analysis of all aspects of the
objective interrelationship between offensive and defensive
weapons and to hear each other out on this issue. However, it
seems to me that there will be little meaning to such
discussions if in tandem with them weapons of war start coming
out of the doors of our laboratories, weapons whose influence
on strategic stability we must not now miscalculate. Common
sense dictates that until we determine together those
consequences, we must not permit anything to go beyond the
walls of the laboratory. We are prepared to negotiate to reach
agreement on this matter as well.

It appears to me this is a practical way to implement the joint
accord you and I confirmed in Geneva concerning the
inadmissibility of an arms race in space and concerning the
ultimate elimination of nuclear arms.

In line with such an approach it would also make sense at the
Geneva negotiations to discuss the issue of eliminating the
danger of a first (disarming) nuclear strike. I would like to

- 4 -

state to you again very definitely: we are not making a bid
for a first nuclear strike, we are not preparing our nuclear
forces for one.

I cannot agree with the way you formulate the issue of first
strike nuclear forces. This issue, of course, is not merely
one of ICBM warheads. For example, there is no difference
between U.S. ballistic missile warheads on "Trident" submarines
and warheads on modern Soviet land-based intercontinental
ballistic missiles as far as their kill capability is
concerned, i.e. in terms of such indices as accuracy, power and
range. And if one considers this issue from the point of view
of warning time, then, for a significant portion of submarine
missiles, where the U.S. has a three-fold advantage in
warheads, the warning time is significantly shorter.

And can we view the "Pershing II" missiles deployed in Europe
with their high accuracy and short flight time to targets on
USSR territory as anything other than first-strike weapons?

Please forgive me for dealing with technical details in a
personal letter like this. But these are vitally important
realities, and we simply cannot get around them.

Believe me, Mr. President, we have a genuine and truly serious
concern about U.S. nuclear systems. You talk about mutual
concerns. This matter can be resolved only through considering
and counting the sum total of the respective nuclear systems of
both countries. Let our delegations discuss this matter as
well.

Mr. President, I would like to give you my brief reaction to
what you said concerning regional conflicts. At the time when
we touched on these issues in Geneva, I stressed that it is
most important to view things realistically, to see the world
as it is. If we recognize the fact that independent states
exist and function in the international arena, then we also
have to acknowledge their sovereign right to have relations
with whomever they wish and the right to ask for assistance,
including military assistance.

Both you and we offer such assistance. Why apply a double
standard and assert that Soviet assistance is a source of
tension and U.S. assistance is beneficial? It would be better
for us to be guided by objective criteria in this matter. The
Soviet Union is assisting legitimate governments which come to
us because they have been and are being subjected to outside

- 5 -

And, as the facts indicate, the U.S. incites actions against
governments and supports and supplies weapons to groups which
are inimical to society and which are, in essence, terrorists.
Looking at things objectively, it is such actions and outside
interference that create regional tension and conflict. If
such actions cease, I am convinced tensions will decrease and
the prospects for political settlements will become much better
and more realistic.

Unfortunately, at present, developments are proceeding in a
different direction. Take, for example, the unprecedented
pressure and threats which the government of Nicaragua is being
subjected to - a legitimate government brought to power through
free elections.

I will be frank: what the United States has done recently
causes concern. It seems that there is a tilt in the direction
of further exacerbation of regional problems. Such an approach
does not make it easier to find a common language and makes the
search for political solutions more difficult.

With regard to Afghanistan, one gets the impression that the
U.S. side intentionally fails to notice the "open door" leading
to a political settlement. Now there is even a working formula
for such a settlement. It is important not to hinder the
negotiations in progress, but to help them along. In that
event a fair settlement will definitely be found.

Mr. President, I would like to have you take my letter as
another one of our "fireside talks." I would truly like to
preserve not only the spirit of our Geneva meetings, but also
to go further in developing our dialogue. I view our
correspondence as a very important channel for preparing for
our meeting in Washington.

The new year will be upon us very soon, and I would like to
send you and your wife our very best wishes.

Sincerely,

M. Gorbachev

POSTSCRIPT

"The fact that the President wrote the letter in longhand obviously made an impression," the Department of State analysis of Gorbachev's letter started. "Gorbachev not only answered in kind, but with an unusual lack of formality." The State analysis continued,

> Gorbachev, however, is characteristically unyielding on substance, whether arms control or regional issues. On the former, he basically reaffirms current Soviet positions, dwelling, as in Geneva, on SDI.

> Gorbachev's extensive treatment of SDI is most interesting for his suggestion that the President's earlier assurances that the U.S. will not develop 'offensive space-based weapons' might serve as 'common ground' for discussion in Geneva. His definition of such weapons – all space-based weapons capable of destroying targets in space or from space – would have the practical effect of barring many potentially promising SDI technologies. But his expression of willingness to discuss the offense-defense relationship in detail appears to take the Soviet position beyond its previous refusal of U.S. proposals for a serious dialogue in this area.

Date: **February 3, 1986**
Subject: **Arms Control – Responding to Gorbachev**
Status: **Declassified (2005)**

BACKGROUND

Gorbachev announced, on January 15, his proposal for a three-phased plan to eliminate all nuclear weapons by the year 2000. The proposal was also sent to Reagan in a letter dated January 12. Today's meeting is called to formulate a response to both Gorbachev's December 24 letter and his January 15 proposal.

Personnel wise, McFarlane resigned as national security advisor at the end of 1985 and was immediately replaced by his deputy, John Poindexter, who became Reagan's fourth national security advisor in five years. McFarlane's resignation was probably a surprise to Reagan, but as the following memo shows, McFarlane had been having problems since Don Regan took over as the chief of staff.

MEMO FOR DON REGAN

From: Bud McFarlane
Subject: Advice to the President
Date: Aug. 1, 1985

I want to raise a matter which seems to me of considerable importance concerning how the President receives advice from his Cabinet and White House staff. There are many models for providing advice to the President and we should pursue the one which the President prefers. The experiences of the first term suggests that the President looks to his Cabinet Officers as the primary source of policy advice. On a given issue that advice often involves the views of more than one Cabinet Officer and consequently once recommendations are received within the White House, they must be faithfully integrated into a single presentation of the issue. In national security affairs, the responsibility for presenting comprehensive policy recommendations has rested with the NSC staff. We have made it our practice to include the views of others on the White House staff in our submission to the President. These include the views of those responsible for the budget, for legislative affairs and for political and public affairs. But the process is oriented toward order through the submission of a single document as opposed to multiple proposals which then must be integrated by the President.

It may be that I am wrong and that the President would prefer to receive the direct views of individual Cabinet and White House Senior Staff officers. If that is the case, then that is how we should proceed. My own experience, however, is with the single integrated approach and consequently if the President prefers another course he would be better served by another National Security Advisor.

As you know, we are entering a period in which the President will deal with a number of issues of great complexity and over which there is a rich diversity of opinion within the Administration – arms control and other East-West Issues are salient cases in point. In order to reach decisions, the President deserves to receive the views of his Cabinet Officers and Senior Advisors in their respective domains. I stress the matter of 'respective domains' for it seems to me inappropriate for example, for a White House staff officer to be offering advice beyond his area of assigned responsibility. But here again, the President's view should govern.

Let me be clear. I am making two points. First, that Cabinet Officers within the national security community should feel free to offer whatever advice they believe appropriate and expect that it will be faithfully transmitted by the NSC staff to the President. Second, that White House staff principles should also feel free to submit to me their recommendations, not on the policy content but on how alternative decisions will be received in their respective domains – legislative, political and so forth. All of these views would then be faithfully submitted to the President in a single – indeed the only – written presentation to the President. I would very much appreciate your confirming to me which of the above or other alternative approaches the President prefers.

SUMMARY

POINDEXTER: Today's meeting is called to formulate a response to General Secretary Gorbachev's letter. The letter is subtle and clever, making some points that appeal to certain domestic U.S. and Soviet audiences, and some that would attempt to drive wedges between the U.S. and allies. The thrust of Gorbachev's letter is seen by some as purely publicity ploy, while others view some areas as unique opportunities to move arms control negotiations forward.

In addition to the substance of the letter and the U.S. response, today's meeting should address the timing of delivery and a public diplomacy plan to handle public information about any response.

[Poindexter then outlines some responses for the President, and all in the room agree that the response should maintain a priority on pursuing common ground - - 50 percent reduction in nuclear arms and an interim INF agreement. All also agree on criticizing those elements of the Soviet proposal that have been previously offered and rejected at Geneva.]

POINDEXTER: These are the areas of U.S. options that require discussion and decision at today's meeting.

Option 1: Have the U.S. express reservations about the Soviet "plan", explore any new elements as appropriate fora, not change the U.S. position, and essentially label the Soviet effort a "publicity stunt".

Option 2: Reframe the Soviet proposal in U.S. terms reserving our opportunity to advance such a reframed proposal where appropriate, and move in the INF area to see whether we can use the Soviet proposal to move toward U.S. and allied goals.

Option 3: Have the U.S. move in all three negotiating areas, making changes in the U.S. NST position during the current round.

WEINBERGER: We should keep our present (November) positions at the Geneva negotiations. The Soviet proposal contains a lot of old Soviet positions. However, I don't favor openly labeling the Soviet action a publicity stunt. To do so would lessen the momentum at Geneva, which the U.S. should not allow to happen.

The U.S. should keep the focus away from the date for abolishing nuclear weapons. One of the most unfair points in the Soviet proposal, which is no change from early Soviet positions, is the way they wish to count strategic systems. The U.S. response should focus on our proposals, which are still valid.

Option 2 offers major concessions. It would accept the 510 Soviet SS-20 warheads in Asia; warheads that are mobile and could still be employed against Europe. It would prohibit French and UK modernization. Option 3, in addition to the INF concessions, would give up our ability to amend the AMB Treaty, which would kill SDI by banning research.

POINDEXTER: To clarify, the INF portion of both Options 1 and 2 seeks an interim INF agreement and would not accept the Soviet notion of freezing French and UK nuclear forces.

CROWE: The Chiefs have sympathy for Option 2 and agree that the Asian SS-20 situation is particularly bad because the present basing locations allow some of the SS-20s in Asia to strike parts of Scandinavia, Turkey, and even, at extreme range, West Germany.

SHULTZ: The SS-20s can be reconfigured to achieve strategic range if one of their three warheads are removed.

ADELMAN: The Soviets have done a lot of propaganda in their proposal. They have, however, moved some on their zero INF option by omitting direct reference to UK and French force levels. The U.S. needs to pick up Option 2.

At the same time, the U.S. should not change our START position or we would be negotiating with ourselves. Any move in Defense & Space would politically hamstring us on SDI. The ABM Treaty needs to remain in place.

The U.S. allies in Asia want a 50 percent cut in Soviet Asian SS-20s as part of an INF agreement. The Soviets appear to have moved a little toward accepting on-site inspections in INF, at least in some public speeches.

Perhaps the way to ensure a real Soviet move would be to offer a draft INF treaty. Then, if the Soviets back away from inspections, the U.S. could challenge them to live with their own speeches.

ROWNY: I'm in favor of Option 2. The U.S. should seize the European INF reduction offer and, at the same time, insist on concurrent reductions in the Soviet Asian forces. It is important to get an agreement on verification details, and Option 2 provides a way to do so.

SHULTZ: I agree with the previous comments on Option 2. Option 2 would befit the President as a man with vision to work for a greater peace. Gorbachev is trying to steal that image.

A phased approach is desirable even though the U.S. need not spell out a second phase at this time. Any first phase would only involve the U.S. and USSR. In later phases other nuclear powers might take part – thus the U.S. could reject Gorbachev's comments on U.K. and French forces for now. The U.S. should provide some details of later phases more than just elimination of nuclear weapons. The U.S. needs to make the point that verification is essential, not only for nuclear weapons agreements, but also for conventional weapons such as MBFR and CDE. The U.S. should also point out that the world would be more peaceful if we had fewer regional flashpoints, there are a number of items we should raise about conventional and chemical weapons arms control.

There is no sense to be in favor of higher INF totals than the Soviets. Our proposal is already for an interim solution of 140 launchers plus proportional reductions in Asia. Our overall view is for an equal global ceiling, the lower the better. The Soviet proposal for zero in Europe ignores Asia. For the U.S. to remain in favor of a global ceiling at lower numbers will be easy to sell to Japan.

Turning to START, the Soviets have not replied to the U.S. proposal, so there is no need to dress up our position. There is an anomaly in the START positions: we call for a ban on mobile ICBMS when we are planning for MIDGETMAN and possibly M-X in a mobile basing mode which would give us greater survivability. When the U.S. Congress picks up this inconsistency, it hurts in our appropriations.

We have three things we need to protect by extending the time for implementation of a first phase: the UK/French modernization program – which we can defer to a subsequent stage, which will let initial reductions take place despite such programs; the visible existence of SDI, as insurance that reductions take place because of it – although at some future stage we will need to discuss with the Soviets questions of possible deployment and the transition to greater reliance on defenses; and the ability to reserve ways to identify in the future some ways SDI can be integrated into the reductions process.

The Soviets want to eliminate SDI. There is a growing perception that the Soviets are at the negotiations to make SDI go away. As an idea, the U.S. and USSR might both agree not to call for amendment of the ABM Treaty so long as reductions continue. Since the time period under discussion is when SDI deployments won't occur anyway, we could propose that the ABM Treaty remain in force so long as reductions go on.

CASEY: The speculation now on how to incorporate SDI in the negotiations is premature. Option 2, in my opinion, offers the opportunity to pocket some Soviet movement while testing the seriousness of Soviet statements about verification.

The U.S. task is to press ahead to define effective verification, determining which aspects are or are not militarily significant. Generally, the concept of a 50 percent reduction still could leave the USSR with a capability for a disarming first strike.

A call for an extended ABM Treaty would be self-defeating for SDI. Therefore we should stick to our present Geneva position on START and Defense and Space. Gorbachev is seeking to undercut the President's broader agenda in arms control and future stability of security. The U.S. should reemphasize the problems with Soviet compliance with agreements they had signed.

In all fora the U.S. needs to stress verification so the focus does not shift to the Soviet positions, allowing them to dominate the thrust of the negotiations.

WEINBERGER: We need to seize any positive elements of their INF position, to retain our own INF proposals as presently construed, and to engage in vigorous conversation about INF to smoke them out.

SHULTZ: It appears that Secretary Weinberger is supporting the State option.

WEINBERGER: The differences in the options are narrow but profound.

MEESE: The U.S. should keep our November proposals on the table. I'm concerned with the provisions of the Soviet proposal that argue for a permanent mismatch in SS-20s: zero in Europe which effectively meant zero for the U.S., while the mobility of the Asian SS-20s would permit the USSR to retain an effective force against Europe.

The U.S. should concentrate on verification – it's the greatest place for a breakthrough. The President must define the course and the goal for SDI. SDI should become a moral imperative for future Presidents.

NITZE: A primary reason for the letter from Gorbachev is because the Soviets feel a psychological need to recapture the high ground – to counter the good position the President established in November. Thus, there are a lot of elements designed to give the appearance of putting the ball back in our court and to curry favor with the specific elements of U.S. and allied publics. However, there are some elements of potential interest in almost all negotiating areas of the letter. The most crucial U.S. decision is to establish our position in INF.

BAKER:

The chess game for world opinions is a central element of the present policy debate. The grandiose Soviet images of zero weapons could prove very enticing in the public relations battle. I don't see how Option 1 will help the public relations questions. Option 2, however, would not foreclose flexibility on our part, and might have a way to work out the Asian deployment question. In my view, the U.S. cannot offer a position that forfeits the Asian balance question.

REAGAN:

I agree with the general thrust of the conversation. I don't believe there is any need for U.S. movement in all three negotiating areas (Option 3).

In reality, the ball is still in their court, but there is a danger in attacking the Soviet generalization as only propaganda. Then the public perceives the issue as, who really wants to reduce?

We need to make the Soviets expose the fact that they are not really serious about reductions negotiations. The U.S. should go to the negotiations, point out that the Soviets have made a general, overall offer, and agree on the overall aims of the process. We should emphasize that what the U.S. seeks now is a practical way forward; a way to achieve verification in a concrete agreement, even if such involves a proposal we have already made.

The U.S. should emphasize the point that we are trying to find a practical way to move forward in implementing the agreed eventual goals.

The U.S. will not give up SDI. We should point out that SDI is not for the U.S. alone – we seek a mutual shift from sole reliance on offensive weapons to an offense-defense mix. We should remember the principle of sharing SDI at the deployment stage.

All the speakers here today agree on the overall goal of SDI. As we continue to develop SDI we need to find a way for SDI to be a protector for all – perhaps the concept of a common trigger where some international group, perhaps the UN, could deploy

SDI against anyone who threatens use of nuclear weapons. Every state could use this guarantee.

We do not have all the answers. When research reveals the practicality of SDI, then we might want to mutually decide what to do.

WEINBERGER: In the meantime, it is vital that the research programs in SDI continue. Anything that restricts research is unacceptable.

REAGAN: **There is no one who wants to curtail SDI. At the same time, there is no guarantee we know how to make SDI work.**

SHULTZ: SDI is the key item. How do we envision getting from where we are now to a defensive world? Mr. President, the agencies owe you a better answer on how to solve the difficult transition problem.

REAGAN: **We need to be careful that our position is not propaganda – if it is, the Soviets will be quick to label it such and negate the value of our position.**

POINDEXTER: Today's discussion has clarified positions. Now we need to consult with the allies and prepare some refined options for decision.

REAGAN: **It is clear that we need to work in INF for total elimination of those systems. If the Soviets try to keep some SS-20s in Asia, perhaps we could counter by putting Pershing II and GLCM systems in Alaska, where they could reach Soviet systems in Asia. The Soviets must know that if there is not complete elimination of INF, we will not eliminate our INF. There should be verifiable measures for destroying INF under an agreement.**

POSTSCRIPT

Reagan's formal response to Gorbachev's December 24 letter, dated February 16, was also handwritten at the suggestion of Jack Matlock (NSC) and Poindexter (actually copied word-for-word from a draft prepared by Matlock). Reagan's letter informed Gorbachev that he welcomed his January 15 proposal to eliminate nuclear weapons by they year 2000, but still needed more time to formulate an appropriate response. Reagan did, however, agree "to the principle of a 50% reduction of nuclear arms" and to "stress once again that we remain willing to reduce those weapons systems which the Soviet Union finds threatening so long as the Soviet Union will reduce those which pose a special threat to the United States and its allies."

Date: **February 22, 1986**
Subject: **Letter from Reagan to Gorbachev**

Dear Mr. General Secretary,

The elimination of nuclear weapons has been an American goal for decades, from our proposals at the dawn of the nuclear age to my vision of a nuclear-free world made possible through the reliance of our countries on defense rather than on the threat of nuclear retaliation. In a 1983 speech to the Japanese Diet and on many subsequent occasions, I have advocated the abolition of nuclear weapons. I have done so because I believe this is an objective which reflects the deep yearning of people everywhere, and which provides a vision to guide our efforts in the years ahead. It was for similar reasons that I have sought to develop concepts and frameworks to guide the efforts of our governments in other aspects of our relations – whether solving the regional tensions that have damaged our relations over the years, or expanding the people-to-people contacts that can enrich both our societies.

It is in this spirit that I have studied with great care your letter of January 14, your January 15 statement to the Soviet people, and your subsequent statements on the prospects for progress in arms control. I believe they represent a significant step forward. ...

First, it will be vitally necessary as we move down this path to ensure the most stringent verification, with measures far more comprehensive and exacting then in any previous agreement. I welcome your recognition of this in your expressed willingness to make use of on-site inspection and to adopt other measures that may be necessary. ...

My second point is that any sustained effort to resolve our basic security concerns must go hand-in-hand with concrete steps to move ahead in other areas of our relationship – non-nuclear military issues, regional problems, human rights, and bilateral ties. ...

Finally, as you know, the United States and its allies must rely today on nuclear weapons to deter conventional as well as nuclear conflict. This is due in large part to the significant imbalance that currently exists between the conventional forces of NATO and the Warsaw Pact. As a result, it would be necessary, as we reduce nuclear weapons toward zero, that we concurrently engage in a process of strengthening the stability of the overall East-West security balance, with particular emphasis on redressing existing conventional imbalances, strengthening confidence-building measures and accomplishing a verifiable global ban on chemical weapons. In addition, our cooperative efforts to strengthen the nuclear non-proliferation regime would become even more important.

Reagan went on to note that movement in the area of INF looks promising, and in terms of defense and space, "I continue to believe that limits on research could be counterproductive and, in any case, could not be verified; therefore, they must not be included in an agreement."

In summary, I would propose that the process toward our agreed goal of eliminating nuclear weapons include the following elements:

Initial Steps. I believe that these steps should involve reduction in and limits on nuclear, conventional, and chemical weapons as follows:

1. *The U.S. and USSR would reduce the number of warheads on their strategic ballistic missiles to 4500 and the number of ALCMs on their heavy bombers to 1500 resulting in no more than a total number of 6000 such warheads on strategic nuclear delivery vehicles. These reductions would be carried out in such a way as to enhance stability.*

2. *In the INF area, by 1987 both the United States and the Soviet Union would limit their LRINF missile deployments in Europe to no more than 140 launchers each, with the Soviet Union making concurrent, proportionate reductions in Asia. Within the following year, both sides would further reduce the numbers of LRINF launchers remaining in Europe and Asia by an additional 50%. Finally, both sides would move to the total elimination of this category of weapons by the end of 1989.*

3. *Research programs on strategic defenses would be conducted in accordance with treaty obligations.*

4. *The U.S. and the USSR would establish an effective MBFR verification regime and carry out initial reductions in manpower levels along the lines of the recent Western proposal at the MBFR negotiations; they would then begin a process of moving on to a balance of non-nuclear capabilities in Europe.*

5. *Concrete and meaningful confidence-building measures designed to make the European military environment more open, predictable, and stable would be initiated.*

6. *An effective, comprehensive worldwide ban on the development, production, possession, and transfer of chemical weapons would be instituted, with strict verification measures including international on-site inspection.*

Subsequent Steps. Subsequent steps could involve other nuclear powers and would aim at further reductions and increasingly strict limits, ultimately leading to the elimination of all nuclear weapons. We would embark on this process as soon as the steps encompassed in the first stage are completed. The goal would be to complete the process as soon as the conditions for a non-nuclear world had been achieved.

Obligations assumed in all steps and areas would be verified by national technical means, by on-site inspection as needed, and by such additional measures as might prove necessary.

I hope that this concept provide a mutually acceptable route to a goal that all the world shares. I look forward to your response and to working with you in the coming months in advancing this most important effort.

Let me conclude by agreeing with you that we should work constructively before your visit to the United States to prepare concrete agreements on the full range of issues we discussed at Geneva. Neither of us has illusions about the major problems, which remain between our two countries, but I wish to assure you that I am determined to work with you energetically in finding practical solutions to those problems. I agree with you that we should use our correspondence as a most important channel of communication in preparing for your visit.

Nancy and I would like to extend to you, Mrs. Gorbacheva and your family our best wishes. It is our hope that this year will bring significant progress toward our mutual goal of building a better relationship between our two countries, and a safer world.

Sincerely,
Ronald Reagan

A White House statement, two days later, also served as a direct message to Gorbachev: "The place to make real progress in reducing nuclear and other forces is at the confidential negotiating table…Real progress is now within our reach."

However, Reagan's calls for the elimination of nuclear weapons proved Thatcher's point two years earlier in her private letter to Reagan warning that calls for the elimination of nuclear weapons would make it more difficult to get big defense budgets. Now faced with a Congress about to reject his defense request, Reagan, in a prime-time television address, used terms like "reckless, dangerous and wrong" before saying,

> I will never ask for what isn't needed; I will never fight for what isn't necessary. But I need your help. We've come so far together these last five years; let's not falter now. Let's maintain that crucial level of national strength, unity, and purpose that has brought the Soviet Union to the negotiating table and has given us this historic opportunity to achieve real reductions in nuclear weapons and a real chance at lasting peace.

Date: **March 25, 1986**
Subject: **RSVP (Responding to Soviet Violations Policy) Options**
Status: **Declassified (2005)**

SUMMARY

POINDEXTER: Mr. President, we are meeting today to review the policy of U.S. interim restraint in the face of the continued pattern of Soviet noncompliance with arms control agreements. We need to consider what appropriate and proportionate response the United States would be prepared to undertake in response to these Soviet violations.

Today's meeting will focus on possible military program options, but setting aside for now decisions on such options. We will be having a second meeting on this issue in mid-April to step up to the decisions required at that time.

As you know, the specific event requiring your early decision is that our eighth Trident submarines begins sea trials on May 20. Unless we dismantle other U.S. strategic systems, such as Poseidon submarines, this new Trident will exceed numerical limits under SALT I (SLBM ceiling) and under SALT II (MIRVed ballistic missile and MIRVed SNDV ceilings).

Mr. President, before we begin a review of the specific programmatic options before us today, I believe it is important to briefly summarize the policy on the issue of U.S. interim restraint that you have set forth during your administration – most comprehensively in your report to the Congress on June 10 of last year.

In May 1982, on the eve of the START negotiations, you decided that the U.S. would not undercut the expired SALT I agreement or the unratified SALT II agreement as long as the Soviet Union exercised equal restraint. You stated that in spite of serious reservations about the inequities of the SALT I agreement and the serious flaws of the SALT II agreement, you were taking this action to foster an atmosphere of mutual restraint on strategic forces as we entered serious new negotiations.

You indicated that this policy was an interim policy to help provide a framework of mutual restraint as we pursued effective arms reductions agreements. You made clear that it required Soviet reciprocity, and that it must not adversely affect our national security interests in the face of the continuing Soviet military buildup.

Unfortunately, our hopes and assumptions of 1982 concerning Soviet behavior did not withstand the test of time. The U.S. scrupulously refrained from any actions which would undercut existing agreements. We kept our part of the bargain. But, as you have detailed in three reports to the Congress on Soviet noncompliance (most recently last December 23), the Soviets have repeatedly violated important provisions of these agreements in spite of our requests for corrective action. At the same time, they have maintained their massive military buildup and, notwithstanding the summit agreement to seek common ground, they have failed to make substantial progress in the Geneva negotiations.

In your report to the Congress on Interim Restraint, last June 10, you stated that you were prepared to go the extra mile in terms of interim restraint by deactivating an additional Poseidon submarine later in the year, but that you would not accept a double standard of compliance and would not accept an adverse impact of Soviet violations on our national security.

In your June report you informed the Congress, as well as the Soviet Union, that the United States would take proportionate and appropriate responses to Soviet violations and that you would consider future deployment milestones of U.S. strategic systems on a case-by-case basis in light of the overall situation and Soviet actions regarding: (1) correction of their noncompliance, (2) a reversal of their unparalleled and unwarranted arms buildup, and (3) their active pursuit of arms reduction agreements in the Geneva negotiations.

To help determine such proportionate and appropriate U.S. responses, you asked Secretary Weinberger to provide his recommendations to you. The recommendations of the Secretary of Defense, the Joint Chiefs, the Secretary of State and the Directors of ACDA and the CIA are before us today. They include specific military responses as well as considerations of a more general nature.

We intend to focus today on the specific programmatic military options rather than on broader issues. We need to understand what specific actions we are capable of taking before fashioning our overall declaratory policy context.

We will proceed in order with the eight programmatic options as shown on the boards of matrices at your right and left, Mr. President.

Secretary Weinberger has the first four original options that were reported to you last December. Each of these were conceived under the assumption of an FY 86 arms control supplemental and in a pre-Gramm-Rudman-Hollings environment. Some of the funding for those options is now contained in the FY 87 budget submission as indicated on the funding matrix.

WEINBERGER: To clarify, the money is in the budget, but it will have to be better defined.

POINDEXTER: Under Option A, OSD would preserve the two Poseidon SSBNs that would have to be cut up when the eighth Trident – the Nevada – goes on sea trials in May 1986, if we were to continue to comply with SALT.

Within a year we could decide what, if anything, is to be done with the submarines. We could overhaul them, convert them or simply leave them as is. The funding line in the matrix covers the overhaul of five Poseidon's to return them to service as C-3 missile SSBN's - it was included in the 86 and 87 budget submission.

Under this approach we would violate both SALT I and SALT II limits, in May 1986, by not commencing required dismantlement activity.

Under Option B, 50 Minuteman III missiles that are now kept in storage would replace 50 of the older, non-MIRVed Minuteman II's and we would add 150 (MK-12) warheads to our forces – a net increase of 100 warheads.

This option is reasonably cheap and could be achieved within a relatively short time, and it seems to have some military utility. It would violate the SALT II MIRV limits.

Option C involves encryption on future ballistic missile flight-testing. I understand this capability is already planned for the Small ICBM, so there is no additional cost on that system. The D-5 would incur additional cost and a possible IOC slip.

At the SACG on this subject last Friday no agency favored encryption of the D-5. A consensus emerged on dropping this option as an RSVP response but keeping our options open to deny information, including encryption, on future ICBM tests.

The last of the original DOD options is the one involving an intensified CBW research and development program, Option C. This type of activity is currently underfunded and represents a real area for technological surprise.

The funding seems reasonable, but the SACG members had trouble relating this response to the overall thrust of Soviet noncompliance. As a consequence, we feel that this program should compete in a normal manner for funds in the DOD budget and not be an element of a response to violations.

Option E is not so much a matter of accelerating the small ICBM milestones, as it is one of ensuring that they are met in a timely manner. State originally felt that the administration's support for Midgetman was beginning to wane on the Hill.

At the SACG last Friday, we concluded that the Small ICBM –Midgetman—was moving about as fast as programmatically possible. We have some big decisions regarding its size and basing mode that are coming up next winter, and forcing the system into the limelight might derail the orderly selection process.

The Midgetman was part of your June interim restraint policy in that it was cited as the U.S. response to the SS-25 violation. We reached consensus at the SACG to include a reference to the small missile in the declaratory policy that would go along with our RSVP decisions. That reference should not prejudice the MIRV status or basis mode outcome.

Option F is a State sponsored response which pushes for earlier IOCs on PENAIDs and MARVs as a treaty compliant answer to Soviet ABM Treaty violations. There are several ways we can go in this area, and most are very threat specific.

We have highlighted two possible excursions – RADR only and MARV – to illustrate the IOC and funding tradeoffs. These options simply accelerate ongoing programs that are paced to the evolving Soviet ABM threat.

Option G is a late entry supported by both State and ACDA in which we would back-fit the first half of the SSN-688 class of attack submarines with Vertical Launch Systems for SLCM. There are some costs here, but we would not have to commit to the full 31 boat line. The conversion could be accomplished during the regular overhaul cycle at the $92 million per unit (and) this option would be compliant with all U.S. treaty obligations.

The last military response option, Option H, originally involved turning the 69 B-52Gs that are planned conventional assets into ACM carriers in the near term. There was strong resistance to putting these assets into a Single Integrated Operational Plan (SIOP) role due to unplanned tanker shortfalls.

We discussed this fully at the SACG and changed the option to simply accelerate the ACM program. Mr. President, as you know the ACM is the new stealth model that will be a big improvement over the present ALCM it will eventually replace. Our funding estimate on this option is rough since it relies heavily on how quickly the ACMs replace the ALCMs and what platform they are retrofitted on.

Mr. President, I know you agree that this has been most helpful. We more fully understand the programmatic options. The matrix on funding, and the eventual method we choose to get those funds is very important and should be carefully refined as we move toward an April programmatic decision.

Besides the funding issue, this decision will turn on both the military significance of the Soviet violations and the appropriateness of our chosen response.

Mr. President, I will now turn over the discussion of the options to your Cabinet members. Secretary Weinberger, would you care to lead off?

WEINBERGER: Our declaration about SALT II is going to be important. We need to state firmly that the U.S. will not continue to comply and what we do thereafter will be done in the most militarily efficient manner possible.

As OSD looked at the programmatic actions we used four criteria to narrow the field. The first was the military significance of the options. Second, we are interested in its affordability. Third, it should be distinguishable from our current programs and, finally, it should be reversible in case the Soviets return to compliance.

With those criterions in mind, we chose to preserve two Poseidons from dismantlement as a visible demonstration that we are no longer bound by SALT. The Minuteman switch to 50 more MIRV systems was chosen because of the low cost and the relatively quick achievement of military capability.

Option C, encryption, is now being undertaken with the small ICBM and the CBW option which could be included in the regular program. According to the most recent draft of Soviet Military Power, chemical weapons in the Soviet Union are on the rise. The recent explosion of an SS-18 is also evidence that the Soviet violation pattern continues.

CROWE: The Chiefs essentially agree with Secretary Weinberger on the choice of options. The four Defense options have more merit than any others.

The Chiefs have consistently argued that the most important response is full funding of the strategic modernization program since it is designed to deal with the Soviet cheating. If we go with the first four options, these must be funded on top of the full strategic modernization program.

Gramm-Rudmann-Hollings will make this all the more difficult. The Chiefs are sensitive to funding for older systems and don't believe that we should spend money unnecessarily. But at the bottom line, we view this decision as a political judgment call.

WHITEHEAD: State does not agree with the choice of Options A and B and opposes a U.S. violation of SALT numerical limits (because) if we are to do so we would start a process of escalation in responses.

State is not unmindful of Soviet violations, however, believes we must look at costs and benefits of options. There is no benefit in returning two old SSBNs to sea, and, if we would simply add 100 warheads to the current inventory of 7,000 that would not be a large increase.

In contrast, there are costs: the Geneva NST attempt to reduce nuclear arsenals would be seen as inconsistent and Congressional reaction on the Defense budget would present severe problems and these options would further handicap us on the Hill. Our allies would be distressed with violations of numerical limits, and, finally, the public will question our rights to these measures.

For all these reasons, the cost outweigh the benefits in violation of numerical limits. State is not soft on violations, but we need proportionality and therefore favor Options C, D, E, F, and G. As a last thought, we need to consult with allies this week – (we got) communications this week from Thatcher and Carrington.

CASEY: We need to communicate clearly to both the Soviets and our own people that we are concerned with the violations by undertaking those actions which are feasible. We should stress that the U.S. is free to take any steps necessary.

Defense should develop contingency plans that go beyond these options. It is most important that we remain resolute in our backing of the strategic modernization program and SDI. With regard to the specific programmatic options, I'm agnostic but feel our choosing the encryption option would lose a moral initiative and be counterproductive since we seek to reverse the Soviet capacity to encrypt.

ADELMAN: The U.S. can take a measure of pride in that we have called out Soviet violations and these are now widely accepted – the question is what to do about it. Worst of all worlds would be, after highlighting issues, not to do anything. It's a matter of our word. We will lose credibility if we continue to live under an equal restraint regime including the fatally flawed SALT II Treaty. The longer this administration abides by that treaty, the more it becomes the Reagan treaty and less the Carter treaty.

We should proclaim that we are no longer bound by SALT and then substitute some form of equal restraint framework. We can look at military options later in an orderly fashion but, we should not exclude breaching numerical limits since the Soviets have been in violation of this provision for the past five years. In fact, today they are over the limit by about two Poseidon's worth of SNDVs.

ROWNY: I agree that if we decide to continue with SALT, the Soviets are going to laugh all the way to the bank. We need to change now to something that gets their attention.

(Option H is the most desirable as) the Soviets are particularly concerned with ACMs, and the sooner we get them the greater the signal we will be sending.

WEINBERGER: I have to disagree with Ken Adelman in that it is not desirable to have an interim restraint framework. I also disagree with State options as being too expensive and fully compliant. However, I agree with the need for consulting, but the allies should not tell us what to do.

REAGAN: **We may be shooting ourselves in the foot by keeping two old Poseidon's, which do not represent a productive military solution. I am concerned that we** are in the midst of a public debate on reducing arsenals and our options should be consistent with that theme and not sound extravagant. Our policy should be one in which we reduce in one area if they reduce in another. The problem here is that the Soviets do not destroy their weapons.

WEINBERGER:	Options allows us to keep and use things we already have. They do provide some military advantage. Our strategic modernization program helps us keep up. We should simply state we no longer adhere – and take whatever steps necessary.

BAKER:	Most of the options are merely symbolic. Our new policy needs to focus on what you, Mr. President, want to obtain from the summit. But what is the magic of doing it now? Why symbolism now?

POINDEXTER:	Because the next Trident goes to sea in May.

REAGAN:	**I still have a problem with the Poseidon's – why use something on its last legs? I would prefer Option B since the missiles are in storage and they can be used to help even up the balance. The public could understand that we don't need to keep good missile in storage.**

CROWE:	Option B provides you the greatest military return on your investment.

REAGAN:	**If we were to take all the options and tie them together, would we still stay even with the Soviets? I feel it's hypocritical to stay with a treaty they are violating. Can we give them a choice to join us now to reach mutual equality before assuming a no restraint policy?**

WEINBERGER:	The Geneva program is doing just this. What you need to decide is what is to be done when the eighth Trident goes to sea. I still feel the declaration was most important, and that we could couple that to urge them to join us in Geneva.

REAGAN:	**I suggest we replace the interim restraint framework with our new START position, and failing that, the U.S. would undertake further programmatic options.**

WHITEHEAD:	It is not true that the Soviets violated all the provisions. They have shown restraint to their numerical levels. If we breach the limits, it will give them an open excuse to observe no limits. Feeble as they are, the limits are useful.

REAGAN: **The Soviets have more to gain by exercising restraint now from an economic standpoint. I learned that during the "fireside chat" in Geneva.**

If we use the thrust that the agreement on the table is what we want to replace interim restraint, we won't be permitting a dangerous superiority to develop. We are just playing catch up.

ADELMAN: The Soviets may not have violated all the provisions of SALT, but it's like the tax code – no provision should be violated. Since SALT II was signed, the Soviets have fielded 4,500 warheads, double their bomber weapons, and deployed two new SSBNs and three new ICBMs. We need a sub ceiling on warheads. I differ with Secretary Weinberger, we need to replace the restraint of SALT with our START proposals – we must be seen as not just shredding treaties, but simply not being bound by SALT II, if violated.

WEINBERGER: I don't have a problem being limited to no more than they have in warheads and throw weights our formulation must be positive, we will be free to buildup.

BAKER: I agree with that approach but stress that we don't need to couple it with new funds.

REAGAN: **What are we doing now in strategic modernization?**

WEINBERGER: We have submitted funding for M-X and Midgetman.

REAGAN: **Anything we do will have funding problems. We will need to explain that new systems are replacements and do not represent an increase in the numbers of weapons.**

ADELMAN: A good solid set of military options will be the key. We can go to the American people with our plan.

CROWE: The immediate problem is the two SSBNs – we don't have to destroy them, just tie them up. Their tubes may have some utility as SDI platforms as the technology matures.

REAGAN: **It makes more sense to tie them up rather than cut up these old boats.**

WEINBERGER: The subs could be used for mobilization.

POINDEXTER: We will return to the subject for a decision in mid-April.

POSTSCRIPT

The discussion continues on April 16, and in between Reagan and Gorbachev exchanged two letters on the arms control negotiations.

Date: **April 2, 1986**
Subject: **Letter from Gorbachev to Reagan**

Dear Mr. President ...

More than four months have passed since the Geneva meeting. We ask ourselves: what is the reason for things not going the way they, it would seem, should have gone? Where is the real turn for the better? We, within the Soviet leadership, regarded the Geneva meeting as a call for translating understanding of principle reached there into specific actions with a view to give an impetus to our relations and to building up their positive dynamics. And we have been doing just that after Geneva.

With this in mind, we have put forward a wide-ranging and concrete program of measures concerning the limitation and reduction of arms and disarmament. It is from the standpoint of new approaches to seeking mutually acceptable solutions that the Soviet delegations have acted in Geneva, Vienna and Stockholm.

What were the actions of the USA? One has to state, unfortunately, that so far the positions have not been brought closer together so that it would open up a real prospect for reaching agreements. I will not go into details or make judgments of the US positions here. But there is one point I would like to make. One gathers the impression that all too frequently attempts are being made to portray our initiatives as propaganda, as a desire to score high points in public opinion or as a wish to put the other side into an awkward position. We did not and do not harbor such designs. After all, our initiatives can be easily tested for their practicality. Our goal is to reach agreement, to find solutions to problems which concern the USSR, the USA and actually all other countries. ...

The issues have to be solved – there is no doubt about it. And above all this bears on the area of security. You are familiar with our proposals, they cover all the most important aspects. At the same time I would like specifically to draw your attention to the fact that we do not say: all or nothing. We are in favor of moving forward step by step and we outlined certain possibilities in this regard, particularly, at the negotiations on nuclear and space arms. ...

I assume that you are also working on all these questions and in the subsequent correspondence we will be able in a more specific and substantive way to compare our mutual preliminary ideas for the purpose of bringing the positions closer together. Obviously, this joint work, including the preparations for our meeting, will benefit from the exchanges of views at other levels and particularly from the forthcoming contacts between our Foreign Minister and your Secretary of State.

I will be looking forward with interest to hearing from you.

Sincerely,

M. Gorbachev

"We must talk about a reply to this," Reagan noted after reading the letter. The reply came the following week.

Date: **April 11, 1986**
Subject: **Letter from Reagan to Gorbachev**

Dear Mr. General Secretary...

Thank you for your letter of April 2. ... It is clear that both of us are concerned about the relative lack of progress since our meeting in Geneva in moving overall relations in a positive direction. While each of us would cite quite different reasons to explain this situation, I agree with your thought that the important thing now is to focus attention on how we can solve the concrete problems facing us. ...

Although I believe we should not relent in our search for ways to bridge critical differences between our countries, I agree with your observation on the desirability of moving step by step when an overall solution to a problem eludes us. I want to assure you that our proposals, like yours, are not "all or nothing at all." We wish to negotiate, to find compromises that serve the interests of each of us, and to achieve as much progress as possible. If we can make a critical breakthrough, that of course would be best. But as we attempt to deal with the key issues, we should simultaneously try to solve as many of the smaller ones as we can in order to develop momentum for dealing successfully with the larger issues. ...

I am pleased that Secretary Shultz and Foreign Minister Shevardnadze will be meeting in May to discuss how we can accelerate the preparations for your visit to the U.S. I would hope, however, that we can begin immediately to exchange ideas regarding practical goals we can set, and therefore look forward to receiving your more detailed letter and your reaction to the ideas I presented to Ambassador Dobrynin. I would also like to suggest that you look again at our most recent arms control proposals – the comprehensive proposal of November 1 and the INF proposal of February 24. I believe there are positive elements in them on which we can build. Both of these proposals were designed to pick up on positive aspects of your proposals and bridge the previous positions of our two sides. They also would provide key elements in implementing the first phase of your proposal of January 15. ...

Nancy joins me in sending our warn personal regards to you and Mrs. Gorbacheva.

Sincerely,
Ronald Reagan

Date: **April 16, 1986**
Subject: **Options in Responding to Soviet Violations**
Status: **Declassified (2005)**

BACKGROUND

Today's NSPG meeting is called to continue the March 25 discussion on whether to stay within the limits of the ABM Treaty.

SUMMARY

After Poindexter reviews the pros and cons of breaking out of the ABM Treaty, the discussion follows.

WEINBERGER: The issue should be settled now – we should simply state we are no longer going to observe the treaty. We should make clear we are not breaking out for the purpose of conducting an arms race, but we will no longer conform to the treaty.

The least cost option is to dry-dock Poseidon submarines, we can save them for future options. Such options will cost about $132 million later, but we don't have to identify this now. Putting the ships in dry-dock is the least expensive approach. We don't have to do anything else like change Minuteman warheads – converting existing Minuteman II missiles to Minuteman III. Such an approach will show the Soviets what the costs of violations are.

SHULTZ: (The official meeting minutes read: "Complained about not having access to military advice.")

Ceilings do have impact. Since 1972 they have dismantled (sic) launchers compared to 144 on our side. By all analysis of military measures, we are winning. Freedom and democracy are on the march. We have the advantage everywhere.

They do have two perceived advantages: conventional forces and the ability to produce nuclear systems. I doubt their superiority in conventional forces. They could not have done the Tripoli raid. With regard to producing nuclear systems, yes, it is an advantage – they have the technology and no political restraint.

There are three areas of violations that have the most significance: Krasnayarsk radar, the second new ICBM, and encryption. Responses are needed, (and) the best response is to get the budget where it ought to be. A flamboyant announcement to break numerical SALT limits is unwise (because) it will hand the Soviets a propaganda windfall. They are ready to expand; such a step will cause us problems with the alliance.

CROWE: The Chiefs understand Soviet cheating and the flaws in the treaty, but the best thing to do is to complete the strategic modernization program. That program takes into account Soviet cheating. We also feel strongly that on the conventional budget, if we can get the money, SALT I and II are irrelevant.

The proposals being considered are a wash. We doubt they will affect the military equation. They may serve as signals, but they will not affect the military balance. Failure to get strategic modernization would.

There are three options the Chiefs could support: the Poseidon's; converting more Minuteman III (which is a good return on investment); or encrypting telemetry on future systems. That aside, when you talk about options, where do we get the money for doing these things if we have problems with the modernization program, problems with money for existing systems?

The treaty does have flaws, but not overriding ones. We are in a chess game between the allies (and) the Soviets. We want the President to be in the best position to get the money he needs on the Hill. We should not make decisions based on legalistic interpretations of the treaty.

CASEY: As long as the Soviets are in violation, we are forced to take whatever steps needed. We need to get the message out that if there is no compliance, there will be no sustained treaty.

We are winning because we are calling the Soviets on their transgressions. The Soviets are moving to deploy new mobile MIRVed systems and a nationwide defense. We need to have R&D to develop penetration aids. If we don't reinfirm the treaty, however, it could slow down SDI. The Soviets SA-X-12 could become the basis of a nationwide defense. Any attempt we make to clarify the

ABM Treaty will be ambiguous and let them creep out. The Soviets could move beyond SALT II, but I'm not sure it makes a difference.

ADELMAN: The political options are not expensive. If we breach a numerical limit we will do it once and for all. If we stay under SALT II we will come up on this decision every year. The allies will be squeamish; they need leadership; the man on the street will understand. You can't keep abiding by SALT II.

REAGAN: **What's the relationship of SALT II to the strategic modernization program?**

[Weinberger reviewed the strategic modernization program.]

SHULTZ: The key is the strategic modernization program.

WEINBERGER: We don't ask for anything beyond the strategic modernization program, we just want to make it clear we will not be bound by a meaningless treaty. (NATO Secretary General) Carrington said he expected us to stop complying with SALT II.

SHULTZ: The State option is an appropriate response to the Soviets – we hold the numerical limit, but we do other things.

REAGAN: **What if we finesse SALT II by saying that our goal is some specific other limit?**

WEINBERGER: We will have to return to the SALT II issue repeatedly.

MEESE: Our audience must be Congress and the allies. Can't we eclipse the whole issue of SALT I and II? We should announce a new doctrine, say what we will do if the Soviets do "x". Make it the basis for bargaining with the Congress.

In this approach we would go beyond the SALT II debate by indicating certain restraints by withdrawing systems from service but not destroying them, by monitoring violations, and by seeking arms reduction measures. We are always battling this issue on the Hill; this would be a way to get a change in the terms of the debate.

REAGAN: **Modernization must be seen as modernization, not as a buildup. I'm willing to bring the number of missiles down if the Soviets will reduce. We can come down to any equal levels if they join us.**

WEINBERGER: This new policy of restraint isn't your policy.

REAGAN:	**We should say in hearings on the modernization program, if that puts us above the Soviets we will reduce.**
ROWNY:	Modernization gets the Soviets attention. We should not give credibility to a flawed treaty; we can still show restraint by adhering to SALT I. We must show that SALT II is dead.
REAGAN:	**People should be reminded that SALT II could not be passed by the Democrats.**
MEESE:	We need to avoid a SALT debate.
NITZE:	There is nothing in the State option about complying with SALT. We are not saying we would be restricted in the future, we are just saying that it's not economic today to overhaul these submarines. There is no point in alienating Congress and our allies.
WEINBERGER:	Carrington is not expecting us to remain within SALT II. The State approach also has us continuing to abide by the ABM Treaty – that will kill SDI.
REAGAN:	**We need to say to people that both sides are modernizing, not engaging in an arms race. The Soviets are ahead in modernization, we are not. This isn't a race to achieve numerical superiority. The end result is no increase in total numbers. Such an approach to modernization lends itself to reductions in warheads and delivery vehicles. We shall eliminate systems as we modernize.**
SHULTZ:	The key is what we do about the submarines.
WEINBERGER:	Put them in dry-docks.
REAGAN:	**Everyone should be able to understand dry-docking and that that means they are not in service.**
SHULTZ:	But it's still a violation.
POINDEXTER:	We still have a few days to think about this.

POSTSCRIPT

A month later, on May 27, Reagan announced that the United States "had long planned to retire and dismantle two of the oldest Poseidon submarines when their reactor cores were exhausted." The statement continued:

> Since the United States will retire and dismantle two Poseidon submarines this summer, we will remain technically in observance of the terms of the SALT II Treaty until the United States equips its 131st B - 52 heavy bomber for cruise missile carriage near the end of this year. However, given the decision that I have been forced to make, I intend at that time to continue deployment of U.S. B

- 52 heavy bombers with cruise missiles beyond the 131st aircraft as an appropriate response without dismantling additional U.S. systems as compensation under the terms of the SALT II Treaty. Of course, since we will remain in technical compliance with the terms of the expired SALT II Treaty for some months, I continue to hope that the Soviet Union will use this time to take the constructive steps necessary to alter the current situation. Should they do so, we willcertainly take this into account.

Date: **June 6, 1986**
Subject: **U.S.-Soviet Relations**
Status: **Declassified (2005)**

BACKGROUND

Reagan sent Gorbachev a short letter, dated May 23, conveying his sentiments after the accident in Chernobyl released 400 times as much radiation as the nuclear bomb detonated at Hiroshima. Some fifty deaths were reported, but the long-term fallout from the radiation exposure is believed to have caused cancer in thousands more. On the subject of arms control, Reagan expressed his "readiness to reach agreement by the next summit on the key elements of treaties to reduce strategic nuclear forces and eliminate intermediate range nuclear missiles, as well as on methods to remove both the threat of an effective first strike from either side and the use of space for basing weapons of mass destruction."

Gorbachev's response, a seven page letter on June 1, dealt entirely with better nuclear safeguards and cooperation in dealing with nuclear safety. He also reiterated his call for Reagan to follow the Soviet example of placing a moratorium on nuclear testing until a test ban treaty could be signed.

SUMMARY

POINDEXTER: The approaching summer break in the Geneva arms control negotiations provides an opportunity for fresh thinking aimed at developing new proposals for the fall. The Soviets clearly want to lock us into a period of ABM Treaty adherence; this presents opportunities and challenges.

SHULTZ: [After outlining the overall state of U.S.-Soviet relations, Shultz concludes] that the Soviets are at a fork in the road where they can either choose to wait out the President – gambling that Congress will cut the defense budget – or go for an agreement that will allow them to reduce their military spending on the premise that Ronald Reagan is their best hope for selling an agreement to the American public. The U.S. priorities for the year should be: restore budget cuts to defense and international functions; work on alliance relationships; and go for a good arms control agreement.

POINDEXTER: An arms control agreement represents both the greatest opportunity and the greatest challenge to the administration. In re-examining our current position, the main issue is the ABM Treaty versus SDI – how to position ourselves so as to bring Congress along in funding SDI while working the treaty issue, developing a concept for transition to a defense-based deterrence, and coming up with a viable concept for sharing.

In addition, the other arms control areas must also be addressed. The interagency group should be tasked to develop proposals for consideration by the NSPG. The output of these deliberations should be a private initiative and/or public speech.

REAGAN: **Gorbachev has an internal dilemma heightened by Chernobyl – we need to reach an agreement which does not make him look like he gave up everything.**

We cannot give away SDI, but we can make clear we do not seek a first-strike capability. I'm thinking of something like an agreement now, that if SDI research proves out, and recognizing that both sides are now free to conduct research under the ABM Treaty, we would, when we get to the point of needing to test, invite the Soviets to observe our test, but that actual deployment by either side would depend on movement towards total elimination of strategic nuclear missiles. In this way, both sides would see SDI not as a threat, but as a defense against a madman.

The meeting came to an abrupt end with Poindexter announcing that there would be a follow-on meeting. The discussion continues on June 12.

Date: **June 12, 1986**
Subject: **U.S.-Soviet Relations**
Status: **Declassified (2005)**

SUMMARY

After Poindexter reviews the June 6 meeting, the discussion follows.

WEINBERGER: The Soviets want an agreement to cut their defense budget.

We should not bargain SDI away; if we agree not to deploy SDI, Congress will not fund it. There is no enormous public pressure for a new agreement. If new proposals are needed, I agree that we should say we are not designing SDI to destroy targets on earth, that there should be no restraints on SDI research and we should go for reduction to zero ballistic missiles to be phased in with SDI deployments. Verification is a major problem and should be discussed first, not last, in any serious negotiations.

CASEY: Soviet proposals are clearly aimed at getting SDI. That is not in our interest. We should stick to our goals: cuts in offensive forces and transition to defense.

At some point we will need to change the ABM Treaty, (so) we should not accept the Soviet proposal to bless it. More work needs to be done on transition and sharing, perhaps along the lines of the open labs proposal. We can possibly accept restrictions on the pace of our transition to defense and should link this to reductions in offensive forces.

WICKHAM: The Soviets are timing their proposals to influence Congress on SDI funding. Their numbers are attractive, but there are hookers – especially in INF and SLCM. We should not undercut SDI; new proposals are not necessary.

SHULTZ: I disagree; we need to be seen as joining the process.

I like Secretary Weinberger's repackaging of the zero-option – as long as the agreement permits SDI we have not given away anything. We need to focus on compliance, (and) SDI can be seen as insurance against Soviet non-compliance.

The stage is set for something dramatic, but the current U.S. proposals are too complicated. The zero-option linked to SDI sounds good to me.

REGAN: I agree that we should work now to develop a new proposal or a repackaging of the current one. If we do not take this seriously, now, the Soviets will wait us out. The right agreement will give the Soviets what they want – reduced costs – and will be good for the allies and good domestic politics too.

REAGAN:	**We do not want a first-strike capability, but the Soviets probably will not believe us.**
	The Soviets have economic problems and Gorbachev has his own internal problems with the hardliners. Chernobyl has altered Gorbachev's outlook on the dangers of nuclear war. The time is right for something dramatic.
	We should go for zero ballistic missiles, agree to go forward with research permitted by the ABM Treaty, invite the other side to witness testing when we come to that. No deployment of SDI until we eliminate ballistic missiles; agree to share SDI with the world.
BAKER:	I agree we need something new. Would we really agree to share before giving up ballistic missiles?
WEINBERGER:	There is also a timing problem with respect to linkage of deployments to ballistic missile elimination. We should develop a new proposal for after the break, but we also need to be careful with any discussion of ABM or we risk being dragged into an agreement.
REAGAN:	**The ABM Treaty issue is okay since research is permitted. We need an agreement to cover what we do when we are ready to test; providing for joint observers or something like that. The issue of the timing of the period of deployment and how deployment is linked to elimination of ballistic missiles needs to be negotiated.**
POINDEXTER:	We will summarize the President's views and circulate them to NSPG principles, and then energize the interagency process.

Tab I of the official meeting minutes is the President's official guidance with respect to the arms control process:

1. The USG should act positively towards Soviet proposals put on the table at Geneva during this round. We should take their proposals seriously and develop appropriate counter-proposals within existing policy guidelines. Our public posture should project this positive/serious stance.
2. I believe the Soviets oppose our development of SDI because they genuinely believe that we seek a first-strike advantage. Accordingly, I propose the development of a new initiative designed to counter this fear and to lead as rapidly as possible to a system of a mutual deterrence based on defense. Development of this dramatic new proposal should commence now and be introduced at the next Geneva round in September. The basic elements of this initiative should include:
    *   Continue our SDI research at our current pace. Acknowledge that the Soviets are free to continue their ABM research.
    *   Agree that when either side reaches the point when ABM research testing is required, then the other side will be invited to observe the testing.

- Agree that there will be no deployment of an ABM system by either side until agreement is reached on reductions of ballistic missiles by both sides. Actual deployments of ABM systems would be linked and phased to actual ballistic missile reductions by both sides.
- Agree that either side will share its ABM system with the other side, after the mutually witnessed testing has demonstrated that the system works. Eventually, our goal would be sharing the ABM systems with all responsible nations of the world.

Date: **July 1, 1986**
Subject: **Program Briefing on SDI**
Status: **Declassified in Part (2005)**

SUMMARY

Poindexter opens today's meeting, which is still heavily redacted, noting the "importance of a program update for participants in view of progress to date, the vital nature of the program, and the need for support from Congress." Weinberger then gives a brief introduction noting "the importance of a boost phase intercept, saying that those who favor exclusively terminal defense only want to kill the SDI program by eliminating its potential to protect people." Weinberger also notes that "Congressional actions threatened the SDI program by trying to force concentration on terminal defense through legislative directive and funding cuts." The discussion follows.

POINDEXTER: Do the new definitions proposed by the USSR relating to the ABM Treaty restrict only tests in space?

ABRAHAMSON: The Soviet proposals would prohibit all laboratory simulations which would give confidence that a space-based system or component would be feasible.

WEINBERGER: The Soviets are attempting to destroy the U.S. program with their new definitions.

REGAN: The briefing mentioned four possible surveillance systems and seven possible weapons. Ultimately, are we going to choose to pursue certain systems while dropping others?

ABRAHAMSON: The program is designed to prevent an Achilles heel – that means delivering two means for each function.

REGAN: Does that mean for each function there will be six systems, two for each phase of a ballistic missile trajectory?

ABRAHAMSON: The multiple systems would not be necessary immediately, but would be designed to deal with a responsive offensive threat.

REGAN:	How many missiles out of a 100 would be knocked down during the boost phase?
ABRAHAMSON:	The goal is about 60-80 percent for each phase, which would contribute significantly to deterrence.
REGAN:	If the layers of defense are each 80 percent effective, one missile would get through.
(Five lines redacted.)	
WEINBERGER:	(Two lines redacted.) Pursuing several concepts for each function is important as a hedge against failure and also because it allows faster progress.
REGAN:	At what point will choices be made to narrow alternatives?
WEINBERGER:	It's a function of funding.
ABRAHAMSON:	Last years cuts have already forced me to narrow options by scaling back three of four laser projects.
CROWE:	If the Soviet proposed definitions are not accepted, would the SDI program be constrained by the ABM Treaty in the early 1990s?
ABRAHAMSON:	That would indeed be the case.
BAKER:	Which Republicans on the Senate Armed Services Committee voted with the Democrats to force SDI to concentrate on terminal defense?
WEINBERGER:	Senator Cohen. Those who sought to force SDI to focus on point defense through legislation or funding cuts will kill the program and play into the Soviets' hands.
POINDEXTER:	Ambassador Nitze, would you please now brief us on your conversation with Senator Gore?
NITZE:	Senator Gore is troubled (five lines redacted).
MILLER:	How much is known of relevant Soviet activities?
ABRAHAMSON:	We have some information which forms the basis for analysis of potential Soviet countermeasures. Work is underway to analyze other possible tactics the Soviets might pursue?
WEINBERGER:	The Soviets are vigorously pursing both strategic offenses and defense and both are a cause for concern.
ADELMAN:	What effect will the loss of space launch capability have on SDI's timetable?
ABRAHAMSON:	One experiment will be delayed two years, although some of the results have been attained through other means, while another experiment will be delayed at least a year.
ADELMAN:	(One line redacted.)

ABRAHAMSON:	This experiment will be delayed at least two months because of problems with Delta rockets.
MEESE:	SDI offers many potential commercial by-products. Can any of them be used as a selling point with Congress?
WEINBERGER:	This argument is very persuasive with foreign governments.
REAGAN:	**Is there some way to convince the program's critics on the Hill?**
WEINBERGER:	The administration has gone out of its way to make sufficient information available to Congress. Opposition to SDI is from basic philosophical differences.
REAGAN:	**General Abrahamson, I want to congratulate you and your staff on progress to date. SDI is a strategic necessity and a crucial part of our three part response to the Soviet strategic threat: modernizing our retaliatory forces; negotiating deep, equitable and verifiable reductions of nuclear weapons; and taking steps now to provide future options for the possible introduction of strategic defenses.**
	We need everyone's support. Please do everything possible in public and in private to obtain the needed political support for the program.

Date: **July 15, 1986**
Subject: **Nuclear Testing**
Status: **Declassified (2006)**

SUMMARY

POINDEXTER:	Today we will be reviewing the subject of nuclear testing. As you know, General Secretary Gorbachev has accepted our suggestion to begin expert level talks on nuclear testing. We have proposed such talks begin later this month, the Soviets have responded positively, and we are now working to establish dates and locations. We will use these talks to advance your goal of improving verification of existing treaties on nuclear testing.
	In addition, as part of the broad review the President has directed, we have been considering what, if any, arms control steps in the nuclear testing area might be appropriate should we reach agreement on such verification improvements.

These developments make it appropriate for the President and his senior advisors to review the important military purposes served by testing so that we can better understand the implications of any negotiated restrictions.

WEINBERGER: Many people say testing is bad, that it leads to war. In fact, there is a military and technological necessity to test; since we depend on nuclear weapons for security, we must make certain they work. This briefing will show that critics of testing are wrong; it has been shown to the allies with great success.

[Frank Gaffney and Dr. Robert Barker brief on the military utility of testing and conclude that changes in the current administration position on nuclear testing restrictions would be an error.]

REAGAN: **Is it correct to say that when the Soviets broke out of the moratorium (from 1958-1961) they did so in a way that made it clear they had been preparing to do so for some time?**

BARKER: It took us a year to conduct a militarily significant test. The Soviets came out swinging, conducting the largest test program in history.

ADELMAN: In 1962, President Kennedy said the United States should never again agree to a moratorium noting that closed societies can prepare for a breakout while open societies cannot.

WEINBERGER: There is one circumstance in which nuclear testing would not be required; if the SDI were to be deployed it would no longer be necessary to test.

POINDEXTER: With regard to expert discussions, we are working with the Soviets on a date and location for the meeting. Dr. Barker, who just briefed us, will lead the U.S. experts group.

We are working on instructions for the experts delegation. Some issues remain to be resolved, none of which deserve attention at this meeting.

In addition, as part of the compartmented review the President directed of our response to Gorbachev's latest arms control proposals, we are examining options for the period following ratification of the Threshold Test Ban Treaty (TTBT) and Peaceful Nuclear Explosions Treaty (PNET).

The first step would be verification improvements, which would allow us to send the existing treaties to the

ADELMAN: Hill for ratification. If we get reduction in strategic offensive forces, we will want to know what options we have. Agencies have differing views and there is no point in going too fast until we see the Soviet response to the experts meeting.

ADELMAN: While the briefing has been well received by the allies, the allies still publicly hope we will get to a Comprehensive Test Ban (CTB). They always vote for such a treaty in international conferences. We also cannot underestimate the importance of nuclear effects testing since the survival of warning systems in a nuclear environment is essential. Finally, despite Secretary Weinberger's comments, even with SDI we will need to test so long as we depend on any nuclear weapons.

WEINBERGER: I agree. I promise to prepare an unclassified version of the briefing and an article or speech on the subject and forward them for consideration.

REAGAN: **Can we say publicly what technical steps we have done to deter terrorism?**

POINDEXTER: We could.

REAGAN: **Reminds me of what Jefferson said: "If the people have the facts the people won't make a mistake." Right now the people don't have the facts on nuclear testing, we should give them the facts.**

POSTSCRIPT

Reagan's July 25 letter to Gorbachev rejected the idea of banning nuclear testing. "With respect to nuclear testing, as you know, we believe a safe, reliable and effective nuclear deterrent requires testing," Reagan explained. "Thus, while a ban on such testing remains a long-term U.S. objective, I cannot see how we could move immediately to a complete ban on such testing under present circumstances."

Date: **July 29, 1986**
Subject: **U.S. Space Launch Capabilities**
Status: **Declassified (2005)**

BACKGROUND

Today's meeting is called to allow NASA Administrator, Dr. James Fletcher, to brief on progress towards restarting space flights after the Challenger broke apart 73 seconds after takeoff. All seven crewmembers were killed in the January disaster, including Christa McAuliffe, a schoolteacher who was the first participant in the Teacher in Space program. The NASA official report blamed a faulty O-ring seal on the right rocket solid booster.

SUMMARY

FLETCHER: NASA's first priority is to begin Shuttle flights as close as possible to the first quarter of 1988. Our second priority is to keep the Space Station on schedule. Our third priority is to replace the Challenger orbiter.

NASA also supports a number of major science and technology programs and the development of Expendable Launch Vehicles (ELV). The replacement of the Challenger orbiter, in my view, is not just a NASA priority, but a national priority. We believe in a mixed fleet of launch vehicles comprised of the orbiter and the ELVs. These are needed for DOD, civil, science, and international launch requirements.

The Space Station is the nation's and NASA's priority. It's your program and we want to keep it on schedule. In order to do so, it will be a very different program with three orbiters to support it. Very soon we will have agreements with Europe, Japan and Canada on the Space Station. We want to assure them we can support it. We were told to look at a private financing plan for a fourth orbiter. We support a Government-sponsored finance plan. To do that we soon will need $500 million to keep it on track. I know financing is difficult, but we need to find it in order to start the program in FY 87.

Finally, NASA is in terrible shape in a number of areas. We need support for the space program, but our morale is bad and we need to get the Space Station back on track. Without your support, everything will unravel. We need a commitment from you, Mr. President.

MILLER: I would like to express my empathy for Dr. Fletcher, and I know it has not been easy....

The DOD says three Shuttles are sufficient, but they would like to have a fourth. They cannot, however, dedicate any budget to it. It is a close call between funding for a fourth orbiter and funding for individual rockets for the added capacity the country needs.

NASA has been overly optimistic in the cost of an additional shuttle. The costs cited, however, for ELVs have been more accurate. If we want to replace the orbiter a billion dollars will be required in 1990, but it would be less with ELVs. The outlays of monies for a replacement shuttle would be greater up front than with ELVs. ...

Congress will be looking at lower budget requirements in the next few years. NASA's budget does not need programs that cost billions of dollars in 1987. Some members of Congress support the shuttle program but others are very proximonious. Congress' estimate of the national budget came in with less than you did, Mr. President. The NASA estimate of their budget was less than what we at OMB thought.

I recommend we wait until 1988 to replace the orbiter to get a better handle on actual costs and what substantial increases we will be looking at in NASA programs. One way to cut down on NASA costs is to cut down on the satellite manifest. In conclusion, no additional launch capacity is needed by NASA and the orbiter program. Since it is not needed, and no clear funding is identified, we recommend you wait. If you must commit to NASA, I recommend we wait on funding.

FLETCHER: I disagree. We expect capacity will increase, and if you look at the NASA chart, we and DOD will need the additional launch capacity. Secondly, the OMB bullets are not exactly correct. I think our estimates are on target and are correct.

MILLER: This is an official sur-rebuttal (laughing). The charts show the demand is down. There is a difference between capability and the demand. They have leveled between the shuttle and ELVs.

FLETCHER: But there is a difference between costs.

MILLER: In amortizing the cost of a shuttle?

FLETCHER: No, you should average the marginal costs.

MILLER: I'm figuring on cost permitted as in...

POINDEXTER: (Interrupting) Let's move on.

WEINBERGER: In 1972, I was at OMB and the nation would not have an STS if we had listened to the OMB arguments. Once we had it (STS) our costs became lower. We need a fourth orbiter, SDI, and the Space Station. We need them all. We are way ahead of where we thought we would be. We will need the orbiter in the 1990 and 1991 period for SDI as I mentioned to you, Mr. President, yesterday.

We need a fourth orbiter to do what needs to be done. There is a national requirement for a fourth orbiter. There are some savings to be derived from other areas and we can cut back on some requirements with a lack of commercial launch business.

There is a need for a fourth orbiter. In 1972 they said there is no necessity for an STS because we couldn't see it. But since that time there has been enormous support.

Funding today is different than what it was in 1972, but we must see it as do-able. European and Soviet capabilities are moving forward; they don't have a public opinion or an OMB (laughing). We support NASA.

DOLE (Transportation): The Economic Policy Council (EPC) will meet tomorrow (and) the private sector is ready to move out to provide launch capability using ELVs. They need the signal that the government will off-load the commercial satellite business from the shuttle. This is an important signal that will have a major impact. They can gear up in 30 to 36 months, leaving the more exact and complex missions to NASA. I say we make no decision on a fourth orbiter until we see what the commercial industry can do.

SHULTZ: I agree with Cap (Weinberger), and the sooner we step up this decision the better.

BROWN (Commerce): There is an additional demand needed for launch capabilities. Our feeling is that we should repair the design on the STS. Perhaps the cost will be high, but we need at least three shuttles. Redesigning an advanced STS and letting private industry ELVs pick up the slack is the way to go. NASA should not be in the ELV business. Industry simply won't start without a decision that encourages commercial satellite launches.

The STS has been a loser. If it turns commercial then it will cost the government. ELVs can carry international, commercial and government payloads. The question of private industry needs and government requirements should wait until the EPC meeting tomorrow.

FLETCHER: I would like to support Secretary Dole, but ELV integration must be done carefully to ensure we can support the manifest and launch requirements without jeopardizing either the shuttle or commercial ELV programs.

MEESE: I don't think there is much difference between the positions of Transportation, Commerce or NASA.

SHULTZ: Oh no, I disagree.

MEESE: However, I support DOD. The budget won't get better and you should invest $500 million now to show continued forward motion of the U.S. Space Program.

BROWN: You suggested more international discussion. Ariane (French space program) wants to talk space cooperation and does not want to put all of their subsidy into competing with the U.S. They are being more cautious since their recent launch failure.

REAGAN: **Can I ask, what is the status of the space plane?**

FLETCHER: It is a joint NASA and DOD project. From the standpoint of technology it can fly in 1995, but in terms of flying regularly and operationally it will be much later.

ALDRIDGE (Defense):   It is a three-phased program. If technology problems are worked out, then we will build it and fly it regularly for assured access to space. It should be clear, however, that it is not a substitute for the STS.

REAGAN: **There has been no mention made of a return from our investment or spin-offs. We have fishing nets made from materials of space-age technology. Sufferers from diabetes are using pharmaceuticals derived from the space programs. We have repaired or salvaged satellites in orbit.**

                      If we do not move forward with the procurement of a fourth orbiter, how much will we delay the Space Station? How much further will other nations move ahead of us? We wonder what the Soviets are cooking up in space and how far ahead of us are they.

FLETCHER: The economies derived from spin-offs have been of great value. We need another manned vehicle in order to ensure we stay ahead in all areas.

TRULY (Associate Administrator for Space Flight):

                      Man involved in spaceflight will in the future be able to do things we have not envisioned today. We intend to continue to emphasize a manned space flight program and will have a need for man in space in the mid-1990s, whether we have three or four orbiters. A fourth orbiter is essential; if we lose another existing orbiter, from just the blowout of a tire, it is a serious matter.

FLETCHER: Conceivably, you could delay the Space Station for one year, but that simply creates one more year of uncertainty. We're not sure, but a delay in a decision now should not delay Space Station deployment.

SVAHN:	What if a three-orbiter fleet were all that we had to build a Space Station? Would we be able to do it?
FLETCHER:	My staff disagrees, but I think we can do it.
BROWN:	We need a decision since both ELVs and the orbiters are needed to replenish satellite constellations. But since the cost of a manned vehicle and insurance rates are greater, I recommend delay of an orbiter replacement decision.
REAGAN:	**I have one question about recent space activities that has nothing to do with dollars. There were recent reports of a man who turned up missing and reportedly was a missile launch specialist who defected to the Soviets. Prior to the Challenger launch, Soviet trawlers were seen speeding away at flank speed from the launch area. Is there any possibility that sabotage could have played a role in the Challenger accident?**
FLETCHER:	We are going to be taking steps to ensure that this will not be a question in the future.
POINDEXTER:	Before we launch again, I would hope we take all necessary safeguards to avoid the possibility of any suspicious activity. There is, however, no evidence to support any assertion of sabotage on our launches. Mr. President, we have overextended our time. We will be talking to you later on your decision on this subject.

POSTSCRIPT

Reagan formally approved the $2.8 billion needed for a fourth orbiter, and the White House statement on August 15' also announced a new direction for NASA:

> It has been determined, however, that NASA will no longer be in the business of launching private satellites. ... Instead, NASA and the four shuttles should be dedicated to payloads important to national security and foreign policy, and, even more, on exploration, pioneering, and developing new technologies and uses of space.

Space launch capabilities are discussed again on February 3, 1987. Shuttle flights resumed in 1988.

Date: **October 11-12, 1986**
Subject: **Reykjavik Summit**
Status: **Declassified**

BACKGROUND

In a letter dated September 15, Gorbachev proposed a "quick one-on-one meeting" in London or Iceland to give "instructions to our respective agencies to draft agreements on two or three very specific questions, which you and I could sign during my visit to the United States." Two weeks later, on September 30, Reagan walked into the White House Press Room and announced,

> General Secretary Gorbachev and I will meet October 11 and 12 in Reykjavik, Iceland. The meeting was proposed by General Secretary Gorbachev, and I've accepted. And it will take place in the context of preparations for the General Secretary's visit to the United States, which was agreed to at Geneva in November of 1985.

SUMMARY

SESSION ONE: **OCTOBER 11, 1985; 10:40 A.M.-12:30 P.M.**

The first meeting started with a private conversation during which Reagan and Gorbachev agreed that verification would be one of the most important aspects of any agreement. After an hour, Secretary Shultz and Foreign Minister Shevardnadze join the discussion, and Gorbachev immediately makes the first Soviet proposal.

- Strategic Arms: A 50% reduction in strategic arms taking into account all forms of strategic arms (all three legs of the triad – air, land and sea).

- Medium Range Missiles: The total elimination of U.S. and Soviet medium-range missiles in Europe, and without an agreement from France and Britain. Regarding INF missiles in Asia, the U.S. should, in the spirit of compromise, withdraw this question, or at least agree to continue negotiations regarding medium-range missiles in Asia while those in Europe are being eliminated.

- A freeze and the commencement of negotiations on the reductions of missiles with a range of less than 1000 km.

- ABM Treaty: With respect to the ABM Treaty, it is important to agree on a period during which both sides obligate themselves not to exercise their right to withdrawal.

- Nuclear Testing: On nuclear testing, we propose that each side continues to act as it wishes during negotiations, while negotiating on: verification; lowering the threshold; reducing numbers of tests; and questions of the 1974 and 1976 treaties.

"What is important," Gorbachev tells Reagan, "is that we get a mutual understanding which permits research and testing in laboratories, but not outside of laboratories, covering space weapons which can strike objects in space and on earth. This would not, however, affect testing of those systems allowed by the ABM Treaty."

The discussion follows.

REAGAN: **Your proposals are very encouraging, although there remains points of difference. For example, in INF, zero in Europe is fine, but there must also be reductions of missiles in Asia. The missiles in Asia are mobile and Europe could be targeted from the ones now in Asia. There also could be reductions in Europe to 100 on each side.**

Regarding strategic weapons, we would also like to go to zero, but we draw the line regarding the ABM provisions you have proposed. The point is that SDI should make the elimination of nuclear weapons possible. We are proposing to sign a treaty now which would supersede the ABM Treaty. You are also researching defensive weaponry, and both sides would go forward within the ABM Treaty. If either reaches the point that they decide it would be desirable to go beyond the ABM Treaty restrictions, they would conduct testing in the presence of representatives of the other country. For example, if the U.S. were first, Soviet representatives would be invited to witness testing. Then, if testing should reveal that a system is practical, we would be obligated to share it, and would have two years to negotiate an agreement to eliminate ballistic missiles and to share.

The reason for this is that we can't guarantee in the future that someone – a madman like Hitler, for example – might not try to build nuclear weapons. A treaty now would also bind our successors.

GORBACHEV: Mr. President, I hope that these are preliminary remarks on your part. I have just made proposals that have not been previously discussed, they require appropriate attention.

In INF, we proposed zero in Europe and that negotiations continue on INF missiles in Asia. The U.S. seems to be moving back from its earlier proposal.

On the ABM Treaty, we are proposing to preserve and strengthen the treaty, you are proposing to renounce it. We want to preserve you; you want to destroy it. We just don't understand this.

Regarding SDI, we have thought the matter through thoroughly. We are not worried about the prospect of the three-layered ABM system. We will respond to it, but not in the same way. But if we do so we will just have the arms race transferred to a new environment. If this is what the U.S. wants, then we can understand why it has made the proposals it has. However, the resulting situation will simply be more dangerous to U.S. allies – and to the U.S. public.

So, Mr. President, I hope that you will give careful thought to the new Soviet proposals. We would appreciate a point-by-point reaction. It is important for us, and for the U.S., to know just what you can accept and what you cannot accept – and why.

REAGAN: **I will look at the proposal, but you are refusing to see one thing: if SDI research is successful, it will make possible the elimination of nuclear weapons. We are accused of wanting a first strike capability, but we are proposing a treaty which would require the elimination of ballistic missiles before SDI is deployed, therefore a first strike would be impossible.**

GORBACHEV: We have thought about this for a year and are well aware of your attitude. However, I am willing to continue the discussion on this subject later if you wish. It seems that our time is up for now, should we continue now or after lunch?

REAGAN: **Let's go to lunch and then continue the discussion.**

SESSION TWO: **OCTOBER 11, 1985; 3:30 P.M.-5:40 P.M.**

After lunch, in an over two-hour session, Reagan and Gorbachev agreed to instruct their negotiators to work out a way to achieve a zero global nuclear missile solution. Standing in the way of a final document, however, was a difference of opinion over the ABM Treaty and what types of defensive testing would be permissible. Specifically, Reagan insisted on testing outside of laboratories while Gorbachev insisted that SDI testing could be unlimited as long as it is done within a laboratory.

SUMMARY

REAGAN:

We are both civilized countries and civilized people. When I was growing up – a little before you were growing up – there had been rules of warfare that protected non-combatants, civilians. Now, with the ABM Treaty, we have horrible missiles, whose principle victims are civilians. The only defense against them is the threat of slaughtering masses of other people. This is not civilized.

I am proposing something to change this, something to be shared. It is not for one country only. It will protect people if a madman wanted to use such weapons – take Qaddafi; if he had them he would certainly have used them. But Qadhafi, or someone like him, will not get a nuclear weapon in our time, it will happen on someone else's time. Mr. General Secretary, please think about us two, together, standing and telling the world that we have SDI, and then asking other countries to join us in getting rid of these terrible, nuclear weapons systems.

GORBACHEV:

Mr. President, my remarks in reply will be less philosophical, more prompted by the nature of what we had been discussing which was practical.

We proposed to enter a period of proceedings to reduce the nuclear weapons of both sides, both strategic and medium-range, and to strengthen the ABM Treaty so we could have the confidence needed while reducing. We think the period should be for a minimum of 10 years with very strict compliance with all the provisions of the ABM Treaty. This is my first point.

The second point, Mr. President, is that we are accommodating you concerning the continuation of laboratory research, to enable the U.S. to see whether it wanted a full-scope three-echelon strategic defense or something else. This, by the way, is consistent with the Soviet plans, too, for the U.S. would not be able to deploy the full system by then, but only some things in it. Within that period both countries would reach arsenals that, while still huge, would be much reduced. During that period anti-missile defense would make sure that no terrorist, or lunatic, or madman could do what he wanted.

Mr. President, right now SDI does not concern us. We do not fear a three-echelon system if the U.S. decides that is what it wants. The Soviet response will be not symmetrical, but asymmetrical. The U.S. has money to do things the USSR cannot do. But, we have a different concern. Our concern is to convince our people, and our allies that they should be prepared to begin reductions while the ABM Treaty is being destroyed. This is not logical, and our allies and people will not understand this.

REAGAN: **The ABM Treaty is a defensive systems treaty. The Soviets built up quite a defense, and the U.S. has not. All we are saying is that in addition to missiles covered by this treaty, here is something bigger that we want the world to have. We are not building it for superiority. We want all to have it. With the progress we are making we do not need 10 years. I could not have said that a few years ago, progress is being made.**

GORBACHEV: We are not going to proceed with strategic defense but will have another approach, which will take less than 10 years.

[Skipping a few minutes.]

REAGAN: **I have one closing remark. You said that you do not need SDI and have a better solution. Perhaps, both sides should go ahead and if the Soviets do better, you will give us your system.**

GORBACHEV: Our solution is not better, but different. Mr. President, I am sorry to say that with regard to sharing I cannot take you seriously. You are even unwilling to give us oil drilling equipment, automatic machinery, even milk factories. For the U.S. to give us the produces of high technology would be a second American revolution. This will not happen, so it is better to be realistic. This is more reliable.

REAGAN: **If I thought the benefits would not be given to others, I would give up the project.**

GORBACHEV: Mr. President, it does not sound like you know what the project contains.

REAGAN: **I have some lists concerning human rights I'd like to give to you.**

GORBACHEV: I will accept the list, and as always, it will be carefully considered.

SESSION THREE:	**OCTOBER 12, 1986; 10:00 A.M. – 1:35 P.M.**

GORBACHEV: The bible said that first had come the first day, then the second, and so on. We are now on our second day – there is still a lot of time before the seventh.

REAGAN: **We should be resting.**

GORBACHEV: Yes, it is Sunday.

Mr. President, I suggest we begin with a review of the progress achieved by the two groups, which met all-night last night. I will let you give your assessment first.

REAGAN: **With a few exceptions, I am disappointed by the progress in the arms control negotiations. With respect to START, I understand there was substantial agreement with gave and take on both sides. It is my understanding that the working group was able to agree on a formulation for the outlines of a 50% reduction of strategic arsenals that should move the negotiations substantially ahead. Both sides should be proud of this achievement.**

On INF, I am under the impression that the sides have come to the conclusion that SRINF, the duration of an interim agreement and verification could be handled in negotiations. But they could not solve the issue of reductions of LRNF missiles in Asia. The question was now fairly simple, not technical at all. We made clear that we required a global agreement; this is not a new issue, but an issue that we must not ignore any longer if we want to make progress. I cannot and will not accept a situation in which sizeable reductions in Europe, even to zero, are not matched by proportional reductions in Asia. You know the reason for this – your SS-20s are mobile. These are not new arguments, and our allies in both Europe and Asia support this position, in fact they insisted upon it for their security.

The U.S. has long called for proportional reductions in Asia. If we reduce to 100 warheads in Europe, and reduced Asian systems in the same proportion, the Asian ceiling would come out to something like 63. 100 in Europe, 100 in Asia is acceptable, in the right context. Why don't we settle now on 100/100 and instruct our negotiators to work out the details?

GORBACHEV: To clarify your proposal, it is for 100 LRINF warheads each for the U.S. and Soviet Union in Europe and an additional 100 for the Soviet Union in Asia.

REAGAN: **Yes, under the proposal we would also have the right to deploy an additional 100 warheads on a global basis on U.S. territory.**

On defense and space, I feel I recognize the basic differences between our approaches. For my part, I recognize that you are not prepared to agree with me, but I am also not prepared to move from my position, which I believe is correct. Recognizing this, I propose that we instruct our negotiators to focus on what I feel are the three critical issues. The first two deserve immediate attention, but I also understand your concern about the third issue. These issues are:

First, how can activities with respect to the investigation of strategic defense be synchronized with out shared goal of eliminating ballistic missiles?

Second, what should the conditions and timeframe be for increased reliance on strategic defense?

Third, until these conditions are met, what common understanding might be reached on activities under the ABM Treaty on advanced strategic defenses?

At a minimum, can we not agree to instruct our negotiators to address these three questions in the hope of using them to move our positions closer together?

GORBACHEV: Despite the fact that the arms control group labored for 10 hours last night, I am also very disappointed. I felt the proposals we brought here were highly constructive in spirit – and not just in philosophical terms. We made real concessions to the U.S. in a number of negotiations and had sought to establish conditions for reducing and eliminating nuclear weapons. But we found that, instead of seeking as we had tried to give an impulse to the discussions, the U.S. was trying to drag things backward.

As I said previously, the Geneva negotiations have reached an impasse so a new approach is needed, as is the political will and ability to think in broad terms, to escape this dead-end. We crafted our proposal with that in mind, and expected the same from the American side.

It does look like it is possible though to record some areas of agreement with respect to strategic systems. We both agreed to reduce by 50% all components in this category, both as to warheads and delivery vehicles.

INF is an issue over which we have both struggled for a long time. The problems are particularly difficult because they involve not just our two countries but our allies as well. We feel that our current position satisfies all the U.S. concerns: we agreed to put aside consideration of the British and French systems; agreed that the problem of shorter range systems exists, and so agreed to a freeze and to enter into negotiations on such systems. As for the Asian systems, they bore no relation to the problem of reducing INF in Europe. Nonetheless, as the U.S. insisted on linking European systems with those in Asia, the Soviets are willing to take Asian systems into account.

Mr. President, I am starting to get the impression that you and your administration are proceeding from the false impression that we are more interested in nuclear disarmament than you are, and perhaps you feel that you can use that leverage to force us to capitulate in certain areas. This is a dangerous illusion – such a scenario will never occur.

You mentioned an interim INF agreement. This is not possible, but if the question of Asian systems can be resolved – not just put into the negotiations but dealt with in specific terms – the U.S. could agree to zero systems in Europe and some sort of equal number in Asia. Is this a correct statement of the American position?

REAGAN: **The problem is that your SS-20s in Asia are mobile and as such we view them in both the Asian and the European category. We feel that if we withdraw completely from Europe and you are left with 100 in Asia, you would gain an enormous advantage. This would pose great difficulties for U.S. relations with our friends in Europe.**

GORBACHEV: It seems clear nothing is going to come of this conversation.

REAGAN: **Perhaps you have some suggestions of your own.**

GORBACHEV: Mr. President, it seems you have forgotten that we agreed to leave out the UK/French systems – a major concern. How can you speak of a zero solution in Europe when the Soviets would be obligated to eliminate their INF missiles while the U.S. allies would retain their nuclear forces.

With respect to the possibility that our systems in Asia could be moved, the subject should not even be discussed at our level. Any agreement to include Asian systems would be verifiable: if there was even a single fact of Asian systems being redeployed, it would nullify the agreement. Thus, your concerns are not serious. Mr. President, if you do not want an agreement you should say so. Neither of us wants to waste our time.

REAGAN: **We do not see French and UK systems as part of NATO. Those governments made clear their forces were for their own defense. If France is attacked, for example, those systems would not be used.**

In fact, the Soviet Union and the United States are really the only two nuclear powers. Other countries have nuclear weapons but they are in a defensive mode. I envision that if the U.S. and Soviet Union were to start the process of reducing their own nuclear forces to zero, and would stand shoulder-to-shoulder in telling other nations that they must eliminate their own nuclear weapons, it would be hard to think of a country that would not do so.

GORBACHEV: I agree, and I also feel that the present opportunity might be the only one in that respect. I was not in the position a year ago, let alone two or three years ago, to make the kind of proposals I am now making. In a year or so from now I might not be able to make the same proposals. Time passes; things change. Reykjavik would simply be a memory.

REAGAN: **We are in the same situation in that respect. But if one were soon to be without authority, it is all the more important to use the time available to contribute something to the world – to free the world from the nuclear threat.**

GORBACHEV: The proposals I brought to Reykjavik leave me with a clear conscience. I can look you in the eye and say that, if it were impossible to reach an agreement, that is all right. But the situation in Geneva has just been marking time, and no agreement has been in sight. Now the U.S. does not appear to feel obliged to take Soviet concerns into account, while the Soviets met American concerns. Could we not agree as follows: eliminate all

INF from Europe leaving the UK & French systems; a freeze and subsequent negotiations on short range systems, and we are willing to find a solution to the problem of Asian systems.

REAGAN: **What do you have in mind for the Asian systems?**

GORBACHEV: We could accept the formula that there be 100 warheads on Soviet systems and the U.S. has 100 warheads on its territory. We can accept this even though it would require time to reduce by an order I cannot even compute. We consider this a major concession – one despite the U.S. buildup in the Pacific basin. This should show you how serious we are to reach an agreement.

REAGAN: **I agree to the proposal you just described.**

GORBACHEV: Good. When is the U.S. going to start making concessions? We have gone through half the agenda and there has been no movement from the U.S. side. The next issue is going to be the test of the U.S.'s readiness to meet the Soviets half way.

We have agreed in principle to a 50% reduction; eliminating long-range INF from Europe; on freezing and subsequently starting negotiations on shorter INF; and on 100 Soviet warheads in Asia with the U.S. the right to the same number on its territory. These are unprecedented steps which require responsible further steps in the implementation phase. This raises the question of verification, an issue which is now acute. You will find that we are going to be more vigorous than you in insisting on stringent verification requirements as we enter the stage of effective disarmament. If it proves impossible to agree on such provisions, it will also be impossible to reduce strategic and intermediate range weapons.

With respect to the ABM Treaty, nothing should be allowed to shake the ABM regime or confidence in an ABM Treaty of unlimited duration. I feel you can agree to this proposition. As I said yesterday, once we decide to reduce nuclear arms, one side has to be certain that the other side could not act behind the back of the other, so it is necessary to strengthen the ABM regime. The Soviet proposal for a ten-year commitment not to withdraw from the Treaty is a step toward strengthening the ABM regime.

In preparing our position, we took into account your personal attachment to the SDI program. Thus, under the ten-year pledge, SDI-related research in laboratories would not be banned. This is not a strict limitation on SDI, and we know where the program stands. You have scored breakthroughs in one or two areas, we know where. But ten years will enable us to solve the problems of reducing nuclear weapons, and so it is necessary. The type of arrangement I'm proposing poses neither a political, practical nor technical impediments to your program.

REAGAN: **We have no intention of violating the ABM Treaty. We have never done so, even though, as you know, we believe you have done more than has been permitted by the Treaty.**

With respect to SDI, I pledged to the American people that SDI would contribute to disarmament and peace and not be an offensive weapon. I cannot retreat from this pledge. The U.S. proposed a binding Treaty providing for the sharing of research which demonstrates a potential for defensive applications. We would share the fruits of our research – and out of our own self-interest. If everyone has access to the relevant technology, it would be a threat to no one. I don't see why SDI could not be made part of the ABM Treaty. I am dedicated to the establishment of mutual defenses against nuclear weapons. I cannot retreat.

[Reagan and Gorbachev went back and forth for another hour, and neither would budge from their positions. They agreed, however, to meet again that afternoon.

SESSION FOUR: OCTOBER 12, 1986; 3:25 P.M.-4:30 P.M.

The fourth and last session at Reykjavik opened with Shultz reading the proposal he had discussed with Shevardnadze during the break:

Both sides would agree to confine themselves to research, development and testing which is permitted by the ABM Treaty for a period of **five** years, through 1991, during which time a 50% reduction in strategic offensive arsenals would be achieved. This being done, both sides will continue the pace of reductions with respect to all remaining offensive ballistic missiles with the goal of the total elimination of all offensive ballistic missiles by the end of the second five-year period. As long as these reductions continue at the appropriate pace, the same restrictions will continue to apply. At the end of the ten-year period, with all offensive ballistic missiles eliminated, either side would be free to introduce defenses.

Gorbachev responds with the Soviet counterproposal:

The USSR and the United States undertake for **ten years** not to exercise their existing right of withdrawal from the ABM Treaty, which is of unlimited duration, and during that period strictly to observe all its provisions. The testing in space of all space components of anti-ballistic missile defense is prohibited, except research and testing conducted in laboratories. Within the first five years of the ten-year period, the strategic offensive arms of the two sides shall be reduced by 50 percent. During the following five years of that period, the remaining 50% of the two sides' strategic offensive arms shall be reduced. Thus by they end of 1996, the strategic offensive arms of the USSR and the United States will have been totally eliminated.

With the two proposals now on the table, the discussion follows.

REAGAN: **Isn't it necessary to pledge something to assure a defense against someone who might come along and want to redevelop nuclear missiles?**

GORBACHEV: It is the Soviet view that for 10 years, while we proceed to the unique historical task of eliminating nuclear forces, we should strengthen the ABM Treaty regime. Why should we create other problems whose prospects are dim and whose consequences are unknown, that leave one side in doubt about reducing nuclear weapons while the other side retains them under the guise of defensive weapons. Why burden agreements by these weights?

The U.S. side would be permitted laboratory research, and of course the Soviet side would too. In the U.S. case this would mean SDI. We are not trying to bury SDI.

SHULTZ: The first is how to handle what is permitted during the 10 years. The second, if I understand correctly, is that the Soviets see a period of indefinite duration for agreement not to depart from the ABM Treaty, while the U.S. side sees 10 years.

SHEVARDNADZE: Under the Soviet proposal, there would be no limit on SDI research, except that it would be confined to laboratories.

[A few minutes later.]

GORBACHEV:	Strict observance means confining work to laboratories. If you agree, we can write it down and sign now.
REAGAN:	**You talk about deployment as if it means space weapons. We already have agreements that prevent that. You are violating these agreements; there is the K-radar, for example. You should knock it down.**
GORBACHEV:	You might be testing objects and say they are not offensive, but there would be suspicions. Testing must be confined to laboratories only.
REAGAN:	**I am not going to destroy the possibility of proceeding with SDI. I am not going to confine the work to laboratories.**

POSTSCRIPT

Although the discussion continued for a few more minutes, with Reagan even asking Gorbachev for "a favor" in agreeing to include the language about testing in space, the two leaders were not going to budge from their positions. At one point, Soviet Foreign Minister Shevardnadze even observed, "if future generations read the minutes of these meetings, and saw how close we had come but how we did not use these opportunities, they would never forgive us."

The reality, however, was that Reagan and Gorbachev were not nearly as close to an agreement as Shevardnadze thought. In fact, according to a very top-secret paper prepared by Poindexter after the Summit,

> Immediately following Reykjavik, the President…concluded that:
>
> (1) The United States would continue to reject eliminating <u>all nuclear weapons</u> in 10 years, and focus attention on the proposals that you handed over to Gorbachev in writing in Iceland which were focused on the elimination of <u>all offensive ballistic missiles in 10 years;</u> however
>
> (2) The United States would stand firm by our long-term commitment to the ultimate goal of the total elimination of all nuclear weapons, but always cast this in terms of a long-term goal which will require the correction of existing conventional force imbalances and other conditions that require us to have the nuclear weapons in the first place.

Another highly top-secret memo, this one from Paul Nitze to Shultz, dated March 11, 1987 (not released until May 2009), suggests that even before Reykjavik the United States was conducting space-based SDI testing. Nitze wrote in that memo that another test was planned for early 1988 and that the test was within the restrictive interpretation of the ABM Treaty although Weinberger wanted to move to the broader interpretation "to add a test of a space-based kinetic-kill interceptor against a target launched into space from earth."

CHAPTER EIGHT

SDI & INF

"There has to be an answer to all these questions because some day people are going to ask why we didn't do something now about getting rid of nuclear weapons."[23]

"I have my own answer: It is possible to proceed immediately with a 50 percent reduction."[24]

"We do not want to be in the position of defending ourselves by saying that we have done nothing when we should have acted."[25]

---

[23] Reagan, speaking at the September 8, 1987 NSC meeting.

[24] Reagan to Gorbachev during their December 9, 1987 meeting in Washington discussing a proposal to reduce both countries nuclear weapons by 50 percent.

[25] Gorbachev to Reagan during their December 9, 1987 working lunch at the White House.

Date: **December 16, 1986**
Subject: **ICBM Modernization**
Status: **Declassified in Part (2005)**

BACKGROUND

Two days before today's meeting, and the day before he was scheduled to testify before Congress on his role in Iran-Contra, CIA Director Casey suffered multiple seizures requiring hospitalization. Three days later he underwent surgery for a malignant brain tumor, and later reports revealed that he was also being treated for cancer of the prostate gland. Unable to resume his duties at CIA, Casey resigned several weeks later and died in May 1987 without ever testifying.

"America has lost a patriot, and the cause of freedom, an able champion," Reagan's statement said following Casey's death. Bob Gates, his deputy, would be nominated to take his place, but his nomination was withdrawn due to controversy over his involvement in Iran-Contra. Gates would serve as acting DCI until William Webster, the former director of the FBI, was confirmed in May.[26] Frank Carlucci, though not at today's meeting, became the new WHNSA after Poindexter, also implicated in the Iran-Contra scandal, resigned on November 25, 1986.

Today's meeting continues the November 18, 1982 and April 14, 1983 discussion over the M-X missile. In the interim, Congress rejected Reagan's call for 100 M-X missiles, instead limiting the program to 50 M-X missiles with an insistence on finding a suitable basing alternative to Closely Spaced Basing. Dr. Alton Keel, Deputy WHNSA, is at today's meeting to brief on the status of a suitable basing mode for the M-X, now called the "Peacekeeper". The presentation introduces the "Garrison Rail Basing System," which would use the national rail system by deploying two missiles on 25 different trains.

SUMMARY

Dr. Keel introduced the meeting by reviewing the fact that several administrations have attempted to find an acceptable basing mode for the Peacekeeper missile; the Scowcroft Commission recommended placing 100 Peacekeepers in Minuteman silos and to start development of a small ICBM, to pursue arms control, and to seek a new survivable basing mode for the Peacekeeper missile. Keel also notes that The Scowcroft Commission recommendation, at first, attracted bipartisan support, but that bipartisan support has faded and Congress has limited deployment of the Peacekeeper to 50 missiles in Minuteman silos.

---

[26] Mr. Gates became DCI in 1991 and served as DCI until 1993. After serving in various academic positions from 1993 onwards, Mr. Gates resumed his career in government replacing Donald Rumsfeld as Secretary of Defense in 2006.

"We have a need to maintain and demonstrate resolve to protect our national security absent the arms control process and the need to develop leverage as we negotiate," Keel also tells the NSC. "We also have a need to resolve the apparent contradictions between our arms control proposals to ban mobile missiles and our plans to develop mobile missiles for our deterrent force."

Secretary Weinberger follows with an explanation of the Garrison Rail Mobile Basing concept and the high cost of the small ICBM in relation to the Peacekeeper garrison rail mobile system. The discussion follows.

SHULTZ: Does the Garrison Rail Mobile Basing system require warning of a Soviet attack?

WELCH: It requires about four hours of warning to be highly survivable.

BAKER: Is the Garrison Rail Mobile Basing the same as the old racetrack system in the Carter Administration?

WELCH: No, it's not the same. The shallow trench system is more similar to the old racetrack system

REAGAN: **Is there a problem in finding locations for the basing sites?**

WELCH: There have been few objections to the locations of the small ICBM bases. These sites have not been discussed in detail and their planned locations have not been announced.

REAGAN: **The small ICBM is strongly supported by members of Congress. Its continued development is essential to national security and to winning further support from the Democrats for the Peacekeeper garrison rail basing concept. It seems to me a low-key announcement of these decisions on ICBM Modernization would be the best approach for now. General Welch, would the small ICBM be deployed on the highways?**

WELCH: The small ICBM may use some local roads but does not depend on them for survivability. We have been transporting Minuteman missiles to and from their silos over these same roads for years and have had few, if any, problems.

KELLEY: The Peacekeeper basing is a political hostage to the small ICBM program on the Hill. However, the small ICBM has strong military value to the country and is fully supported by the Joint Chiefs of Staff. My recommendation to you, Mr. President, is to move forward with both the small ICBM and Peacekeeper garrison rail basing as soon as possible.

REAGAN: **I've approved a low-key announcement on Friday, the 19th of December.**

SHULTZ: Mr. President, I strongly support the Scowcroft Commission's recommendations to develop small ICBM and Peacekeeper garrison rail basing. The two programs are linked and should be considered as a package. Some critics may try to exploit the idea that garrison basing depends on warning – we need to deal with that issue carefully and tactfully.

Mr. President, having both programs in development would help with our objective of getting an equitable arms control treaty. In the past the Peacekeeper program has been plagued by less than full support from within the Department of Defense. The Chiefs do not support the plan for Closely Spaced Basing for Peacekeeper. It would be helpful if everyone would express their views on the present program so that the President would then know where everyone stands. We are going to need everyone's support this time or Congress will not approve the program.

KELLEY: The Chiefs fully support the recommendation to proceed with development of both the small ICBM and the Peacekeeper garrison rail basing.

WEINBERGER: There are concerns within the Department of Defense over the cost of the small ICBM, but the DOD would fully support the President's decision.

MEESE: Congressional support is the real issue. The President should invite the Congressional leadership down to the White House to be briefed and to discuss the issue with the President. This would give them the feeling that they are participating in this important decision and generate considerable goodwill.

WEINBERGER: I agree. Meeting with Congressional leaders would be a good idea.

KEEL: Mr. President, General Welch and Dick Godwin have been pre-briefing Congressional leaders and their reactions have been favorable so far.

ADELMAN: The small ICBM also needs to be supported in such meetings.

DOLE: The Department of Transportation strongly supports the garrison rail basing for the Peacekeeper missile.

WEINBERGER: Should we try to have a Congressional leadership meeting before the Friday announcement?

REAGAN: **Is there time to organize such a meeting?**

WEINBERGER: The DOD is ready to announce on Friday, but I'm concerned that there is not enough time to organize a Congressional leadership meeting, especially since Congress is not in session.

KEEL: We need to go ahead with the announcement on Friday. Mr. President, we will see what is possible with Congress.

[The minutes indicate Reagan concludes the meeting with a funny story and thanks everyone for the recommendations.]

POSTSCRIPT

On December 19, as discussed, Reagan announced his decision to proceed with the Garrison Rail Basing System and the full-scale development of the small ICBM.

Date: **February 3, 1987**
Subject: **The SDI Program**
Status: **Declassified (2005)**

BACKGROUND

Today's meeting is called to review the SDI program. The participants reference NSDD 192 (signed October 11, 1985) covering SDI and the ABM Treaty. The meeting also discusses adopting the LCI (legally correct interpretation) versus the RI (restrictive interpretation) of the ABM Treaty. NSDD 192 can be found at online at www.thereaganfiles.com.

SUMMARY

Carlucci introduces the meeting with a prepared statement by acting DCI Gates warning that the Soviets are working on their own ABM systems as well as new generations of offensive and defensive systems. The discussion follows.

WEINBERGER: Mr. President, if you want to deploy SDI, especially in light of continued Soviet activity, we need to consider the most effective way to proceed.

            We have nothing to deploy now, nor do we anticipate anything upon which to base a deployment decision in the next year. There is nothing we should take off-the-shelf and consider for deployment. Rather, we need to focus on deploying something that is both effective in its own right and a part of a later, integrated system.

We have been looking at options, various paths and degrees of concurrency. The progress we have made is astonishing.

Space-Based Kinetic Kill Vehicle (SBKKV) technology is most promising, and the most likely to yield earliest results. We are in a position to recommend further testing of SBKKV, looking at the possibility of an initial deployment in the 1993/4 time frame.

We do not need to decide more about this now than to decide that we should focus on deploying a phase of SDI capability as an initial deployment. We will be unable to achieve our overall objectives at once.

We should see if with proper testing and development we can recommend an initial deployment of 60 garages carrying SBKKVs capable of killing some 2,000 weapons in boost phase. So we will need to be in a position to give the okay to the necessary testing and development.

We will need to be able to conduct realistic tests. The Delta 180 test proved that we could distinguish metal within the plume generated by the engine's firing. Delta 181, having found the missile in the plume, should test if we can hit the missile. We can't conduct such an intercept under the restrictive interpretation (RI). However, under the legally correct interpretation (LCI) of the ABM Treaty, we can do the Delta 181 test, and see if we can hit the missile. If the answer is yes, then we are well on the road to a useable technology.

We should think of the concept of phased SDI deployments like building a house. The first phase deployment is like laying the foundation of the house; the second phase can be like putting up the walls; the third, the ceiling.

We need to be able to move to planning for such activity now. Specifically, we need you, Mr. President, to decide the following:

1) That the concept of phased deployments is ok;
2) That you would like to deploy the first phase as soon as we can; and

3) That we can immediately restructure the SDI program to follow the LCI.

[Reads large sections of NSDD 192.]

In October 1985, you set certain criteria for moving to the LCI. It is now February 1987, Mr. President, and the costs of maintaining the RI are now very high because of the astonishing success of the SDI program.

We could move to the LCI immediately. There may be no need for an announcement. You could simply allow us to do the planning under the LCI to prepare you to decide if you feel we can really support the 1993 option that I have suggested. Other options may also arise and be okay.

We don't need you to announce a deployment decision or a date. All we need is the okay to press on under the LCI and the associated funding.

There is no rush to field something before the end of your administration. However, without an okay to move to the LCI, I fear that we will have to conduct ineffective testing and, as a result, we may lose funding for the SDI program.

CARLUCCI: Cap (Weinberger), the first issue under discussion is simply the concept of phased deployment.

WEINBERGER: Well, on that, phased deployment is the only way to go. We simply will never be able to do it all at once. Programmatically, it is the only way. The Soviets may get there first.

I am not interested in a point defense. The first phase deployment must be an area defense.

CARLUCCI: What do you say to the arguments on the hill that phased deployments could lead to instability?

WEINBERGER: The logic of the argument is faulty, and that is key. The same players argued that we should not deploy M-X without a defense. SDI may be the only thing that keeps the Soviets at the negotiating table. They agreed to the ABM Treaty only after ABM passed the Senate by one vote.

The Soviets may not sign any agreement if we don't press forward. We should press forward. It will provide much better leverage.

As long as the first phase involves a boost-phase capability, it is not destabilizing.

CARLUCCI:	Do others see any problems with the concept of phased SDI deployments?
CROWE:	The Chiefs support SDI and the concept of phased deployments. They do feel that SBKKV technology is very promising. However, they feel that they simply do not have enough information now to decide to deploy anything in 1993.
WEINBERGER:	I agree. We don't know enough now to decide.
CROWE:	I agree. We do have problems yet to resolve, especially in C3. The software issue is very tough. At this point the single biggest challenge may be battle management.
WEINBERGER:	However, we are making great strides in computational capabilities to: (1) discriminate decoys from warheads, and (2) to compute the trajectories needed to kill vehicles in flight. We are experiencing a real expansion of knowledge.
CROWE:	But it still remains a challenge. In addition, a heavy lift vehicle is needed, both for general national needs and to meet the challenging requirements of a 1993 deployment option. We need more information on whether we can build a suitable heavy lift vehicle by 1993.
WEINBERGER:	The Soviets are already building heavy lift capability.
REAGAN:	**Didn't we already approve pressing forward towards heavy lift capability in NASA's management plan?**
CROWE:	That was based on a different timetable.
BUSH:	But, was that for SDI?
WEINBERGER:	It supports both civil and defense needs.
SHULTZ:	I didn't know that the Secretary of Defense had made specific recommendations in December, or, for that matter, that the President was briefed on this subject. However, I have informed myself on the issues involved (and) General Abrahamson has briefed me several times lately on the status on the SDI program.
	In my view, we have done well on the issue of survivability. I also share the sense that we have accomplished many important things. I am equally impressed by the unanimity of the view of the Chiefs, expressed on several occasions that it is not to the U.S. benefit if the Soviet Union departs from the ABM Treaty.

Phased deployment will require that we depart from the ABM Treaty. It is my view that we should not start on phase one unless you know what will follow in the entire integrated system. This must be considered prior to any deployment decision. However, once you satisfy our conditions, the only way to proceed is in a phased manner. This is very sensible to me.

But we are not in a position to decide on a phased deployment now. I agree with the Chiefs that there are problems to be resolved, like C3, and we need more information on phases two and three.

So, Mr. President, in summary, I agree both with Cap and with Bill Crowe.

CARLUCCI: Do you mean that you agree conceptually with the idea of a phase one, on which phases two and three could build?

SHULTZ: We need to know the next steps, phases two and three, before we cross the ABM Treaty by deploying phase one. If phase one is simply countered by the Soviet Union breaking out, that is not good.

WEINBERGER: Mr. President, there is not a lot of daylight between our positions (State and Defense). By the time we need to consider a real deployment of phase two or three, we can determine if we need more SBKKVs or something based on other technologies. By 1993, we will be in a position to make such a decision.

We need to keep our options for 1993 open. There is no need to decide today even if the initial deployment should be SBKKVs.

The Soviets could counter SBKKVs only with great effort, and in the process, our defenses would introduce great doubt into their military planning.

It is not our idea just to deploy a phase one system and stop, but to go on to make ballistic missiles obsolete. The first phase system should make a start and contribute to this overall goal. We should only deploy something if it will be an integral part of the whole system.

We are making great strides. ...

SHULTZ: (Interrupting) With respect to the 1993 option, it is my sense that when questioned, General Abrahamson smiles as he says 1993. Others, who have managed similar programs, say we should add a few more years to that estimate. 1993 is, at best, the earliest possible date, the most likely date is later. This must be kept in mind because it plays with what we do in Geneva.

WEINBERGER: Only a few years ago the earliest projections were 1998/9. It is now realistic to talk about 1993.

I base my estimates not only on General Abrahamson's view but also on the view of my oversight group. It has recognized Abe's optimism, and feels that it is realistic.

ADELMAN: It would be imprudent to go forward with phase one if we needed phases two through four to maintain stability. We must judge that phase one is good for us on its own merits.

WEINBERGER: I agree, and I believe that we can meet that challenge.

SHULTZ: If we are to protect the 1993 option at all, we will need heavy lift capability. So, we should press on with the pursuit of that heavy lift capability now.

CROWE: We could get along for a while (in 1993) without a new heavy lifter.

WEINBERGER: We could use available Titan IVs.

MILLER: Do we need a different heavy lifter than NASA wants?

WEINBERGER: No.

REGAN: But are we talking about two vehicles: one for OSD and another for NASA?

WEINBERGER: No, just one vehicle.

[The official meeting minutes show that Carlucci moves the conversation to the LCI of the ABM Treaty, asking Secretary Weinberger to begin the discussion.]

WEINBERGER: The issue of the LCI and the program are interlocked. To move to phased deployment, we need the most economical and effective way to test. For example, under the RI we have to use Delta 181 to test, trying for a near miss. This is a silly way to test, especially if the LCI is legally correct.

The ABM Treaty forbids the deployment of ABM components based on other physical principles (OPP) without prior agreement. But even in the absence of such an agreement about deployment, it places no restrictions on the development or testing of such devices. This position has been sustained by our legal experts. We should be able to do anything we wish short of deployment. It would be a monstrosity of logic to follow the RI for some number of years and then attempt to shift to the LCI. We should opt now to go for the most effective path.

CARLUCCI: Do we need integrated testing now?

WEINBERGER: Yes. We don't need a test this year, but we need to begin planning for such a test this year. The first such test could come in 1988/9.

CARLUCCI: You don't mean 1988. The budget is already submitted.

WEINBERGER: It could begin in 1988. We could reallocate funds.

CARLUCCI: So you hold the possibility of such a test in calendar year 1988?

WEINBERGER: I don't know the exact date, but I do know we need to begin planning for it now.

MEESE: It seems we have general agreement from all administration lawyers that the LCI is acceptable.

ADELMAN: Yes, we had, but there is new evidence. We need to look at the new evidence to be prudent. It may not have a bearing on the issue, but we must be sure.

WEINBERGER: There were discussions by Ellis – loose conversations at the SCC some thirteen years after the treaty was signed. Ellis should be retired.[27]

SHULTZ: We need to adopt a strategy to support the LCI because we need the LCI to achieve the full potential of SDI.

We need a strategy because we need to garner support effectively, in a manner that can be supported by Congress. Nothing will be gained by an announcement or reprogramming if Congress cuts SDI funds.

I believe that there is a way to accomplish this via a process of discussion with the Senate and the House, and with our allies also. Judge Sofaer sent me a copy of a memorandum tasked by the NSC staff which provides such a plan.

Three main issues must be handled, and this can only be done in collaborative ways with Congress if we are to avoid having our water cut off:

1. Sofaer has already focused on the negotiating record and we have made this available to some in Congress. Attacks from these quarters have diminished. We need to make this record available to others in Congress so they can see for themselves.

---

[27] Reagan appointed General Richard H. Ellis as the US Commissioner to the U.S.-U.S.S.R. Standing Consultative Commission on March 12, 1982.

2. We need to consider the common law of treaties. We must examine more fully the practice and understand what both parties have been doing under the treaty over the years.

The ACDA General Counsel also recently put out a paper on this and Sofaer began receiving calls about it before he even had a chance to read it himself.

ADELMAN: That was just a compilation of the various statements collected.

SHULTZ: It was released on the record and made immediately available to the press, so this needs to be dealt with. Sofaer has completed a draft memorandum on this subject and he is confident that we have a case. But he requires more time to work on it and prove that it is correct.

3. Representations were made at the time of ratification that also must be dealt with. Secretary of Defense Laird did say that the U.S. understood the treaty as presented under the narrow interpretation when he was asked. Some in the Senate are now claiming that that is the interpretation that the Senate ratified. We need to work this through carefully before engaging on this point so that we put ourselves in a position so that we can successfully assert our position in light of what we and the Soviets have been doing.

In short, I agree with Cap. Cap is right – we need to move to the LCI. However, we need to do it effectively (and) we need to convince and win support before we move.

At the same time it is conceivable that the negotiations could result in an agreement on prohibited activity that would help us, especially on moving to the SDI testing we desire, and would build support for SDI.

Max (Kampelman) is now authorized to listen and probe, and to adhere to our position that the LCI is legally correct and that's that. He will continue to do this. This is a satisfactory tactic for now, but we may find a moment in the near future where movement is a good idea.

Right now we are not ready or able to examine options internally. We also need some sort of process to allow the implementation of the LCI. Sofaer suggests a five to six month program. I don't see why five to six months is a problem. There is nothing we need to do to the FY 88 budget for now, and current Congressional appropriation language limits us to the narrow interpretation.

I fully agree with your hope, Mr. President, of moving to a world with fewer nuclear weapons and ballistic missiles. The proposal made at Reykjavik was a good one (and) the immediate agreement to reduce offensive arsenals by 50% would be even better.

If we are able to deploy a perfect SDI shield, great. It would mean that we have achieved the "zero ballistic" situation called for at Reykjavik. That is where the SDI program is going, and we should recognize it.

This possibility also means that we will need enhanced defenses against cruise missiles, bombers, and conventional forces. All of this will cost more money, in addition to the costs of SDI deployments.

The level of real spending for the Defense budget is orders of magnitude too low. We need to get this reality in play. We need, and will need, more than three percent growth. There is no reason why higher levels can't be supported by our economy. We need to make the public realize that if they want a safer world they have to pay for it and it will be more expensive. We need to get this into play while we have some time to go.

In summary, I support the LCI. We need a process so that we can implement it effectively, so that it will be supported. We also need to show our public where SDI is taking us and what our future needs will be.

WEINBERGER: I like the part about your supporting Cap. We do have a major disagreement on the subject of negotiating what is prohibited. To engage in such a negotiation we will eventually have to prohibit something, and I don't know what that could be.

SHULTZ: We need to see if there is anything. We can't discuss this now within the administration, so we can't prepare to negotiate. If the Soviets realize our situation … they will be able to press us knowing we will never agree.[28]

WEINBERGER: The Soviets want to strengthen the ABM Treaty. If we sit down to negotiate they can only conclude that there is something that we are prepared to prohibit. But we have a position under which nothing which is based on

---

[28] The minutes state, referring to this particular Shultz statement, "the resulting reconstruction may not be accurate even in its basic thrust."

other physical principles (OPP), save deployment, is prohibited.

Further, I believe that five to six months of study will impact on our program and is unnecessary. The common law of treaties is not applicable here. It has only been since 1983/4 that we have had the possibility of using OPP. Laird's remarks should not bind us; he was talking about traditional technologies. We really don't need to spend six months working up good arguments. We need to stay away from negotiations on what is permitted and prohibited.

George Shultz is correct that we can never leave ourselves with our deterrent down. We will need air defense and improved conventional capability. It is vital that we don't take down our strategic offensive nuclear capability before enhanced conventional capability is in place. Therefore, we need to watch the reductions schedules.

In any case, all agree that any additional prohibitions are almost certainly going to be unverifiable. There should be no additional agreements on prohibitions. We should prepare a strong case for the LCI and press on.

ADELMAN: All agree to the need to move the program to the LCI. To make a deployment decision we will need integrated testing. You would not buy a car based on the assurance that all the individual pieces were fully tested but the car was never assembled and driven.

We need to do three things:

1) We need to look at all the legal evidence to ensure that we are correct.
2) We need to have a clear idea of the specific tests under the LCI vice the RI, and, why each is needed.
3) It is fine to talk about activities in the ABM under the ABM Treaty as long as we are trying to get the Soviets to buy the LCI.

We should go nowhere beyond the LCI. Anywhere beyond the LCI is a wilderness, a swamp, especially since we don't really know what the Soviets are doing in advanced defenses and what they are driving for.

MEESE: The five to six month study that Sofaer suggests can be done in three months. We should consider concurrently going forward with the planning needed to restructure the program.

The idea we should pursue is not to see if we can sell the LCI, but to sell it. We will need a massive, big deal sales job – and it should be seen as a big deal.

Go up and do it. Make the effort massive if needed. I will help with assets. If it really looks like it will take four months, lets find out by pressing for three months.

[Shultz leaves to go to a Congressional hearing.]

REAGAN:

Why couldn't we just go ahead and restructure the SDI program without making any announcement? We could let others bring up any problems and we could respond to them.

We could, and should point out that we are not going as far as the Soviets have gone under the ABM Treaty. We may have only five years to prepare since the Soviets are already installing battle management radars.

If the Soviets press on with both their offensive and defensive improvements we will be hurting. Why should we go to Congress? Just do it.

CARLUCCI:

You already issued an NSDD which made commitments.

REAGAN:

How does the NSDD read?

[The minutes show that Weinberger handed Reagan a copy of NSDD 192 and that Reagan started reading parts of the NSDD to the NSC.]

It is a good position, well stated, and has stood the test of time. It also permits us to move as I've suggested.

WEINBERGER:

You will note, Mr. President, it sets as one of the conditions "adequate funding."

CARLUCCI:

The problem with your approach, Mr. President, is that if we surprise the Congress, they could simply cut SDI funding.

ADELMAN:

I agree. We should not attempt to bushwhack the Congress; it will simply result in funding cuts.

REAGAN:

(Reads more of NSDD 192 to the NSC.)

ROWNY:

Mr. President, the SDI program is now approaching critical mass so it would be good to announce your intention to restructure the program.

NITZE: To build the support that we will need, Mr. President, you must inform them of your restructuring.

WEINBERGER: You don't need to ask them, but in order to get them to support your action you do need to tell them.

REAGAN: **(Reading from NSDD 192)**

The U.S. SDI program will continue to pursue the course currently set for it by my previous guidance. Under this course, there can be absolutely no doubt of the U.S. intention to fully meet its treaty commitments. As we do so, we will continue to demand that the Soviet Union correct its behavior and come into full compliance with its obligations, especially in those cases like the construction of the Krasnoyarsk radar and their telemetry encryption, among others, in which there are no grounds for doubt about their non-compliance. In sharp contrast to Soviet behavior, our clear and principled restraint with respect to our own SDI program, and the price we are prepared to pay in exercising that restraint, demonstrates by our deeds, our sincerity towards negotiated commitments.

The whole story is in the NSDD. It covers the Soviet violations. It explains that I evaluated the price involved in my decision. It sets the criteria that "as long as the program receives adequate support." It's all laid out.

The NSDD makes it clear that my decision not to restructure the program in 1985 was temporary, but that I clearly retained the right to move to the broader interpretation when needed.

CARLUCCI: Mr. President, we are agreed on a number of points:
1. We are agreed on the concept of phased deployments.
2. We are agreed on the need for more priority on the heavy lift vehicle.
3. We are agreed on moving to the LCI when the correct foundation is laid.

We now need to discuss the arms control aspects, including the issue of negotiating permitted/prohibited activities, and the process of implementing the points made above. We will carry on this discussion at next week's meeting to focus on these areas.

We need to be able to implement our decisions effectively and the only way we can do this is if our deliberations on this sensitive issue stay within this room.

MEESE:	I want my lawyers to get with Sofaer to see how we can help.
REAGAN:	**We do need to effectively work this issue with the Congress.**
WEINBERGER:	Don't forget you, Mr. President, and not the Congress, interpret treaties. The Congress can't impose an interpretation of the treaty on you because of constitutional grounds.
CARLUCCI:	Our next meeting will be next Tuesday.

Date:	**February 10, 1987**
Subject:	**Arms Control and SDI**
Status:	**Declassified (Unknown)**

SUMMARY

Carlucci opens today's meeting with a reminder of the importance of security; asks that no notes be taken out of the White House Situation Room, and tells the participants that the NSC staff is responsible for note-taking and participants can come to the White House to review the notes as needed.

Carlucci then introduces the issue by presenting a list of options for discussion and decision. The options could not be located in briefing material for this meeting, but Option C was found in a March 11, 1987 memo from Paul Nitze to Shultz that was not released until 2009. Option C is reproduced below because it is central to the discussion.

OPTION C

Continue U.S. position on non-withdrawal from the ABM Treaty through 1996 and the right to deploy thereafter unless otherwise agreed. Propose an agreement on the treatment of advanced defenses during this period along the following lines:

- *a. Establish thresholds for devices which are based on other physical principles (OPP) beyond which such devices would be considered "components";*
- *b. Base these thresholds on physical phenomena (i.e., for directed energy devices consider power [watts of output] and the size of the optics [diameter in meters]; for kinetic kill vehicles consider velocity;*
- *c. Agree that below the thresholds identified, there would be no constraints on testing, but above the thresholds testing would be subject to constraints to agree on testing in an ABM mode; and*
- *d. Agree that sensors (other than radars) would be free from any constraints on testing except testing in conjunction with a kill mechanism.*

The discussion follows.

SHULTZ: I think we should not decide on Option C now. I prefer we not discuss it in such an open meeting. It will leak and we will lose it. I suggest we use this option in some other mode, that we not pursue it further in such a leaky meeting.

We are in a good position. Max is authorized to listen and probe. If pressed he can simply repeat our position. I think we should simply stay in this mode for now.

WEINBERGER: I think that Option C is a bad approach….

SHULTZ: Don't make me respond about Option C. We may need to be creative at some point soon, but not now.

WEINBERGER: It is important that we don't negotiate what is permitted and prohibited under the ABM Treaty. And, we certainly should not suggest we are willing to conduct such negotiations in advance of having an end-game in sight.

SHULTZ: I am not sure that we should discuss Option C now in this forum. Should we do so?

WEINBERGER: Whether now or later, it will have to be discussed.

The Soviets want to kill the SDI program. Option B offers the only option protecting what we want.

CARLUCCI: George, if you don't want to talk about Option C now, when would it be appropriate?

ADELMAN: I agree. We should talk about it now.

WEINBERGER: We agreed to reduce forces by 50 percent. Option B has this as an end by 1991, we would then be free to deploy, not negotiate.

We need to discuss the concept behind Option C because it will be discussed in Geneva.

The current structure of the SDI program is hurting us already. Delta 181 was designed originally to be an intercept; it is now redesigned to miss.

We need to decide on what we are going to do about the LCI of the ABM Treaty.

I agree that we have to consult with Congress and our allies, but we don't need to get into haggling with the Soviets over how many watts will be permitted for a laser and the like.

If we can keep them convinced that we will hold on to SDI, we will get them to agree to offensive force reductions.

REAGAN: **To ensure that the Soviets understood that we are not interested in a first strike capability, I put on** the table at Reykjavik the idea of making an agreement in advance that we would share the benefits of SDI. I made the point that it had to be an agreement in advance so that it was clear to all that they agreed we could go forward with our efforts.

Since then, I've had another thought. Now the Soviets want an agreement but are determined to force us to give up SDI. How about looking at going forward with deployment, but of an international SDI and international defense against any ballistic missile.

CARLUCCI: Mr. President, we are already staffing that general idea in the Arms Control Support Group (ACSG).[29]

REAGAN: **This approach would take SDI out of the bargain. This done, I can see no reason why we could not move forward with reductions.**

ADELMAN: We should not have this associated with the UN. If placed there it would be a real loser.

We can't forget that nuclear weapons are needed to deter war in Central Europe. We will not be able to roll that back in our lifetime. We should not associate this idea with the elimination of all nuclear weapons.

REAGAN: **[According to the minutes, Reagan "delivers a series of remarks on why MAD was an unacceptable basis for the future."]**

A major part of the way we deter requires rethinking and the associated arms control environments, renegotiation. The Soviets don't want an all out arms race with both the U.S. and NATO.

ADELMAN: However, Europeans still need nuclear weapons.

CARLUCCI: Secretary Shultz, what do you think about the idea of a broad international defense?

SHULTZ: The idea needs to be made more concrete before it can be fully evaluated. It must have sufficient detail to be as realistic as cuts in START and INF. This will need some definition.

I do think that the "non-deployment" period is the key, but delinked from the "zero ballistic missile" idea.

I don't think that this is the moment to spring a new concept on the Soviets, but we need to be ready to deal.

WEINBERGER: If we did need to trade some defense for offensive reductions, we should remember that we offered them

---

[29] The work is actually being done under a special compartmented study entitled THRESHER RAIN.

ten-years of non-deployment, plus sharing, and were scorned.

We don't have to make such a trade! We should show them that it is in their interest, too, to seek offensive force reductions. If we bargain about how much SDI we will give up we will simply set ourselves up for a fall. Once we signal that our approach involves such a trade, we have a real problem.

SHULTZ: You already offered seven-years of non-deployment (in the July 25, 1986 letter to Gorbachev).

WEINBERGER: That offer entailed no real cost to the SDI program.

REAGAN: **I want to return to the idea that I just suggested.**

From the very first we made it clear that we were prepared for and argued that we should share the benefits of the SDI program for the benefit of all. Our public diplomacy themes have stressed that:
1. **We want to deploy SDI and render ballistic missiles obsolete, effectively eliminating them;**
2. **We don't intend to simply deploy more defense over our offensive capability; and**
3. **We have offered to share the benefits.**

The idea I have fits perfectly with these themes. We can make it clear that we intend to go forward, with no restraints, based upon an agreement in advance that we will seek a system that is designed to hit any missile. An international group can be established to monitor what we are doing.

With such an agreement on defense, then, we can press forward with offensive reductions.

WEINBERGER: This would certainly put us in a high moral position. And if the USSR does not agree we could still go ahead. We would not wait to obtain Soviet agreement, would we?

REAGAN: **Hell no! We will press forward.**

WEINBERGER: I agree with Ken Adelman. I think that the Europeans would not be happy about this.

NITZE: The Soviets would clearly try to gain control of the international group by loading it with those whom they can influence.

REAGAN: **But it would take the SDI program out of the picture, (removing it from controversy and delinking it from offensive force reductions).**

ADELMAN:	We would still have the threat of suitcase bombs.
CARLUCCI:	We will have this staffed thoroughly. As we do, we will add options as appropriate.
WEINBERGER:	If someone still feels we need an option now, Option B is available. Don't offer anything beyond 1991. In fact, I'd rather not offer anything so we can avoid giving any false impression that we are ready to trade.
CARLUCCI:	We also need to consider some other actions:

1. Start consultations immediately with Congress and allies,
2. Continue our legal research, which could take an additional three months.

BUSH:	On SDI?
CARLUCCI:	Yes, on the legal aspects of ratification, whether the testimony to Congress in 1972 gave Congress the impression that they were ratifying the more restrictive interpretation of the treaty and whether this binds current action, and on case law, the issue of subsequent practice.
SHULTZ:	Yes, we need to do the consultations and the work, but you, Mr. President, need to be in a position of saying that you haven't made any decision. If you are not in that mode than it really isn't consultations.

We need time to go through the appropriate records. It's hard to determine how much time we will need to do this right. We can go through the legal homework in three months but have no idea how long it will take to lay the necessary foundation with Congress.

Nunn is already personally going through the negotiating record.

WEINBERGER:	Nunn is already acting like a presidential candidate.

If we delay for three, six, or twelve months, we will be blocking experiments that we need and increasing the hopes of those who want to block us permanently.

We need to be in the posture of taking steps to support the LCI, not arguing about its validity. Let's not take actions that aid others to tie our own hands.

CARLUCCI:	Cap, could DOD submit to the President a report on how, specifically, the SDI program would be restructured if authorized, including what changes to testing and why?
WEINBERGER:	We would be glad to.
CARLUCCI:	Mr. President, once again we have a number of actions that we should agree to pursue. These include:

1. Completing the legal research;
2. Completing the DOD report on restructuring the SDI program;
3. Beginning consultations with Congress and allies; and
4. Continuing our work on modifying our arms control positions.

Can we all agree on these as tasks to be accomplished?

[No objection.]

SHULTZ: Cap, you need to be sure that any money you plan to use in a restructured SDI program, which goes beyond the restrictive interpretation, is permitted by law.

CROWE: We need to be sure we understand the terms of any consultations. We can do some additional staffing involved with programmatic detail to buy some additional time. At the same time, the quicker we are free to move the program freely the better.

WEINBERGER: We can treat the restructuring of SDI as the basic proposal for consultation. The idea of sharing has always scared the pants off some.

SHULTZ: We need to remember to stress that we are offering to share the benefits of SDI, not the technology. The whole idea of going to "zero ballistic missiles" is that this is a clear way for the entire world to share the benefits achieved by the SDI program.

ADELMAN: Frank (Carlucci), on your fourth point, the present situation is the best for now.

Option C would have been a good option in 1981. Now it is a swamp. It is unverifiable. On top of all else, it is not clear the Soviets themselves would be interested in this.

SHULTZ: Mr. President, I would strongly advise you not to go into Option C in a public meeting.

ADELMAN: The President asked my views on the options, and I am providing them. Option B sets the date for the end of the non-deployment commitment period at 1991. This walks us back from Reykjavik.

I am not opposed in principle to negotiating what is permitted and prohibited during some non-deployment period as long as there is a clear green light to deploy at the end of the period.

WEINBERGER: With respect to Option B, I see no inconsistency or problem with the Reykjavik proposal. The Soviets didn't accept it when offered, so we can withdraw it. The situation has changed. We have had much more technical progress since then.

      With respect to Option C, I think that we need to discuss this now!

SHULTZ: We can't discuss Option C now. The technical work needed to do so is not done. I don't think that we should task this work to be done either since the work will leak. Therefore, I don't want to talk about this now.

ROWNY: The most important aspect of the consultations is the way they are done. We need not give the impression that our options and thinking is open-ended. We need to assert that the LCI is correct.

BALL: We can't let Nunn manage us. We have maintained support for SDI, but we are working on some very thin margins. Reykjavik let us resolve five major issues associated with last year's budget in a favorable way. We will not have that type of device available this year.

      We will need allies on the hill. SDI funding will be a fight no matter what we do, but we also must consider that we will also need help on other key issues. We must consider the overall impact of the SDI funding fight.

REAGAN: **If we were to approach the SDI program along the lines that I have suggested in this meeting [an advance agreement of international sharing], then I would love to see Congress try to cut the funds for SDI.**

SHULTZ: Yes, we need to build support to (put) SDI into the very core of an arms control agreement that people want. It must become the insurance policy we need, and in turn the agreement itself will insure SDI.

[Reagan discusses Chernobyl.]

CROWE: Mr. President, your idea about international sharing would require a new order of negotiation and a whole new set of specifics.

ROWNY: Mr. President, you must take steps to ensure that such a proposal is not viewed as being too far afield from the current negotiations (to be) a diversion.

CARLUCCI: Mr. President, our time is up. I believe that we have reached an agreement on the following points:

1. We should complete the legal research as quickly as possible.
2. DOD will provide a detailed report on the specific steps we would take if the President were to authorize the restructuring of the SDI program.
3. We will begin consultations with Congress and allies as soon as possible, and as soon as terms of those consultations can be developed and approved by the President.
4. We will staff out the President's new concept for a "compartmented" or closely held priority study.
5. All will provide the President their views on the options discussed today.

George (Shultz), you need to find an appropriate way to discuss your views on Option C so that the President can reach a view or decision on that option as well as the others.

POSTSCRIPT

Reagan, on February 17, sent joint letters to Speaker Wright and Senator Pell (Chairman of the Senate Foreign Relations Committee) transmitting a report on Compliance with Arms Control Agreements. The short cover letter noted:

> In previous reports to the Congress, the United States has made clear its concerns about Soviet noncompliance. These concerns remain. The United States Government takes equally seriously its own commitments to arms control agreements and sets rigid standards and procedures for assuring that it meets its obligations. The United States has been and remains in compliance with all current treaty obligations and political commitments.
>
> In view of the continued pattern of uncorrected Soviet violations and the increasing magnitude and threat of Soviet strategic forces, I decided on May 27, 1986, to end the U.S. policy of observing the SALT I Interim Agreement (which had expired, and which the Soviets were violating) and the SALT II Treaty (which was never ratified; which, had it been ratified, would have expired on December 31, 1985; and which the Soviets were violating). These agreements are now behind us, and Soviet allegations and the facts of Soviet compliance with regard to these agreements are therefore not discussed in this year's report. For our part, we will continue to exercise utmost restraint in our strategic force programs as we press for equitable and effectively verifiable agreements on deep reductions in U.S. and Soviet nuclear arsenals.

About three weeks later, on March 3, Reagan announced that a new round of arms control negotiations would soon begin with the Soviet Union.

And a month later, Reagan sent Gorbachev a letter, dated April 10, reminding him that "it has been a long time since you and I last communicated directly. … Together we can make the difference in the future course of world events. Let us pray that you and I can continue our dialogue so that the future will be one of peace and prosperity for both our nations and for the world."

That same day, April 10, Reagan was in Los Angeles and used the opportunity to give a major speech on U.S.-Soviet relations to a luncheon organized by the Los Angeles World Affairs Council. "From the very first days of this administration, I have insisted that our relations with the Soviets be based on realism rather than illusion," Reagan told the group. Today, though, he was ready to challenge the Soviets "to join us in a mutual 50 percent cut in our strategic nuclear arsenals in a way that strengthens stability." Reagan went on to characterize U.S.-Soviet relations as "proceeding," saying there was neither a "great cause for excitement" nor a "great cause for alarm."

On April 16, after Shultz returned from talks in Moscow, Reagan told the press he was still "optimistic about an agreement this year," and the day before the Geneva negotiations were set to begin, May 4, he issued another statement saying he had "directed our U.S. START negotiator to intensify efforts to reach agreement on reducing strategic offensive nuclear arms by 50 percent." "I am firmly convinced that a START agreement is within our grasp, even this year, if the Soviets are prepared to resolve the remaining outstanding issues," the statement continues. "And most important among these issues is the need, for the purpose of ensuring strategic stability, to place sub-limits on ballistic missile warheads."

Date: **May 21, 1987**
Subject: **Political Issues for the President's Trip to Europe**
Status: **Declassified (2005)**

SUMMARY

REAGAN: **Today's session will focus on my upcoming trip to Europe. The European trip will include stops in Venice, Rome, Berlin and Bonn. I want today's discussion to focus on the political agenda at the Venice Economic Summit. With Gorbachev seeming to be taking the initiative domestically and in arms control, it is necessary for the West to demonstrate cohesion and movement in Venice.**

I am particularly concerned that our political statements do not fall back from where we were last year. The keys will be a strong statement on terrorism

and a clear agreement on how the West will want to move East-West dialogue forward.

Secretary Shultz, will you please start the meeting with an assessment of how the political agenda is coming along.

SHULTZ:

The President will be in his usual summit role: the President is the leader of the Western Alliance and that responsibility is underlined particularly at summits.

The President's colleagues are facing difficult situations. Mrs. Thatcher has decided to cut short her participation and will be in Venice only for the Monday evening dinner discussions. She will depart Tuesday following the lunch. This will leave a gap since she always provides strength and dynamism to the discussions. She has been an especially effective collaborator with the President and we will want to rely on her to help secure our key objectives. We are disappointed that she will be leaving early, but of course she has a particular problem – her reelection campaign.

In addition, Mitterrand and Chirac will be there, but not always at the same time. They are split on many issues and will be bringing that division to Venice. Both will be looking over their shoulders in the jockeying for position leading up to next year's presidential elections. Fanfani will be representing Italy, but in essence they have no government. Given his caretaker role there is not much strength to come from him. The President's good friend, Nakasone, is nearing the end of his term. Still the Japanese have always insisted on a strong security statement and the President will want to rely on Yasu's (Nakasone's) support at the summit.

Prime Minister Mulroney has generally been supportive of our efforts, but he comes with a very much weakened base at home....

Chancellor Kohl will be preoccupied with his key concern, finalizing the German position on INF. It is important that this be sorted out before the summit so that it does not dominate the discussions and the news coverage. In sum, as we look around, the leadership role at the summit will fall on the President's shoulders more than ever. In the past, we have been able usually to count on the host country for support and some leadership, but this will not be the case in Venice.

A second reason why the President's role is so critical is that Europe is facing a period of internal doubt. The 40th Anniversary of the Marshall Plan is an occasion for reflecting on past accomplishments, but also for speculation on what the next era will be like. The Europeans have expressed anxiety, for example, over growing U.S. Congressional protectionist sympathy and about the agriculture issue in the Uruguay Round. Defense spending has leveled off both here and in Europe and the national commitments to NATO's three percent spending increase has waned. Some Europeans are worried about the increasing calls in the U.S. for withdrawals of our forces in Europe. Others voice the concern that the INF process could lead to a "denuclearization" of Europe. The Europeans are now making tentative moves toward improving defense cooperation, but they are not certain exactly where they want to go. These European doubts were emanating at a time of increasing effectiveness by Soviet public diplomacy campaigns, particularly in portraying Gorbachev as a leader who is working hard for disarmament and an improvement in East-West relations.

While the Europeans appear to be wringing their hands, this is not to suggest that things are falling apart in Europe. In fact, much of what we see is the result of the successes of our common policies. Together we have produced a democratic tradition that has brought freedom and prosperity to a continent that was reeling from the impact of a devastating war 40 years ago. The market-oriented, capitalist economic systems have clearly shown their superiority over the centralized, dictatorial systems. We are developing technology for the future at an impressive rate. On the arms control front, the Soviets have come to adopt many of our viewpoints – indeed, the movement the Kremlin has shown is directly attributable to the President's policies. In sum, things are working well, but we will have to rally the troops in Venice.

On the political agenda, we will focus on East-West relations, terrorism and South Africa. …

On East-West relations we will want to share our assessments of Gorbachev's domestic and foreign policies. The FRG (West Germany) currently has the most enthusiastic interpretation of the General Secretary, while the UK takes the most skeptical approach.

However, even Mrs. Thatcher has described him as a person with whom we can do business. We all know that change is taking place in the USSR, but we will want to maintain a realistic appraisal of events there. ...

It would be unthinkable not to have a political statement come out of the Venice discussions. Some – notably France – will oppose or drag their feet. The Japanese have tabled a good draft statement on East-West relations. ...

Finally, there are a couple other issues we need to resolve. The first is the increasingly difficult dispute we have with the French over the conventional arms negotiations format. We have got to resolve this one. Cap and I need to get together with the President to discuss it. Lord Carrington is pushing hard to get past these procedural differences.

WEINBERGER: We might just want to leave the French out of these negotiations.

SHULTZ: The Europeans very much want the French involved given the "Atlantic to the Urals" nature of the talks. ...

The discussion shifts to terrorism, and picks up a few minutes later with Weinberger talking about an arms control agreement. "We may be close to a major European arms agreement," Weinberger tells the NSC. "The Soviet movement toward our position is a direct result of the alliance's firmness in staying together and deploying the INF missiles. This decision demonstrated the strength and resolve of the alliance – nothing else will bring the Soviets to the table so quickly."

Gates notes that the CIA does not expect any surprises from Gorbachev because he "feels he has the ball rolling" and will want to keep it that way.

USIA Director Wick explains that he received some disturbing news: "Many Europeans feel that Gorbachev is more committed to an arms control agreement than Ronald Reagan by a surprising 8-1 margin in the FRG." Wick suggests a concerted effort to counter the Soviet disinformation campaign.

Adelman remarks that he is concerned that the "alliance continues to fiddle around and has not reached an INF decision. ... We need to move toward a global zero-zero agreement, not one that leaves 100 in Asia." "On START," Adelman continues, "the Soviets are simply not doing anything."

Carlucci wraps up the meeting a few minutes later:

> When the President goes to the summit he will bring strength to the group at a time when the other leaders are being buffeted by internal difficulties. There has been a lot of work done in preparation for this summit. Venice presents us with a number of challenges, but lots of opportunities as well.

POSTSCRIPT

Reagan held his 41st live news conference on the grounds of the Hotel Cipriani in Venice, Italy following the G-7 Summit on June 11. Reagan called the summit one of the most successful and productive of his presidency "because it put form, substance, and institutional framework on those initiatives (created last year) and locked in a process which will better enable us to navigate the dynamic new world of international economics." Moving to arms control negotiations, Reagan continued,

> As most of you also know, we're currently engaged in a highly sensitive discussion with the Soviets that could lead to an historic arms reduction treaty on U.S. and Soviet intermediate-range missiles. Progress has been made here in Venice. And today and tomorrow Secretary Shultz will be meeting with the NATO foreign ministers in Reykjavik. I'll be anxious to have his report about the views and recommendations of our allies. So, I'm particularly grateful I had this opportunity in Venice, not only to discuss these arms reduction efforts with our allies, but to agree again on the importance of reminding the Soviet Union of the progress that needs to be made in other arms negotiations, especially the reduction of strategic intercontinental nuclear forces.

Reagan spent the next day in the Federal Republic of Germany where his first stop was in Berlin to give a major foreign policy speech in front of the Brandenburg Gate, just steps away from communist East Berlin. Going against the advice of most of his advisers, and with speakers placed in the direction of East Berlin, Reagan challenged General Secretary Gorbachev to "tear down this wall."[30]

Reagan then went on to Bonn for a meeting with Chancellor Kohl (the meeting minutes could not be located) before boarded Air Force One for the flight home.

Date:	**September 8, 1987**
Subject:	**Review Of United States Arms Control Positions**
Status:	**Declassified in Part (2005)**

SUMMARY

CARLUCCI: This is the meeting we have all been waiting for, an opportunity to review our options prior to Secretary Shultz's meeting with his counterpart. Mr. President,

---

[30] Peter Robinson, How Reagan Changed My Life, Regan Books (2003). Reagan, according to Robinson, said in the limo on the way to the speech when asked if he was going to go with the line "tear down this wall,": "The boys at State are going to kill me, but it's the right thing to do."

	would you care to make any initial remarks before we begin?

REAGAN: **For several years we've had consistent arms reductions goals: to get verifiable deep reductions and to preserve our ability to move to a safer world through SDI. It appears we are near agreement in INF. Now we must finish the task in other areas.**

I don't accept the suggestions of some that it is too late for us to get a START agreement before I leave office. I want a START agreement, but only if it is a good one, one we can verify and which enhances our security. At the same time, I believe fully in our policy of seeking a stable transition to strategic defenses. We must set the stage for one day deploying effective defenses, and seek to do so in a manner that will strengthen strategic stability. George's meeting next week is a chance to move toward these two goals.

I want your thoughts today on how we can best use that meeting. Are we better served by movement in our position, or are our current positions the best way to gain our objectives? I'm looking forward to your views so we can help prepare George for his discussions.

CARLUCCI: We have a host of arms control issues we could consider, (but) I would hope we can resolve some at the cabinet or sub-cabinet level with papers so that we can keep this meeting on START and Defense and Space issues.

We need to look at all the issues in the context of our overall strategy. We have done papers on each of the areas with options. As we go through the upcoming week we will want to bring many of these options to decision.

With that introduction, let me ask Secretary Shultz if he wants to frame the way he intends to approach his upcoming meetings with Shevardnadze.

SHULTZ: The President has had success in imposing the full U.S. agenda on the Soviets, and we will come into this next meeting with Shevardnadze covering our entire four-part agenda. This will not be an arms control meeting only, and I know, Mr. President, you will do the same in your meeting.

Mr. President, you should compare the situation today to that which we faced in 1984 when you invited Gromyko to come down from the UN the first time. At that time there was little going on in any of the areas. Now, however, there is a lot going on in each of the four areas: human rights, bilateral, regional issues, and arms control.

On arms control, with respect to INF, the major points are basically agreed to. We have a verification regime that is more intrusive than any other we have ever negotiated. Even after adjusting that regime to reflect zero-zero, we should be able to move to put the verification in place.

However, Mr. President, we are not doing right by our negotiators. We need decisions now in the INF areas. There are four or five issues of the second order that are just hanging us up. We need to make decisions and get the Treaty on the table before Shevardnadze gets here. I would like to make sure we have that done so that I can focus the conversations with Shevardnadze on START, not INF.

CARLUCCI: I understand the decision paper is ready, but we've just gotten it.

SHULTZ: Well, can we have decisions today? I would like to get this behind us so that we can go on further in the agenda.

WEINBERGER: Reaching quick decisions under the pressure of a meeting is not a good way to proceed.

CARLUCCI: Cap, I think we can clear the decks by tomorrow. We are close to closure on most issues and we need another day or so to make sure that our staff has a chance to consider the paperwork received. Why don't we go ahead now and discuss START. George, would you like to start?

SHULTZ: No, I think I would rather not. Let's let the others speak.

REAGAN: **With respect to the INF issues, as I understand it we are talking about our positions, not a problem with the Soviet (position). We need to step up to what we need to agree. Maybe we ought to stick in a few giveaways at the same time, but we ought to press forward on decisions.**

CARLUCCI: We will bring a decision paper to you by tomorrow. Now, let's turn to START. Secretary Shultz, would you like to open the remarks?

SHULTZ: No, I'd rather listen to others speak.

CARLUCCI:	(Speaking to an NSC staffer) Please put up the first chart on START options.
	Looking at the chart, the most momentous decision we face is the one involving mobile missiles. The Soviets have put a heavy emphasis here. The assessments are that we have reasonable verification of mobile missiles if they are in a deployed, peacetime mode, but that it would be very, very, low in a non-deployed mode. Mr. Gates, isn't that correct?
GATES:	Yes.
CARLUCCI:	I think that the chart correctly reflects the State position.
SHULTZ:	I don't want to be associated with any position or any views. I don't feel that it's appropriate for me to be associated with any view in a group like this. All that will happen is that it will leak and it will undercut my position with Shevardnadze. I propose, Mr. President, that I will provide you my views privately.
CARLUCCI:	Can someone in the room from the Department of State talk for the Department?
SHULTZ:	What I am talking about is the problem with the process. You've got to find another way to work the process.
WEINBERGER:	That's ridiculous. We must be able to meet and discuss issues.
CARLUCCI:	Can anyone explain the State position?
SHULTZ:	I have no intention of telling you my position. You know my rationale. And, by the way, Frank, you know the rationale for the State position. Why don't you review it?
CARLUCCI:	(Starts to review the State position.)
WEINBERGER:	(Interrupting) The treatment of mobile ICBMs is the most fundamental issue. Our position now is that we should have no mobiles. There is no way we can verify them, and to move now would just mean that we would get nothing for it.
	I think that we should have a firm position not to allow mobiles. We had such a position in the past. Nothing has changed and no one can tell me what we'll get for it. So I have to ask – what is compelling us to move for a change?
CARLUCCI:	I would note that we are pursuing mobiles ourselves.
WEINBERGER:	If we could ban them, there would be no need for us to move to mobiles.

This would be a much better situation. If we move in this general area, once again I don't know what we're going to get for it, Mr. President.

CARLUCCI: It may be that it is the necessary step to get a START agreement.

WEINBERGER: That may be the case, but then we will get an unverifiable agreement.

CARLUCCI: Do you really believe that? I mean, is it really that bad? We have some verification on deployed missiles.

WEINBERGER: We can verify current deployments but we can't verify total capability.

CARLUCCI: Let's stop for a second and get the DCI's view.

GATES: Mr. Webster isn't here yet, but he has written out the points he wants to make.

[Fourteen lines redacted.]

Overall, we are able to monitor some aspects of a mobile missile agreement well and others poorly. The policy agencies must make the judgments of military risk associated with our monitoring capabilities and our uncertainties. The singular question becomes, "how much risk are we willing to take?"

ADELMAN: Mr. President, I would note that the problems that we face in START are similar to the problems we will face in INF verifying SS-20s.

KAMPELMAN: Obviously, I am not speaking for State (Laughing.)

There is no reason for us to move in mobiles now without getting something in return from the Soviets. We don't need to go unless we get something appropriate.

But the negotiators need to know, if the situation permits or requires, that you're going to give them some flexibility. I'm not making a suggestion that we decide today, but we ought to know that in return for sub-limits or in view of our interest in deploying U.S. mobiles, that we do want to have the ability to entertain the possibility of moving on mobiles in that context.

CARLUCCI: We all agree that no one is proposing that we just put mobiles on the table. Isn't that clear?

WEINBERGER: That's good, and I agree, but you've got to remember that sub-limits are not verifiable if mobiles can be produced. A ban is needed, not anything else. If we don't have a ban, nothing is verifiable. We should not give up things to get a treaty that is not verifiable.

REAGAN: **Well, Cap, I think we have to figure that they're going to have mobiles whether we ban them or not. We will have to have them too.**

WEINBERGER: It's a little harder for them to have mobiles if we ban them. If there is no ban, it will be impossible to verify any sub-limits. For example, in the INF area, because there is a ban, if we find any missiles it is a clear, naked violation. If there is no ban, it is easier for them to have violations under the sub-limits to have more missiles that are mobile than those permitted by a treaty.

CARLUCCI: Well, let's concede then that they can or will cheat. The President's point, though, is if they're not banned, we can have some too.

WEINBERGER: True, but our exercising the right to make such deployments will be very, very tough with Congress.

CARLUCCI: Would a situation in which there is no ban be easier? By that I mean, no ban, and no agreement.

SHULTZ: I would note that the only missiles that people want these days are mobile. Ours are mobile at sea and they are survivable. Mobile missiles are less of a threat to bring on a first strike because they are not targetable.

                 The resistance that we are having to M-X is not to the missile, it's to a missile that is not survivable. The rail mobility may be an answer for M-X, and road mobility for Midgetman. If it were not vulnerable being put in silos, it would be more politically supportable. If you confine us both to fixed ICBMs, you are building a very destabilizing force.

CARLUCCI: Well, doesn't our insistence then on a ban on mobiles drive the Soviets to sea?

WEINBERGER: We're at sea already, but we also have many fixed ICBMs today. The Soviets have mobile missiles on land and we do not. It's going to be very hard for us to get mobile missiles on land. Therefore, there is a relative advantage to us if we can get them to agree to a ban. Trading a ban for sub-limits is an empty trade because the sub-limits will become unverifiable.

SHULTZ: It is very easy for the Soviets to deploy more missiles and it is hard for us. Therefore, a START agreement may be very, very important for us.

                 First of all, INF will look very naked if long-range strategic missiles can replace the targeting that is provided by INF missiles – that will make it an empty agreement. And second, given that they deploy missiles much more easily than we do, an unconstrained world would not be good for us. The numbers that we got at Reykjavik for START are very good, Mr. President – 6,000, the 1,540, which was half of the heavy force, and a bomber counting rule that is very, very, good.

The Soviets are on-again, off-again, with the 4,800 sub-limit. If we can get those four, that is 6,000, 1,540, the bomber counting rule, and, 4,800, those numbers by themselves buy you a very good agreement if we can get them. We shouldn't overlook how important a START agreement is if these numbers are in.

Our problem is that we have a very limited political capability to deploy missiles. When it does come to making deployment decisions, in my view, it will be easier if our missiles are mobile.

WEINBERGER: I have no doubt that I agree with you on the need for START, but that is no reason for us to give in to Soviet demands. We've got a good agreement in INF because we hung tough – we can do the same in START….

The argument is not only on mobile missiles and verification, but it is also the fact that they have mobile missiles now and we don't. We need to ensure that we will have enough stuff left after an agreement to provide for deterrence. I feel they want a START agreement and I believe we will get a good one if we'll just hold. As far as giving flexibility to a negotiator, I think that is simply another way of telling him he can give up on the issues.

ADELMAN: Mr. President, I see no evidence at all the Soviets are interested in START. It is very unlikely you are going to get an agreement on this area in this administration under the terms we are asking. What we need to worry about is thinking about the precedents for the future and for this reason we should not go any further because probably we are not going to get an agreement.

ROWNY: It's in our interest to push for START now. We can defer the issue of what to do about mobiles very safely. That is not a make or break issue.

REAGAN: **You've got to remember that the whole thing was borne of the idea that the world needs to get rid of nuclear weapons. We've got to remember that we can't win a nuclear war and we can't fight one.**

The Soviets don't want to win by war, but by threat of war. They want to issue ultimatums to which we have to give in.

If we could just talk about the basic steps we need to take to break the log jam and avoid the possibility of war. I mean, think about it, where would the survivors of the war live? Major areas of the world would be uninhabitable. We need to keep it in mind that that's what we're about. We are about bringing together steps to bring us closer to the recognition that we need to do away with nuclear weapons.

CARLUCCI: Well, where can we get some motion in this area?

ROWNY: No motion is needed on mobiles. We may be able to get some motion on sub-limits. The 1650 sub-limit is the problem. If we could get rid of that lower sub-limit we may be able to move the Soviets. SLCMs (submarine-launched cruise missiles) are also not an area that we need to do anything about. The crucial issue is Defense and Space.

CARLUCCI: Okay on sub-limits, let me see if I can at least summarize what I think I have heard. We all agree that 4,800 is needed. We've seen some flexibility on the 3,300 number before. Everyone has questions on all the others. I guess that's the best summary I can give. Let's move to Defense and Space.

REAGAN: **I have a friend who tells me that in the Soviet Union their right-wingers are starting to call Gorbachev "Mr. Yes" because he agrees with everything that I propose.**

CARLUCCI: Mr. President, our current position is shown on the chart. The options are as listed.

WEINBERGER: We have to be very careful in this area, Mr. President, because what we want to do is get rid of nuclear weapons, and if we handle this badly, we will not be able to get rid of them. We can't live with nuclear weapons if they are used. We can't get rid of them because there are no defenses against them. We must do nothing to inhibit our ability to defend against nuclear weapons. We need to defend early —we need to defend our continent, not just a few sites.

The Soviets want to insist on a lengthy period of non-withdrawal from the ABM Treaty in return for START. If the Soviets want a link, we will have to make sure that there is no inhibition on our rights to deploy without any additional negotiations or further equivocation. The earliest I think we can deploy is 1995....

We need no further restrictions on our right to deploy. We should make every effort to hold firm. No talks for two years or more, no negotiations, no six month notification, none of that. All we are doing with this type of stuff is blocking ourselves in. Anyone who believes that the Soviets will not deploy as soon as they can when they get their system is wrong.

[The minutes show that Reagan is shaking his head "yes."]

All the options are ways to get us to agree, but the Soviets have their own objective. Their objective is to block the SDI program. Nothing here is verifiable, and we can't do anything before 1995. But what the hell, we don't need to do anything before that time period either.

CARLUCCI: You know, Cap, under the current ABM Treaty we are free to move to deployment within six months by simply withdrawing.

WEINBERGER: Yes, but withdrawing from the ABM Treaty carries a lot of political baggage. We need Soviet agreement that at an appropriate time they can raise no objection to our deployment.

CARLUCCI: Do you object to simply giving them six months notice?

WEINBERGER: No, not if it's before 1995.

CARLUCCI: We had a non-withdrawal for 1996 at one point, you know.

WEINBERGER: Yes, but we're walking back from that, and we're really making progress. (Laughter.)

REAGAN: **Why can't we agree now that if we get to a point where we want to deploy we will simply make all the information available about each others systems so that we can both have defenses. So that if either side is ready to deploy, both agree to make available to the other all the results of their research.**

WEINBERGER: I don't believe that we could ever do that.

HERRES: Mr. President, there is a great risk in exchanging technical data. Much of our technology is easily convertible into other purposes and into an offensive area.

ADELMAN: Mr. President, that would be the most massive technical transfer the western world has ever known. We would make the Toshiba incident[31] look piddling. If they understood our system that well it would be easy for them to move to countermeasures.

WEINBERGER: So let's make sure that we not bind ourselves so that we can get there first. They've been working for 17 years.

ADELMAN: It would be okay if we both got there together.

WEINBERGER: But we need to get to the point where we are talking about deployments, not research.

REAGAN: **Once we deploy something, won't they know about the system? So won't they try to counter it anyway, so what difference does it make if they get the information and counter it their way or if we simply provide it to them.**

WEINBERGER: The key here is the price that they are asking for is too high. We ought to just hold tough.

KAMPELMAN: At this point, Mr. President, I would like to make a pitch for our negotiators. They have been at it for 30 months and they haven't given up the store.

In the INF area we have a fantastic agreement, or are on the verge of a fantastic agreement. In START, we are at 50 percent without giving up the store, and in principle, we have what we want. No one at the table is considering proposals that would jeopardize U.S. security. And, Mr. President, I would note that in my opinion none of the options that are under consideration on that chart would undermine the SDI program. There is nothing there that can give us or will cause us to give up the SDI program.

So we have some negotiating room. I'm not arguing that we need to make a move in Defense and Space unless we get something in START. If they come around in START, we may need to move in Defense and Space. We can evolve our position. For example, now at the end of our period of non-deployment we want the Soviets to agree to legitimize deployment for either of us and the Soviets simply say no. The Joint Chiefs are concerned that they may be readier to deploy than we are, and the figure of 1995 assumes that we have full funding for SDI. But, on the other hand, Mr. President, we have

---

[31] The Toshiba incident, in 1987, involved a subsidiary of Toshiba supplying the Soviet Union with precision equipment to make ultra-quiet submarine propellers in violation of allied trade restrictions put in place to deny the Soviet's high-technology. After U.S. intelligence uncovered the sale, the U.S. military banned Toshiba products, which also strained U.S.-Japanese relations.

the right to withdraw on six months notice from the ABM Treaty and we don't need any legitimization by the Soviets. At some time we may wish to, simply in emphasizing our right to withdraw from the ABM Treaty on six months notice.

REAGAN: **I don't want to make this a part of the START agreement though.**

KAMPELMAN: START and Defense and Space treaties should not be linked. If the Soviets say "okay" in START then we could consider options in Defense and Space. We should be able to protect our SDI program.

WEINBERGER: All that's fine, Max, except how do you define the SDI program?

KAMPELMAN: I see it as an exploratory research program that may allow us at some point to come to the assessment of the feasibility of deploying defenses.

WEINBERGER: That's what I thought. That's not the program I see, and we need the unequivocal right to deploy now.

KAMPELMAN: Our proposal doesn't do any damage to that.

WEINBERGER: Our proposal should include that we intend to deploy as quickly as we can after the end of withdrawals.

KAMPELMAN: (A) six month withdrawal from the ABM Treaty can still cover that.

CARLUCCI: This is going to be a real fun week. Mr. President, we'll get the issue papers to you this week for decision.

REAGAN: **There has to be an answer to all these questions because some day people are going to ask why we didn't do something now about getting rid of nuclear weapons.**

You know, I've been reading my Bible and the description of Armageddon talks about destruction, I believe, of many cities and we absolutely need to avoid that. We have to do something now.

CARLUCCI: We certainly need to avoid Armageddon.

WEINBERGER: The answer is SDI.

POSTSCRIPT

Before Shultz left for Moscow, Soviet Foreign Minister Shevardnadze hand-delivered an eight-page letter on arms control from Gorbachev to Reagan during his September 15 White House meeting. Gorbachev's letter acknowledged that an INF Treaty is "within reach," but an agreement still needed to be reached on verification and a global zero solution. In terms of reaching an agreement on the ABM Treaty, Gorbachev wrote:

Things are not as good with regard to working out agreement on the ABM Treaty regime, on preventing the extension of the arms race into space. Whereas we have submitted a constructive draft agreement that takes into account the U.S. attitude to the question of research on strategic defense, the U.S. side continues to take a rigid stand. However, without finding a mutually acceptable solution to the space problem it will be impossible to reach final agreement on radically reducing strategic offensive arms, which is what you and I spoke about in both Geneva and Reykjavik.

Reagan responded the next day with a short letter emphasizing that the Shevardnadze meeting was a constructive and useful step toward "our common search for peace."

Date: **October 14, 1987**
Subject: **Upcoming Shultz-Shevardnadze Meetings in Moscow**
Status: **Declassified (2005)**

SUMMARY

CARLUCCI: Secretary Shultz is hosting a lunch for President Duarte, Mr. President, so he cannot be here right now. Max Kampelman is representing Secretary Shultz. Max, can you give us a setting for the Moscow trip?

KAMPELMAN: I talked to the Secretary before I came. He reassured me that he intends to cover the full agenda of U.S. concerns. It is his hope that we'll not spend the full meeting in Moscow on INF, though important issues, like verification, do remain.

The Soviets did raise the German issue again and we may have to deal with it. However, I received a personal message from my counterpart, Mr. Vorontsov, who indicated to me that he hopes that we would be able to move to resolve this promptly.

CARLUCCI: We may have just seen a crack in the Soviet position on this earlier today.

KAMPELMAN: I would expect that because the Soviet negotiators are really not first-drawer....

The primary emphasis we should have is on START, and Mr. President, Reykjavik provides a good basis for this. The Soviets have come part of the way towards us on things like sub-limits and throw-weight. The Soviets have said that START is the root problem and they're ready to seriously work to resolve the START differences. If they are serious, we are ready to see where we can go too. They know, for sure, that in no way will they be able to block SDI.

REAGAN: **I hope they know that.**

KAMPELMAN: After Geneva, they knew that you were serious, (and) they realized that SDI is real and that they have to learn to live with it.

CARLUCCI: That's what Shevardnadze said to me during his visit.

KAMPELMAN: We need to tie SDI into a stabilizing process. From this point of view we can also minimize the domestic problems with respect to SDI. In a sense, we can strengthen SDI out of this stabilizing process rather than weaken it. The Soviets have indicated interest in Chemical Weapons (CW). We have a problem dealing with this area, but we have the same teams ready to deal with it in Moscow as we did in Washington. We will have working groups in each area; one of them will be in CW. I don't know if testing will come (up) at this meeting.

CARLUCCI: I think we solved that in Washington, at least for the time being.

KAMPELMAN: We need to ensure that we keep the show on the road with respect to nuclear testing. We have to sort out who will be the head of the U.S. delegation, and be ready for the talks that will start by the first of December.

CARLUCCI: Mr. President, we do have some significant INF issues.

REAGAN: **(Interrupting) I'd really (like) to return to SDI.**

Some group did an excellent film that I saw at Camp David over the weekend. It really refutes the scientific groupies that have it all wrong. I think if the American public saw this film, they would understand a hell of a lot better.

LINHARD: Sir, the group was the American Defense Preparedness Association, a civilian group. They have a regular series of awards for SDI achievement and you have routinely supported their functions.

REAGAN: **Can we help these further?**

LINHARD: We have to be careful that we maintain the proper White House involvement. But there's no reason why you can't help this group, and we have been supportive in the past.

WEINBERGER: The public really needs some additional information. The public is with us, and the more information we give them the more supportive they will be.

SEC. BAKER: The Wirthlin Poll agrees with what Cap (Weinberger) just said. However, there is some confusion out there about exactly what SDI is. The film may be able to help.

REAGAN: **(Speaking to Senator Baker) Can we kind of push this along?**

SEN. BAKER: Yes, we'll get on with it.

CARLUCCI: Are there any other comments on INF?

WEBSTER: I have a comment which I think I want to make at this point. I think I need to speak for the technicians.

We're very concerned about the verifiability of the INF Treaty, and especially the current position, which does not remove the infrastructure of Soviet INF forces. We should have no infrastructure remaining, although I know there is some price on the NATO side. I think we should forbid all operations in training and have the personnel leave the bases that are being eliminated, and we need strong on-site inspection.

But more than anything else, Mr. President, there should be no effort to close on these nut-cutting details in Moscow, but rather come back and work it with the experts who can work on this issue. We need time to look at the issue....

CARLUCCI: Mr. President, we've looked at this very issue twice and there are significant impacts on NATO that have to be considered.

WEBSTER: I understand that we have looked at this before, but I want to make sure that we consider verification in light of the ratification problems we're going to have.

GRAHAM: I agree with Judge Webster. I understand the Soviets don't want to give us data on their non-deployed missiles anyway.

KAMPELMAN: Mr. President, Judge Webster has experts of his on each delegation. It is very clear that we have to work hard on verification, and we'll do so.

WEBSTER: We need to ensure that this is the case.

CROWE: I agree with the DCI's concerns. I'm more than happy to abide by whatever restrictions we need to ensure that they are met.

CARLUCCI: Let's turn to START. The Soviets have offered us a limit of 3,600 or 60 percent of total weapons on each of the three legs of the Triad. The JCS looked at this and found it not to be acceptable. Last time we met we looked at sub-limits, and we have a dazzling array of options in sub-limits involved.

I understand yesterday there was a discussion of the sub-limits issue with the Chiefs and the Secretary of State. I thought perhaps we might have the Chiefs comment on this area.

WEINBERGER: I think that's a very good idea. The Joint Chiefs examined priorities with respect to sub-limits. Admiral Crowe, maybe you could speak for the Chiefs.

CROWE: Our discussion was sparked by the offer of the Soviets to limit each leg of the Triad to 60 percent. As Mr. Carlucci said, because of uncertainties in the future we think it's unwise to limit our flexibility by accepting this proposal. However, based on a request by Mr. Carlucci, we did review the priorities involved with the sub-limits issue, and I'd like to report on those now.

Our number one priority is the 6,000 RV limit. Number two is protecting the bomber counting rules achieved at Reykjavik which permits us to compensate for other aspects of the agreement.

WEINBERGER: I would note, Mr. President, that Admiral Crowe told me yesterday that the finding of military sufficiency in the START area rests most heavily on maintaining the bomber counting rule.

KAMPELMAN: Mr. President, you got this in Reykjavik. Many people have run Reykjavik down often (and) this is certainly one of the accomplishments of that meeting.

CROWE: This was a spectacular accomplishment of that meeting which allowed us possibilities in other areas. But let me return to priorities. Number three, we feel that we should pocket the 1,540 limit on heavies. We need to pocket this limit in some way.

CARLUCCI: The Soviets have already agreed to the 1,540 limit.

CROWE: Our fourth priority is the 4,800 limit on ballistic missile reentry vehicles.

Those priorities are the vital priorities. Those are the ones we absolutely have to have. Beyond that we have opinions on the others.

Number five, we need to have acceptable counting rules for ALCMs and ballistic missile reentry vehicles. Number six would be the ban on mobiles. Number seven would be the limit of 3,300 or 3,600 on ICBM RVs. We'd be willing to delete this in order to avoid the 60 percent being applied to all three legs of the Triad.

WEINBERGER: The Soviets want an INF and a START agreement. We should stand firm, and we'll get them. They may try to link this stuff to Defense and Space, but if we can hold in Moscow on no linkage, we can get the progress we seek.

I agree with the priorities the Chiefs stated. The ban on mobiles, however, is important. There's a lot of discussion currently about whether we have wavered on this subject. I would note, Mr. President, though that Congress has not given us funds for either M-X or Midgetman in sufficient numbers. So we need to keep trying to get the ban on mobiles.

ROWNY: Mr. President, I have one question for the Chiefs. What about throw-weight?

CROWE: Ed (Ambassador Rowny), we would very much like to see a 50 percent reduction in throw-weight, but it's not clear to us that we can measure throw-weight.

For example, we just revised the throw-weight estimates for the SS-24 by some 15 percent. However, that 15 percent change in throw-weight can translate into a 300 percent change in yield. So the delta between what we can measure and what we want is just too significant, and we don't understand how we can make those measurements.

CARLUCCI: That change on the SS-24 – doesn't that put that into the heavy class?

WEINBERGER: Mr. President, they're ahead of us in throw-weight by a significant amount – 5.3 to 1 as I understand, and we are concerned about throw-weight.

WEBSTER: I agree with the Chiefs, though, that it's extremely difficult to measure.

CROWE: We would certainly like it, but as I said we don't believe we can find a measurable number.

REAGAN: **Are all those numbers – are they all counting warheads?**

CROWE: Yes, that's right, Sir.

REAGAN: **Therefore, all the 6,000 are warheads, and the 1,540 are heavy warheads inside the 6,000. Isn't that true?**

CROWE: Yes, that's true.

REAGAN: **What is the 4,800 number?**

CROWE:	That's the number of reentry vehicles on ICBMs and SLBMs only.
REAGAN:	**And what is the 3,600 number?**
CROWE:	That's on the ICBMs, but I would note Mr. President, that the 4,800 is the important one.
KAMPELMAN:	We feel the 4,800 number is essential.
CARLUCCI:	In light of the Chiefs' discussion, I don't see any point in going through the six substantive options in our paper and the two timing options, unless there's someone who wants to talk about them.
	From what I see, it would be very hard for us to make a move on any option before Moscow. Therefore, I think, Mr. President, we have consensus to stay with the flexibility which you have already provided, and you have already given us some flexibility on the 3,300 sublimit, and we can work on the remainder of this in Moscow.
KAMPELMAN:	The Soviets do want a START agreement, and that gives us leverage.
	There is a time element involved. They know if they want a START agreement during this administration, they have to move quickly. The Senate Foreign Relations Committee members told me that they expected that the absolute deadline would probably be a March-April time frame for them to have enough time to ratify such a treaty during this administration. I told this to the Soviets.
REAGAN:	**When we started, we had the Triad, and they had most land-based things. They had a chip on their shoulders and said that we were trying to restructure their forces.**
	Why couldn't we just get the numbers we want and let them structure their forces anyway they like? Are we really trying to restructure their forces?
KAMPELMAN:	We certainly are.
CROWE:	We are nice guys, Mr. President, but I agree we want to affect their force structure.
CARLUCCI:	Yes, we are trying to affect their force structure.
REAGAN:	**But if they want the land-based stuff, so what?**
CARLUCCI:	Mr. President, we're after the most destabilizing systems and the most destabilizing systems we've identified are associated with land-based systems. We're trying to affect that now.
WEINBERGER:	The Soviets have got air defenses and they have a heavy investment in heavy missiles. We need to change

these relationships in order to give us a level playing field.

CARLUCCI: The Chiefs have done a good job on setting priorities (and) we should be able to build on this.

Let's turn to Defense and Space. We have three options, which I can summarize as hold firm, extend our non-deployment commitment to 1996, or accept one or the two Soviet positions.

The first Soviet position provided is a set of lists and labs; the other would be for us both to agree to abide by the strict interpretation of the ABM Treaty. However, the Soviet version of the Treaty is just as strict as the Senate.

WEINBERGER: No, no, it's much worse. It is more strict than the strict interpretation held by the Senate. We also need to force them to delink the Defense and Space area from START.

KAMPELMAN: Okay, we do want them to delink, but we may reach a point where having a START agreement in hand, we need to face linkage again. At that point it may be that we will be able to help ourselves by having something in the Defense and Space area. All I'm asking is we keep this in the back of our minds.

WEINBERGER: That's what they did in Iceland to us. We need to delink and not discuss Defense and Space until START is standing alone on its own two feet.

I dislike having things in our minds until we need them. We can get a stand-alone START agreement if we just hold firm. I think they want their START, and the Chiefs' priority has given us a way to get there – if we can hold firm.

KAMPELMAN: I don't know of anyone offering a different position at this point.

CARLUCCI: I understand that ACDA is considering extending the period for 10 years. Dave Emery, would you mind giving us the ACDA view?

EMERY: ACDA thinks that extending the Treaty through 1996 would give us reserve leverage useful in achieving progress in START.

CARLUCCI: Well, I'm not sure I understand that completely. But we did have a ten-year position at one time and we changed and dropped it back to seven-years, and the Soviets complained about that. But we do have a good position.

No one supports moving to the Soviet position. Therefore, Cap, we're spared your speech on lists and labs. Are there any other issues?

KAMPELMAN: In Geneva, we are dealing with the lists and labs. We're handling them by asking a lot of questions, and that's very useful. Is there a study of the Joint Chiefs on the labs and criteria?

CROWE: No, we received a briefing from Abrahamson and we concluded that the Soviet list of criteria is not in our interest. We could build a list of things that we could accept.

CARLUCCI: But would Cap (Secretary Weinberger)?

WEINBERGER: Yes, of course, if the list allows us to do whatever we want anywhere. I want no restrictions. Any restriction on testing is too restrictive. It's just a scientific matter. You're asking me not to think about something. If we had taken this attitude we would never have had the auto or the cinema industry.

For example, Mr. President, you'll note that on their list, the electromagnetic masked accelerator is restricted to 1.2 grams per fathom. That's certainly too restrictive. (Laughing.)

GRAHAM: I second everything that Cap (Weinberger) said. Nothing worries the Soviets more than having U.S. technology focused on a problem. They will try to set a framework of constraints on our technology and then gradually tighten it.

WEBSTER: I agree, too. We have less than 10 percent confidence in our ability to verify any of these restrictions.

NITZE: We should have a study on this area and understand why we don't like the Soviets' limits and what we could accept as limits. It's going to be very hard to argue with Congress if we don't have any study. It would be a real morass.

WEINBERGER: I can argue very comfortably without a study that no restriction is a common sense position. No study can tell us what we need, and no study can look into the future and determine what restrictions will hurt us or not. This seems fairly obvious to me.

CROWE: Paul (Ambassador Nitze) though does have a point with respect to Congress.

KAMPELMAN: I agree, it is something we have to be concerned about.

CROWE:	We will be asked about how we looked at criteria. We will look at this.
ROWNY:	I'm very encouraged, Mr. President, by dropping some of the sub-limits, and I believe we probably could get a deal on START now that will help with INF ratification and the like.
CARLUCCI:	Well, this meeting has helped quite a bit. Let's avoid leaks. Leaks would be absolutely fatal to us in our ability to achieve our negotiating aims. Do not debrief your staffs.
CROWE:	On INF I would make one point. The Chiefs are very interested in modernization in other areas that will be needed to reorient to the new military situation after INF. We should not look at the INF agreement as a money-saving device. We are going to devote that money into other areas. We absolutely need the High Level Group's Montebello Decision to be implemented.[32]
WEINBERGER:	I fully agree with the Chiefs. We need modern systems (and) we also need modernization of conventional forces after an INF agreement to ensure we have proper deterrence.
REAGAN:	**I know that we need modernization, (and) we certainly need to replace our older systems.**
WEINBERGER:	Especially modern conventional systems.
CROWE:	And a buildup of modern short-range nuclear forces.
CARLUCCI:	Thank you very much.

POSTSCRIPT

Shultz, accompanied by Carlucci and Nitze, went to Moscow for meetings with Gorbachev to try and finalize an INF agreement before the Washington Summit. The conversation quickly dispatched with INF because both sides agreed that the issue was done. Gorbachev explained: "I think Mr. Shultz put it right when he said that the most important issue now is no longer intermediate and shorter range-missiles, but the prospects for resolving the problem of strategic offensive weapons, and the shifting of negotiations to the plane of practical decisions." In fact, Gorbachev was ready to settle the outstanding space, SDI research and strategic weapons issues and, as he said, "leave only technical issues for Geneva" in the hopes of having the START Treaty ready to be signed at the 1988 Moscow Summit.

---

[32] October 27, 1983 decision of the NATO Nuclear Planning Group that the policy of the Alliance is to preserve the peace through the maintenance of forces at the lowest level capable of deterring the Warsaw Pact threat.

Gorbachev also presented a new START proposal, offering a 50 percent reduction in nuclear forces linked to a 10-year agreement not to withdrawal from the ABM Treaty. To appease Reagan's SDI testing interest, Gorbachev conceded testing in space as long as "it is understood that there should be no weapons in space."

Shultz said he thought the two sides were closer than ever to an agreement, however, the U.S. is more concerned with a reduction of ballistic missiles than nuclear weapons because ballistic missiles are the most destabilizing offensive weapons due to their short flight time. Gorbachev then wrapped up the meeting:

> I have an impression that you still cannot decide what it is you want. Maybe it is Ambassador Matlock who informs you in such a manner that you still cannot figure it out? Do you want the Soviet Union to develop successfully, or you don't want that? (Do you want) the Soviet Union to develop in the direction of greater democracy or in the opposite (direction)? (Do you want) us to have stagnation or to move forward?

"It is up to you to decide," Shultz responded. "But I can give you my opinion: what is happening in your country is very interesting, and I follow all these changes very closely."

The venue switched to the White House one week later for meetings with Soviet Foreign Minister Shevardnadze and Reagan. Shevardnadze brought with him a new letter from Gorbachev (dated October 30) proposing a Washington Summit in early December to sign the INF Treaty and to discuss Defense and Space. The meeting minutes for the Shevardnadze-Reagan meeting could not be located, but an hour after the meeting, Reagan, Shultz and Shevardnadze stood before the White House press to announce that Gorbachev would be coming to Washington, on December 7, with the expectation of signing an agreement eliminating all U.S. and Soviet INF nuclear forces.

Date: **December 7-10, 1987**
Subject: **Washington Summit**
Status: **Declassified in Part**

BACKGROUND

By the time Gorbachev flew to Washington for the Summit, all that was left on the INF Treaty was for Reagan and Gorbachev to sign the documents, which they did as one of the first acts of the Summit. The signing of the INF Treaty was an historic event because it was the first time an entire class of nuclear weapons was eliminated. Nevertheless, the INF Treaty only required each side to reduce their nuclear forces by about four percent, meaning that by the time the INF agreement was fully implemented in 1991, the Soviet Union destroyed 889 of its intermediate-range missiles (compared to 677 for the U.S.) and 957 shorter-range missiles (compared to 169 for the U.S.).

With the INF Treaty signed early in the Summit, Reagan and Gorbachev were free to use the rest of the Summit to discuss START negotiations, SDI, and any other area of U.S. – Soviet relations the leaders wished to discuss. The following is a summary of some of the more important meetings between Reagan and Gorbachev during the Washington Summit.

SUMMARY

DECEMBER 8, 1987; 2:30 P.M.-3:15 P.M.

[Although Reagan and Gorbachev held working sessions before this meeting, the minutes could not be located.]

REAGAN:	**I suggest we take up the discussion where it left off (from this morning).**
GORBACHEV:	With your permission, I will complete my presentation from this morning.
REAGAN:	**Please do so.**
GORBACHEV:	I believe that you, Mr. President, feel like I do following the signing of the INF Treaty. The two sides have begun to discuss the key problem of reducing nuclear weapons. There is also the concern about conventional and chemical weapons. This is becoming very important. It is coming to the forefront of concern. I do not wish to overdramaticize, (and) there is no need to panic, but the Soviet side is in the process of assessing whether harm is being done to equality, to the balance of security.

We have been listening to what is being said in Europe, and we have the feeling in Moscow that it was hoped in Europe that we would give due attention to chemical weapons (and) to conventional weapons. We should discuss these issues (and) we should give instructions to our colleagues to move forward.

Turning first to conventional weapons, I remember how we began the process of eliminating medium-range and shorter-range missiles. … When we began to discuss this question there was the issue of British and French arms. We debated it, and the Soviet side decided to set it aside. Then we discussed missiles in Europe and in Asia. At Reykjavik it had been decided each side could retain 100 warheads, with the Soviet warheads in Asia. Later we decided to go to complete zero. We had moved step by step, (and) all these things had gone into the treaty we just signed.

This experience should not only help with strategic offensive arms discussions, it should also help with conventional weapons. In the West it is said that the Soviet Union has superiority in armed forces and weapons. In the East it is said that NATO has a superiority in weapons. And both sides are right – each side has the data proving its case. We should agree to sit down (and then) see who is trying to outsmart whom, and who is serious. We should look at the asymmetries. It should be a process, we should go step by step.

We should move forward toward a mandate for negotiations between the two alliances. Perhaps we should lock our negotiators in a room, give them some food, of course, but we should instruct them to prepare proposals. Some are saying that the Soviet Union should take certain steps even before this is done, they say the Soviet Union has an advantage in Central Europe. No one talks about NATO's advantages in Southeastern Europe, which exists, and in an area close to the Soviet borders.

This should be put in the final document. We should put our cards on the table, (and) we should think of first steps to lessen confrontation. There is the concept of corridors, of thinning out forces in certain corridors. There is the question of discussing military doctrines, and we should seek a common concept of sufficiency, sufficiency for defensive purposes. I will not expand on this list, but the atmosphere created by signing the INF Treaty was not less important than the Treaty itself. We should talk about my suggestions, this will be well received by the allies of both countries, and in Europe generally.

Turning to chemical weapons ... after a valuable British initiative and the Soviet position had overcome certain hurdles... work went forward toward a convention to ban all these weapons, among all the participating countries, including the United States. Then there came a slowdown, someone was holding back the process. It could be either the Soviet Union or the United States. We know it is not us because we stopped production of these weapons. We are in fact completing a facility to destroy chemical weapons. ... Perhaps it is the U.S. side. Perhaps the U.S. has some concerns – maybe it is the binary weapons program; the U.S. has already funded production of 155 mm shells.

Verification is also very important. The U.S. is still proposing verification only of state facilities. That will include all the Soviet Union's, but not all the U.S.'s. There is no equality there.

The final document of the Summit should express a common view that would make it possible to give momentum to the negotiating process. This will enrich our meeting, and it would be welcomed by the peoples of Europe, the peoples of the world.

I wished to raised these two questions by way of concluding our initial meeting. I can confine myself to this at this point.

REAGAN: **I do not think anyone on the U.S. side does not favor more disarmament. We think the main priority should be to move forward in START, but if we continue on that path, we would face the question of short-range, or battlefield, weapons. It would only be possible to eliminate them if we first restore a balance in conventional weapons. We should find a way to move forward on this, but I want to remind you that it is not armaments that create distrust, but distrust that creates armaments.**

GORBACHEV: Confidence cannot grow in an empty place. The arms control process will help it grow, that was dialectics under the Marxist approach.

SHULTZ: The U.S. side wants to work with what has been said about conventional weapons and chemical weapons, but the question is not so much one of language as content.

The U.S. side would like to see the mandate being worked on in Vienna finished as soon as possible. It is pretty well along, including discussion of human rights. The Soviet side made proposals, and the U.S. side made proposals, and it was the Helsinki framework which held all these things together. So the two sides need to deal with all these aspects. That is what the U.S wants to do, then, as you said Mr. General Secretary, the two sides should proceed on to deal with the asymmetries. They should try to move toward an equal situation at lower levels. The U.S. side has some ideas, perhaps they parallel those of the Soviet side.

Like the Soviet side, the U.S. side made a point of moving forward as a member of an alliance. This is not something the U.S. and the Soviet Union could just do together. Most of the arms under discussion on the Western side belong to the U.S. allies. But, it is true that the U.S. and the Soviet Union have important parts, and could energize things.

GORBACHEV: I support what Secretary Shultz has just said concerning the linkage of allies. The working group should work on this topic during the visit. They should develop ideas, and when they are done the two sides should consult with their allies. Then Mr. Carlucci and Soviet Defense Minister Yazov can meet and move the process forward.

SHULTZ: I am all for meetings between defense officials of the two sides, but we have to be careful about acting as if the U.S. and Soviet sides could work things out, and then consult with the allies. We cannot have it that way, it will not work. The allies see the importance of the issues, but the two sides need to go about it right. We should come to grips in Vienna with all the topics that have been discussed – this means not only a mandate for negotiations on conventional weapons, but also a mandate for confidence building measures. We should get that done in the early part of next year.

GORBACHEV: We share your view that the topic is important, and agree that we should not rush, but I have reservations after I heard you (Shultz) say it. The Warsaw Treaty Organization put proposals on the table 18 months ago and has still not received an answer. As I told the President, I did not come to Washington to bicker, but to do real politics. At the stage we are at, recriminations and complaints just serve to delay things. (Pointing to the main negotiators.) They feel this on their skins – one needs to be persistent to succeed.

With regard to the substances, the U.S. side said there is general agreement. But I have one question: I do not want to link conventional disarmament to Helsinki. Helsinki includes many things....We should tackle conventional disarmament straight on, we should not make a package. The U.S. made Jackson-Vanik 15 years ago ... and over 15 years the U.S. has been unable to untie it.

SHULTZ:	The U.S. side is prepared in the working groups to discuss conventional arms in relation to the CSCE process. …
GORBACHEV:	The formulation in the statement could stress cooperation with allies – that is important.
SHULTZ:	You better believe it.
GORBACHEV:	That is, if the President agrees.
REAGAN:	**I do.**
GORBACHEV:	What about chemical weapons?
SHULTZ:	That is a more severe problem. For 50 years there has been a moral consensus against them. This has been broken. It is important to try and put it back together.
GORBACHEV:	Is the Secretary referring to the 1925 convention?
SHULTZ:	I am. It worked, more or less. Actually, the fact that some countries possessed these weapons had probably had some deterrent effect. But there are now many countries which have or could have them. They have been used in the Iran-Iraq war. At the same time, there is the problem of verification. There is a need for a broad consensus, but it will be hard to get….
GORBACHEV:	Does the U.S. side see the goal, for the two sides and for others, as speeding up the drafting of the convention?
SHULTZ:	It does, as long as we go about it realistically.
REAGAN:	**Any country with a fertilizer plant can make chemical weapons (so) it is an almost impossible task to know that they are not being made.**
SHULTZ:	We thus have an impossible, but necessary task. Chemical weapons are potentially destabilizing.
GORBACHEV:	There is no cause for panic. I wish to draw the President's attention to another issue. We have noticed that in European political and journalistic circles there is discussion of how to compensate for the elimination of INF missiles in Europe. If such thinking prevailed, it would be very dangerous. We should interact and take a common stand. There could be new weapons, of great new capacity. If all the talk of reinforcing or adding new forces in Europe became true, the whole process would be more difficult. This is especially true since we agreed to eliminate INF missiles over a certain period of time.
REAGAN:	**It is here that we need to take the most steps to create trust. There is a legacy of mistrust because of Soviet expansionism.**

GORBACHEV: Compared to American expansionism, the Soviet side is a small child.

REAGAN: **We do not think so. There have been four wars in my lifetime, and the U.S. has not gained an inch of territory.**

Under the U.S. system, it is not enough just to say something, you have to do something. We have people here from every part of the world. There is a kind of dual loyalty. The first question asked is what you are. More and more people have to name three or four places. There is a pride in where one's parents and ancestors are from, Americans are proud of them, as well as of being American. So there are elements in our country that had big resentments over what happened where they had come from. Signing the treaty is therefore not enough, there is also the question of getting it ratified.

GORBACHEV: The Supreme Soviet is even larger than the U.S. Senate. It has some 2,000 members, and I expect ratification will be a sharper process than usual. It has opened up many questions. There is the question of why the Soviets have been so generous towards the Americans – we are eliminating four times as many missiles (than the U.S.). But, it used to be that parity had been recognized. So, the question is why it is being broken. We will need to tackle this even before the formal ratification process.

It was not easy to take the first step toward disarmament. People asked how it was possible to have disarmament with the U.S. when the Soviet Union was ringed with U.S. bases. People asked how I could bow down to the U.S., and do more.

I have just seen a recent Gallup poll in the U.S. and the Soviet Union. It was an independent poll, and it showed that there are not many enthusiasts for the Treaty in the Soviet Union. About half the Soviet people expressed certain doubts….

REAGAN: **Your comments underline the need for trust. If you genuflected before me, I will stomp my foot.**

GORBACHEV: I am not referring to myself, personally. I am one thing, but pride is a matter for a nation, and I represent a nation. We have to deal with each other on the basis of equality, of respect, of taking each other's concerns into account. We need to make real policy.

The U.S. side accuses the Soviet side of all sorts of sins. What is needed is to look forward, instead. During the 45 years since the world war, so much has piled up that if we just went on with complaints – on the Soviet side there are all sorts of doctrines to complain about: the Truman doctrine; the Eisenhower Doctrine; the Carter Doctrine – we would put each other on trial. This is not the constructive polices people want. I advise the Vice President to reflect on that. Unless policy reflects what the people want, you could win an election, but not succeed in the long term.

REAGAN: **The U.S. side welcomes moves toward democratization in the Soviet Union, toward glasnost.**

GORBACHEV: I wish to say a few words about that. It is people's greatest wish to go to bed and wake up in the morning to see everything changed for the better. But even in fairy tales, the hero's have to go through trials, and in real life things are even harder. I will continue to fight conservatism, to fight those who sought to shackle people in dogma. But I will also fight adventurists, the equivalent of the Red Guards in China who want to push ahead without thinking.

It will not be easy. The present leadership has taken a firm stand to move along that path. Certain politicians, perhaps Ambassador Matlock, are looking for an opposition. There is opposition in every single Soviet, it would be foolish to deny it. We are children of our time, but of political opposition, there is none. There would be debates, there would be differences of view, and exchanges of views. But I can assure you, Mr. President, the Soviet side will be moving ahead toward democratization. That is, if the U.S. side permits us to do so. I would ask that the American side lets the Soviet side do it our own way.

REAGAN: **There was a U.S. President who had once said something very profound. That was Franklin Delano Roosevelt. In America there had also been people who had thought that government should have more control of people. Roosevelt had asked where, if people did not have the capacity to run their own lives, we would find among them the tiny group that could run not only their own lives, but those of others.**

I do not want to offend you, Mr. General Secretary, but I recently talked to a U.S. scholar who visited your country. On his way to the airport he had a taxi driver, a young man finishing his education but

also driving a taxi because he needed money. The professor asked the young man what he was going to be and the taxi driver replied that he had not yet decided. When the professor got to the Soviet Union, he basically had the same conversation with a taxi driver also finishing his education. The professor again asked what he would be, and the Soviet driver replied: "They haven't told me yet."

GORBACHEV: Mr. President, I know you like anecdotes about the Soviet Union, and it is indeed a country rich in anecdotes. I have only one request: that you, Mr. President, not ask Ambassador Matlock to collect anecdotes for you. That will stop relations entirely – that would be the biggest joke.

SHULTZ: Perhaps I can get a word in edgewise. People are waiting for the working groups to start, (and) there has been discussion of strategic arms this morning. Notes have been exchanged, there are things to work with.

The General Secretary and the President also had a discussion about conventional and chemical weapons, so that is additional material. There is one area that has not been touched on, perhaps we can reach it tomorrow, that is regional issues.

GORBACHEV: Agreed.

After a short discussion on the agenda for the next day, Gorbachev closes the meeting with his final remarks.

GORBACHEV: In the previous two hours we made an important event. It was a bridge to the future, and we are ready to build it over. By the time you, Mr. President, come to Moscow, the two sides of the bridge should be locked together.

REAGAN: **We should meet in the middle.**

GORBACHEV: I fully agree.

DECEMBER 9, 1987; 10:35-10:45 A.M.

[Reagan started the meeting by passing to Gorbachev a baseball from Joe DiMaggio. Mr. DiMaggio asked President Reagan to ask Gorbachev he would sign the ball. Gorbachev said he was happy to comply.]

REAGAN: **In the coming two days, we will be working hard to set in motion the other things that need to be accomplished in order that the people of both sides could work hard in the winter and spring to make a summit in Moscow possible next summer. I am prepared to keep my people working at his, in addition to what the two of us will discuss this morning and tomorrow.**

GORBACHEV: I welcome this approach. It is not only my feeling, but also that of the Soviet leadership, to continue to work at these issues, and to make the process even more dynamic, not only in the main area of arms control, but in other areas as well, in order to prepare a good visit by you to Moscow, which would also be productive and important.

A good time for a visit, when it is not too hot, would be early summer, perhaps June or late May. This will allow time for the process of ratification and also will allow for time for a lot of work to be done on a new document on strategic arms and other issues.

REAGAN: **Agreed.**

GORBACHEV: In my conversation with Mrs. Reagan the other night, I indicated that a program could be arranged which would include time for meetings between the President and myself, meetings of working groups, but also one or two days during which the President and Mrs. Reagan could see the country.

REAGAN: **That would be nice. I cannot agree to a date, however, until I know when some other things (like the Economic Summit) would be taking place. I need some time before agreeing to a date, but I do want to go to Moscow.**

This visit has been a short one, but perhaps some time before I leave office, you and Mrs. Gorbacheva can return, not for a Summit, but simply to see the country, and California specifically, since one has not seen America without seeing California.

GORBACHEV: I agree, that is a very good idea. There should also be regular meetings between the leaders of our two countries, and not always official visits. If we wish to restructure our relations and improve our dialogue and cooperation, all these things could be done in a more normal way, including visits to the U.S. to get to know the country. Such a trip would be important to get a deeper knowledge of the U.S., and would be a possibility.

DECEMBER 9, 1987; 10:55 A.M-12:35 P.M.

REAGAN:

Yesterday was a very proud day. But, as you Mr. General Secretary said, we have to keep working.

I want to return to some of the subjects we talked about in our first meeting, especially the relationship between strategic offense and defense. Our experts met the day before on START and had had a good discussion. The U.S. stressed two important issues: verification and counting rules. On verification, our ideas built on what we had learned from the INF negotiation. Counting rules are also important; issues like sublimits cannot be decided until we know exactly how different types of weapons are to be counted. However, I'm encouraged by the Soviet willingness to compromise between 4,800 and 5,100 ballistic missile warheads. If it is possible to come to agreement on this, I would be prepared to be forthcoming on an ICBM sublimit. (Gorbachev makes a note at this point.)

The Soviet side also discussed sea-launched cruise missiles and suggested new ideas for their verification. You, Mr. General Secretary, also expressed a readiness to examine verification of mobile missiles. We appreciated your suggestions, and while we have some doubts, we are willing to study your concepts.

Moving to a discussion of the U.S. defense and space position, the arms control working group is taking up these issues today. Each side seems to understand the other's position on START, but this isn't true in Defense and Space. I want to urge that the two sides move together in a direction in which we are already going separately.

Specifically, if it were possible to agree on a treaty reducing strategic arsenals by 50 percent and preserve the opportunity for effective strategic defenses, the two sides would stand on the threshold of a new and stronger regime of strategic stability. Offensive nuclear weapons helped keep the peace for 40 years, but now it is necessary to look to the future.

We hold awesome responsibilities, and our only means to avoid nuclear war is to be prepared to strike each other's homeland with devastating consequences.... Our successors, and more importantly, our peoples, deserve better. For my part, I want to strengthen peace by finding new ways to save lives rather than threaten to avenge them. Providing a better, more stable basis for peace is the central purpose of SDI.

Effective defenses against ballistic missiles can strengthen stability in a number of ways. First, they would significantly increase uncertainty about whether missiles could penetrate defenses to destroy the other side's capability to retaliate. This would become even more important after a 50 percent reduction in strategic offensive arms.

Second, defenses would provide an alternative to accepting massive devastation if a missile were ever launched in error or against either side by another country.

Third, defenses could reinforce arms reductions. Fifty percent reductions, combined with increasingly effective defenses, could offer a real hope of protecting people, not just weapons.

Finally, defenses would underwrite the integrity of arms reductions by reducing the advantages of cheating.

In short, the combination of effective defenses and a 50 percent reduction in strategic arsenals would establish a whole new concept of strategic stability. ...

I noticed your March 1, 1987 remarks in <u>Pravda</u>, which focused on the issue of deployment. I think that was the right approach, and am prepared to negotiate a period during which neither side would deploy strategic defenses beyond those permitted by the ABM Treaty. The length of the period could be agreed once the terms are settled. At Reykjavik, you talked of ten years. I think it will be possible to agree on the length of the period once the terms are settled.

Moreover, in order to reassure you that the Soviet Union will not be surprised by events during the non-deployment period, I am also prepared to commit to a package designed to increase predictability for both sides. Frank Carlucci will describe the package in a moment, but in brief, I'm offering predictability during a non-deployment period of certain length. In return, I need to protect the existing U.S. – and Soviet – right to conduct, in the words of Marshal Grechko (Soviet Minister of Defense, 1967-1976), "research and experimental work aimed at resolving the problem of defending the country against nuclear missile attack." Both sides need a clear right to deploy defenses after that period.

The U.S. is seeking a separate, new treaty of unlimited duration that would go into effect at the same time the START Treaty went into effect. This second treaty would contain a period during which both sides would commit not to deploy defensive systems currently prohibited by the ABM Treaty. After that period of time, both sides would be free to deploy such defenses without further reference to the ABM Treaty, after giving six months notice of intent to deploy. During the non-deployment period, both sides would have the right to pursue their strategic defense programs, conducting research, development and testing, including testing in space, as required. Our negotiators in Geneva could explain in detail the U.S. concept of deployment.

As you will see, I'm trying to create a future in which the two sides would have reduced strategic offensive arms by 50 percent and could pursue their respective strategic defense programs as common elements in a new regime, which you have called "strategic stability." In that context, I took special note of your interview with Tom Brokaw the week before, in which you acknowledged the existence of a Soviet analogue to SDI. This is a step in the right direction.

This is a summary of the U.S. position. Secretary Shultz, would you please comment in further detail?

SHULTZ: I'm handing out a Russian text of what I've described as elements on which negotiators in Geneva might build.

First, there would be a period of time during which both sides would commit not to deploy defensive systems currently prohibited by the ABM Treaty. It should be possible to agree on an appropriate time period.

Second, after that period, both sides would be free to deploy defenses not currently permitted by the Treaty after giving six months notice of an intent to deploy and without any further reference to the ABM Treaty.

Third, during the non-deployment period, both sides would have the right to pursue their strategic defense programs, conducting research, development and testing, including testing in space, as required.

Fourth, to enhance strategic stability, promote predictability, and ensure confidence that prohibited deployments were not being undertaken during the non-deployment period, the U.S. proposes that the two sides meet regularly to do three things:

1.   Exchange programmatic data and briefings on each side's strategic defense program;
2.   Arrange for agreed mutual observation of strategic defense tests and visits to strategic defense research facilities; and
3.   Arrange for intensive discussions of strategic stability to begin not later than three years before the end of the non-deployment period.

All of this should be seen in light of the fact that the period in question would span several presidential terms....

I suggest that Mr. Carlucci briefly describe the type of confidence building measures the U.S. has in mind under its proposal.

CARLUCCI: Such confidence building measures would be designed to give each side the predictability it needs. The U.S. has earlier put proposals for "open labs" on the table in Geneva, but has received no response. ... The U.S. would be prepared to open up such facilities as Livermore Labs and Stanford Research; the Soviet side might be prepared to open up its own facilities. ...

With respect to joint observation of actions in space, the U.S. is aware of the Soviet near-space vehicle. We have our Shuttle. If, for example, the U.S. sought to conduct a sensor experiment in space, the Soviet near-space vehicle could be maneuvered close enough to satisfy Moscow that no offensive weapon was being tested. Such activities could be undertaken without compromising the security or integrity of the programs involved on either side. ...

REAGAN: **You, Mr. Gorbachev, heard enough from U.S. representatives. I invite you to share your reactions.**

GORBACHEV: I do, in fact, have a few words in response. First, I cannot on the level of principal support the proposal just outlined. The thrust of that proposal is to invite the Soviet Union to join the U.S. in undertaking a kind of SDI program. I said before that Moscow has no intention of developing its own SDI; I even urged you, Mr. President, to renounce the program. If the U.S. proceeds, the Soviet side has made clear it would develop a response. But that response would take a different path from SDI.

What then, are the proposals of the Soviet side? The ABM regime has worked well for 15 years. True, some concerns have been expressed with respect to compliance with the Treaty, including in the recent past. But, a mechanism for dealing with such problems exists in the Standing Consultative Commission (SCC), which has worked well in the past. Such concerns could be discussed and removed. But, in fact both sides have basically observed the Treaty in the past.

But, we are now entering a new phase, a phase of reducing strategic offensive arms. Not only will it be necessary to continue to observe the ABM Treaty, it should be strengthened – as was agreed at Reykjavik – through a commitment not to withdraw from the Treaty as strategic arms are reduced. On the basis of such an approach, which presumes an interpretation of the Treaty consistent with that which had been used since Day One of its existence, it would be possible to begin work on the specifics of reducing strategic arms by 50 percent.

Mr. President, you have yourself said that SDI is not up for negotiation. If you are now proposing to structure our discussion of strategic offensive arms reductions by linking that subject to SDI, I have to say it will be a slow process. It will take time first of all just to define SDI. Space is a new area for both countries; there is no criteria for making judgments. Both sides would be groping in the dark. Such an approach would lead the dialogue down a blind alley.

I want to underscore that I objected in principle to SDI. If America wishes to pursue the program, that is its business – to the extent its activities are consistent with the ABM Treaty.

But if there is a real desire for accommodation on both sides, the Soviet approach is a practical one. Taking into account the U.S. desire to implement SDI, Moscow simply proposed that neither side use its right to withdraw from the Treaty for ten years. Two to three years before the end of that period, there could be a discussion of what to do next. If the U.S. had decided to deploy SDI, it could say so. But, during the ten years of the period the Soviet side would have the assurance that, while strategic offensive arms are being reduced, the U.S. would observe the ABM Treaty and not use its right to withdraw. This is something the two sides could agree on.

As for SDI research, it could continue, and the U.S. could decide what to do after ten years. If the U.S. were to violate the ABM Treaty during that period, the Soviet side would be released from any obligation to continue reductions, and would have the right to build and perfect weapons, as well as to cancel its anti-satellite (ASAT) moratorium. But, that would occur only if the U.S. decided to deploy SDI.

The Soviet Union, for its part, did not want a new sphere for the arms race. It did not want to deploy SDI. Moscow did not know what, precisely, it wanted to do in the areas involved. Therefore, we proposed a straightforward approach: 50 percent reductions in strategic offensive arms; agreement on a period of non-withdrawal; observance of the Treaty as it has been observed in the past. As for SDI, the U.S. could do research. Should it ultimately decide to deploy, that would be up to the U.S., but after the termination of the withdrawal period. This proposal made it possible to implement 50 percent reductions in strategic weapons in the context of non-withdrawal from the ABM Treaty, and to continue research. Before the end of the ten year period, there could be a discussion.

For the Soviet side, it would be less expensive to explore ways other than through SDI-type deployments to ensure its security. Thus, SDI is not acceptable from a political standpoint; it is not acceptable from a military standpoint (because it is destabilizing); it is not acceptable from an economic standpoint. It could wear out the Soviet economy; it is up to the U.S. to decide if SDI made sense for itself in economic terms; the Soviet Union decided it did not. Should the U.S decide to deploy SDI at the end of a non-withdrawal period, the Soviet side would have to respond. But, that response would be less costly than SDI.

In conclusion, I suggest that we seek a solution which enables the U.S. to develop SDI, but in a way which does not make SDI an obstacle to progress in the reduction of strategic arms. I just outlined the Soviet proposal for guaranteeing peace. For the U.S., the answer is SDI. For the Soviet Union, the answer is different: nuclear disarmament; maintenance of the ABM regime; and no extension of the arms race to space.

REAGAN: **I have my own answer: It is possible to proceed immediately with a 50 percent reduction. Any other options are years ahead for both sides. It would be better not to link the two concepts. ...**

As for SDI, I have a counterargument to your suggestion that the program would step up the arms race. I see it as essential to the realization of a non-nuclear world. The secret of nuclear weapons is spreading inexorably. If the U.S. and Soviet Union ever reach the point where we eliminated all nuclear arms, we would have to face the possibility that a madman in one country or another could develop a nuclear capability for purposes of conquest or blackmail. The situation is not unlike that after the agreement to ban the use of poison gas. People had kept their gas masks.

There will always be a need for a defense. The U.S. and Soviet Union could eliminate their nuclear arsenals without fear of nuclear attack by other countries if we have a reliable defensive shield.

In this context, I'm encouraged by your acknowledgment of a Soviet program akin to SDI. I'm grateful for your words because a future based on an ability to counter any attack would be based on real stability, not the stability that comes from the ability to destroy.

GORBACHEV: The American press distorted the thrust of my remarks to Brokaw. I did not say that the Soviet Union had its own SDI. I said the Soviet Union is engaged in many areas of basic research, including some covered on the U.S. side by SDI. I did not go beyond this, and the Soviet Union will not deploy SDI, and I urged the U.S. not to do so. We will find a different path. The U.S. will not draw us into an SDI program.

On the other hand, if the U.S. wants to reduce strategic arms, it will have to accept a ten year period of non-withdrawal from the ABM Treaty. At the end of that period the U.S. could decide what it would do. The Soviet side could accept that, although it was definitely against SDI.

As for the prospects for a START agreement, I'm ready to cooperate and respond to the major U.S. concerns. Moscow is ready to reduce heavy ICBMs by 50 percent. As for sea-launched cruise missiles, yesterday I shared my ideas on verification with you, Mr. President. I am also ready to look again at the sublimits question. So, I am ready to work to achieve a treaty, but if you, Mr. President, want to link that process to SDI, if it had to involve SDI, there would be no START treaty either with you or your successors.

SHULTZ: Perhaps, Mr. General Secretary, you can describe a possible work program, in view of the previous discussion. Both sides seem committed to achieving a START agreement. Work is already underway among experts.

The President did not mean to suggest that a START treaty be linked to Soviet acceptance of SDI. In fact, he said there should be no linkage to anything.

GORBACHEV: A START treaty must be linked to the ABM Treaty.

SHULTZ: The question is not one of whether the Soviet Union liked or did not like SDI. Neither side could tell the other how to see to its own defense. But, the proposal you, Mr. General Secretary, outlined seemed on the surface not to be inconsistent with what the U.S. wants.

For our part, the U.S. believes that the proposal the President made was consistent with the ABM Treaty. You might not agree with that assessment, but the point is that it makes no sense to set out down a certain path when both sides know they did not agree on what, superficially, they seemed to agree on….

The Soviet side asked for predictability. The President's proposal guarantees that there would be no deployments against the Soviet Union for a certain period. The President had said it should be possible to agree on the number of years such a period would last. The President also said that, when the period ended, either side could do what it chose.

The question remained, what would happen in the meantime? We tried to get at that question through the means that Secretary Carlucci described. These would give the Soviet side confidence in what the U.S. is doing. We would hope Moscow would reciprocate by permitting similar access.

The President's proposal also incorporated the Soviet idea that, before the end of the agreed period, there would be agreement in advance to discussions of the situation created as a result of strategic reductions and the results of research to that point. This discussion would take place several years in advance of the end of the period. While each side would have the right to do what it wished at the end of the period, this discussion would allow both to take into account facts which had emerged in the interim. This could have an impact on the ultimate results.

So, the President's proposal was not an effort to link Soviet acceptance of SDI to a START treaty – even though we cannot understand why Moscow is opposed to SDI. Rather, it is an attempt to give the Soviet side greater confidence that it understood what was going on, on the U.S. side. But, to agree on radical reductions of strategic arms, based on an understanding of the status of the ABM Treaty both sides know in their bones is not shared, makes the U.S. side uncomfortable and is probably unwise....

GORBACHEV: Why can't the U.S. accept the Soviet formula: 50 percent reductions in strategic arms; a ten year non-withdrawal period; discussion two to three years before the end of that period on what to do next. This is a simple approach. There is no reason to encumber the discussion of 50 percent reductions.

SHEVARDNADZE: It is important to consider another factor – if the President were to pay a return visit to Moscow, there must be a decision on what such a visit might produce. I've been operating on the assumption that the purpose of the visit would be to sign an agreement on 50 percent reductions in strategic arms in the context of the preservation of the ABM Treaty for an agreed period, as Secretary Shultz and I publicly stated. This has been the basis for all our discussions. If the two sides start to open up philosophical questions about what might happen years from now, the President's visit could not be crowned by signature of an agreement. ...

Finally, there can be no question of the INF Treaty becoming the end of the process. It cannot stop. Nuclear proliferation is a growing problem, which makes it all the more important to maintain the momentum of nuclear arms reductions. The President's visit could provide a major stimulus to this effort. As for SDI, it is not and has not been a subject for discussion. Secretary Shultz has made it clear that it is the President's program, but there is a need to clarify certain questions or there would be no START agreement.

DOBRYNIN: I want to reiterate General Secretary Gorbachev's point that the ABM Treaty has worked well for 15 years. Now, the U.S. seems to be proposing that, at the Washington Summit, the two leaders in effect announce that this Treaty of unlimited duration would cease to be. That is the effect of the President's proposal – there would be three years of negotiations, and then there would be an open arms race.

REAGAN: **You are forgetting something – prior to Mr. Gorbachev becoming the General Secretary, there were violations by the Soviet Union of the ABM Treaty. The Krasnoyarsk Radar is the principal example. But, there are differences of interpretation, and we believe that the Treaty allows research into weapons which it did not specifically address. The Treaty dealt with ABM interceptor missiles; it did not ban research into development of other systems not even envisioned at the time. SDI clearly was covered by the clause which covered "other physical principles." It is not an interceptor missile, but there are real questions of when the Soviet side will begin to abide by the ABM Treaty.**

SHULTZ: I propose to seek to outline where broad agreement seems to exist.

First, the two sides agree on the concept of a period of time – as yet undecided – when there would be no deployment of antiballistic missile systems beyond what was permitted by the ABM Treaty. There is agreement that, at the end of the period, either side could do what it chose to do. The U.S. has sought to pick up on the Soviet proposal that there should be agreement in advance that the two sides would discuss problems of strategic stability well before the period ended.

| | Where there is no agreement is on the question of what actions could be undertaken during the period in question. The U.S. would have no problem agreeing to the formula, "the ABM Treaty, as signed and ratified," because it considers its SDI program to be consistent with that concept…. |

GORBACHEV: These differences emerged only in 1983. Prior to that, there were no differences, as Congressional hearings and Pentagon reports made clear. Only after SDI had been proposed did the U.S. seek to make the Treaty fit the program. A lawyer had been found to make the case, but, as Bismarck said, a lawyer could be found to justify anything. What is going on is obvious to everyone. The U.S. should have more respect for the Soviet side than to expect that they would not see through this.

If the U.S. wants a 50 percent reduction, there has to be a commitment of ten years on the ABM Treaty. There could be nothing on SDI before that, in any case. The issue is not complex, but the U.S. side is making things "foggy."

REAGAN: **I'm not the one making things "foggy." I want to make things clear: I did not want to talk about links to SDI, but about 50 percent reductions, about how the hell the two sides are to eliminate half their nuclear weapons. I want to talk about how we can sign an agreement like the one we signed yesterday – an agreement, which made everyone in the world so damned happy it could be felt in the room at dinner last night. Let's get started with it.**

GORBACHEV: I'm ready, we should make clear that we are working on agreed reductions and are making progress. We should also indicate that, as we begin this important process, we reaffirm our commitment not to withdraw from the ABM Treaty for ten years. This should not be a problem, the period could be for nine years if that would help.

SHULTZ: The issue should be set aside for a moment. I feel there has been some progress, there has been agreement on the concept of a certain period. There is agreement on what should happen at the end of that period. The two sides are not there yet on actions to be permitted during that period, but that can be worked out. But there is clear agreement on the need for major cuts in strategic arms.

Indeed, I feel electricity at this point. That is the place to start.

GORBACHEV: I would like to return for a moment to the issues of sub-launched cruise missiles (SLCMs). If this question is not resolved, there can be no agreement. We clearly outlined our position, what is the U.S. position?

REAGAN: **I think that is an issue for the experts.**

GORBACHEV: The experts will not be able to do anything without guidance from the top.

SHULTZ: Mr. General Secretary, I'd like to remind you that the U.S. has problems with the verification of SLCMs. You said the day before that the Soviet side had some ideas for dealing with verification. We are ready to study them. If we are satisfied that they are workable – and that is a big question – it would be a realistic basis for proceeding. At this point, I am not in a position to respond to your proposal for a SLCM ceiling of 400 missiles.

GORBACHEV: Ironically, the U.S. has no answer on this and other issues I raised, only more demands of the Soviet side. But, this is not the kind of momentum that is needed. The U.S. is simply squeezing more and more concessions out of its partner. Verification of SLCMs should be more of a problem for Moscow than Washington, in view of the U.S. advantage in numbers of SLCMs. Once there is agreement on a number, the verification problem could be resolved. If it proved impossible to satisfy the U.S. on verification, we will remove our insistence on a numerical limit.

SHULTZ: We will study the proposal.

GORBACHEV: Good, this has been a good conversation, it made it clearer what both sides want. In closing this phase of the discussion, I want to emphasize the importance I attach to reductions of strategic arms – a key issue in our relationship, and one which requires a responsible approach from both sides. Obviously, no agreements are possible except on the basis of equality.

REAGAN: **I, for one, have no desire to come to Moscow to be disappointed.**

GORBACHEV: I did not mean to suggest any linkage. If the President wishes to come to Moscow without a START agreement, he would be welcome. But, Mr. President, you should say so. For my part, I feel that there is, in fact, a common understanding that the visit should be marked by the signing of an important document. The Soviet side wants to push towards that goal. If the President is operating from a different set of assumptions, all he has to do is say so. The Geneva negotiators would probably be just as glad to spend their time playing soccer. But, I assume that this administration shares my assessment that an agreement is possible. The President's visit would be a very important one; but if he wished to finesse the question of a treaty, he should say so.

SHULTZ: Mr. General Secretary, you have heard with your own ears what the President has just said. For myself, I can assure you that whenever I go off to meet with Shevardnadze, the President makes it clear in no uncertain terms what he wants me to accomplish. I think the President has made his views on a START agreement pretty clear to the General Secretary as well a moment before.

GORBACHEV: I agree that this is important, but one has to decide beforehand in building a bridge whether it should go across a divide or alongside it. The Soviet approach is that there should be a good treaty by the time President Reagan comes to Moscow. If there is another view in Washington, it would be best to make that clear. In Russian, there is a saying, "If you respect me, don't make a fool of me. Tell me what you want."

SHULTZ: I hope this doesn't mean that you, Mr. General Secretary, are giving up.

GORBACHEV: No, on the contrary, that is why I urged against any link between START and SDI. There should be a good treaty by the time of the President's visit.

REAGAN: **I think that is what I said earlier. I said that we should be seeking to eliminate strategic weapons. So, one objective, whether or not the U.S. deployed SDI, would be 50 percent fewer missiles. But, this should only make the two sides more interested in defense, since we would both become more vulnerable to other nuclear states.**

GORBACHEV: It will be a long time before that is a problem, since even after a 50 percent reduction, the U.S. and USSR arsenals will still vastly outweigh those of other states.

The discussion then shifts to a long discussion on regional issues. Reagan and Gorbachev then join their wives for a working lunch.

DECEMBER 10, 1987; 12:40 P.M-2:05 P.M.

Reagan and Gorbachev continue to discuss regional issues, like Afghanistan and Central America, during the first half of their working lunch. But, with this being the last opportunity the two leaders have together in Washington, Gorbachev then shifts the discussion to his overall reflections on the Washington Summit.

GORBACHEV: I will soon be saying goodbye. I have arrived at the conclusion that this third summit has been a landmark. It has witnessed important agreements and other questions had been discussed intensively. Most importantly, the atmosphere has been good. There have also been more elements of mutual understanding, and I would like to acknowledge President Reagan's efforts towards making this a successful summit, as well as to the contributions of other American participants.

I would like the momentum achieved at the Summit to continue. On my way to lunch today at the White House I rode with Vice President Bush. We had looked out of the car and seen Americans responding warmly to what happened in the negotiations. When the car stopped at a red light, I jumped out and had had a spontaneous conversation with some passerby. When it was time to go, I did not want to leave the conversation.

SEC. BAKER: This is known by the American politicians as "working the crowd."

GORBACHEV: I have always had this style – throughout my entire career. I became well-known around the world over the past two years because of my position. Before that, however, I spent my entire career in the provinces, and developed this style then, and there was nothing to change. In the Soviet Union, there is more common sense in the provinces than in the nation's capital. If our Ambassadors reported information based only on sources in the capital, I would have to seriously question their reporting.

REAGAN: **I agree with that more completely than with anything else you have said over the past three days. I often wonder what would happen if I, with other leaders, just closed the doors of our offices and quietly slipped away. How long would it be before people missed us?**

GORBACHEV:	In my case, within 56 days of my "disappearance" earlier this year, people began to say that I was dead or had been dismissed. In fact, I had done good work during this period on many things…
SEC. BAKER:	This conversation, between the President and General Secretary, has given me the impression that, as politicians, you both are alike in many ways: you are both strong personalities; you know what you believe; and you know where you want to go. This augurs well for our two countries.
GORBACHEV:	I agree. I do not often hear such complimentary assessments – most people try to see the problems….
REAGAN:	**I also agree with the General Secretary – I could never understand why he opposed me on so many things.**
GORBACHEV:	The areas of agreement will increase and the areas of disagreement decrease, provided both sides move.
REAGAN:	**I would like to return to the subject of Iran. Some of my harsh feelings toward Iran came from the fact that in 1978, I was there with Nancy for several days. We shopped for rugs in the bazaar – and I'm still trying to get even.**
SEC. BAKER:	Secretary Shultz and Foreign Minister Shevardnadze have left to compare the final draft of the Joint Statement. I will go see if it is ready.
REAGAN:	**The General Secretary and I have the right to feel good about the Summit. When we first met in Geneva, I told you, Mr. General Secretary, that ours was a unique situation. We represented two countries that could initiate another world war. Or, we could make sure that there would not be another world war.**
GORBACHEV:	I remember that conversation.
REAGAN:	**Both the General Secretary and I have problems with bureaucracy.**
GORBACHEV:	I also agree with that.
REAGAN:	**When I was in the military during World War II, there were filing cabinets full of obsolete records. I asked, going up the chain of command, for permission to destroy these documents in order to make space for current records. The answer came down through the chain of command that the request was approved – so long as copies were made of the records to be destroyed.**

GORBACHEV: Mr. President, your anecdote reminds me of a joke about Russian business. Someone bought a case of Russian vodka, and then emptied out the bottles by pouring out the vodka. He then returned the bottles for money which he used to purchase more bottles of vodka. This is Russian business – that joke is 30, maybe 40 years old.

REAGAN: **That reminds me of the joke of a man who was driving down the road and spotted a chicken running alongside his car. The man sped up, yet the chicken ran right along side him. Then the chicken went into high gear, passed the car, and turned off on a side road. The driver of the car followed down that side road, saw a farmer and stopped to ask him if he had seen a chicken pass by. The farmer said he had seen the chicken and, in fact, had raised it. The driver asked if it was true the chicken had three legs. The farmer said yes, explaining that both he and his wife liked to eat chicken legs. Then they had a son, who also liked to eat chicken legs. So the farmer decided to raise a chicken with three legs. The driver then asked how the chicken tasted. The farmer told him that he did not know – he had never been able to catch it.**

GORBACHEV: Do you know the Russian writers Ilf and Petrov? They wrote humorous, satirical novels. They left as a heritage notebooks consisting of thoughts and ideas for writing future books. I particularly liked one idea in their notebooks. A man was accused of driving a government-owned car to a public bath. To defend himself, the man said that he had not been to the bath for two years. The same could be true of our governments. We do not want to be in the position of defending ourselves by saying that we have done nothing when we should have acted.

CHAPTER NINE

GOING FOR THE GOLD

"I want to leave as a legacy as complete and coherent an arms reduction position as I can."[33]

"It is our impression that we have to tango alone, as if our partner has taken a break."[34]

---

[33] President Reagan to his NSC advisors, May 23, 1988.
[34] Gorbachev letter to Reagan, Sept. 20, 1988.

Date: **February 9, 1988**
Subject: **U.S. Options for Arms Control at the Moscow Summit**
Status: **Declassified in Part (2005)**

BACKGROUND

Reagan had a significant shift in personnel when Secretary of Defense Weinberger resigned in November 1987. Carlucci, most recently serving as President Reagan's National Security Advisor, moved back to the Pentagon to become Reagan's second and last Secretary of Defense. Colin Powell was then promoted from within the NSC to be the new National Security Advisor, becoming the sixth and last person to hold the position in the Reagan administration.

SUMMARY

POWELL: Mr. President, the purpose of today's meeting is to review and identify U.S. options for arms control outcomes at the (Moscow) Summit. Would you like to make a few remarks?

REAGAN: **We have important issues to discuss today. If the Soviets and we have a Moscow Summit, it could be the most important meeting of all. We now have a range of arms control options, but depending on how we use our time, our options will narrow.**

I need your honest assessments of what we can and should achieve in Moscow. I would like to use the remaining months of this administration to the best advantage.

I meant what I said in the State of the Union – we should all have our work shoes on. At the same time, I know how much must be accomplished before we can conclude another arms agreement with the Soviets. I will not rush to an agreement for agreements' sake, so we should use this meeting to identify the option that should be protected and the work that is required to protect them. If we are to achieve our objectives, all the departments and agencies will have to work hard and work together.

POWELL: Thank you, Mr. President. Today I would like to review a number of areas as we think about what we have to do with respect to the upcoming summit. Let me take a moment to review where we stand in our internal preparations for completing a START agreement.

To complete a START treaty, we need to do two things. First, we have to finish determining our initial position. Second, we have to reconcile that position with conflicting Soviet positions.

I have no idea if the Soviets are prepared for serious negotiations, (and) the tactics in Geneva suggest that they may not be. But for their own reasons, the Soviets might be anxious to complete work on a START treaty this year with this administration. That's why it is of some significant concern that we have so much remaining to do to complete the details of our own initial START positions.

For example, our START treaty calls for three protocols: The Conversion and Elimination Protocol; The Inspection Protocol; and The Throw-Weight Protocol. I see serious problems with our progress on all three of these documents.

We tabled a Conversion and Elimination Protocol in Geneva, in October, supposedly after a thorough interagency review. After it was tabled we began to get comments from agencies. As a result, a revision to our Conversion and Elimination Protocol was submitted yesterday to the President for the President's approval with literally a dozen changes, many of them substantive. Even as this revision is being considered, many additional changes are still coming in from agencies.

On the Inspection Protocol, we have not yet reached agreement on many sensitive issues (including): verifying compliance with RV-carrying rules; verifying compliance with ALCM-carrying rules; the conduct of close-out inspections; rules for suspect-site inspections; tagging treaty-limited items; and procedures for perimeter/portal monitoring. Instead, the current draft has placeholders in all these areas and has, essentially, a shallow listing on basic notification inspection procedures similar to INF. Even with a large number of issues we have had to defer, some have formally objected to the tabling of this version of the critical Protocol.

Finally, on the Throw-Weight Protocol, while limiting Soviet ballistic missiles, throw-weight has been a policy objective of this administration since 1981. We are far from interagency agreement on how to define and measure throw-weight. The current draft Protocol lists three different options for computing throw-weight. It reflects significant disagreement on rules for flight-tests, and there is no agreement on verification and monitoring ability of the Protocol provisions.

Finally, in addition to the Protocols, we have a number of problems with our draft treaty itself. Many of these involve policy decisions. Among the outstanding issues are: How we would limit and verify mobile ICBMs if we offer our position on mobile ICBMs; How we would count and verify ALCMs; How we would ultimately resolve the issue of SLCMs; and how we would limit non-deployed missiles. To deal with all these problems, we have established an ambitious formal START interagency work program, and it will complete our initial position, but even if we follow it, it's not going to be done until mid-April.

If a sound agreement is to be reached, we really need to get on with it now. We need to think about the alternatives to signing a treaty because of the difficulties we face. We could consider recording a joint statement, or perhaps a framework agreement as we consider the summit. We should note that every one of the agencies at this table has told us that our START work program is too ambitious focused at mid-April. So, we do really need to think about alternatives, and I would like to have your views on this subject. Secretary Shultz, would you like to start us off?

SHULTZ: Mr. President, it's my impression we can get there if we give it the right priority and effort. We will need to work on many of the details, and we will need to make judgments in a number of areas. For example, we will need to make a judgment on the balance of the intrusiveness of inspections we require and the impact of the intrusiveness (on) our own security. These issues will be no easier eight months or two years from now.

The real question is how important is this to us. I think it is important because the Soviets are a lot better than we are at producing and deploying ballistic missiles that are targeted at the United States, and that's just the cruel truth. And, it has to do less with our technology and our ability to build missiles than it does with our politics.

Congress blocks our ability to deploy such missiles. A clear example is what's happening to the ICBM program. So, it benefits us to have placed equitable and stabilizing limits on forces, especially ballistic missiles. This is an issue of our national security.

I understand that we also have a problem, and many of us are uneasy at the idea that we are working against a deadline of a summit, but I'm not negative on that. I think that negotiating against the summit is what we need to do because deadlines cause tough decisions to be taken. I wouldn't be the negotiator for Jimmy Carter because he would want agreement for agreement's sake. But I have no fear that we will go bananas and grab a bad deal off the table under your leadership.

I remember when Frank Carlucci and I walked away from Gorbachev in Moscow when they refused to give us a summit date. I called back and asked him (Reagan) whether he wanted us to do anything different and he said no, just press on. So from my point of view, with Ronald Reagan as President, the fact that we are working with a deadline is an advantage, not a problem. As to how intractable the details are, I can't judge, although I have a feeling I'll get into them fairly quickly now. (Laughing.)

I think we're far less along in our work towards the START treaty than we could have been, and partially it's because of INF – INF just took up too much time. My position is that we should all pledge to make an all-out effort. It would be wrong if we were not to do so – it could lead to a very grave mistake.

On the other hand, Mr. President, I think I'd be very concerned if we moved towards a framework, especially if we moved in that direction too soon. Framework's not a good idea; Congress would want us to observe a framework; we'd have no verification; we'd have no leverage on Soviet behavior; we really should press for a treaty. And with respect to verification, I know there are a lot of concerns, especially about cuts in the intelligence assets in the out-year budgets. We need to really watch this; it's going to be a harder verification problem in START. We need to step up to the issue of funding for intelligence assets to accomplish this.

REAGAN: **(Interrupting) From my past experiences as a labor negotiator, maybe we need to do this: we need to go for the gold. You need to put down what the ideal agreement would be. After you've done that, you can decide among ourselves what our bottom lines should**

be – what you can and what you can't give up beyond; also where there's no bargaining – those items on which we can't bargain. And we should set up the things that are not essential. Now, once we have that, then you can see the negotiating pattern of what you absolutely must get, what you could try for but still have a good agreement if you didn't get, but the bottom line is you've got to go for the gold.

CARLUCCI: I don't disagree. We should go for the gold; we should work as hard as we can. Our question, though, that has been asked today, Mr. President, is how realistic is that really. In all candor, it'll be very, very, difficult to get from where we are today to a START treaty by the summit.

I've been up to three times now on the INF Treaty, with Bill Crowe, to the Hill, and we've been questioned very toughly on each trip. We have to be certain that the verification to the START treaty is very, very good. Therefore, I think we should condition public mindset that negotiations will continue beyond the summit. We should take the line that if we get an agreement by the summit, that's fine, if it takes by October, that's fine, if not, whatever we do it will be a benchmark for the future and we'll just keep negotiating.

I agree completely with Secretary Shultz that we should not go for a framework – a framework would be an absolute disaster. So, therefore, we ought to tell the public that we're going to continue to negotiate towards a good START agreement, and if we get it by the summit, that's okay.

CROWE: I'd associate with Secretary Carlucci. The Chiefs are down in the trenches and they're worried. The INF Treaty provided some good lessons, but START is becoming fifty to one hundred times more difficult. There are at least three areas I think are tough – by the way, you mentioned getting to bottom lines, you know, it's awfully hard to get a real bottom line in Washington. We get a bottom line often acceptable to the negotiators, but not acceptable to the military.

With respect to the three areas, the first is the bombers and ALCMs. The Soviets are trying to erode our position in both these areas. We need to make sure that we maintain a good ALCM counting rule and that we protect the ability for us to deploy conventional ALCMs.

The Soviets are going to press us on all three. These three are bottom lines.

Second, we have verification. For START, we must be able to do better than monitor simply what's in being, but we must also be able to monitor what's in production. We also have to exchange data early, not at the end, because we won't be able to make the decisions we need to make in the process unless we get the information early. We need the information to make decisions.

CARLUCCI: (Interrupting) I must say, Mr. President, we've devoted an immense amount of time lately on the Hill discussing one site, Magna, Utah. We are going to have some real problems with the Defense contractors at handling a whole bunch of sites.

POWELL: Mr. President, in the INF Treaty, we had 135 sites in the Soviet Union to look at. We are going to have to give you a magnitude (of) about 1,800 Soviet sites in the START treaty.

CROWE: Yes, Mr. President, that one plant caused us an awful lot of problems on the Hill. So we have to get out in front and notify and coordinate with the contractors and with the Congress before we sign a treaty.

We were hit pretty hard on the Hill, Mr. President, for not talking to them before we signed. Therefore, all the above – these three areas – all pose questions about whether the time frame that we are working against is realistic. I agree that we ought go forward as Secretary Shultz suggests as hard as possible, but we ought to do it with our eyes open.

REAGAN: **There are things that we simply can't retreat on. One of them is verification.**

CROWE: But we're still developing our approach to verification. Mr. President, we've gone a long way, (and) the Chiefs have gone a long way, with respect to intrusive verification techniques, and we are prepared to go even further. It's not only tough intellectually… it's tough emotionally.

CARLUCCI: Others suggested that we need to select the plants that we are going to monitor in advance, and, in fact, on the Hill they suggested that we should, in advance of signing a treaty, have selected and completed the security upgrades at those plants before we sign.

POWELL:	Judge Webster, do you have anything you want to add?
WEBSTER:	The monitoring problem is ours. Certainly, there are a greater number of places that we have to monitor than in INF – as Colin Powell said, moving from 150 sites to over 1,800. And in INF, we had no types of missiles that we had to monitor after the elimination, and in a START treaty, we are going to have to monitor some 15 to 20 different types of systems.

We're going to come to loggerheads very quickly with the Joint Chiefs, and the issue will be the amount of the infrastructure that we want to destroy to make the thing monitorable against the amount of infrastructure they need to maintain to do their mission. The Congress knows about all the cuts that we're taking in our overhead assets in the out years; we need to work on that.

Mr. President, I'm also worried that we may spook Congress on the INF treaty if it looks like on the Hill that we're rushing the START treaty. You must know that we face major monitoring problems in a tough economic environment. However, for all those reasons, I support what Secretary Carlucci said – the prospects of getting to where you want to be soon are simply not so good.

SEN. BAKER: I'm a little troubled by the feel of this meeting. It's almost as if we've all decided that we can't do it. If this attitude sets in, we simply won't be able to do it.

Now, we are vulnerable in some respects in that we set a date and some of you, if we don't get a START treaty at that date, will fail. But I don't think we should worry about that. We should go forward with an honest effort to get a START treaty and we ought to pursue that START treaty. In fact, I would argue that if we don't get a START treaty we might not have been right chasing an INF treaty.

I remember, Mr. President, discussions we had in Miami while we waited for an energetic Pope to finish innumerable photo ops, and you, Frank, and I sat in the room, and I watched Frank walk you through a long list of detailed decisions, and you made them one after the other to allow us to get down on an INF Treaty. I always felt that that was one of the most important meetings I had the honor to attend during my tenure here.

Unless we decide to press on seriously forward, let Colin Powell drive this action, and get the President involved in making decisions where he needs to make them, its going to drift away from us, and that would be the wrong legacy for you, Mr. President.

EMERY (ACDA): I wanted to say exactly what Senator Baker said but he said it first. The interagency process has its drawbacks; it's slow and it's ponderous. To meet your goals and the expectations of the public we need to identify key issues and cut through the system and get decisions as we need them. We may finish if we do this. We need to give it a good try.

REAGAN: **We must not ignore certain things. First of all, the situation is not the same as in INF. In this case, the Soviets want a START treaty too. In INF we were the demandeurs, they had the SS-20s, we had to force them out of them.**

But, in this case it's very evident that they, too, want a START agreement. They feel they need START. In that context I can't be too pessimistic.

One thing of interest is that they have an innate eye to protect the homeland at all cost, and it may be that they recognized after Chernobyl that facing the nuclear forces they face, they couldn't do this. So, I think we must press.

POWELL: I think we have, therefore, Mr. President, a decision, and the decision is that we'll go for the gold, and we will drive towards that end. We will need high-level involvement now. We can't stand situations where we don't get agency inputs when required. A lot of this will fall on the Secretary of Defense, the Joint Chiefs, and the Director of Central Intelligence. We're going to throw it into overdrive. …

Mr. President, with respect to Defense and Space, basically our current position is that we should pursue a separate treaty on the Defense and Space area and that we should pursue a treaty that best protects SDI. Unless the Cabinet has any reason to relook at this issue, I'd like to press on to another subject. (No objections.)

I'd like to turn to testing. With respect to the nuclear testing area, two options are presented:

1. To pursue the signing at the summit of a necessary additional verification protocol to permit TTBT (Threshold Test Ban Treaty) and PNET (Peaceful Nuclear Explosions Treaty) ratification, or

2. To pursue the signing at the summit of an executive agreement that permits the joint verification experiments to proceed.

A majority of your advisors strongly prefer the first option. The problem we face in pursuing this is that the Soviet position is that we must first conduct joint verification experiments (JVE), which involve monitoring nuclear tests in each other's sites. We've suggested, and it is the judgment of our testing experts, that there's simply not enough time to conduct these test prior to the summit date. We've suggested to the Soviets on four separate occasions that we may do the verification Protocols JVE's in parallel and not delay the verification Protocols waiting to complete the JVE's. Up to now, they have refused.

Other advisors have another point of view. They suggest that we should not attempt to press forward and break the linkage between JVE's and protocols because we need to accelerate our efforts in this area. The issue then, before us, is whether we should attempt to press forward towards the TTBT and PNET Protocols, and I believe a majority of your advisors support this course. Can I have the views of the Cabinet?

SHULTZ: The alternatives that you outline are well stated. We certainly don't want to let the Soviets think that we really want the TTBT and PNET Protocols so we have to pay a price for them. We should be able to get those Protocols anyway. The major argument for getting them is domestic.

We want to avoid being blind-sided by the Congress. Mr. President, you ought to remember at Reykjavik how we had a rather involved to do with the Congress – you on the phone with Speaker O'Neill and we had others on the line trying to work out a situation on the eve of your meeting with Gorbachev. The Congress is much more restrictive on testing than we would like. We need to avoid this by the current process. In addition, I don't see anybody out there wanting to test above 150 kt. Therefore, I don't see us paying a price for this. We ought to move ahead.

CARLUCCI: I'm a little confused by all this. Are you arguing that we drop CORRTEX?

POWELL: No, no, there's no change here. We want CORRTEX, the only issue is should we be pressed to break the linkage with JVE's.

CARLUCCI:	Well, then there's no change. I don't hear anything new, and on that basis I think we ought to press forward.
GRAHAM:	Neither we nor the Soviets will learn anything at all through the JVE's that will affect our position. The Soviet position is simply not logical, and they may cave based on that.
SHULTZ:	The way this happened is kind of strange. The Soviets were inflexible at Reykjavik, but they got more flexible after Reykjavik. In my ministerial meeting in Moscow after Reykjavik, they suggested they had a better method for verification than our CORRTEX, and Shevardnadze seemed to display quite a bit of information about it. And I suggested why don't we do some tests comparing the two. Shevardnadze agreed. After that we were not able to put together the test program, although Ken Adelman tried. I think right now that it may not be a big thing to break the linkage between JVE's and the Protocols.
WEBSTER:	It's our view that the Soviets will probably not want to break that linkage – that they will want the JVE's.
SHULTZ:	I think you're right at one level. But the Soviets also want to ratify these treaties. They want to show that something negotiated with the United States can be ratified. So I think we're going to see a different attitude at the senior level in the Soviet Union, and the issue as I see it here is do you want me to try to encourage this at the senior level and break that linkage? Do all agree?
POWELL:	I believe that's the view totally around the table. So I think we're going to press in that direction. That's all the major points I think we can cover today. We do need to do some more work on the ABM Treaty Review and the Krasnoyarsk radar, but I think we'll refer that back to staff. Does anyone else have anything to say?
SHULTZ:	There is something new that I think we ought to look at, and that is the factor of Secretary Carlucci meeting with his counterpart and Bill Crowe with his counterpart. I think we can create a constructive atmosphere out of these meetings and we ought to do so. This is a very positive development.
CARLUCCI:	I'll be happy to do this, but I want to make sure you understand we've been very clear with the Soviets that we don't want this to evolve into a parallel arms

	control channel, and therefore any meeting that we're going to have must be carefully structured to avoid this.
SHULTZ:	I agree.
POWELL:	Thank you, Mr. President.

Date: **February 26, 1988**
Subject: **NATO SUMMIT, March 2-3, 1988, Brussels, Belgium**
Status: **Declassified (2005)**

SUMMARY

"All sixteen alliance leaders will be attending the NATO Summit in Brussels on March 2 and 3," Reagan opens today's meeting. "This will be the first NATO Summit in six years. The alliance has much to celebrate, including the INF Treaty, but it also has to confront some important problems."

"Some in Europe are nervous that the U.S. is getting too close to the Soviets," Kampelman adds. "On the other hand, if we are doing nothing and not involved in active negotiations, some Europeans would also complain."

"This is the natural condition of the alliance," Reagan responds. "But everyone should understand that I will do all that I can to reach meaningful and useful understandings with the Soviets – not for agreement's sake, but for the security of the alliance as a whole."

A short discussion follows, after which Reagan brings the meeting to a close,

> I feel comfortable about the preparations for the Summit. Our objective must be to convince our allies to keep up their defense expenditures. We must all go through the motions of convincing the Soviets we are serious, and will maintain our guard. In the final analysis, I don't think General Secretary Gorbachev wants to engage in an arms race with the United States, but our task is to convince him not to try.

POSTSCRIPT

The White House issued the following statement immediately after the NATO Summit:

> The meeting of the NATO alliance concluded with extemporaneous remarks by President Reagan concerning the values of the alliance in the free world. …

> The President cautioned that, while General Secretary Gorbachev speaks of reforms and restructuring, many of the Soviet policies are unchanged. The President referred to the words of Demosthenes when he said: "Surely, no man would judge another by his words and not his deeds. That certainly is true when considering the Soviet Union. I am not a linguist, but I recall the Russian proverb: Dovorey no provorey. That means trust but verify."

On April 14, the Soviets announced they would begin pulling troops out of Afghanistan starting May 15, and that all troops would be withdrawn by 1989.

Date:	**May 23, 1988**
Subject:	**U.S. Options for Arms Control at the Summit**
Status:	**Declassified in Part (2005)**

SUMMARY

REAGAN: **This is our last chance to meet as a group before my final meeting with General Secretary Gorbachev. Last week we discussed areas other than arms reduction. Today I want to focus on START, Defense and Space, and the ABM Treaty.**

I need your advice in two areas. First, what should we try to accomplish in Moscow to further our START and Defense and Space goals? Second, what are we going to do about what George Shultz referred to at our last meeting as a "time bomb?" I mean, of course, the ABM Treaty Review.

We've been putting off decisions in this area, but we can't do so forever. I need your advice on how to proceed.

Looking to the future, even though we weren't able to have START and Defense and Space treaties ready for signature at this meeting, we must not stop our efforts.

I want to leave as a legacy as complete and coherent an arms reduction position as I can.

POWELL: We've discussed a number of the issues in the last two NSPGs. Today, we'll focus only on those arms control issues where additional discussion is needed.

Among them, the ABM Treaty Review is extremely important. As the President has said, it is a "time bomb."

First, a procedural point: we agreed that there would only be a START/Defense and Space Working Group at the Summit – no other Arms Control Working Groups.

Well, let's start in on cruise missiles as our first substantive issue. Up to now, we've been insisting on a discounting rule in which we would attribute ten ALCMs to every ALCM heavy bomber under the START counting rules. The Soviets want our bombers to count with a higher number. Lately, they have been hinting that they may accept operationally realistic loads – smaller numbers – if we would accept a different number for each type of bomber associated with ALCM carriage.

For example, right now, most agencies would agree that if the Soviets would accept ten or less of the U.S. B-52 bomber, we could accept six or more for the BEAR-H bomber and eight or more for the BLACKJACK. I think that's the way, Mr. President, this issue plays out. Perhaps Secretary Carlucci would like to start the discussion.

CARLUCCI: The basic problem we have is that we have no loading information at all on the BLACKJACK bomber. We prefer all be counted as ten, but we are not opposed to the other figures.

We prefer to count ten across the board for all ALCM-carrying bombers. We're just not certain that eight is the right number for the BLACKJACK.

REAGAN: **If we count six and eight, wouldn't that give them somewhat of an advantage? I mean, couldn't they load a hell of a lot more on their bombers than those numbers? (Four lines redacted.)**

CARLUCCI: Mr. President, we need discounting to avoid bumping into the 6,000 limit.

SHULTZ: I don't have any expertise on how to load a bomber, but I understand that by counting six for BEAR-H and eight for the BLACKJACK, we use parallel procedures like our counting ten for the B-52H. In other words, Mr. President, I think they're fair numbers.

CARLUCCI: I think that would be okay if you want to go that way.

REAGAN: **Well, we should recognize that we do this kind of thing better than they do. It's an area of natural superiority, isn't it?**

CROWE: Yes, it is, and they know it is. So I'm not sure that they're going to give us this. But certainly the numbers we've just talked about have an element of fairness.

CARLUCCI: Ron Lehman thinks that we need more flexibility for the B-52 so that we can change the number when we go to the B-1.

POWELL:	General Burns, Ambassador Nitze, do you have any comments? (Neither offered any.)
ROWNY:	I think what we ought to do, Mr. President, if they say that they want six and eight for their bombers and will give us ten for ours, we ought to grab it and run.
CARLUCCI:	That's okay by me.
CROWE:	That's okay by me too.
POWELL:	Okay, let's now move to mobile ICBMs. The decisions on mobile ICBMs verification are pending. If they're ready for the Summit, and I believe they will be, the issue will be what number to use with them.
	Some feel that we should not propose any number associated with mobile ICBMs until the Soviets accept our complete verification package. Therefore, only after accepting such package should we talk about either a range of numbers like 500-700 or a single-point number like 700 or a number that's imbedded in the 1,540 heavy warhead limit. Others feel we should put down the numbers at the Summit so that we can have a complete and coherent position.
SHULTZ:	I guess I'm taking the negotiator's point of view – kind of in between. We have not laid down our verification regime which we should get down as quickly as we can and then have a back and forth on verification. If it looks agreeable to the Soviets, then we ought let the negotiator use his judgment when he puts a number down. We need to emerge from the Summit with a clear statement of what we're for.
	We should not give them a number until the thrust is clear that the regime we propose will make it. But we can't wait until we've got it all marked down before we begin to talk numbers.
CARLUCCI:	I agree. Let's lay down our verification regime first before going any further, and certainly before putting down numbers.
	From our point of view, Mr. President, we don't know if we're going to have mobile ICBMs because of the Congress. The worst of all worlds would be to agree to let them have mobiles and then not get a U.S. mobile program ourselves. Therefore, it's very important that we get the verification first.
SHULTZ:	You know, I took it from the remarks made by General Welch last Friday, that the issue is whether they will accept the basing mode scheme we have in mind, and

the material Bill Webster circulated shows high marks for being able to verify deployed systems.

CARLUCCI: Yes that's true, but the problem is in non-deployed systems.

CROWE: I think a lot of our verification is generally in good shape, except for the area of suspect-site inspection.

POWELL: I think the whole package will be there shortly. OSD, as I understand it, wants to complete the entire package and get Soviet acceptance, not just have a feel that the Soviets think the package is pretty good. State, on the other hand, wants to have the package presented, and if there's any receptivity on the Soviets' part, put down the number so that we have a complete numerical picture.

SHULTZ: I hope, Frank, that you don't mean by complete that they must sign up to all the language we put down.

CARLUCCI: No, all we want them to do is to agree on the type regime – just to agree with us on the fundamental points.

SHULTZ: We agree. Let's just stop the discussion there.

REAGAN: **Will someone tell me why we wouldn't be better off with no mobiles? It seems like their mobiles are bigger than ours and they have a bigger program.**

SHULTZ: If we have no mobiles, then we're only going to have fixed silos. Fixed silos can be taken out by accurate weapons. They're an invitation to a first strike.

CARLUCCI: You know, Mr. President, we don't advocate "launch-on-warning," but they do have two types of mobiles ready to deploy and we have none. They've out done us. It would be no good to endorse mobiles if we had none for ourselves.

SHULTZ: We must be able to deploy what we want to deploy under a treaty or no arms control makes sense.

CROWE: We do have mobiles now, Mr. President, at sea, and, if fixed ICBM silos become very vulnerable, it would be more of a problem for them than for us because they have a higher percentage of their forces in ICBMs.

SHULTZ: I agree, they're going to mobiles no mater what we do.

WEBSTER: I agree, they are going to mobiles.

POWELL: Except, perhaps the SS-24 plant explosion will settle them down a little bit.[35] (General laughter.)

Whatever the number, should it be within the 1,540 or not?

---

[35] The SS-24 plant, in the Ukraine, was reportedly the only Soviet plant that produced the rocket motors for the long-range Soviet missiles.

CARLUCCI:	This has always been our position. We have always taken the position that they should be forced to trade off between mobiles and heavies.
SHULTZ:	No, no, no, that's not right. We had a number of 1650 at one time and we dropped it. You know, we want to get 50 percent reduction from heavies, we shouldn't come out with that as an alternative to mobiles.
CARLUCCI:	I agree, so let's put the number in as a subset for the 1540.
SHULTZ:	No, no, no, 1540 should be heavy only.
CARLUCCI:	From the beginning, we said we wanted to force the Soviets to trade heavies for mobiles.
POWELL:	I can see that this is not as much of a subordinate issue as I thought. Chiefs, do you have anything you would like to add?
CROWE:	No.
POWELL:	The Chiefs are open-minded about this. If we get it in the 1540 number, that's okay, but if not, that's okay too.
REAGAN:	**Tell me again, the 1540 number is 1540 warheads, right?**
SHULTZ:	That's right – 1540 warheads on heavy missiles.
SEC. BAKER:	Treasury agrees with the Joint Chiefs.
ROWNY:	We need to get the heavies. If we get a flight-test ban for future heavy flight tests, that's okay. If not, let's put the mobiles under 1540. That would force them to get rid of heavies that way.
BURNS:	The whole mobile issue can be looked at as a litmus test to whether the Soviets really want a START treaty soon. If we get a lot of interest in our mobile verification scheme, and serious interest, then we're probably on course.
	If not, that'll give us a good indicator that the Soviets are not serious about trying to get a treaty soon. 1,540 is a good number to play with, maybe we ought to see what the traffic will bear.
REAGAN:	**In Moscow, then, the key will be how the Soviets react to our verification scheme. We'll need to make some decisions in Moscow once we see their reaction.**
CARLUCCI:	Yes, we could pick a number or a range of numbers.

POWELL: Mr. President, you summarized correctly. As for range, I guess the numbers would be 500-700. Let's turn to Defense and Space.

We still need to complete our position on Defense and Space – both on sensors and on testing in space.

On testing in space, State basically takes the position that this idea ought to be negotiated with the Soviets, whereas OSD thinks it should be a unilateral declaration.

Secretary Carlucci, would you like to start on this subject?

CARLUCCI: We favor a unilateral declaration on sensors. …

SHULTZ: You know, this discussion highlights the fact that we can't get straight internally what we want. How can we possibly negotiate with the Soviets when we can't even articulate to each other what our position is in a meeting like this?

CARLUCCI: We know what we want. We want sensors to run free. We have language to that effect.

POWELL: But we need to pin down both the sensors, Frank, and testing in space.

CROWE: The idea of sensors has a lot of appeal, but we must be careful about capturing unintended effects. We don't want the Soviets crawling all over our space vehicles.

Right now we don't have any definition of sensors; we need to work on that. And, we certainly can have no discussion of testing in space until we've gotten the sensors nailed down.

REAGAN: **You're very concerned about sensors – about the distinction between sensors and weapons. You don't have any idea of putting nuclear weapons in space, do you?**

CROWE: No, I'm just talking about regular weapons, like kinetic-kill vehicles. But, we still have a problem with sensors because some sensors can turn into weapons if you get the power up high enough.

GRAHAM: You know, Mr. President, one way to look at it is to say, let's not look at anything on the ground, you can look at anything you want in space, and what you should look for is to make sure that whatever is up there isn't shooting down ballistic missiles.

ROWNY: I tried to solve this and I recommended to you Option C.

WEBSTER:	Option C may capture some of my intelligence assets.
ROWNY:	No, it only refers to things in the ABM Treaty terms – it makes no definitions, just explanations, but in a backhanded way it lets you know what it means.
SHULTZ:	Once again this conversation confirms my overall view – we work hard to try to understand what we want, but we have not yet found something we're ready to put down on paper and sign. The only thing we can do right now is listen and keep our options opens and look for the right opening. We're not in a position to state anything.
POWELL:	We may still be able to solve the sensors issues prior to the meeting, but probably not the testing issue.
CARLUCCI:	Well, I think we're in a defensive crouch. We also have to deal with the Soviets and with Congress.
SHULTZ:	Yes, Mr. President, it's kind of hard, because we're trying to talk the Soviets into giving us what the Congress will not give us and they know it. At the same time, as we work on that problem, among ourselves we can't agree on how to put down an explanation of what the hell we want.
POWELL:	The Soviets may come at us again with a short Defense and Space Treaty, tracking the Washington Joint Statement, but still maintaining all the ambiguity.
SHULTZ:	You know we could tell them, as we did before, that the Washington Joint Statement is okay, but at the same time not only do we agree on the language but we also agree that we don't agree on what the language means. Therefore, it does not settle anything. We probably want to settle the issue on supreme national interest and on duration.
POWELL:	You probably won't be able to solve the supreme national interest issue until all the other elements, including duration, are solved.
CARLUCCI:	It's not clear to me that you want to solve duration until everything else is solved.
POWELL:	Let's turn to the issue of the ABM Treaty Review. The issue here is should we do it on the margins of the Summit?
SHULTZ:	As you know, Mr. President, this Review must start by October 3. The Soviets say we ought to get going and get it out of the way. The Review has one major problem, the K-Radar. Other than that, we've been reviewing the Treaty for the past three years. So the

question is, where do we want to be at the end of the Review? I would think that we want to be at the following position: The K-Radar is a violation and it should be destroyed. But, they stopped construction on it, and they said that if we sign a Defense and Space Treaty they would take it down. I also believe that getting out of the ABM Treaty this year is not in our interest. That's what we've been told by the Joint Chiefs.

So where we want to be at the end of the year is basically where we are right now. There's certainly no material breach call; that would end the ABM Treaty. One way to do this at the Summit is to simply say that we've been discussing the ABM Treaty for three-years, so we'll have a short meeting on the margins and clear the books.

If we don't do it at the Summit, we need to put a review process in motion. I've got to tell you, it's not likely that they going to destroy the Krasnoyarsk Radar.

CARLUCCI: I'm here to tell you, George, that if you come out of the Review with the K-Radar not down and you don't declare a material breach, you'll never see a START Treaty. There can be no review until the K-Radar is down, or if we do have such a review, you've got to call a material breach. And calling a material breach is not the end of the Treaty.

POWELL: Helms will put great pressure on us on the Hill to conduct the Review.

CARLUCCI: I would prefer to kick it down the street a bit.

ROWNY: I think what we ought to do is let him hear from the President. You know, he may tear the thing down once he hears our strongest card. Once we have you, Mr. President, talk to him face to face to tell him that it's got (to) come down.

REAGAN: **Well, the K-Radar isn't the only issue. I have questions on other radars, don't I?**

UNKNOWN: Gomel.

SHULTZ: How can you claim a material breach and still retain the ABM Treaty? And by the way, when we call material breach for that, they'll call a tit-for-tat at Flyingdales.[36]

CARLUCCI: Well, but we can take compensatory measures.

POWELL: There'll be a lot of pressure on the Hill to do a hell of a lot more than just take compensatory measures.

---

[36] Ballistic Missile Defense system in Yorkshire, England.

SHULTZ: There isn't going to be any change in the current situation by the time we get to September or October. Why do you want to talk to yourself in that environment? All that's going to happen is that we are going to be perceived as walking away from the ABM Treaty.

CROWE: Tell me, what's the difference between destroying and simply keeping the K-Radar in a condition where it won't work?

POWELL: Our position is that the K-Radar has to come down. We need to have it come down because it is a violation, and in order to put us back into compliance with respect to the ABM Treaty.

GRAHAM: Mr. President, it would take them a lot of time to rebuild the radar, but less time for them to re-equip it.

SHULTZ: Yes, time is essential – and an essential consideration when we picked this item in negotiating the Treaty. The feeling was that time would give warning.

NITZE: At the time we negotiated the Treaty we expected it would take five to ten years to build this kind of radar. You can equip one in a much shorter time. So you'd lose the breakout protection that's involved in the radar. On the other hand, if we don't conduct a review before the 3rd of October, we ourselves will be in violation of the Treaty.

CARLUCCI: Well, that's just a technical violation.

SHULTZ: Do we want to handle this at the Summit? The question is do we want to handle this at the Summit, and if not, then what do we do?

CARLUCCI: The point, George, is that you're prepared to come out of the Review without taking the K-Radar down and with no declaration of material breach, and I simply am not there.

SHULTZ: I disagree. What would you do?

CARLUCCI: I'd take compensatory measures.

SHULTZ: What do you mean – more money on SDI?

CARLUCCI: Well, that's one way to go.

SHULTZ: Fat chance.

WEBSTER: Couldn't we do something with confidence-building?

SHULTZ: Yes, we've tried that in the Predictability Protocol, trying to work something on confidence building that might provide an out. But let's not kid ourselves, the Soviets know they have a violation on their hands – it's just a matter of how to handle it.

HOWE:	Well, the way I see this, the question is, do we do this Review at the Summit, early thereafter in perhaps late-June, or later in September or October. But before you can decide the timing, you've got to ask yourselves, if the K-Radar is still there, what do we do about material breach? How do we handle the K-Radar? You have to answer that question first.
SHULTZ:	You know, we all agreed that there would be no START treaty until the K-Radar is down. That's something we should point to.
CROWE:	You know, it's strange that the K-Radar and START are linked. How about another option? Couldn't both sides just decide to change the dates of the Review – maybe slip it for a year by mutual consent?
ROWNY:	I say let the President take his run at Gorbachev and see if they take it down, and then decide what we do after that.
SHULTZ:	I guess we could try for a one-year delay.
CARLUCCI:	No you can't. You would leave the President completely politically vulnerable. We've already got dozens of letters from Jesse Helms on why we aren't conducting the Review.
CROWE:	So what?
SHULTZ:	We all agree that it's a violation. What we're struggling with is how to handle it.
POWELL:	Mr. President, we owe you a recommendation. But this, at least, has given you a good feel for the debate on this issue.

I'd like to turn to one final issue, and that's nuclear testing. Right now we have two documents that we're going after – the Joint Verification Experiment (JVE) agreement, and the Peaceful Nuclear Explosion Treaty (PNET).

The JVE, Mr. President, is 167 pages long and 37 annexes in all. So far it's under control, but I need each of the Cabinet members to pay very close attention to the input because if they don't, we're never going to finish this treaty in time for you to sign it.

For example, I've had at least one agency recently that's given me two absolutely conflicting inputs. You have to know that I'm going to be absolutely vicious in getting this treaty complete. So please review the inputs that we get on testing from your agencies and make sure they represent your views.

On PNET, we have two problems. One is that the articles are just starting to come back to Washington for review, so we need your cooperation in reviewing them. Secondly, the Soviets have suggested that rather than use CORRTEX on any shot above 50 kilotons, we use CORRTEX on all shots. But we know that CORRTEX is not useful on lower range. We're going to have to sort this one out. ...

If there are no other questions, that will conclude the meeting.

POSTSCRIPT

Two days before the Summit, on May 27, Reagan explained his objectives for the Moscow Summit in NSDD 307, which said in part:

- Continue to advocate a legally binding sublimit of 3,300 ICBM RVs...
- Provide the Soviets details of our proposed verification scheme for mobile ICBMs. ... Based on Soviet receptiveness to this verification approach, I will make the decision in Moscow whether to discuss specific numerical limits on mobile ICBMs and, if so, what limits to propose.
- If warranted to Soviet movement in other areas, I am prepared to agree to allow testing and modernization of silo-based heavy ICBMs subject to appropriate restrictions on the modernization of such missiles (but not on other ICBM modernization) and subject to the United States having an equal right to heavy ICBMs.
- Building upon the Reykjavik formula for heavy bombers carrying gravity bombs or SRAMs, we will seek to resolve additional issues concerning air-breathing weapons in a single, integrated package as follows:
  - While continuing to prefer a counting rule of ten ALCMs per bomber, if the Soviets accept our approach to counting rules, we can accept an outcome which meets the following criteria:
    - No more than ten ALCMs per B-52;
    - No less than six ALCMs per BEAR-H and no less than eight ALCMs per Blackjack;
  - No sublimit on ALCMs or bomber weapons;
  - No restrictions on conventionally-armed cruise missiles;
  - 1000 km range cut-off for counting nuclear-armed ALCM (acceptable only if the Soviets agree to the remaining elements of our proposal);
  - Acceptance of the U.S. position on bomber and bomber weapon distinguishability and verification;
  - No constraints on ALCM inventory; and
  - Acceptance of the limited right to convert ALCM bombers to non-ALCM bombers and non-ALCM bombers to conventional bombers set forth in the U.S. draft of the Conversion or Elimination Protocol.
- On sea-launched cruise missile, if the Soviets appear interested in moving from their current position to a declaratory approach, we will base such an approach on a reciprocal non-binding declaration of acquisition plans for all nuclear-armed SLCMs regardless of their range. If such a scheme were agreed to, the United States would declare it has no plans to acquire more than 1,500 nuclear-armed SLCMs.

•   We will continue the expanded data exchange begun in Geneva.

NSDD 307 also listed Reagan's four priorities at the Summit (Resolving issues related to the joint summit statement; Seeking Soviet agreement to the ALCM position set forth above; Setting forth additional details of the U.S. approach to mobile ICBM verification; and Continuing the expanded data exchange), and concluded with a statement on Soviet non-compliance with the ABM Treaty:

> We will reaffirm in Moscow our long-standing concern with Soviet failure to comply with and to correct Soviet violations of the ABM Treaty. We will make it clear that we will not sign any strategic arms agreements, either in START or in Defense and Space, while the issue of the illegal Soviet Krasnoyarsk radar remains unresolved, and that we consider the only appropriate resolution to be dismantlement or destruction of the radar.

> The third five-year review of the ABM Treaty must be conducted by October, 1988. We will not attempt to conduct the review in Moscow on the margins of the Summit, nor will we plan on delaying it past October. Within those parameters, interagency consideration of options for the timing and forum of the review should be expedited. Taking into account developments during discussions in Moscow, especially with regard to Krasnoyarsk, I would like to be able to decide the U.S. position on timing and forums of such a review as soon as possible following the Moscow Summit.

Date:	**May 29-31, 1988**
Subject:	**Moscow Summit**
Status:	**Declassified**

BACKGROUND

Shultz, Powell and Nitze flew to Moscow in February to discus with Gorbachev where progress could be made towards reaching a START agreement. The meetings lasted the good part of the day with the topics spanning all areas of U.S.-Soviet relations. Both Shultz and Gorbachev emphasized that they were "determined" to get a document ready to be signed when Reagan visited in May. "Once the Soviet side has accepted a U.S. proposal, the U.S. side takes it back," a skeptical Gorbachev told Shultz. "This is becoming routine."

Gorbachev was right to be skeptical because by the time Reagan flew to Moscow in May, a START agreement was off the table.

SUMMARY

In the first private meeting, Reagan handed Gorbachev a list of a dozen or so names that he said were "brought to my personal attention, by relatives and friends." In accepting the list, Gorbachev reminded Reagan that in terms of access to education, employment and health care, Blacks and Hispanics in the United States are far behind Whites, and even though there are lower living conditions in the Soviet Union than in the United States, the socio-economic gap is not as large. The discussion followed.

REAGAN:
> **I wish to take up another topic that has been a kind of personal dream of mine. I have been reluctant to raise it with you, but I am going to do it now anyway. If word got out that this was even being discussed, I would deny I said anything about it.**
>
> **I am suggesting this because we are friends, and you can do something of benefit not only to yourself, but to the image of your country worldwide. The Soviet Union had a church – in a recent speech you liberalized some of the rules – the Orthodox Church for example. Would it be possible for you to rule that religion is part of the peoples' rights, that people of any religion –whether Islam with its mosque, the Jewish faith, Protestants or the Ukrainian church – could go to the church of their choice.**
>
> **In the United States, under our constitution, there is complete separation of church and state. People endured a long sea voyage to a primitive land to worship as they pleased. What I have suggested could go a long way to solving the Soviet emigration problem. Potential emigrants often want to leave because of their limited ability to worship the God they believe in.**

GORBACHEV:
> The problem of religion in the Soviet Union is not a serious one. There are not big problems with freedom of worship. I was baptized, though I am now a non-believer, which reflects a certain evolution of Soviet society. All are free to believe or not believe in God. That is a person's freedom. The U.S. side is actively for freedom, but why is it then that non-believers in the U.S. sometimes feel suppressed? Why do non- believers not have the same rights as believers?

REAGAN:
> **They do. I have a son who is an atheist, though he calls himself an agnostic.**

GORBACHEV:
> Why are atheists criticized in the United States? This means a certain infringement of their freedom. It means there is a limitation on their freedom. I read the U.S. newspapers – there should be free choice to believe or not to believe in God.

REAGAN: **This is also true for people in the United States. Religion could not be taught in the public schools. When we said freedom, that means the government has nothing to do with it. There are people who spend considerable money to build and maintain schools that are religious. I heard that you recently lifted restrictions on such contributions. There are people volunteering to restore churches. In my country the government cannot prevent that, but cannot help either. Tax money cannot be spent to help churches. It is true that there are private schools with the same courses as public schools but with religious education – this is because there are people willing to pay to create and support them. But in public schools supported by taxes, you cannot even say a prayer.**

GORBACHEV: After the revolution, there were excesses in that sphere. As in any revolution, there were certain excesses, and not only in that sphere but in others as well. But today the trend is precisely in the direction you mentioned. There has been conflicts between the authorities and religious activists, but only when they were anti-Soviet, and there have been fewer such conflicts recently. I am sure they will disappear.

          When we speak of perestroika, that meant change, a democratic expansion of democratic procedures, of rights, of making them real – and that referred to religion, too.

REAGAN: **Can we take a look at religious rights under the U.S. Constitution? There are some people – not many, but some – who are against war. They are allowed to declare themselves conscientious objectors, when they can prove that their objection is a matter of faith not to take up arms even to defend their country. They can be put in uniform doing non-violent jobs – they could not escape from service – but they could not be made to kill against their religion. In every war there are a few such people, and sometimes they perform heroic deeds in the service of others. They can refuse to bear arms.**

          If you can see clear to do what I asked – ruling that religious freedom was a right – I feel very strongly that you would be a hero and that much of the feeling against your country would disappear like water in hot sun. If there is anyone in this room who

later said I have given such advice, I will call the person a liar and say that I never said that. This is not something to be negotiated, not something someone should be told to do.

I have a letter from the widow of a young World War II soldier. He was lying in a shell hole at midnight, awaiting an order to attack. He had never been a believer, because he had been told God did not exist. But as he looked up at the stars he voiced a prayer hoping that, if he died in battle, God would accept him. That piece of paper was found on the body of a young Russian soldier who was killed in that battle.

GORBACHEV: Mr. President, I still feel that you do not have the full picture concerning freedom of religion in the Soviet Union. We not only have many nationalities and ethnic groups, but many religious denominations – Orthodox, Catholic, Muslim, various denominations of Protestants, like the Baptists – and they practice their religion on a very large scale. You are going to meet the Patriarch and visit monasteries. If you ask the Patriarch, he will tell you about the religious situation in the Soviet Union.

With their wives waiting and time running out, Reagan and Gorbachev agreed to break protocol (at least in private) and call each other "Ron" and "Mikhail". But before the two joined their wives, Reagan wanted to tell one quick story:

REAGAN: **There was one thing I've long yearned to do for my atheist son – I've long to serve him the perfect gourmet dinner, to have him enjoy the meal, and then to ask if he believed there was a cook. I've wondered how he would answer.**

GORBACHEV: The only answer possible is yes.

Reagan continued to meet with Gorbachev on a daily basis over the next few days, and because no significant agreements were in the works, he again pushed Gorbachev on human rights and religious freedom. The President and First Lady also pressed the human rights issue by visiting monasteries and meeting with Soviet refuseniks, dissidents and other human rights cases to draw public attention to the cause of religious freedom.

At Moscow State University, "looking ahead to the future of the relationship and the challenges of the modern world," Reagan told the Soviet students and faculty:

"We do not know what the conclusion will be of this journey, but we're hopeful that the promise of reform will be fulfilled. In this Moscow spring, this May 1988, we may be allowed that hope: that freedom, like the fresh green sapling planted over Tolstoy's grave, will blossom forth at last in the rich fertile soil of your people and culture."

A few more meetings with Gorbachev followed, and on the final night of the Summit, the President and First Lady were the honored guests of the Gorbachev's at the Bolshoi ballet. Dinner followed at the Gorbachev's private Dacha outside Moscow, and the next morning was spent quickly thanking everyone for their help: a stop at the Embassy at 9 A.M.; the Gorbachev's at 10 A.M.; the official departure ceremony at 10:45 A.M.; and then an 11:00 A.M. lift off to London where the Reagan's had a 5:15 P.M. date for tea with Queen Elizabeth II. Tea was followed by a 6:15 P.M. one-on-one with Prime Minister Thatcher, and then a 7:30 P.M. dinner with members of the British Parliament.

On the tenth and last day of the trip, Reagan spent an hour in the morning with Japanese Prime Minister Takeshita, and then spoke at Guildhall about how the causes of peace and freedom still bring Britain and the United States together. Reagan referred to his trip as "quite possibly… a new era in history, a time of lasting change in the Soviet Union."

Date: **September 20, 1988**
Subject: **Letter from Gorbachev to Reagan**

BACKGROUND

There is no indication from the list of NSC and NSPG meetings compiled by the Reagan Library that Reagan even held another meeting on the Soviet Union or arms control negotiations following the Moscow Summit. There are also no letters found between Reagan and Gorbachev until Gorbachev's September 20 letter (four months after the Moscow Summit), in which he candidly says about arms control, "It is our impression that we have to tango alone, as if our partner has taken a break."

Gorbachev's final letter is also important as it reflects on the progress the two countries have made: eliminating nuclear weapons for the first time; the highest standard ever of verification agreements; agreement on human rights issues; and an agreement to abide by the ABM Treaty. The letter is also significant because Gorbachev is clear that he would be willing to sign another agreement drastically reducing offensive strategic arms before Reagan leaves office. No reply from Reagan could be found.

SUMMARY

Dear Mr. President,

I take advantage of the visit of by Minister of Foreign Affairs Eduard A. Shevardnadze to Washington in order to continue our private discussion.

In one of our conversations in Moscow it was suggested that we might have a chance to meet once again this year to sign a treaty on drastic reductions in strategic offensive arms in the context of compliance with the ABM Treaty. Regrettably, this goal that both of us share has been set back in time, although I continue to think that it can still be attained, even if beyond this year.

I take come consolation in the awareness that still in effect is our agreement to do the utmost in the remaining months of your presidency to ensure the continuity and consistency of the fundamental course that we have chosen. As I recall, you said you would do your best to preserve the constructive spirit of dialogue, and I replied that in that respect our intentions were quite identical. And so they are indeed, which is a source of great hope for our two peoples.

Four months have gone by since the summit talks in Moscow – a short period of time given the dynamic and profound development in international affairs and those that fill the political calendar in the Soviet Union and the United States. Still, a great deal has been accomplished in putting into effect the jointly agreed platform for the further advancement of Soviet-US relations. For the first time in history, nuclear missiles have been destroyed, and unprecedented mutual verification of the just been process of nuclear disarmament is becoming an established and routine practice. In several regions of the world, a process of political settlement of conflicts and national reconciliation has got under way. The human dimension of our relations, to which we have agreed to give special attention, is becoming richer. Ordinary Soviet people continue to discover America for themselves, marching across it on a peace walk, and right now, as you are reading this letter, another public meeting between Soviet and US citizens is being held in Tbilisi.

Someone might object that in the past, say in the 1930s or 1970s, Soviet-US relations also had their upturns. I would think, however, that the current stage in our interaction is distinguished by several significant features. The four summit meetings over the past three years have laid good groundwork for our dialogue and raised it to a qualitatively new level. And, as we know, from high ground it is easier to see the path we have covered, the problems of the day, and the prospects that emerge.

A unique arrangement for practical interaction has been established, which is supported by fundamental political affirmations and, at the same time, filled with tangible content. This has been facilitated by the principal approach on which we have agreed already in Geneva, ie.. realism, a clear awareness of the essence of our differences, and a focus on active search for possible areas where our national interests may coincide. Thus, we gave ourselves a serious intellectual challenge – to view our differences and diversity not as a reason for permanent confrontation but as a motivation for intensive dialogue, mutual appreciation and enrichment.

Overall, we have been able to achieve fairly good results, to start a transition from confrontation to a policy of accommodation. And this is, probably, not just a result of a frank and constructive personal relationship, although, obviously, personal rapport is not the least important thin in politics. Paraphrasing a favorite phrase of yours, I would say that talking to each other people learn more about each other.

And yet, the main thing that made our common new policy a success is, above all, the fact that it reflects a gradually emerging balance of national interests, which we have been able in some measure to implement. We feel, in particular, that it is favorable to the development of new approaches, of new political thinking, first of all in our two countries – but also elsewhere. The experience of even the past few months indicates that an increasing number of third countries are beginning to readjust to our positive interaction, associating with it their interests and policies.

Ironically as it may sound, it is our view that the strength of what we have been able to accomplish owes quite a lot to how hard it was to do.

It is probably not by a mere chance that the jointly devised general course in the development of Soviet-US relations is now enjoying broad-based support in our two countries. So far as we know, both of your possible successors support, among other things, the key objective of concluding a treaty on 50 percent cutbacks in Soviet and US strategic arsenals. In the Soviet leadership, too, there is a consensus on this.

And yet it has not been possible to bring the Geneva negotiations to fruition, a fact about which I feel some unhappiness. It is our impression that we have to tango alone, as if our partner has taken a break.

In another letter to you, I have already addressed the matter which you raised in your letter of August 12 regarding compliance with the ABM Treaty. I think you would agree with me that it would be unforgiveable if our mutual complaints of violations of the ABM Treaty resulted in undermining what we have been able to accomplish to rectify Soviet-US relations through the efforts of both sides.

I would like Eduard Shevardnadze's visit to the United States and his talks with you and Secretary Shultz to result in reviving truly joint efforts to achieve deep cuts in strategic offensive arms. Our Minister has the authority to seek rapid progress on the basis of reciprocity in this exceptionally important area.

Today, the process of nuclear disarmament is objectively interrelated with the issues of deep reductions, and the elimination of asymmetries and imbalances, in conventional arms and complete prohibition of chemical weapons. In these areas too, there is a good chance of making headway toward agreements.

I am confident, Mr. President, that you and I can make a further contribution to the emerging process of settlement of regional conflicts, particularly to a consistent and honest compliance with the first accords that have already been concluded there.

In Moscow we also reinforced the foundation for a dynamic development of our bilateral relations and helped to open up new channels for communication between Soviet and American people, including your people and artists. All these good endeavors should be given practical effect, and we stand ready to do so. I am aware of your deep personal interest in questions of human rights. For me, too, it is a priority issue. We seem to have agreed that these problems require an in-depth consideration and a clear understanding of the true situation in both the United States and the Soviet Union. Traffic along this two-way street has begun and I hope that it will be intense.

Our relationship is a dynamic stream and you and I are working together to widen it. The stream cannot be slowed down, it can only be blocked or diverted. But that would not be in our interest.

Politics, of course, is the art of the possible, but it is only by working and maintaining a dynamic dialogue that we will put into effect what we have made possible, and will make possible tomorrow what is yet impossible today.

Sincerely,

Mikhail Gorbachev

Date:	**December 7, 1988; 1:05 – 1:30 pm**
Subject:	**Reagan/Gorbachev Meeting at Governors Island, New York**
Status:	**Declassified**

BACKGROUND

Reagan sent to Congress, on December 2, 1988, the Annual Report on Soviet Noncompliance with Arms Control Agreements. "This year's report reaffirms our 1987 findings of Soviet violations or probable violation of the ABM Treaty," the four-paragraph press statement noted. The report continued:

> We are particularly concerned about the Krasnoyarsk Radar, which is a significant violation of a central element of the ABM Treaty. We have made clear to the Soviets that their failure to correct this violation by dismantling the Radar in a verifiable manner that meets our criteria casts a shadow over the arms control process. We cannot conclude new strategic arms control agreements while this violation remains uncorrected. We also reserve all our rights under international law to take appropriate and proportionate responses, including the possibility of declaring a material breach.

> We have discussed these violations repeatedly with the Soviet Union and have given them every opportunity to meet our concerns. If the Soviet Union is genuinely

interested in a more constructive and stable long-term relationship, it will take the necessary steps to correct its violations.

A day latter Reagan used his weekly radio address to review the state of U.S.-Soviet relations.

> *My fellow Americans. ....This will be our last such meeting, and I must admit that I would not have predicted after first taking office that someday I would be waxing nostalgic about my meetings with Soviet leaders. But here we are for the fifth time, Mr. Gorbachev and I together, in the hope of furthering peace.*
>
> *And always in my mind, I go back to that first summit held in 1985 at a private villa on the shores of Lake Geneva. At the first of our fireside talks, I said to Mr. Gorbachev that ours was a unique meeting between two people who had the power to start World War III or to begin a new era for humanity. The opportunity for such a new era is there and very real.*

In his speech at the United Nations, directly before his meeting with Reagan and President-Elect George H.W. Bush, Gorbachev announced that the Soviet Union would begin unilateral disarmament actions by reducing conventional forces by 500,000, and removing thousands of tanks and tens of thousands of troops from Eastern Europe. The unilateral Soviet cuts, apparently, caught many in the U.S. by surprise, and as the memorandum of conversation between Reagan, Bush and Gorbachev show, Reagan and Bush barely acknowledged the Soviet announcement.

SUMMARY

GORBACHEV: I hope that what I said at the UN did not contain any surprises. I had wanted to address the logical construction of what had been done in recent years, as a matter of real policy. This is our fifth meeting. It is not a negotiating session, but at the same time it is our fifth meeting, and it is special, taking place as it does in this group.

REAGAN: **It is a pleasure for me to commemorate our meetings. I well remember standing in front of the house before the lake in Geneva, waiting for you for that first meeting. Most of my people thought at the time it would be our only meeting.**

GORBACHEV: It is true that we have much to remember, and much to look forward to as well. This is true not just in a personal sense. The most important thing we have done is begin a movement in the right direction. Vice President

Bush is here listening, but probably thinking to himself, "let them talk."

MEDIA: Mr. Gorbachev, why did you announce troop cuts during your UN speech?

GORBACHEV: As I just told the President and Vice President, what I announced was a continuation and implementation of what I first outlined on January 15, 1986.

I appreciate what the President and I have accomplished in recent years. We have made a joint analysis, undertaken joint efforts, and taken real, specific steps forward. Today, at the UN, I outlined certain additional ideas that demonstrated the realistic nature of the policy and added to it. This was an invitation to work together, and not just to the U.S. What I said was grounded in common sense and experience.

MEDIA: Mr. Gorbachev, do you expect the NATO allies, including the U.S., to reduce as well?

GORBACHEV: I made clear that these cuts were unilateral steps, undertaken without reference to the Vienna mandate. I have been discussing the range of disarmament, humanitarian and economic questions with the U.S. and our Eastern partners. As for today's meeting, it is not for negotiations; I was invited to New York by the President and Vice President. I hope it will be a useful meeting.

MEDIA: Is there opposition to the cuts you announced in the Soviet Union?

GORBACHEV: No.

A few minutes later, after the media is escorted out, Reagan presented Gorbachev with a commemorative photo of their first meeting in Geneva. "We walked a long way together to clear a path to peace, Geneva 1985 – New York 1988," Reagan inscribed on the photo.

GORBACHEV: Those are good words, and I especially appreciate that they are written in your own hand. Thank you, Mr. President.

I will tell the larger group the same thing later, but I wish to say here as well that I have highly valued our personal rapport, and the fact that in a rather difficult time we were able to begin movement toward a better world.

REAGAN: **As I'm leaving office, I am proud of what we have accomplished together. One reason for all that we have accomplished has always been that we have been direct and open with each other.**

GORBACHEV: Agreed.
REAGAN: **We have accomplished much, but there is still much yet to do. There is a strong foundation for the future. What we have done has been based on the values that have guided our hand, the values we subscribe to in this nation. That commitment to promoting trust and confidence remains. George, would you like to add anything?**
BUSH: No, except that the picture President Reagan gave to you, Mr. General Secretary, was also symbolic of the distance our two countries have come. I do not get to be the President until January 20, but with reference to the three year span since the picture was taken, I would like to think that three years from now there could be another such picture with the same significance. I would like to build on what President Reagan has done, as I told you when we met at the Soviet Embassy, even before the presidential campaign had gotten underway. I will need a little time to review the issues, but what has been accomplished could not be reversed.

Wrapping the meeting up, "Now you can tell the press you raised it again," Gorbachev joked after Reagan brought up human rights. With what must have been a smile, Reagan handed Gorbachev a list of names, as he had done at their previous meetings, and in accepting the list Gorbachev couldn't resist another one: "Perhaps they have already left."

"I want to remind you of something I said at our first meeting in Geneva," Reagan started his closing remarks. "I am not sure I told the Vice President about it. I told you that we were two men in a room together who had the capability of bringing peace to the world. Now, all these years later, I think it is evident that we had decided to keep the world at peace." "It all began at Geneva," Gorbachev replied.

CONCLUSIONS

Although Gorbachev was ready to sign a START Treaty at the 1988 Moscow Summit, it took until 1991 for Gorbachev and President George H.W. Bush to finalize the agreement. Once it was signed, Bush and Gorbachev agreed to no more than 6,000 nuclear warheads atop a total of 1,600 ICBMs, SLBMs, and bombers which meant reductions of 25–35 percent over seven years. Months earlier, the Soviets dropped their requirement that limitations on SDI research be linked to a START Treaty. Gorbachev, however, reiterated that if the United States violated the ABM Treaty, the Soviets might pull out of START. Gorbachev also agreed, in 1989, to dismantle the Krasnoyarsk Radar.

Before leaving office in January 1993, Bush and Russian Federation President Boris Yeltsin also agreed to a START II Treaty, which called for the elimination of MIRVed ICBMs and reductions to strategic warhead limits on each side of between 3,000 and 3,500 by the year 2003. The Treaty, however, never entered into force.

In 1997, President Clinton agreed with President Yeltsin to immediately begin negotiations on START III once START II entered into force. The two agreed that START III negotiations should include a limit of 2,000–2,500 deployed strategic nuclear warheads by the end of 2007. Although the Russians ratified START II in 2000, since the U.S. Senate never ratified it, Putin announced in 2002 that Russia was no longer bound by START II.

President George W. Bush, in December 2001, announced that the United States was withdrawing from the ABM Treaty to build a national missile defense system. Reaction was mixed from Russia and China – perhaps from skepticism that the program would even work.

The United States and Russia, in 2002, signed another arms reduction treaty, SORT (Strategic Offensive Reductions Treaty), capping the total number of deployed warheads at between 1,700 and 2,200. SORT, however, is viewed as a weak treaty, in that either country can withdrawal on three months' notice; verification is not seen as effective; and most importantly, warheads already deployed were only required to be removed and placed in storage instead of being destroyed.

Tensions escalated again in 2007 when Bush announced U.S. plans to deploy a missile defense system in Poland and the Czech Republic. Putin threatened to respond with the deployment of short-range missiles along the Russian border. The situation seemed to be defused in 2009 when President Obama reversed the 2007 announcement of a land-based missile defense system for Poland and the Czech Republic. The most recent START negotiations, in 2010, are working towards a limit of 1,550 strategically deployed warheads.

GLOSSARY

ABM:	Anti-ballistic missile
ACDA:	Arms Control Disarmament Agency
ACM:	Advanced cruise missile. The ACM was supposed to replace the ALCM.
AFL-CIO:	American Federation of Labor and Congress of Industrial Organizations
ALCM:	Air-launched cruise missile
ASAT:	Anti-satellite weapon
ATB:	Advanced technology bomber.
AWACS:	Airborne Warning and Control System
C-3:	The Poseidon C-3 missile succeeded the Polaris missile beginning in 1972. 620 were built between 1970 and 1978.
CBI:	Caribbean Basin Initiative
CBW:	Chemical and Biological Weapons
CCC:	Commodity Credit Corporation run by the Department of Agriculture
CDE:	Conference on Disarmament in Europe
CCEA:	Cabinet Council on Economic Affairs
CIA:	Central Intelligence Agency
COCOM:	Coordinating Committee for Multilateral Export Controls. COCOM was established after World War II with the participation of 17 Western bloc countries to embargo arms from going to Warsaw Pact countries.
CORRTEX:	A method developed by the United States and proposed by Pres. Reagan to test for the underground detonation of nuclear weapons. CORRTEX is an abbreviation for Continuous Reflectometry for Radius versus Time Experiments.
CTB:	Comprehensive Test Ban
D & S Treaty:	Defense and Space Treaty
DABM:	Defenses Against Ballistic Missiles
DCI:	Director of the Central Intelligence Agency
DOD:	Department of Defense
DST:	Defense and Space Talks
ELV:	Expendable Launch Vehicle
EXCALIBUR:	U.S. Government nuclear weapons research program that was part of the ballistic missile defense program and the SDI.
Flyingdales:	A ballistic missile early warning defense system located in Yorkshire, England.
FRG:	Federal Republic of Germany
GLCM:	Ground-launch cruise missile
GNP:	Gross national product
GRU:	*Glavnoje Razvedyvatel'noje Upravlenije* (Main Intelligence Directorate for the Soviet Union)
ICBM:	Intercontinental ballistic missile
IEEPA:	International Emergency Economic Powers Act. A U.S. federal law that allows the President of the United States to identify any unusual extraordinary threat that originates outside the United States and to confiscate property and prohibit transactions in response to that threat.
INF:	Intermediate-range nuclear force
IOC:	Initial Operating Capability
JVE:	Joint Verification Experiments

KGB:	*Komityet Gosudarstvennoy Bezopasnosti* (Soviet Committee for State Security)
MAD:	Mutual assured destruction
MARV:	Maneuverable Re-entry Vehicle
MBFR:	Mutual and Balanced Force Reductions
MIDGETMAN:	Name given to the small intercontinental ballistic missile developed in the 1980's. The small ICBM was designed to be launched from a mobile so it would be both difficult to destroy and serve as a deterrent against a Soviet first strike.
MIRV:	Multiple Independently-targetable Re-entry Vehicle
MPS:	Multiple Protective Shelters
MX:	The "Peacekeeper" missile. A land-based intercontinental ballistic missile that became the subject of intense fighting between the President and the Congress.
NATO:	North Atlantic Treaty Organization
NORAD:	North American Aerospace Defense Command
NSC:	National Security Council.
NSPG:	National Security Planning Group. A smaller and more senior component of the NSC. NSPG meetings usually discussed covert military activities.
NSDD:	National Security Decision Directives. Pres. Reagan issues hundreds of NSDD's during his two-terms. Declassified NSDD's are online (thanks to the Federation of American Scientists) at http://www.fas.org/irp/offdocs/nsdd/index.html
NST:	Nuclear and Space Talks
OMB:	Office of Management and Budget
OPEC:	Organization of Petroleum Exporting Countries
OSD:	Office of the Secretary of Defense
PENAID:	Penetration Aid
Pershing I/II:	American medium range ballistic missiles. The 19887 INF Treaty signed by Reagan and Gorbachev saw the elimination of the Pershing missile and the Soviet's SS-20 missile.
PNET:	Peaceful Nuclear Explosions Treaty
ROE:	Rules of Engagement
SACG:	Senior Arms Control Group
SALT:	Strategic Arms Limitation Talks
SALT I/II:	Strategic Arms Limitation Treaty
SAM:	Surface-to-air missile
SBKKV:	Space-Based Kinetic Kill Vehicle
SDI:	Strategic Defense Initiative
SIG-DP:	Senior Interagency Group – Defense Policy
SIOP:	Single integrated operational plan
SLBM:	Submarine launched ballistic missile
SNDV:	Strategic nuclear delivery vehicle
SOUTHCOM:	United States Southern Command
SSBN:	The Navy's designation for submarines that are nuclear powered and carrying ballistic missiles equipped with nuclear warheads.
SSN:	Submarines that are nuclear powered. They are lighter weight and considered fast attack submarines.
START:	Strategic Arms Reductions Talks
STS:	Space Transportation System
TASS:	Official press agency of the Soviet Union
TNF:	Theater nuclear forces

TOW:	Tube-launched, optically tracked, wire-guided
TRIAD:	The TRIAD refers to a nuclear arsenal composes of (1) strategic bombers; (2) land-based missiles; and (3) ballistic missile carrying submarines. Pres. Reagan advocated a strong TRIAD system to deter a Soviet first strike because it would be virtually impossible for the Soviet's to destroy all three legs of the TRIAD in a first strike.
TTBT:	Threshold Test Ban Treaty
UN:	United Nations
USSR:	Union of Soviet Socialist Republics
WHNSA:	White House National Security Advisor; Assistant to the President for National Security Affairs; National Security Adviser.

NOTES

All documents used in this book, unless otherwise noted, were found at the Ronald Reagan Presidential Library (RRPL), in Simi Valley, Calif. All public statements came from the Public Papers of the President of the United States. At the Reagan Library, the National Security Council (NSC) and National Security Planning Group (NSPG) meeting minutes, unless otherwise noted, are located in the collections of the Executive Secretariat, NSC Meetings Files or the Executive Secretariat, NSPG Files.

Since I have used NSC and NSPG meetings interchangeably and refer to the meetings by date rather than by number, the following list identifies the meeting by date and notes the corresponding location at the Reagan Library. For example, NSC 6, which took place on March 6, 1981, is located in the Executive Secretariat, NSC: NSC Meetings Files in a folder labeled "NSC 6". Similarly, NSPG meeting minutes would be found in the collection titled Executive Secretariat, NSC: NSPG records, and then the relevant NSPG meeting number.

National Security Decision Directives from the Reagan Administration are also located at the Ronald Reagan Presidential Library in a special collection called National Security Decision Directives.

All letters between Reagan and the Soviet leaders, unless otherwise noted, were found in the collection of the Executive Secretariat, Head of State Files. USSR.

INTRODUCTION

Draft NSDD 1: *The Reagan Revolution, 1: The Politics of U.S. Foreign Policy.* (Trafford 2003.) Thornton, Richard C. p. 71.
Oct. 15, 1981: Letter from Brezhnev to Reagan. Box 37 (8106615).
July 6, 1981: NSC 16: East-West Trade Controls.
Dec. 21, 1981: NSC 33: Poland.
Sept. 22, 1982: NSC 61: Pipeline Sanctions.
March 19, 1981: NSC 5: Pakistan; Sinai Peacekeeping; Foreign Military Sales; Middle East.
Oct. 13, 1981: NSC 22: Nuclear Force Negotiations.
Letter from Thatcher to Reagan. RRPL: Exec. Sec, NSC: UK Head of State Files. See also Exec. Sec., NSC: European and Soviet Affairs Directorate. Box 90902. Mrs. Thatcher: Visit Feb 85 (1).
"further elimination": RRPL: Files of Howard Baker, box 4. Folder: Nuclear Weapons 3/19/1987. Poindexter's paper, "Why We Can't Commit to Eliminating All Nuclear Weapons Within 10 Years," is attached to a memo from Carlucci to Howard Baker dated March 18, 1987 with the subject line, "Nuclear Weapons Issues."
Sept. 8, 1987: NSPG 165: United States Arms Control Positions.

CHAPTER 1

March 6, 1981: Letter from Brezhnev to Reagan. Box 37 (8100630).

My Dear Mr. President,

In writing the attached letter I am reminded of our meeting in San Clemente a decade or so ago. I was Governor of California at the time and you were concluding a series of meetings with President Nixon. Those meetings had captured the imagination of all the world. Never had peace and good will among men seemed closer at hand.

When we met I asked if you were aware that the hopes and aspirations of millions and millions of people throughout the world were dependent on the decisions that would be reached in your meetings.

You took my hand in both of yours and assured me that you were aware of that and that you were dedicated with all your heart and mind to fulfilling those hopes and dreams.

The people of the world still share that hope. Indeed the peoples of the world, despite differences in racial and ethnic origin, have very much in common. They want the dignity of having some control over their individual destiny. They want to work at the craft or trade of their own choosing and to be fairly rewarded. They want to raise their families in peace without harming anyone or suffering harm themselves. Government exists for their convenience, not the other way around.

If they are incapable, as some would have us believe, of self governance, then where among them do we find any who are capable of governing others?

Is it possible that we have permitted ideology, political and economic philosophies, and governmental policies to keep us from considering the very real, everyday problems of our peoples? Will the average Soviet family be better off or even aware that the Soviet Union has imposed a government of it's own choice on the people of Afghanistan? Is life better for the people of Cuba because the Cuban military dictate who shall govern the people of Angola?

It is often implied that such things have been made necessary because of territorial ambitions of the United States; that we have imperialistic designs and thus constitute a threat to your own security and that of the newly emerging nations. There not only is no evidence to support such a charge, there is solid evidence that the United States, when it could have dominated the world with no risk to itself made no effort whatsoever to do so.

When World War II ended, the United States had the only undamaged industrial power in the world. Our military might was at it's peak – and we alone had the ultimate weapon, the nuclear weapon, with the unquestioned ability to deliver it anywhere in the world. If we had sought world domination then, who could have opposed us?

But the United States followed a different course – one unique in all the history of mankind. We used our power and wealth to rebuild the war-ravaged economies of the world, including those nations who had been our enemies. May I say there is absolutely no substance to charges that the United States is guilty of imperialism or attempts to impose it's will on other countries by use of force.

Mr. President, should we not be concerned with eliminating the obstacles which prevent our people – those we represent – from achieving their most cherished goals? And isn't it possible some of these obstacles are born of govt. objectives which have little to do with the real needs and desires of our people?

It is in this spirit, in the spirit of helping the people of both our nations, that I have lifted the gain embargo. Perhaps this decision will contribute to creating the circumstances which will lead to the meaningful and constructive dialogue which will assist us in fulfilling our joint obligation to find lasting peace.

Sincerely,
Ronald Reagan

April 30, 1981:	NSC 8: Theater Nuclear Forces.
May 22, 1981:	NSC 9: USSR Standing Consultative Commission.
May 25, 1981:	Letter from Brezhnev to Reagan. Box 38 (8190204-8190205).
May 27, 1981:	Letter from Brezhnev to Reagan. Box 38 (8190206-8190207).
July 6, 1981:	NSC 16: East-West Trade Controls.
July 9, 1981:	NSC 17: East-West Trade Controls.
New York Times,	July 2, 1981. "Reagan Aides Call Strains With Haig 'Fact of Life". A3.
Sept. 15, 1981:	NSC 21: Economic Assistance for Poland.
Sept. 22, 1981:	Letter from Reagan to Brezhnev. Box 37 (8103356-8105534).
Oct. 13, 1981:	NSC 22: Nuclear Force Negotiations.
Oct. 15, 1981:	Letter from Brezhnev to Reagan. Box 37 (8106615).
Oct. 16, 1981:	NSC 23: East-West Trade Controls.
Nov. 17, 1981:	Letter from Reagan to Brezhnev. Box 37 (8106607).
Dec. 1, 1981:	Letter from Brezhnev to Reagan. Box 37 (8190038-8190057).

CHAPTER 2

Dec. 10, 1981:	NSC 31:Poland.
Dec. 15, 1981:	Working lunch with Cardinal Casaroli. RRPL: Exec. Sec. NSC Subject Files: Records, 1981-1985. Box 49 Memorandum of Conversation President Reagan (December 1981) (1)(2).
Dec. 19 1981:	Poland. See NSC 33.
Dec. 21, 1981:	NSC 33: Poland.
Dec. 22, 1981:	NSC 34: Poland.
Dec. 23, 1981:	NSC 35: Poland.
Dec. 23, 1981.	Letter from Reagan to Brezhnev. Box 38 (8190210).
Dec. 25, 1981:	Letter from Brezhnev to Reagan. Box 38 (8190211 8190212).
Eight Sanctions:	See Public Papers; Dec. 29, 1981.

I.   Suspending all Aeroflot service to the United States;
II. Closing the Soviet Purchasing Commission;
III. Suspending the issuance or renewal of licenses for the export to the U.S.S.R. of electronic equipment, computers and other high-technology materials;
IV. Postponing negotiations on a new long-term grain agreement;
V.   Suspending negotiations on a new U.S.-Soviet Maritime Agreement;
VI. Requiring licenses for export to the Soviet Union for an expanded list of oil and gas equipment and suspending the issuance of such licenses, including licenses for pipelayers;
VII. Not renewing U.S.-Soviet exchange agreements coming up for renewal in the near future, including the agreements on energy and science and technology; and
VIII. A complete review of all other U.S.-Soviet exchange agreements.

CHAPTER 3

Jan. 5, 1982:	NSC 36: Poland.
Jan. 15, 1982:	Letter from Reagan to Brezhnev. Box 37 (8200225-8204854).
Jan. 21, 1982:	Letter from Brezhnev to Reagan. Box 37 (8200225-8204854).
Feb. 4, 1982:	NSC 39: Scope and Interpretation of Oil and Gas Equipment Controls.
Feb. 26, 1982:	NSC 43: Terms of Reference for Mission to Europe on Soviet Sanctions.
March 25, 1982:	NSC 44: Debrief of Under Secretary Buckley's Trip to Europe.
April 16, 1982:	NSC 45: NSSD 1-82 (U.S. National Security Strategy).
April 21, 1982:	NSC 46: START.
April 27, 1982:	NSC 47: NSSD 1-82 (U.S. National Security Strategy).
May 3, 1982:	NSC 49: START.

CHAPTER 4

CHAPTER 5

P.S. Mr. Chairman,
In thinking through this letter, I have reflected at some length on the tragedy and scale of Soviet losses in warfare through the ages. Surely those losses, which are beyond description, must affect your thinking today. I want you to know that neither I nor the American people hold any offensive intentions toward you or the Soviet people. The truth of that statement is underwritten by the history of our restraint at a time when our virtual monopoly on strategic power provided the means for expansion had we so chosen. We did not then nor shall we now. Our common & urgent purpose must be the translation of this reality into a lasting reduction of tensions between us. I pledge to you my profound commitment to that goal.]

July 18, 1984:	Letter from Reagan to Chernenko. Box 39 (9480793).
July 26, 1984:	Letter from Chernenko to Reagan. Box 39 (8490829).
July 28, 1984:	Letter from Reagan to Chernenko. Box 39 (8490829).
July 31, 1984:	Letter from Chernenko to Reagan. Box 39 (8490847-8491054).
Sept. 18, 1984:	NSPG 96: Next-Steps in the Vienna Process.
Nov. 16, 1984:	Letter from Reagan to Chernenko. Box 39. (8491139) (1 of 2)
Nov. 30, 1984:	NSPG 100: Soviet Defense and Arms Control Objectives.
Dec. 5, 1984:	NSPG 101: US-Soviet Arms Control Objectives.
Dec. 10, 1984:	NSPG 102: Geneva Format and SDI.
Dec. 17, 1984:	NSPG 104: Substantive Issues for Geneva.

CHAPTER 6

Feb. 22, 1985:	Letter from Thatcher to Reagan. RRPL: Exec. Sec. NSC: Head of State File. United Kingdom: Prime Minister Thatcher (8590152-8590923). See also Exec. Sec. NSC: European and Soviet Affairs Directorate. Box 90902. Mrs. Thatcher: Visit Feb 85 (1).
March 11, 1985:	Letter from Reagan to Gorbachev. Box 39 (8590272-8590419) (1 of 2).
March 24, 1985:	Letter from Gorbachev to Reagan. Box 39 (8590272-8590419) (1 of 2).
April 30, 1985:	Letter from Reagan to Gorbachev. Box 39 (8590475-8590495).
June 10, 1985:	Letter from Gorbachev to Reagan. Box 40 (8590683-8590713).
June 22, 1985:	Letter from Gorbachev to Reagan. Box 40 (8590683-8590713).

Buchanan's May 27, 1985 memo to Chief of Staff Regan had the subject line, "The Defense Consensus." In his 6th point on why "defense no longer commands the concern, priority, and interest it did in 1980-1981," Buchanan wrote: "In our desire for arms control, the Administration itself has made the argument that the Defense Program has so re-built our armed forces that we can now negotiate from a position of parity with Moscow if not strength – though no such parity exists. We are, in part, victims of our own success. Even many Republicans think we are armed to the teeth." RRPL: WHORM Sub. File FG001 casefile 315674.

Time, September 9, 1985. Gorbachev's full statement was: "Without such an agreement (on SDI) it will not be possible to reach an agreement on the limitation and reduction of nuclear weapons either. The interrelationship between defensive and offensive arms is so obvious as to require no proof. Thus, if the present U.S. position on space weapons is its last word, the Geneva negotiations will lose all sense."

Sept. 20, 1985:	NSC 121: Visit of Soviet Foreign Minister Shevardnadze.
Nov. 21-22, 1985:	The Geneva Summit. Executive Secretariat, NSC System Files (851041 (1)(2)).
"held hostage:	RRPL: Files of Robert E. Linhard. Folder: Geneva Summit Records, Nov. 19-21 1985 [4 of 4]) OA 92178.

CHAPTER 7

| Nov. 28, 1985: | Letter from Reagan to Gorbachev. Box 40 (8591143-8591239). The idea to send a handwritten letter originated with Jack Matlock, a senior member of the NSC responsible for Soviet affairs. Matlock, before becoming Ambassador to the Soviet Union in December 1987, wrote many of the initial drafts of letters that Reagan would send to the Soviet leaders after he joined the NSC in July 1983. |

Dear Secretary General Gorbachev,
Now that we are both home & facing the task of leading our countries into a more constructive relationship with each other, I wanted to waste no time in giving you some of my

initial thoughts on our meetings. Though I will be sending shortly, in a more formal & official manner, a more detailed commentary on our discussions, there are some things I would like to convey very personally & privately.

First, I want you to know that I fond our meetings of great value. We had agreed to speak frankly, and we did. As a result, I came away from the meeting with a better understanding of your attitudes. I hope you also understood mine a little better. Obviously there are many things on which we disagree, and disagree very fundamentally. But if I understood you correctly, you too are determined to take steps to see that our nations manage their relations in a peaceful fashion. If this is the case, then this is one point on which we are in total agreement -- and it is after all the most fundamental one of all.

As for our substantive differences, let me offer some thoughts on two of the key ones.

Regarding strategic defense and it's relation to the reduction of offensive nuclear weapons, I was struck by your conviction that the American program is some how designed to secure a strategic advantage -- even to permit a first strike capability. I also noted your concern that research & testing in this area could be a cover for developing & placing offensive weapons in space.

As I told you, neither of these concerns is warranted. But I can understand, as you explained so eloquently, that these are matters which cannot be taken on faith. Both of use must cope with what the other side is doing, & judge the implications for the security of his own country. I do not ask you to take my assurances on faith.

However the truth is that the United States has no intention of using it's strategic defense program to gain any advantage, & there is no development underway to create space based offensive weapons. Our goal is to eliminate any possibility of a first strike from either side. This being the case, we should be able to find a way, in practical terms, to relieve the concerns you have expressed.

For example, could our negotiators, when they resume work in January, discuss frankly & specifically what sort of future developments each of us would find threatening? Neither of us, it seems, wants to see offensive weapons, particularly weapons of mass destruction, deployed in space. Should we not attempt to define what sort of systems have that potential and then try to find verifiable ways to prevent their development?

And can't our negotiators deal more frankly & openly with the question of how to eliminate a first-strike potential on both sides? Your military now has an advantage in this area -- a three to one advantage in warheads that can destroy hardened targets with little warning. That is obviously alarming to us, & explains many of the efforts we are making in our modernization program. You may find perhaps that the U.S. has some advantages in other categories. If so, let's insist that our negotiators face up to these issues & find a way to improve the security of both countries by agreeing on appropriately balanced reductions. If you are as sincere as I am in not seeking to secure or preserve one-sided advantages, we will find a solution to these problems.

Regarding another key issue we discussed, that of regional conflicts, I can assure you that the United States does not believe that the Soviet Union is the cause of all the world's ills. We do believe, however, that your country has exploited and worsened local tensions & conflict by militarizing them and, indeed, intervening directly & indirectly in struggles arising out of local causes. While we both will doubtless continue to support our friends, we must find a way to do so without use of armed force. This is the crux of the point I tried to make.

One of the most significant steps in lowering tension in the world -- & tension in U.S.-Soviet relations -- would be a decision on your part to withdraw your forces from Afghanistan. I gave careful attention to your comments on this issue at Geneva, and am encouraged by your statement that you feel political reconciliation is possible. I want you to know that I am prepared to cooperate in any reasonable way to facilitate such a withdrawal, & that I understand that it must be done in a manner which does not danger Soviet security interests. During our meetings I mentioned one idea which I thought might be helpful & I will welcome any further suggestions you may have.

These are only two of the key issues on our current agenda. I will soon send some thoughts on others. I believe that we should act promptly to build the momentum our meeting initiated.

In Geneva I found our private sessions particularly useful. Both of use have advisors & assistants, but, you know, in the final analysis, the responsibility to preserve peace & increase cooperation is ours. Our people look to us for leadership, and nobody can provide it if we don't. But we wont be very effective leaders unless we can rise above the specific but secondary concerns that preoccupy our respective bureaucracies & give our governments a strong push in the right direction.

So, what I want to say finally is that we should make the most of the time before we meet again to find some specific & significant steps that would give meaning to our commitment to peace & arms reduction. Why not set a goal -- privately, just between the two of us -- to find a practical way to solve critical issues -- the two I have mentioned -- by the time we meet in Washington?

Please convey regards from Nancy & me to Mrs. Gorbacheva. We genuinely enjoyed meeting you in Geneva & are already looking forward to showing you something of our country next year.

Sincerely yours,
Ronald Reagan

Dec. 24, 1985:	Letter from Gorbachev to Reagan and Secretary Shultz's analysis. Box 40 (8591293) and (8690024-8690124).
Feb. 3, 1986:	NSPG 127: Arms Control – Responding to Gorbachev.
(Aug. 1, 1985):	McFarlane Memo to Chief of Staff Don Regan re: "Advice to the President". RRPL: WHORM Subject File FG001, #446044. Memo, Aug. 1, 1985
Feb. 22, 1986:	Letter from Reagan to Gorbachev. Box 40 (8690146-8690267).
March 25, 1986:	NSPG 130: RSVP Options.
April 2, 1986:	Letter from Gorbachev to Reagan. Box 40 (8690146-8690267).
April 11, 1986:	Letter from Reagan to Gorbachev. Box 40 (8690146-8690267).
April 16, 1986:	NSPG 131: Responding to Soviet Violations.
June 6, 1986:	NSPG 134: U.S.-Soviet Relations (SDI).
June 12, 1986:	NSPG 135: U.S.-Soviet Relations (SDI).
July 1, 1986:	NSC 132: Program Briefing on SDI.
July 15, 1986:	NSPG 136: Nuclear Testing.
July 25, 1986:	Letter from Reagan to Gorbachev. Box 40 (8690529).
July 29, 1986:	NSC 134: U.S. Space Launch Capabilities.
Oct. 11-12, 1986.	Reykjavik Summit. RRPL. Executive Secretariat, NSC System Files (8690725(1)).
"Poindexter Paper":	RRPL: Files of Howard Baker, box 4. Folder: Nuclear Weapons 3/19/1987. Poindexter's paper, "Why We Can't Commit to Eliminating All Nuclear Weapons Within 10 Years," is attached to a memo from Carlucci to Howard Baker dated March 18, 1987 with the subject line, "Nuclear Weapons Issues."
"Nitze to Shultz":	RRPL: Files of Howard Baker, box 4. Folder: Paul Nitze 4/23/87 [March –April 1987].

CHAPTER 8

Dec. 16, 1986:	NSC 140: ICBM Modernization (M-X)
"America has lost":	Public Papers of the President of the United States, May 6, 1987.
Feb. 3, 1987:	NSPG 143: The SDI Program.
Feb. 10, 1987:	NSPG 143A: Arms Control and SDI.

"Option C":   RRPL: Files of Howard Baker. Folder: Paul Nitze 4/23/1987 [March 1987-April 1987] box 4. Memo: Nitze to Shultz, March 11, 1987, "Broad Interpretation." Document was withheld from release by George W. Bush under E.O. 13,233 until 2009.

May 21, 1987:   NSC 147: Political Issues for the President's Trip to Europe

"tear down this wall"   June 12, 1987.

Sept. 8, 1987:   NSPG 165: United States Arms Control Positions.

Sept. 15, 1987:   Letter from Gorbachev to Reagan. Box 41 (8790986-8791196).

Oct. 14, 1987:   NSPG 168: Upcoming Shultz-Shevardnadze Meeting in Moscow.

Shultz Moscow meetings: Notes from the October 23, 1987 meeting in Moscow are based on a National Security Archive translation of the conversation released by the Gorbachev Foundation and part of Briefing Book No. 238: The INF Treaty and The Washington Summit: 20 Years Later.

Oct. 30, 1987:   Memo from Shultz to Reagan re: Oct. 30, 1987 letter from Gorbachev to Reagan. Box 41 (8790986-8791196). The letter could not be located.

Washington Summit: RRPL: Executive Secretariat, NSC System Files 8791377.

CHAPTER 9

Feb. 9, 1988:   NSPG 176: U.S. Options for Arms Control at the Moscow Summit.

Feb. 26, 1988:   NSPG 177: NATO Summit, March 2-3, 1988.

May 23, 1988:   NSPG 190: U.S. Options for Arms Control at the Summit.

NSDD 305 (April 26, 1988), "Objectives at the Moscow Summit," listed the U.S. objectives at the Moscow Summit.

- Stressing the importance of progress in Soviet human rights performance;
- Making maximum practical progress toward an agreement for a fifty percent reduction in U.S. and Soviet strategic nuclear forces;
- Following through on the progress made on the regional agenda, including emphasizing to the Soviets the importance of completing a prompt withdrawal from Afghanistan, reaffirming our objective of a genuinely independent non-aligned Afghanistan in which the Afghan people are free to determine their own future, and actively engaging the Soviets to be helpful in resolving other regional issues on our agenda;
- Consolidating progress and moving forward on bilateral issues, including exchanges and, where warranted, economic relations.

May 29-31, 1988:   Moscow Summit. Executive Secretariat, NSC System Files (8890497, 8890511).

"becoming routine":   RRPL: Exec. Sec. NSC Systemt Files: Memcon, Feb. 22, 1988: "The Secretary's Meeting with Gorbachev Feb. 22." Sys. II 90190.

Sept. 20, 1988:   Letter from Gorbachev to Reagan. Box 41 (8890725-8890750).

Dec. 7, 1988:   Reagan/Gorbachev Meeting at Governors Island, New York. Executive Secretariat, NSC System Files (8890931, 8890944).

ACKNOWLEDGMENTS

Projects like this start and end with the work of all those at the Ronald Reagan Presidential Library. Without their tireless work – from organizing the estimated 50 million pages of documents, to coordinating with the various agencies to get documents declassified, to putting up with my constant demands for more and more information – works like this would not be possible. At the Reagan Library, I would like to especially thank Mike Duggan, Shelly Williams and Cate Sewell, whom I am sure put in more work on my behalf than I will ever know. The same could be said for Diane Barrie, Kelly Barton, Steve Branch, David Bridge, Greg Cumming, Sherrie Fletcher, Lisa Jones, Meghan Lee, Ira Pemstein, Ben Pezzillo, Bruce Scott, Jenny Mandel, Josh Tenenbaum, Raymond Wilson, Martha Huggins, Kimberlee Lico, Gordon Kaplan and Mike Pinckney, some of whom have moved on to other places, like the Nixon Library, and others who have just moved on. I feel very fortunate to have had the chance to work with each of them, and for anyone who spends even an hour inside the archive, it's evident that the Reagan Library is a superb archive thanks to the hard work of the archivists.

I would especially like to thank Richard Reeves for giving me the opportunity to become an expert on the Reagan Library. I first met him, back in 1995, when I was senior in high school and his wife was looking for a personal assistant a few hours a week. Somehow, when she called my high school, luck brought the note to Don Walz, my Academic Decathlon teacher, and for whatever reason he decided to pass the message on to me, saying something like, "You should do this job, it is a great opportunity." Years later, when I was a senior at UCLA, I saw Catherine O'Neill on television talking about her job as the director of the United Nations Information Centre in Washington, D.C. I immediately applied for an internship there, and on my first day in the office she suggested that I immediately interview with her husband for the research assistant position. I doubt she remembers, but she told me that if I got the job working for her husband I'd learn how to do a book if I ever wanted to do it on my own. Those words stuck with me when I wasn't sure I'd be able to complete this project.

I'm especially thankful for having had the chance to interview David E. Hoffman about his Pulitzer Prize winning book, *The Dead Hand: The Untold Story of the Cold War Arms Race and its Dangerous Legacy.* (Doubleday, 2009.) Mr. Hoffman graciously spent a few hours with me talking about his book and his knowledge of U.S.-Soviet relations. In many areas *The Reagan Files* has benefited from his expertise.

Professor Laura Kalman at the University of California Santa Barbara has also made a significant contribution to this book. I first met her at the Reagan Library while she was researching her book *Right Star Rising: A New*

Politics, 1974-1980. (W.W. Norton & Company, 2010). She took time to comment on various parts of this book, and in more than one case saved me from embarrassing errors.

I am also especially grateful to Timothy Connelly of the National Historical Publications Records Commission for granting me the opportunity to learn about the process of editing historical documents by participating in the 2010 summer editing institute at the University of Wisconsin. There is no question that the editing institute saved me from making many novice editor mistakes. Lynette Smith provided some last-second important copyediting, and Karrie Ross deserves a big thank you for her efforts designing the front and back cover.

There are also very few people who took the time to read every single page of *The Reagan Files* when it was just a manuscript. For their time, and their unwavering friendship, I'm very much indebted to Dr. Johannes Burge and Daniel Burge. Johannes, in particular, served as an outstanding reminder that although finishing the book would require years of work, doing so would provide an important contribution to Reagan scholarship. Daniel, a recent graduate of the University of Puget Sound, came into this project while it was wrapping up, but was still able to make important suggestions that I almost always adopted. Both Jessica Zetley and Sol Zetley have also been kind enough to take the time to read parts of the manuscript and offer important comments and suggestions. Jessica, in particular, is owed an enormous thank you for her unwavering love and support despite our troubles over the past couple of years. Another good friend, Ardalan Haghighat, has been acting as my de facto editor on and off for the last few years.

As with most of my accomplishments in life, nothing much is accomplished without the support of my family. For that I am eternally thankful to have had the financial support to complete this book from my mother, Dr. Synthia Saltoun, and my step-father extraordinaire, Norman Siever, both professors at Los Angeles Valley College. I have also been fortunate to have the support of my grandmother, Beverly Saltoun Bernstein, and my grandfather, Andre Saltoun, both of whom have read various parts of the book and made important contributions. Dr. Lee Sharp, an honorary grandfather, has also provided tremendous help by both commenting on the manuscript and providing me a bed to sleep in and food to eat while I was researching in Washington D.C. Although I rarely see eye-to-eye on anything with my father, Joseph Ebin, including foregoing starting my legal career so that I could put this book together, I owe him a big thank you for his constant reminders that excellence, in whatever the field, is usually rewarded. I also owe a big thanks to my sister, Rebecca Saltoun Ebin, who from the first day I started working on this project made me think it was the coolest thing in the world I could be doing. I couldn't have agreed more.

INDEX